D0052433

Reckoning with Homelessness

The Anthropology of Contemporary Issues

A series edited by
Roger Sanjek

A full list of titles in the series appears at the end of this book.

Reckoning with Homelessness

Kim Hopper

CORNELL UNIVERSITY PRESS
Ithaca & London

First published 2003 by Cornell University Press
First printing, Cornell Paperbacks, 2003

Printed in the United States of America

Library of Congress Cataloging-in-Publication Data

Hopper, Kim.
Reckoning with homelessness / Kim Hopper.
p. cm. — (The anthropology of contemporary issues)
Includes bibliographical references and index.
ISBN 0-8014-4068-8 (cloth : alk. paper) — ISBN 0-8104-8834-6 (pbk. : alk. paper)
1. Homeless persons—United States. 2. Homelessness—United States.
3. Poor—United States. I. Title. II. Series.
HV4505 .H665 2002
305.5'69—dc21
2002011089

Earlier versions of material included in chapters 4, 5, and 6 have appeared in "Symptoms, Survival, and the Redefinition of Public Space," *Urban Anthropology* 20 (1991): 155–175; Technical Reports to the U.S. Census Bureau under Joint Statistical Agreements 90-18 and 90-19, May 1991; and "Margins within Margins" in *Margins of Insecurity: Minorities and International Security,* ed. S. Nolutschungu (Rochester: University of Rochester Press, 1996), 213–249.

Cornell University Press strives to use environmentally responsible suppliers and materials to the fullest extent possible in the publishing of its books. Such materials include vegetable-based, low-VOC inks and acid-free papers that are recycled, totally chlorine-free, or partly composed of nonwood fibers. For further information, visit our website at www.cornellpress.cornell.edu.

Cloth printing 10 9 8 7 6 5 4 3 2 1
Paperback printing 10 9 8 7 6 5 4 3 2 1

For my parents, Roy and Marie—
Home is where we start from

The housing industry trades on the knowledge that no Western country can politically afford to permit its citizens to sleep in the streets.

Anthony Jackson, *A Place Called Home*

Contents

Acknowledgments

To tell a tale of homelessness in his latest novel (*King: A Street Story*), John Berger resorts to the voice of a shanty-town dog. While this book has no key informant quite so strategically placed, it has amassed (more than) its share of debts. With apologies for grouping peaceably in print what would (in some cases) be fracas in practice, my thanks to the following:

To my comrades-in-arms at the outset of this errantry: Ellen Baxter, Robert Hayes and Stuart Cox, the Fathers John (Duffell, Felice, and McVean), Diane Sonde, and David Beseda.

To Sue Estroff, Shirley Lindenbaum, Katherine Newman, and Roger Sanjek, who early on spied something resembling anthropology in my field dispatches and encouraged its cultivation. To the late Elliot Liebow, for showing this upstart an elder's esteem. To Jim Baumohl, for policing my syntax, playing wrangler to my unruly arguments, and collaborating on God knows how many drafts of joint undertakings.

To the advocates at the New York and National Coalitions for the Homeless, and the National Law Center on Homelessness and Poverty, for insisting that what passes for a line item on a budget these days remains a scandal nonetheless.

To government officials who ignored the clove of garlic around my neck and, not without misgivings of their own, admitted me to the outer reaches of the inner circles of policy making and report writing.

But this is, after all is said and done, a book. For critical comments on earlier drafts of chapters, I owe huge thanks to: Mireille Abelin, Joan Alker, Martha Are, Steve Banks, Sue Barrow, Jim Baumohl, Gary Blasi, Mary Brosnahan, Marti Burt, Frank Caro, Jack Doyle, David Giffen, Kostas Gounis,

Marg Hainer, Jill Hamberg, Chester Hartman, Mary Ellen Hombs, Fred Karnas, Ken Kusmer, Gene Laska, Anne Libby, Margaret Lock, Anne Lovell, Maryse Marpsat, Elizabeth Martin, Michael Meyer, Deborah Padgett, Debra Rog, Peter Rossi, David Rothman, Roger Sanjek, Diana Silver, Luisa Stark, Norma Ware. For access to unpublished historical material, I want to acknowledge the keepers of the Stuart A. Rice Archives (at the Harry S. Truman Library, Independence, Missouri) and the Community Service Society Archives (Columbia University, New York). For assistance in preparing the manuscript, thanks to Donna Brophy and Caitlin McMahon. And on the editorial front, may I salute the discerning eye and deft hand of Cathi Reinfelder.

Last and forever, it would have been a different book (and a vastly different life) were it not for Nancy and Jude, who took in a wayfarer and restored his sense of home.

While working on this project, I've received support from the Ittleson Family Fund, the Woodrow Wilson Foundation, the Charles H. Revson Foundation, and the National Institutes for Mental Health, for which I'm grateful. Half the author's proceeds from the sale of this book will go to support the work of The Jazz Musicians Emergency Fund (800-432-5267; jazzfndtn@aol.com).

A note on the photographs:

The historical pictures of the Municipal Lodging House come from the Municipal Archives, courtesy of Edwin A. Brown (*Broke: The Man Without The Dime*, 1913). The shots from the early 1980s (all taken by the author) are more problematic. Images of the street-dwelling homeless not only illustrate but also, ineluctably, participate in that "spectacle of the degraded pauper" that has been a mainstay of American relief policy. They appear here as a necessary part of the record.

PART I

CLASSIFICATION AND HISTORY

[1]

This Business of Taking Stock

> It must be some kind of experiment or something, to see how long people can live without food, without shelter, without security.
>
> Homeless woman, Grand Central Station, winter 1980

As introductions to homelessness go, mine as a newly arrived graduate student in New York in 1972 was hardly traumatic. But it was an uneasy mix of the grim, the wrenching, and the comic. There were, first of all, those inescapable images of the city's forsaken: the half-naked man cavorting in the steam pouring out of vents at a street construction site early one morning, wraithlike in the glow of mercury-vapor lights; the sobbing figure of a woman sitting on the stone steps of a church, the still body of a man lying prone on a sidewalk, the plaintive importuning of a beggar at the subway turnstile—each studiously ignored by passersby. There was even then the wandering army of men and women given to animated, sometimes agitated, conversations with unseen companions in what sounded like a pidgin of obscene and foreign tongues. I had recently finished a six-month stint as a psychiatric aide on an acute ward and my initial reaction was that I knew these people, or had known them in a former life as patients.[1] In a city that was centuries away from a subsistence economy, it seemed incredible that they belonged nowhere, had no refuge however mean to retreat to, and were the responsibility, apparently, of no surrogate protector.

Scruffy enough in my own attire, I was occasionally taken for a fellow traveler. Leafing through a translation of Virgil's *Aeniad* on the used books stand at the old Salter's Bookstore across from Columbia University, I was joined one day by one of the Upper West Side's regulars. Reading over my shoulder, he pronounced the translation sound. I replied, in a perverse moment of pride at having endured three years of high school Latin, that while it was a serviceable job, the original was so much more lyrical—and then went on to recite (from memory, not sight translation) the opening line of that epic poem: *Arma virumque cano, Troiae qui primus ab oram. . . .* My companion was unimpressed: "You're not scanning correctly," he retorted, exasperated, and proceeded to give, in a voice befitting their grandeur, an alternative reading (in Latin) of the poem's first ten heroic lines. To my hopelessly outclassed ear, it sounded like the rendition of someone long familiar with the text.

I came, too, to know the limits of tolerance of those who were the unwitting accomplices of a graduate student's casual charity. Confronted with the sight of my sharing a table with a large, zanily outfitted woman—and her even larger grocery cart of belongings—the owner of the West End Cafe (who knew me as a regular, all-hours customer) was hard-pressed to let us stay long enough to finish our coffee. After we were thrown out, I did, however, demur at her suggestion that we continue our conversation at my dorm room. I saw her irregularly on the street thereafter, and would remake her acquaintance at a Catholic Worker House of Hospitality a decade later.

Suffice it to say that I, like any half-sentient city dweller of that period, was acquainted with the obvious. I did the requisite tour of the Bowery, visited some of the seedier bars in the Lower East Side's repertoire, and succumbed regularly to the entreaties of panhandlers—some of whom I occasionally queried, only to be fobbed off with (what I was later to learn were) stock responses. A vague resignation, almost an absentmindedness, slowly displaced my initial disorientation. I grew accustomed to random, visible suffering as a routine fact of urban life. I suppose I figured this was part of what acquiring a New Yorker's toughness was all about.[2]

At the same time, I managed to miss altogether some subtler, more enduring signs of street poverty. One in particular stands out. Every morning, beginning around six, the queue begins to form at the St. Francis Breadline on West 31st Street Men and women have been lining up here for sandwiches and coffee for more than sixty years. Minutes after the food is gone, so are the recipients. But if one looks closely, a trace of their presence remains: the lower five feet of the beige brick wall against which they stand is several shades darker than the rest of the wall. The stain, a sort of signature, runs for half a block, becoming invisible only when it meets a darker brick in the adjacent building.

Only gradually would I come to understand that these folks were something other than the hapless conscripts of a failed psychiatric campaign. But then I was a slow learner. Even before my own alternative account took shape, I would run across puzzling parallels in the historical literature.

There were the elderly homeless poor in the eighteenth-century French countryside described by Olwen Hufton:

> The aged woman was a more common figure than the aged man: a black bundle of rags with permanent backache and prone to incontinence . . . and with ulcerated varicose veins.[3]

Then there was "Rags," a turn-of-the-century "knight of the road" who could have stepped out of a New York City tableau eighty years later:

> . . . a massive, hairy, lousy gentleman dressed in an assortment of clothes, including four coats, three pairs of pants, and three shirts. In each pocket was something—books, needles and thread, old pieces of iron, scraps of paper. His outside coat was covered with approximately fifty different badges and buttons. Rags was a walking trash can.[4]

Nearer to home and my own generation was the legacy of Jack Kerouac and crew. Among the latter was Neal Cassady, whose childhood had been spent in Denver flophouses with an alcoholic father and whose career as a writer and wayfarer (lastly with Ken Kesey's Merry Pranksters) came to an amphetamine-accelerated end. In the span of a short lifetime, he managed to join two radically different modes of homelessness: skid row and hippie nomadism.

The closer I looked, the more I saw of both continuities and discontinuities. Meanwhile, the numbers of the street-dwelling poor continued to grow. By the later '70s, my own perplexity, inquisitiveness, resignation—or some mixture of all three—had given way to a half-informed anger at the misbegotten policies of the mental health system. I spent the summer of 1976 doing fieldwork on an acute psychiatric ward, on which the average length of stay of (oft-returning) patients was two weeks. That experience, revisited repeatedly during a long-running interdisciplinary seminar on ethical issues in behavior control which recruited clinical participants from that ward, convinced me that to understand this small arc of these inmates' life circuit, one would need to know more about their lives on the outside. So when chance beckoned, in the form of a phone call from Ellen Baxter in 1979 asking me to join a research project, I leapt at the prospect.

It would take a year and a half of interviews and observations, getting to know both the terrain and the people who made it their home, before we would set down what we had learned in *Private Lives/Public Spaces* (1981). In the end, it came down to something rather elemental: the "terribly complicated" business, as George Orwell had called it, of learning to survive on next to nothing. First and last, as one of our informants reminded me on the occasion of the opening of a new drop-in center, the folks on the street were "people just maneuvering as best as they are able." Much later still, I would come to appreciate the maneuvering that had occurred before the threshold of homelessness had been crossed. And again, it had been in front of my eyes all along.

A Brief Look Backward

Thirty-five years ago in New York City, vagrancy was a crime, practiced (if a status can be said to be practiced) chiefly by elderly white men, who tended to congregate along a grubby mile-long corridor of the Lower East Side known as the Bowery. Here was located the city's "skid row," an area known for its cheap lodgings, rough taverns, petty commerce, and broken lives. In these tawdry surrounds, urban missionaries tirelessly plied their trade in soup and sermons, as they had been doing for nearly a century. Small knots of men pooled their change for bottles of wine and retired to vacant lots or street corners to drink it. Spot labor pools provided sporadic employment for some, while others turned to varieties of street enterprise: panhandling, unloading trucks, taking grimy rags to the windshields of motorists at stoplights. "Jackrollers," muggers of the lowest order, preyed on the unwary or insentient. Discipline was lax, limited to periodic forays by the police, as likely to net a sober man as the habitual drunk. Night brought an end to the unruly sociability of the day and evening. Commercial flophouses operated at 60 percent capacity, while missions (where the berths were free) ran at triple their official capacity. By the early morning hours, perhaps a few dozen men could be found sleeping outdoors, huddled in weedy lots or ruined buildings, sprawled in doorways, or tucked away in abandoned vehicles.

The Bowery was at once familiar and alien, a place where poverty, disengagement, and "antisocial behavior patterns" intersected in a laboratory-like demonstration of "what sociologists have commonly referred to as 'anomie,' in this case lack of adherence to norms held by the society at large."[5] For a population untrammeled by the usual ties that bind and reportedly immune to obligations that order, Bowery men were remarkably well behaved, seldom venturing beyond the confines of skid row. The reverse was not true. Haunt of the permanent stranger, the Bowery erected few barriers to the curious. Sociologists found this convenient: "For the price of a subway ride, [one] can enter a country where the accepted principles of social interaction do not apply."[6] So did ordinary citizens: The lure of its notoriety was such that sightseeing tours regularly included it along their scheduled routes, a practice that dated back to the 1930s.[7]

The last three decades have seen dramatic changes in this social niche.

Vagrancy is no longer a status offense; it was decriminalized by the Supreme Court in early 1972.[8] By early 1980, when our work began in earnest, the average age of a man in the shelter system was in the midthirties; for the first time in the institution's history, most new applicants for shelter were African American. While hardly insignificant as a species of "deviance," chronic alcoholism had yielded ground to psychiatric disorders and polymorphous expressions of "substance abuse." Spot work was considerably harder to come by. Punk rock clubs occupied the street-level floors of old flophouses. Authors, lawyers, and arbitrageurs had taken up residence in newly renovated units along the mile-long stretch of the Bowery.

Other things had changed little. The lodging houses (those that had resisted the nascent stirrings of gentrification in the area) and the missions continued to do brisk business. (Both operate at full capacity, though with different clienteles, today.) One or two of the bars, the predatory elements, the unsolicited windshield washing, and the tour buses were still there. A palpable air of dissolution still clung to the place. Its century-old reputation as the city's back-burner melting pot of "tramps, panhandlers, whores and vagrants"—minus, perhaps, the commercial sex—showed no sign of abating.[9]

To be sure, the Bowery no longer could lay claim to being the city's exclusive niche of vagrancy. Visible evidence of those without a bed for the night was scattered far and wide throughout Manhattan. And there was soon to be a shift in lexicon. Following the lead of advocates and the courts, the press would retrieve an old Victorian term, long favored by students of the problem. Instead of "derelicts," one now referred to "homelessness."

What follows is a hybrid account, joining the hand-to-mouth immediacy of having been there with the luxury of looking back—one troubled participant's attempt to assay the career of homelessness among single men in the last quarter of the twentieth century.

Mongrel Methods, Applied Work

To begin with, a word about methods. In practice, *ethnography* means carrying out two distinct kinds of inquiry, pursuing two ways of knowing: what might be referred to as "framework" and "fieldwork." They relate to one another as context and story, disciplinary backdrop and case-at-hand, history and action. But however formulated, a full anthropological account invariably includes both.[10]

Framework is concerned chiefly with "track[ing] the condition"; it monitors the changing configuration of local limits and pressures within which the object of study is situated.[11] It includes all activities directed at the documentation of *setting* in its most encompassing sense—from the genealogy of a program, to the history of a neighborhood or client population, to the shifting configuration of relevant goods and services, to changes in the economic and political armature of a city. With respect to homelessness, archival and library work provided the indispensable material for constructing "a usable past"[12]—the history of poor relief in New York City from almshouse to shelter, the legacy of skid row as an urban neighborhood, the rise of the "de facto" mental health system in the wake of deinstitutionalization, the fallout of the postwar deindustrialization of the north, and the changing configuration of the African American family over the last thirty years. *Framework* also refers to the intellectual backdrop against which a "problem" is defined: the work that has "gone before" and accounts for this particular question being of some interest to the field. Here, my most obvious debts are to earlier studies of homelessness in Gotham (especially those by Stuart Rice, Charles Barnes, and Nels Anderson) and of the makeshift economies of the poor, as well as the Columbia Bowery Project's reconnaissance of what was mistakenly taken to be the twilight of that disreputable corridor. Conceptually, Ephraim Mizruchi's construct of "abeyance mechanisms"[13] and their role in accommodating surplus populations, and Victor Turner's analysis of "liminality" and the dicey uncertainty of transitional states[14]—which Jim Baumohl and I have used to reinterpret homelessness—furnish the essential flooring.

Fieldwork, on the other hand—the storied, venerable "nothing quite like being there" trial of initiation and renewal—has been de rigueur for anthropologists at least since the 1913 edition of *Notes and Queries*.[15] That was when W.H.R. Rivers (psychiatrist, anthropologist, hero of Pat Barker's *Regeneration* trilogy) insisted on "intensive participant observation studies, to be carried out by a sole researcher in a small population, over a period of at least a year."[16] This alone was to count as real anthropology. The logic was straightforward: Attempts to understand unfamiliar lives are fraught with hazards best weathered by the passage of time, trial and error, interpretive courage, and a steady dose of humiliation. Doing ethnography means taking risks and marking time; one needs room to maneuver, to construct an authentic public self which, once out there, can cease to be a cause for worry. It is notoriously inefficient, in part because the method (for which one is always, perhaps even intentionally, poorly prepared) is as much ordeal as it is discipline.[17] If close documentation is fieldwork's singular strength, it can also be its crippling obsession. Not surprisingly, then, reports from the field are typically composed of unequal measures of hard-won self-understanding, reinvented technique, and snippets of freshly appreciated ways of life.[18] Fieldwork, like alpine mountaineering, commonly reads better retrospectively, preferably in large-format photo-essays, than it wears at the time of its undertaking. But when it works, there is nothing like it for capturing a once-alien way of life.

It does, however, require time and the lenience of muddling through. Done on the cheap, in trimmed-down "rapid" format, the negotiated process of establishing a presence is often finessed, and (depending on questions asked) the abbreviated approach risks distortions. The basic commitment, after all, is to render a faithful ("just") reconstruction of the native(s') point(s) of view, and that project can unfold as a much-corrected enterprise. Recent manuals may have demystified qualitative data collection and analysis to some extent, but few would dispute that a sustained ethnography takes practice to pull off. Being well positioned at the outset (e.g., conversant with the work or problem at hand, familiar with key players, able to connect personally) is no small advantage. At the same time, even among those of us who keep the anthropological faith, recourse to "mixed methods" (quantitative and qualitative) is increasingly commonplace. Indeed, in the precincts of mental health services research in which I increasingly ply my trade, it is all but expected. "Keeping things complicated" may well serve as the watchword of classical anthropological method, but in applied work there are times and purposes for which a judiciously pruned version is the preferred one. Much hangs, however, on that "judiciously."

As will be immediately obvious, this inquiry is an unprepossessing example of the sort of "no name anthropology" that, as Stanley Barrett suggests, has been slogging along in the bush while the fireworks of postmodernism command the attention and dazzle the tourists.[19] This anthropology takes seriously the blunt empirical test put to the documentary: to take on the impossible task of "getting it right." Even fiction, literary critic James Wood argues, operating as it does in a realm of "discretionary magic" and free to cultivate belief by toying artfully with what is familiarly real, risks alienating the reader when it toys too much and crosses over into the insistently fantastic.[20] The documentary's tool kit is smaller and its difficulty greater (or at least different), especially if among those it means to address are reader-characters intrinsic to the story. We arrogant comparative few, who dare take stock of the lives of others, do so with an implicit vow of fidelity. Though it may require stretching the tolerances of instruments, putting them to uses not sanctioned by their inventors, even demonstrating how they come up short (though not for want of trying), the trick is to pace off (not defy) the limits and to expose (not invent) the workings inside. Such work requires commitment—hedged (to the irritation of true believers) when need be by reflection, declared more often than not in advance of the late-coming cavalry of evidence. This sort of anthropology, it might be said, operates at the edges of secular faith.

With that ingredient, finally, we arrive at the mixed accounting promised here as a "reckoning." If more plumbing than poetry, that does not mean it should be done without heart or craft.[21] For suffering to be depicted without sentiment, for the hazards of moral narcissism to be averted, some rigor is required. There the discipline can assist.

At the same time, this isn't conventional anthropology either. It shamelessly raids history and grafts quasi-ethnographic methods onto more standardized social science techniques, the better to drive the inquiry forward as contexts and concerns change. Venues and times shift radically—the evolution of the New York City almshouse, the street and shelter scene circa early 1980s, the retrofitting of present-day "hybrid" institutions, the vagaries of a census count, the wisdom of mounting an outreach effort at a municipal airport, the legacy of the courts and mixed record of organized advocacy—and they shift for good reason. In tracing the career of homelessness through this varied terrain, this book is also a log of evolving *work*. It charts the course of one applied anthropologist's two-decades-and-counting engagement with homelessness, from the time that problem originally took shape and thenceforth as it ramified into an assortment of domains. Where the work turned and found focus in large measure mirrored the social concerns spun out of the initial shock of discovery—accurate numbers, measures of pathology (the glaring exception missing here being substance use), reasons for the use and rejection of proffered help, and, eventually, the design of durable solutions. Because that anthropologist was also an activist, it chronicles too the corrective strategies hatched by a nascent advocacy movement and the present-day predicaments that are their progeny.

Ethnographic inquiry on this front was never a self-contained endeavor. Conducting the original investigations, formulating and translating the results, countering alternative readings, shepherding and correcting implications as they rippled far from home—these tasks became part of what the work demanded. As fresh projects took shape, novel problems presented themselves: properly reading history to recover the origins of vestigial practices, adapting ethnographic methods to more cramped confines, wrestling anew with issues of informed consent, collaborating with advocates, dueling with critics, advising not-for-profit organizations, testifying as an expert witness in class-action lawsuits, paying homage to (while taking issue with) a tribal elder, chafing in the harness of contract work, turning state's evidence as a civil servant. Such concerns take shape as "methodological" issues throughout this book. They may look out of place in a purportedly anthropological text. But these are precisely the sort of work-related issues that the majority of contemporary graduate students will face as they finish their doctorates and enter the labor market.[22]

The work at hand includes a roughhewn ethnography—the account of Bowery flophouses, city shelters, and street life, circa 1980–84—but even this segment was a domesticated version of classical tradecraft. I would spend full days and whole nights roaming the streets, observe intake procedure at a city shelter for hours at a time, crash occasionally at a flophouse or mission, and spend two weeks working alongside erstwhile homeless men at a resort hotel in the Catskills. But I was never without a place or company of my own to return to. Danger was a sporadic concern, but never the stubbornly hovering presence it can be for those who live on the streets or in the shelters. Nor, obviously, was livelihood. The briefer sketches that make up (sometimes substantial) parts of other chapters are harder to justify as ethnography, if only because the time devoted to them was more limited and the issues at stake more circumscribed. Consider them instead as hobbled versions of the real thing, making the extra effort to compensate with other methods, and trusting to relevant seasoned work (my own and others') to get it right. The assessment of the roles of advocacy and ethnography in framing homelessness as a social problem with which this book concludes are as much confession as history, and so should probably be read with Nietzsche's warning in mind about pride getting the better part of memory when reconstructing a contested past.

This book concerns not only the "visible poor" (so termed in a fine book of historically informed policy analysis by Joel Blau[23]) but also their invisible counterparts. Indeed, if the analysis put forth here has merit, it is about the absence, finally, of any air-tight distinctions between these two "populations." For the most part, though, I join the tangled crowd of researchers and advocates in addressing myself to the "literally homeless": those without conventional housing (even if only secured through the kindness of kin or friends) for the night, who take up lodging instead in municipal or private shelters, or retreat to the interstices of public space.[24] Always, however, that completing counterpart (the shadow shelter provided in that informal market) should be borne in mind. For "public shelter" is fundamentally the untold story of how those two modalities of support fit together, reciprocally compensating for one another, such that a local "structure" of homeless relief—part official relief, often under an "emergency" rubric; part routine making do, as the welcome and tolerance of accommodating others allow—might be identified. That structure is part and parcel of the evolving mechanisms of "abeyance" described below. The need to understand such a structure if we are to make sense of contemporary poverty is the best argument for an anthropology of makeshifts.[25] That this will mean merrily plundering our store of improvised methods and fashioning new hybrid approaches in the process is the tacit companion argument.

Just to clarify what is missing here, to underscore the unobtrusive character of the makeshifts I have in mind, let me describe one that tumbled, ready-made, on my doorstep. If the anecdote of comeuppance recounted at the outset of this chapter led me to look more closely at what I had assumed I already understood, this one—a part of *life,* I thought for so long, not *work*—went by with scarce a second notice, another notch on my hardening urban soul.

Emma's Story

This time the lesson concerns the habits and habitat of someone I knew. Let me call her Emma. By the mid-1970s, that same graduate student who had been upstaged by a sidewalk classics scholar had moved into his own apartment not far from the university. Long before it would find infamy as "crack alley," the block was a quirky stretch of school yard, warehouses, old law tenements, and a Catholic nursing home with a courtyard graced by a huge oak. On the floor above me in our five-story walk-up lived Emma, an elderly woman of Greek heritage.

To my knowledge, Emma had never been hospitalized, though hers was a decidedly strange way of life. She inhabited a world bristling with menace. Nearly each night, for years, I would find notes slipped under my door, advising me of the latest CIA agent or front operation in the neighborhood. Although electric with urgency, the notes asked for no action on my part, so I would simply smile in knowing conspiracy the next time I ran into her. Late in the game, before some signal reached her warning that I too was not to be trusted (possibly because she had determined that I was *not,* after all, Kris Kristofferson making a movie in the building), I was astonished to discover that some of the notes were scribbled in the margins of postcards that had been mailed to her from Paris some forty years earlier.

Emma was no homebody. She had lived for half a century with her mother in the apartment. On her own now, she set out on daily excursions that took her far and wide on the Upper West Side. Dragging eighty pounds of belongings in a grocery cart behind her, topped off with a rabbit in a portable hutch, she made her way through the streets with a pronounced limp and an occasional flurry of invective. Though she had been robbed repeatedly, she continued her wanderings, ending up home in the early evening. Eyeing me critically each time I made the offer, she would sometimes let me wrestle the load up to her floor.

A philosophy professor, the late Peter Putnam, had somehow met and befriended Emma. He enrolled her in community art classes and, at her request, combed through mounds of her "pseudo-Byronic" poetry looking for something publishable. Emma would occasionally show up unannounced at faculty–student affairs, and Peter would raid the cold cuts or cartons of Chinese food to put something together for her. He got on with her better than anyone else, but even he could run afoul of her fickle suspicions. Once, in a snit, she dumped a pint of black paint over the windows of his apartment.

Night was especially difficult for Emma. Alone in her rooms, she could occasionally be heard wailing, crying, fending off the thought rays of the CIA, or shouting in arguments with adversaries who, it turned out, had long since departed this earth. My next-door neighbor, an elderly Irish widow, would bang on the ceiling with her broom whenever Emma "went off." And, after a while, the ruckus would cease. If it went on too long, the super would traipse on up to look in on her.

For the eight years I knew her, Emma lived a hair's breadth away from homelessness. But for the kindness of our building super (Cournelius Jouwstra, a man who had abandoned the formal ministry years before, on the night before his investiture, to pursue what he felt to be a more honest vocation); but for the solicitousness of the neighbors who would look in from time to time to see that she had enough to eat, and would never think of calling the authorities to complain of her ravings; but for the rent-controlled apartment she had inherited from her mother; but for the sure sanctuary she found in that ramshackle tenement—she could have wound up one of the city's rag-wrapped street dwellers.

When Ellen Baxter and I began our research on homeless adults in the early 1980s, there were times when a trick of shadow or a familiar quirk of gait would suggest that Emma had at last fallen through. It never happened. The "but fors" held true. She remained, a bit more enfeebled for the wear and tear, a tenant. Years later, it would dawn on me that it is these "but fors" that make for the difference between the margins and the street.[26] I may have made Emma's acquaintance, but I failed, for some time, to make the connection.

Course of Inquiry

This study charts the reemergence of homelessness in New York City in the 1980s and carries the story through the late 1990s, with special attention to the situation of homeless men. I focus on men for three reasons. First and foremost is a methodological and archival given: Male gender shaped the terms of access and affiliation in my own ethnographic efforts and dominates the historical record. The social history of vagrancy within which this inquiry is located is largely a history of men on the road or on the skids. Second, since the mid-1980s, the wheel of social opinion has turned inexorably forward once again—focusing on families rather than "unattached" men, as happened earlier in the 1930s—to the detriment of the men who first gave evidence of the new homelessness. Public sympathy, outraged exposé,[27] and the largest share of public resources are now targeted almost exclusively at the plight of homeless women with children. Where men do participate in specialized public programs, it is chiefly by virtue of disability; otherwise, they are sent to warehouses—and even that option (however mean, it is still unearned) is increasingly under attack. The stain of disgrace and danger, seemingly indelible when it comes to homeless men, is (or was until recently) provisionally lifted for purposes of salvaging families. Finally, this study highlights the situation of men, especially the young African American males who make up the bulk of the shelter population in New York, because this group has proved most vulnerable to the dislocations of deindustrialization.[28]

The text follows a divided course, mirroring my dual objectives: first, to come to a better understanding of the wellsprings of homelessness in American society and the complex of attitudes brought to bear on it as a social problem; and second, to take retrospective measure of practical attempts to remedy and ethnographic efforts to document. The remainder of this chapter sets out a framework for interpreting contemporary homelessness in light of long-standing dilemmas of classification. Chapter 2 draws on the official annals of vagrancy, the almshouse and the municipal lodging house, as well as the observations and commentary of contemporaries, to reconstruct the main contours of the history of homeless men in New York City. Its aims are to challenge the revisionist view of them chiefly as passive victims and to identify continuities and discontinuities in the public response (formal and informal).

Part II puts fieldwork to use as a vehicle for understanding homelessness from the ground up. Chapter 3 retraces the original ethnographic work, done with Ellen Baxter from 1979 to 1983, and argues that reasons of adaptation best explain why men choose to live on the streets. Two ethnographic sketches follow. Chapter 4 examines one contemporary niche of homelessness, the metropolitan airport, stressing the fragility of the contingencies that made it preferable (for the time being) to available formal alternatives. Chapter 5 updates the picture of the streets, drawing on add-on (what Sue Barrow calls "bootlegged") ethnography done in the course of assessing the 1990 census count. Chapter 6 examines in some detail the largely neglected story of homelessness among African American men, and attempts to set that record a little straighter. This chapter also provides a more sustained account of how macroeconomic developments, local culture, and individual agency interact in the production (and prevention) of homelessness.

Part III, Advocacy and Engagement, turns to applied matters in other sectors. Chapter 7 recounts the story of national advocacy for the homeless poor since 1980 (to which I've served as unofficial participant observer), with particular attention to still-ongoing litigation in New York City. Finally,

Chapter 8 tries to bring it all back home: to ask what ethnography has wrought in telling the story of contemporary homelessness and to suggest how it might proceed—if not to make the world a better place, at least to rig the chances that pockets of it might be a little less cruel.

Dilemmas of Classification

Like "the poor," those whom we understand to be "the homeless" historically "emerge when society elects to recognize [homelessness] as a special status and assigns specific persons to that category."[29] Not unmet need *per se,* but a distinct set of "practices" and a formal social response—often taking shape under circumstances of exigency or confrontation—distinguish the homeless poor in the most elementary fashion. Whether as recipients of emergency relief, as workers (or dodgers of work) of a particularly rough and disreputable sort, as wanderers or squatters, as the merely displaced, or as veterans of life on the street life—those who make up a period's official roster of houseless poverty are the product not of a natural distinction drawn but of a cultural decision taken. Are they members of our moral community or not? Conventions of recognition and legitimation apply to the homeless no less than they do to those who never leave the safe confines of hearth and home.

For this reason, the literature on homelessness in times past, though voluminous and varied, can be an unreliable guide, leading the unwary to deceptively familiar terrain.[30] Studies of the indigent on the Continent in the late feudal period or ancien régime make frequent mention of an itinerant poor who, but for their mobility, turn out to be all but indistinguishable from the poor at large.[31] Owing to the dislocations following the dissolution of the monasteries, the tangled skein of Poor Laws, and the upheavals caused by land enclosures and the rise of industrial towns, the English story is even more detailed and disputed.[32] Huge tomes have been assembled on the history of the vagrant and fine studies have appeared of the tramp,[33] both of which highlight the uncertainty of work in newly free and increasingly flexible labor markets. Some anecdotal and autobiographical material aside, until recently little was known about the history of homeless women.[34]

Definitional quandaries have long plagued discussions of American homelessness. As anyone who has ventured even a brief look at the past can attest, the historical record on this phenomenon—even the use of the term itself—is extraordinarily uneven. In part, this reflects linguistic convention, prevailing ways of thinking about social problems, and the efforts of advocates, reformers, and other interest groups to shape public perception and ways of talking. Invariably, of course, when raiding the past for instances of homelessness, scholars must be tacitly guided by some notion of what should count as such an instance. Still, even when we think we have stumbled across unmistakable constancies over time, caution is the rule in interpreting them. One period's "vagrant," for example, may be another's "tramp," only to show up later as a "migrant worker." But the common denominator of their homelessness is not necessarily the obvious one of their "lacking customary and regular access to a conventional dwelling."[35] In fact, if we mean to investigate ways of life, and not merely irregular shelter, the surface picture is deceptive. For in this instance, intermittent lack of shelter was secondary to the circumstances of available labor; members of all three groups would vigorously protest being lumped with what, to all appearances, was the indistinguishable "bum" with no interest in work at all.[36] Most pertinent for our purposes, with the exception of time spent on the road or in makeshift quarters at the work site, these men were rarely without housing and almost never procured it at public expense. Their work was marginal, their lives reflected that fact, and their housing—disreputable though it may have been—followed suit.[37]

If classifying ways of life as homeless is difficult, shifting from persons to places to take the measure of local homelessness merely serves up a different set of problems. Cheap residential hotels, boarding and rooming homes, even flophouses, all served a varied clientele that one would be hard pressed to lump together as homeless. Public relief, on the other hand, looks like a promising lead: the mid-nineteenth century police station–house denizen, for example, is easily recognized as a municipal lodging house client half a century later. But lengths of stay in both forms of shelter were regulated, records made no distinction between lodgers and nights of lodging, and when capacity was exhausted additional demand was simply turned away. There is simply no way of gauging unmet need from the imperfect records of sheltering agencies. Similarly, it may seem not much of a stretch to discern the kinship between one era's shanty settlements and another's, but documentation of such places is haphazard at best and their occupancy uncertain. And Central Park's Depression-era Hooverville, with its substantial constructions and active political organization (including a voting rights campaign), is a far cry from the isolated hovels that punctuated the New York City landscape sixty years later.

The above examples mostly have to do with the recognizably shelterless. What about the thousands of routinely displaced poor, those for whom coping with irregular lodging arrangements (let alone frequent moves or "residential instability") was a staple fact of life? Or the elderly indigent man, interviewed by Charles Barnes in 1912, who was without lodging only because he *would not* go to the city almshouse; he simply could not accept that there was no useful work for which he was fit? Or the thousands of southern blacks who took to the road in the wake of emancipation as an expression of newborn freedom to move about as one wished?

Official records are not only incomplete but may be misleading. To be homeless during the early years of the Great Depression in New York City meant only that one did not meet settlement standards (one year of domicile) and thus was ineligible for local relief; instead, one signed up for assistance through the Federal Transient Program. Significant numbers of "homeless families" were assisted in their own homes.[38] Fifty years later, local jurisdictions across the country scrambled to respond to a rapidly mounting need for emergency shelter by resorting to a variety of makeshifts—shared living arrangements, converted congregate settings, commercial lodgings, quasi-therapeutic facilities, minimally refurbished warehouses—all listed under "homeless assistance."[39] For similarly strategic reasons (qualifying for aid that would otherwise be out of reach), labeling one's own hardship as homeless may occur.[40] Conversely, others hunkered down in homemade street-dwellings will defiantly reject the term.

Scholarly monographs come with their own hazards. In the mid-1960s, the Columbia Bowery Project defined as *homeless* anyone who was poor, had severed the ties with family and community, and lived alone in lowly quarters, only one type of which proved to be a public shelter (the rest were single-room-occupancy hotels [SROs] and flophouses).[41] But, as noted above, that same group of lodgers ("unattached to a family, they had few possessions, enjoyed recreational drinking, worked intermittently, and traveled often") historically accounted for the core of the residential hotel population.[42] With few exceptions, too, researchers have directed their attention to those currently without shelter, missing many who are intermittently in that condition—not only those who manage to cadge a berth on a friend's couch or living room floor, but seasonal workers who continue to replicate the century-old rhythms of on-again, off-again employment.

Finally, consider how cultural factors and political mobilization may determine what gets expressed as homelessness. It was only recently that the ready availability of shelters for battered women, coupled with a feminist campaign against tolerance of domestic violence, led to the emergence of a new species of need from behind the scrim of homebound privacy.

Framing Constructs: Abeyance and Liminality[43]

It would take an elastic notion of homelessness to accommodate this unwieldy mix of station and circumstance. Indeed, the suspicion quickly mounts that seeking to impose order on the hodgepodge of dislocation, extreme poverty, migrant work, unconventional ways of life, and bureaucratic expediency that have, at one time or another, been labeled *homeless* may well be a fool's errand. Pathology, deviance, moral weakness, unreason, resistance, and victimization have all had their day as reigning constructs. Their proponents remain active in contemporary debates, selecting from among the available data evidence in support. Not surprisingly, they often appear to be talking past one another—if, that is, they are talking about the same thing.

A different approach is taken here. I borrow two concepts from anthropology and historical sociology—liminality and abeyance, respectively—that force us to move away from surface appearance in favor of underlying processes. Although these processes have occasionally given rise to various forms of homelessness or provisional shelter throughout history, their usual mode of operation is different, forcing us to notice not how frequently homelessness happens but how rarely. They direct our attention to de facto preventive mechanisms that go unnoticed as such—like those "but fors" that enabled my neighbor Emma to remain housed.

Abeyance

For Mizruchi, *abeyance* solves the generic problem of a mismatch between the (relatively scarce) available positions in a society and the (typically excessive) supply of potential claimants. As he sees it, various mechanisms have been devised to absorb surplus people and neutralize the potential mischief of idle hands. Such functionally inclusive "status slots" take shape under a variety of auspices: the state (frontier settlements, public works, compulsory education), breakaway religious orders (monasteries, abbeys), or countercultural movements (alternative communities). They have in common the makings of sustenance and industry—functional equivalents of work—and if necessary lodging, for redundant people who might pose a threat to social order.[44]

Applying the notion to any setting as beleaguered as New York in the closing decades of the twentieth century is no challenge. Throughout the 1980s, the word commonly used to characterize its large public shelters was *warehouse.* One might assume the term owed its currency to the provenance of such places: hastily converted armories, recycled hospital and school buildings—mothballed properties, in short. With Mizruchi's scheme in mind, the usage is more telling. The "integration and surveillance" functions of abeyance are ideally performed by social forms that

> [are] materially uncompetitive with participation in main-line economic activities . . . [Thus] they do function as warehousing activities in capitalist soci-

eties, since they hold personnel out of the labor force at a cost that contributes to the maintenance of low wages in the economic sphere.[45]

Note how abeyance subtly reframes the scandal of homelessness. Contrary to the moral calculus of advocates, the decisive issue becomes not *whether* homelessness will be "solved" but *how;* not whether adequate resources will be devoted to this problem, but how what counts as "adequate" will be determined; not whether a coherent response will take shape, but how the relative proportions of relief and repression that make for "coherent" policy will be calculated; not whether, when all is said and done, some measure of discomfort will be exacted of ordinary citizens, but how this potentially divisive spectacle will be held in check. The question is how people with insufficient resources to purchase housing on the market (and unable or disinclined to turn to friends or family) will be accommodated, and this remains the question even if such reabsorptive mechanisms never proclaim themselves as "solutions to homelessness."[46] After all, the last two prolonged periods of redundancy and homelessness this country experienced, in the Progressive Era and the Depression, were solved by the domestic mobilization for world war. Nor was combat or wartime industry the end of it. Homelessness resurged in the wake of demobilization after World War I, and likely would have done so in the late 1940s save for the abeyance measure called the G.I. Bill. Land giveaways and like concessions have long been used by governments eager to stave off "the evils of a collection of landless, disgruntled ex-soldiers," such as prowled the newly industrializing American landscape in the wake of the Civil War.[47]

Reframing homelessness as the problem of redundant people lacking sufficient resources (money or kin) to secure housing redirects our assessment of the social response to homelessness. It may make better sense to think of "regular access to a conventional dwelling" more as *work* than *residence,* in ways analogous to those used by economists in measuring "regular access to a conventional job." Just as the official "unemployment" rate is understood to be but a pale index of the true extent of joblessness, so are "literal" homeless rates poor indicators of real residential instability. Analysts must learn to take account of the absorptive capacities of non–homeless institutions and informal practices (such as doubling up) in the same way as labor economists have learned to examine alternative "employments" in military service, prisons, hospitals, and the informal economy.[48] This will mean tracking the institutional hybrids other than shelters—functional equivalents of yesterday's almshouses, bridewells, asylums, workhouses, city homes, and police stations—that are pressed into service to lodge the otherwise homeless poor.[49]

Liminality

Liminality refers to various "states of passage" through which designated members of a culture travel at specified times of "transition." For the duration of passage, such people are "betwixt and between," suspended between the well-known roles they have left behind and the unknown demands of a new life. Because they occupy no fixed position, they are considered dangerous. Special precautions are taken to sequester them away from ordinary social life. Deputized guides are there to expedite the process and serve as mentors. Initiation rites are the best known example in traditional societies, but other critical periods of transition (entering marriage, assuming leadership, taking religious vows, apprenticing in a profession) may be similarly treated. Typically undertaken in secret or in ritually segregated settings, such rites entail taxing ordeals through which initiates are guided. For the duration of passage, the usual social markers of distinction are erased—a "leveling" process that, along with the experience of shared suffering, encourages intense and enduring bonds of solidarity among initiates. But no matter how rigorous the ordeal or sublime the "communitas" experienced en route, the frank expectation is that the initiate will return to ordinary life and resume her responsibilities.

Liminality, with its peculiar blend of peril and privilege, may even extend to those who temporarily remove themselves from the sway of convention. Pilgrimages, religious retreats, secular festivals, even wilderness treks—all briefly suspend responsibility and court uncertainty. Crises, too, may do it: consider the suspension of routine that follows natural disasters (epidemics, floods), civic disturbances (wars or revolutions), or private misfortunes (a death in the family). And the annals of medical anthropology, both at home and abroad, are filled with accounts of the strategic exploitation (whether done consciously or not) of the liberating potential of the liminal experience of affliction.[50] All such states share core elements: suspension of the rule of the commonplace; intermingling with unfamiliar others in strange settings, often mobile circumstances; and a heightened sense of uncertainty, of things being unfinished and in process.

It is this last property, the fact that the process sometimes takes place without experienced guides in poorly mapped territory, that makes for a certain indeterminacy. Occasionally, that is, the process stalls, the return fails to take place as projected, and the liminal period becomes extended. Should this persist, the built-in expectation of a return (on the part of both voyager and awaiting community) may attenuate, eventually giving way to a routinization of the displacement itself. A kind of forgetfulness sets in, the tug of broken ties and forgone appointments weakens, the becalmed voyager finds a substitute normalcy taking shape (as happened with "shelterized men" during the Great Depression). What began as a moratorium on business as usual morphs into a form of life in its own right.

In the momentous dislocations of the late Middle Ages, for example, various outlaw groups contrived to make a virtue of livelihood out of the necessity of displacement. In the process, haphazard mobilities became durable institutions. The Franciscans and other mendicant orders trace their origins in this fashion; so does English wayfaring. More colorfully, the bands of "wandering scholars" who traversed the circuit of monasteries in the fourteenth century turned liturgical mischief into unruly livelihood, until the church hierarchy decided it was unamused by the goliards' parodies of sacred hymns and cracked down on the practice. Gypsies over the ages have survived on the edges and in the interstices of settled life.[51]

Sometimes, too, the routinization of displacement creates a social and cultural *limbo,* that place of forgotten confinement supposed by Catholic theologians in the past to be situated just this side of hell. Its pain was singular, because punishment was not its raison d'être. Limbo was an invention of ecclesiastical logic, not jurisprudence, reserved for those souls born too early in history (righteous pagans) or dying too early in life (unbaptized infants) to be held to the test of confessing Christ as savior. Limbo was a celestial holding mechanism. Unlike stalled liminality that manages to create an alternative destination, limbo describes a state of suspended resolution, an anomalous way-station for those with nowhere else to go. Downsized corporate executives are a modern-day example of lives in limbo; they embody a "living contradiction" of the American promise—talented managers out of work.[52] Unless comparable positions open up in the market or in public employ, their predicament may persist without ever being resolved. The sense of being in one's proper station may stay elusive.

Liminality is plainly relevant to homelessness when dislocations coincide with critical transitions, like the move to set up an independent household.[53] But liminality opens two other possibilities. First, it can give birth to new livelihoods. What begins as a way-station en route to established roles can be institutionalized, becoming part of the abeyance process proper. This may happen directly, as with the normalization of extended unemployed adolescence in the high school,[54] or at one remove, as with the burgeoning not-for-profit shelter and service industry established to manage homelessness as a standing social problem.[55] Second, although liminal passage is usually undertaken for specific reasons, in known territory, with every expectation of return, that cultural process may be upset and the markers dislodged. When that happens, the stage is set for forced improvisation. In late-twentieth-century America, life-course transitions in general have become more individualized, less bound to strategic family decisions, less subject to custom's scripting.[56] Certain forms of liminality are riskier, more easily derailed; the stranded casualties, alternatives devised, and inventiveness brought into play all should be documented.

Implications

Why open the analytic frame to these brassy newcomers, abeyance and liminality? In a phrase: fidelity to forms of life—improvised, reordered, parched, or scuttled as circumstances may dictate. No matter how finely ground the lens, how penetrating the depth of field, or how fine the composition, a focus on literal homelessness will be distorted because it misses features integral to the fuller story. It skips the messy history, sells short the exhausted support structures, ignores alternative patterns of support that keep vulnerable others housed, and neglects the steady throb of an economy uninterested in these workers. A twin concern with abeyance and liminality, on the other hand, could revivify the ethnographic corrective on this subject.

In the first place, it would speed the development of an anthropology of makeshifts, one tuned to the unscripted complexities of unconventional residential arrangements, muddled-through transitions, persisting lack of settlement, and patchworked livelihoods. As Carol Stack did in tracking the "call to home" that yesterday's African American urban migrants are heeding by returning South in growing numbers today,[57] it would attend to long-dormant kinship bonds, hidden resources and moldering debts, the resources of social capital, and application of newly acquired skills in venues left long ago. It would examine the regulatory nightmare of "hazardous housing"—illegally converted multiple dwellings that accommodate thousands of New Yorkers (some recent immigrants, some disabled, some simply dirt poor) in a shadow market, a practice implicitly endorsed when the city cuts back on building inspections.[58] It would inquire into the strategic disregard that enables public housing authorities to ignore standing evidence of widespread illegal doubling up in their own units, over a period of twenty years. And it would try to take the measure of alternatives to homelessness—directing our attention toward *displacement that doesn't happen* and demanding our considered judgment as to why it doesn't.[59] It would muster and channel our investigative energies to describe those hidden local utilities (informal, often legally proscribed) that enable poor households to survive on their own. It would attend carefully to their practical logic, abiding values, and flexible skills (what James Scott calls *mētis*[60]). It might even examine how official programs and policies contend with them.[61]

So what, in the end, is the image of homelessness that takes shape in these pages? Shorn of romance, rebellion, and (in substantial measure) unreason, it is a far more routine fact of life on the margins. Materially, it emerges out of a tangled but unmysterious mix of factors: scarce housing (especially of the "disreputable" sort), poorly planned and badly implemented policies of relocation and support, dismal prospects of work, exhausted or alienated kin. Culturally, a distinctively American genealogy can be traced in the grand themes that weave through this account: distancing and abandonment; utility, work, and worth; the limits of kindness and reach of kinship; the mixed blessings that come from bucking the system and holding out hope for a more humane alternative. And though it explains little and may be glimpsed only occasionally in the pages to come, any outreach worker could tell you that list would be incomplete without one more: how misery can come to prefer its own company.

Rectifying homelessness will require both attention to the structural roots of widespread dispossession and some measure of direct action. A structural analysis of the huge barreling forces that make for the scandal of homelessness today does nothing to exculpate those of us who must live with the wreckage. It doesn't solve the mundane dilemmas of whether to give to panhandlers, to volunteer in soup kitchens, to argue with your parish over the conflicted clemencies of "harm reduction," to support local shelters absent any plan to move their residents on to housing, or to train outreach workers in the arts of reaching people who have every reason to distrust the system those artful workers will pass them on to.

I don't believe there is, or can be, a "progressive," structurally informed response to panhandling, for example. Immediate suffering, no matter how predetermined its genesis or gratuitous its appearance, demands a response that a social science of injustice cannot plot. We may wonder, with an exasperation that matches our former youthful allergy to the same apparatus, "Where is the state when you need it?"—but that merely postpones the reckoning. These are matters of moral suasion, of conscience, and they *ought* to remain troubling and unsettled. If they have a connection to macro-order analyses it is indirect; such encounters serve to remind us that behind the bloodless abstractions of poverty counts and statistical trends are lives of gritty substance, in sometimes unnerving proximity, that make unspoken claims for a fair share of the commonweal. Wrestling with such questions, refusing to consign them to some ready-made algorithm of "to-give-or-not-to-give" (the "broken window" theory, for instance[62]), seems to me good practice in contemporary citizenship.

At the same time, some street-level providers worry about the long-term effects of their rescue and life-support work.[63] Others, increasingly dependent on public funds for their operation, find that vocal advocacy and organizing efforts sit uneasily with the town fathers.[64] Conversely, what a Yonkers cleric on our local shelter board insists upon seeing as "a ministry of restoration," I cannot help but *also* fathom as the dirty, unpaid work of routine system maintenance. Nor are the implications of these small-time Faustian bargains lost on would-be clients: At a meeting of the National Coalition for the Homeless in Nashville in 1993, one homeless critic sardonically congratulated the assembled advocates for "doing a real good job of managing homelessness." I see no way around such binds except to recognize them as contradictions to be lived with—even as we work with the blunt institutional forces at our command to staunch the flow of new casualties—not inconsistencies to be rid of.

But all that fancy talk is where this anthropologist ends up. This book is about the rough road he followed to get here.

[2]

Unearned Keep: From Almshouse to Shelter in New York City

> Dependent homeless persons have always been a problem in New York City and whether by discipline or charity, or both, the attention of the public has been challenged on numerous occasions. Each time the public seems to have met the challenge in the easiest and most expedient manner, with very little reference to previous experience and with only intermittent, casual interest in the future.
>
> Nels Anderson, *The Homeless in New York City*

When tradition stubbornly resists change while all around evidence mounts that change is needed, an anthropologist's curiosity is piqued, especially one working on the home front. Such appears consistently to be the case with cultural images of vagrancy in the United States for the last two centuries. An idiom of impairment (mental, moral, or physical) has dominated official discourse in the face of persistent indications that a contrary, more complicated picture is warranted. Homeless men did the dirty work of early industrialization—laying track, cutting timber, building bridges, digging irrigation ditches and canals, working mines. But they also swelled the ranks of redundant workers when seasonal demand fell off, depressions hit, or machinery displaced men. "Casual labor" may have been essential to the flexible demands of an expanding economy, but this fact earned such men little respect and much suspicion in its off seasons.

No doubt, the burden they posed could be difficult at times, but even depictions of that burden tend to amplify their deviance and diminish what they share in common with the rest of us. Homeless men may have lined up by the thousands for food and lodging in municipal shelters and soup kitchens, but more often they prevailed upon kin and friends to put them up. Some took to tramping in a determined attempt to avoid work, but others hit the road because they knew of no other way of looking for it. Organized bands may have challenged the established order (say, in pitched confrontations with a local constabulary), but such run-ins were rare and the symbolic threat—that a livelihood could conceivably be had outside the regular wage relationship—was always the deeper affront. Twice, when all else failed and even experts despaired of restoring these torpid figures to useful employment, homeless men were drafted in a war effort by a government that had all but forgotten them.

Not that a concern with impairment is irrelevant to the story of homelessness. Disease, disability, and death have always been more prevalent among men on the road or in the shelters. It is the imperial power of affliction—the way a concern with "what's wrong with" such men rules public debate and restricts analysis of causes to "risk factors" located in troubled individuals—that I mean to question here. Long-standing cultural currents figure in such displacements: a deep-seated ambivalence toward dependency, anxiety about the shaky purchase of the work ethic among unsettled men, fears of mobility itself (people without ties were thought to be without norms as well), resentment by ordinary working people of their own ordinary working lot, the deep distrust shown by organized charity toward those of its charges who prove uncooperative or indifferent. All were variations of a theme: These men are "not like us." This insistence makes the annals of U.S. homelessness a tangled tale of contempt, pity, and, curiously, blank disregard.

This chapter attempts to balance the books somewhat. It shifts from men to practices and from beleaguered institutions to networks of subsistence. It accentuates the issue of redundancy and the logic of holding unneeded men in "abeyance," the ironies and ambiguities involved in implementing the English poor law principle of "less eligibility,"[1] the role of kinship in the shadow market of shelter, and the nagging complaint that poor people "misuse" public shelters. It also examines the distancing maneuvers at work in some then-contemporary accounts of homeless men. I make a deliberate effort to view *shelter* not as a material space but as a social utility, one met by a variety of formal and informal means. Only some of those means are classified as "homeless relief" at any particular time, which should raise questions about the segregation of "the homeless" as a distinct class.

A Miscellany of Refuges

New York has traditionally dealt with its "vagrant poor" through a haphazard mix of repression, segregated shelter, and energetic charity, all bracketed (Nels Anderson reminded us in the early 1930s) by an apparent indifference to a broader poverty seemingly impervious to lasting redress. Public relief buffered individuals against the dislocations of the labor market, eased the burden on kinship in sorely strapped households, and alleviated the plight of widows and orphans. But it did not do so eagerly. Historians of social welfare have stressed the exemplary value of the "spectacle of the degraded pauper."[2] The ruinous nature of that broader poverty, however, made degradation a relative thing. Nor could a bracing lesson for the poor be allowed to become too unsettling an assault on the sensibilities of the better off. In the event, elemental shelter proved an embarrassed affair of mirrors: The marginality of the city's homeless poor has consistently been mimicked by the means pursued to deal with them.

Early Poor Relief

Formal provision for overnight sheltering of the indigent in New York City dates from 1886, when the state legislature passed the Municipal Lodging House Act, authorizing the city to establish facilities for the overnight lodging of the homeless poor. Statute in this instance lagged well behind common practice. Spurred by recurrent depressions, the noisome importuning of beggars, and the specter of visible suffering, the city had long played host to "soup houses," public work programs, and temporary shelters intended to ease the lot of the desperate poor. Such measures also served to mask evidence of their presence and to mute the threat to property.

Under both Dutch and British rule, early poor relief in the colonial city was a patchwork of local and county control, canonical and secular authority, church collections and disbursements from the public treasury. Where kinship failed or proved unavailable in time of need, custom stepped in. Eligibility for relief had little to do with merit and everything to do with where one last called home. Religious duty and outpost solidarity alike made it "unthinkable" that any of one's neighbors should go begging. As had been the case in sixteenth century Europe, mobility and scale proved to be the undoing of casual relief. Custom was simply unequal to the demands of circulating strangers when their numbers grew markedly.[3]

Colonial households commonly included boarders, among whom were dependent strangers put up at town government expense. Nonetheless, by the late seventeenth century, the city (working with local churches) found it necessary to rent a separate building for use as emergency housing for residents without friends or family to provide for them. In 1734, it erected its first formal almshouse—a multipurpose "House of Correction, Workhouse and Poorhouse"—on the grounds of present-day City Hall. So thoroughly was the morality of poor relief at that time imbued with the inflections of kinship, that residents were referred to as "Family" in the posted rules of the house. But as the references to "correction" and "work" in its name suggest, and the enabling legislation makes clear, this was something more than a step-household for the kinless poor. In fact, it was a catch-all for the delinquent and lost. In the Charter of 1731, it was expressly provided that this was to be a place of confinement for "Beggars, Servants running away or otherwise misbehaving themselves, Trespassers, Rogues, Vagabonds, and poor people refusing to work." A close look at the terms coupled in that grouping reveals what historians have confirmed more generally: so closely allied was the social status of "vagrant" with that of "slave" in the colonial period that New York's almshouse served as "a sort of calaboose [jail] for unruly slaves." "Here," in the terse description of a later historian, "slaves were kept for correction, and the very poor sheltered."[4]

Discipline, whether as enforced work or frank punishment, appears early in the almshouse's history. Inmates' routine was strictly regimented, with repeated efforts to find ways of occupying the idle. Useful work was an obvious option. But contracting out pauper labor, or applying it to public works projects, encountered objections from "free labor." Owing to the large proportion of the almshouse's residents who were mothers with children, elderly, or disabled, even had suitable projects been available, enforcing compulsory work would have been awkward. Still, however impractical as a rule it may have been, this concern with disciplining paupers suggests the extent to which the dependent poor had become a suspect class. Relief soon gives way to rehabilitation, and a jaundiced eye settles on those who profess to have no other option. By the mid-eighteenth century, a more discriminating approach is apparent *outside* the almshouse as well. Street-sweeps, designed to rid city thoroughfares of vagrants, mendicants, "Negroes," and "common prostitutes" were initiated in the early 1800s and periodically renewed, in an effort to "discountenance" the lawless poor and "remove" those without proper residence in the state. Otherwise, the commissioners of the almshouse fretted, the mistaken impression might be had that our "poor are but illy provided for."[5]

Late in the 1700s, a plaint was raised that recurs throughout the following century and extended well into the twentieth. Critics, motivated as much by morality as by concerns over squandered public funds, charged that the poorhouse was subject to rampant misuse. Instead of the instrument of "wholesome penitentiary" originally intended, it had become "too much a common receptacle for idle, intemperate vagrants, many of whom have no lawful residence [here], and who by pretended illness or otherwise . . . greatly incommod[e] those who are real objects of charity."[6]

Yet for all the allegations of misuse, neither this facility, nor any subsequently set up to harbor the indigent, would solve the problem of people whose predicament could not be neatly classified, let alone those who preferred to slip the strictures of official relief altogether. The almshouse aggregated a myriad of custody and care chores that had previously been distributed throughout the community. It nursed the terminally ill, took in the chronically disabled, put up deserted children and newly arrived strangers, and punished those whose behavior fell outside the jurisdiction of penal institutions. Into so broad a compass fell not only the luckless or criminal, but "friendless laboring people and vagabonds" as well. And therein lay the perplexity at the heart of this attempt to reason the needs of a variegated poor. No matter how stringently the almshouse of the late eighteenth and early nineteenth centuries attempted to winnow the ranks of applicants, reaching on occasion to supplement its usual regimen of "terror and economy" with such exotic imports as the "stepping mill",[7] the homeless poor continued to patronize it. English poor law stipulated that provisions for the dependent poor were to be "less eligible" (attractive) than the lot of the most menial laborer. But operating by that standard proved difficult—less because of the perversities of the poor than because of the wretchedness of prevailing alternatives. Institutionalized "terror" found it difficult to compete with the everyday squalor and routine degradations of slum life in the tenements and cellar dwellings available to the indigent. To anyone with even a fleeting acquaintance with local conditions, that is, making the public provision for the poor "less eligible" than what the market offered would have seemed an invitation to cruelty.[8]

Consolidation of the Institutional Response

The mid-nineteenth century marks a crucial point in the transition from what might be called a *domestic* mode of relief, based in (sometimes subsidized) households, to an *institutional* one, based in separate facilities operated by the state. But among the dependent poor there were those for whom neither the residual reach of kinship nor the mushrooming stock of institutional alternatives proved workable for long. Footloose, indigent, occasionally stranded, sometimes chronically without means or mettle, these formed the company in whose name public shelters would first be established.

Early in 1866, the Department of Charities and Corrections, "feeling the great evil of homelessness among the honest poor," opened a lodging house for three months. A decade later, a citizens' group, the "Night Refuge Association," repeated the experiment. Nor were these the first. For years, the police had routinely put up the stranded or shelterless, certainly well before

1857 when legislation was passed requiring each borough to designate a station house "for the lodging of vagrant and disorderly persons." Demand for these crude refuges soared with economic downturns and declined chiefly when vagrancy statutes were enforced. No one considered these arrangements satisfactory—in fact, they were repeatedly condemned as offenses to decency and hygiene—but they did provide an alternative to the stricter regimens of the almshouse and workhouse. Indeed, in their informality, the police stations were a new form of relief: unstructured, part-time, entailing no further submission to authority than agreeing to behave oneself for the night. This practice of offering the "soft side of a plank" to the city's vagrant poor inaugurated a policy of improvisation that has endured to the present.[9]

The poor of the nineteenth century city were everywhere apparent. Begging was commonplace. Rag-pickers foraged through garbage for discarded items and scrap food. "Wild children" roamed the streets. Poverty's hidden reaches were vaster still: a huge reservoir of sickly, poorly paid, badly housed, and frequently unemployed people, whose margin of day-to-day survival provided only a hair's breadth of protection against overt "beggary." As it grew larger and more conspicuous, poverty took on more menacing overtones. Physically, the danger was epidemic disease; morally, it was pauperism, the contagious example set for the working poor; socially, as the draft riots of 1865 and periodic outbursts of gang violence served to remind, it was latent anarchy. Charity reformers became convinced that the outcast poor were forming lumpen societies of their own, impervious to the civilizing effects of the city proper.[10]

A sequestered program of relief, one explicitly designed to contain an alien threat, seemed the appropriate remedy. Specialized institutions were set up to deal with properly "classified" subgroups of the poor—in New York City, both the asylum (1839) and the workhouse (1850) had been added to the almshouse and penitentiary by the mid-nineteenth century—and for once the location of such facilities perfectly mimicked the social status of their inmates. "[D]ivinely arranged as a home for the unfortunate and suffering . . . a place of quiet reformatory meditation for the vicious," the four islands of the East River were pressed into service for this express purpose. By 1886, they were home not only to the men's and women's almshouses, workhouse, and penitentiary, but to fourteen hospitals, two insane asylums, a home for the indigent blind, a house of refuge for juvenile delinquents, and the city's Potter's Field.[11]

That the poor continued to make use of such facilities—"instead of looking to prison as a terror, they look forward to it as an abode of care, an asylum from wretchedness," as one exasperated alderman put it—says something about the folly of the original mission. Not for the last time, brave plans for an architecture of deterrence and rehabilitation foundered, checked by the sheer scale of need and the wiles of "an intractable and slippery poor" whom want had left desperate and taught to be canny. The dream of the well-ordered poorhouse, dispensing care to the infirm and exacting useful work from the indolent, may have outlasted the century, but its practical legacy was failure. The poorhouse (or "City Home") and the shelters to which the more vigorous or cantankerous of its traditional clientele would be shunted remained outposts of institutional discards and people for whom no other option worked.[12]

Alternatives to the "Island of Penance"

For its part, private charity did little to ease the lot of the disreputable poor, preferring instead to pioneer new disciplinary techniques for their edification. Aside from the few emergency measures described above, the earliest privately organized efforts were taken to harbor unemployed seamen, to rescue abandoned street-urchins, or to salvage women suspected of prostitution. In the post–Civil War period, a host of evangelical "rescue missions" opened their doors on the Bowery, several of which remain in operation today. Spontaneous assistance, organized by citizens' groups during times of dire need, distributed food, fuel, and clothing to the needy. Such drives were fiercely opposed by "scientific charity," which railed against "indiscriminate" almsgiving by misguided do-gooders with a fervor nearly matching its denunciations of the "tramp evil." To demonstrate the advantages of a well-ordered municipal shelter, the Charity Organization Society (COS) opened its Wayfarer's Lodge in 1893. Lodgers were required to repay their hospitality with a few hours of chopping wood. Such "work tests" would become much the rage among reformers seeking to disestablish the police station house system and would later be installed (if erratically enforced) in the public shelters.[13]

Police Station Houses

In the years before the practice of police station lodgings became law, overcrowding in those already providing the service had reached horrendous proportions. With an aggregate capacity of four hundred, on bad nights in the winter of 1856 the station houses were quartering three times that number and still turning away the majority of applicants, "to walk the streets or find repose in the public markets." Emergency shelter may seem an odd mission for an urban police force, but in the latter half of the nineteenth century, the police spent as much time on "social welfare" responsibilities—dispensing food and lodging, searching for lost children—as they did on crime control. Both were aspects of an ambitious agenda of managing the "dangerous classes" of paupers, tramps, and criminals, especially those who dodged the island-based institutions of poor relief and correction. The lodgings offered by the police not only confined the wayward but also, at least to a limited extent, helped to regulate and sustain the "floating proletariat" necessary to meet the irregular demand for labor. Wretched surrounds, limits on stay, restrictions on interactions among the lodgers, and the simple fact that they were open only for a few hours each night, all effectively served to dampen any nascent stirrings of solidarity among those who made use of them.[14]

"Never was parody upon Christian charity more corrupting to human mind," wrote Jacob Riis, in describing the station houses (where he, as a newly arrived Danish immigrant, had stayed). Such places taxed the descriptive talents of even seasoned observers. The following passage, describing two rooms at the Fourth Precinct, appears in the report of the Committee on Outdoor Relief of the State Charities Aid Association in 1877:

> Each of these rooms is 50 feet long and 10 feet wide. Along its whole length runs a wrought-iron framework about eighteen inches high, which is just sufficient to hold up a series of broad planks, a pile of which appears at one end. When a lodger comes in he takes one of the planks, places it on the frame so that it slants a little from head to foot, and lies down with his boots for a pillow and his coat for a covering. If there are few persons in the room he may have two or three planks, but after he is asleep he is likely to be rudely dropped to the floor by having the extra planks jerked from under him. On a cold night, all are taken early, and 50 men and 50 women lie heaped on this long platform that is too rude to be called a bed. Next the aisle is occupied; and finally, as more come in, they will crawl under the platform, until a mouse could hardly thread his way among this mass of humanity. Such a lodging-house at 12 o'-clock on a "full" night is almost as vile as the "Black-hole" of Calcutta. The heat necessarily comes up through the gratings in the floor, and brings with it the ventilation of cells; the presence of 60 or 70 unwashed, gin-steeped bodies adds stenches undescribable; while the snores of stentorian breathers, the groanings of wakeful lodgers, and driveling of drunken ones, the scream of some frightened dreamer, and the querulous wail of a sick child, unite to make a Babel of horrible sounds. A single flickering gaslight sends feeble rays through the laden air, and every ray touches a pile of rags which in the morning will hatch out a tramp.

In the eyes of local commentators, the character of those who regularly made the rounds from one station house to another was the appropriate equal of the sites themselves: the "lowest and most repulsive form of pauperism . . . creature[s] more degraded, more utterly worthless in human economy, it is impossible to find. . . ." Such "bummers" or "revolvers" were estimated to account for between two-thirds and three-quarters of all lodgings. As with the early almshouse, a makeshift established to meet the emergency needs of the situationally distressed had become a way of life for a relatively small proportion of the desperately poor. People stranded by bad luck who were referred to the station houses "generally retreat[ed] in disgust" after a glimpse of the premises.[15]

The police had their own complaints. Contemporary medical doctrine held that foul odors ("miasmas") emanating from garbage or rotting animal matter were the proximate cause of much disease. This not only explained the presence of so much morbidity and mortality in the filthy warrens of the poor, but implicated the station house lodgings as breeding grounds for all manner of infirmity. Complaints about the danger posed to officers quartered nearby form a running commentary on the station houses from the time the practice commenced.[16]

The cops were not the only ones to complain. Unemployment was installed as a routine, predictable fact of economic life during the nineteenth century, claiming many thousands during the worst depressions. At such times, the station houses became a public issue for the simple reason that "many industrious, homeless persons were of necessity lodged [there] with the vagrant and disorderly poor." During the Panic of 1873, for example, when a quarter of the city's labor force was out of work, station houses turned away 2,000 applicants each night for lack of space.[17]

When makeshifts begin to buckle, the simplest response is to suppress demand. Enforcement of vagrancy statutes—a conviction meant a stint in the workhouse—was periodically intensified in an effort to divert some lodgers to "the Island" and to discourage others altogether. In the winter of 1876, for example, this policy cut applications for lodgings by two-thirds, a fact the police oddly took to mean that "poverty and its consequent suffering has been much less than is generally supposed." Eighteen years later, the policy was repeated with similar results. Though the station houses had become "an urban scandal," they were furnishing 150,000 lodgings annually.[18]

Sleeping Rough

Even in relatively prosperous times, there were those who, by habit, inclination, or stubborn pride, sought refuge outside the formal apparatus of relief altogether. Lacking family or friends to put them up, or unwilling to impose, they "misused" spaces and resources dedicated to alternative purposes in order to survive. When available, some bedded down on hay barges in the river. Until the 1880s, shantytowns were common fixtures in Central Park; other squatments turned up on parcels of vacant land as far south as 40th Street. Many of the homeless poor slept in the parks. With no neighbors nearby to disturb, the police allowed the Battery at the foot of Manhattan to be used as an encampment for hundreds of tramps.[19]

Zeisloff's is the most detailed description. He not only situated homeless men and women in the grubby niches of the "New Metropolis," but gave them faces, histories, reasons for being there. He surveyed the various places luckless people found refuge at night, spoke to members of the "great army of vagabond men and women" he met there—people "with apparently nothing about them to appeal to the charitable mind"—and limned "the dreadful routine of their lives," as they circulated among the "parks, the cellars [of lodging houses], the saloons, the station houses, the Island."[20] Notably absent in that list was the newly opened Municipal Lodging House.

The Rise of the Municipal Lodging House

The first Municipal Lodging House opened as a direct consequence of the campaign to shut down the police station houses. Convinced by Jacob Riis that the station houses were beyond reform, Theodore Roosevelt (then president of the Police Commissioners Board) ordered them closed in February 1896. No alternative having been arranged for the thousands making use of them, one was hastily constructed. In what may properly be considered the first official municipal shelter, the city secured a refurbished barge in the East River, at the foot of East 26th Street. It remained open until May, at which time lodgers were simply referred to the COS's Wayfarer's Lodge. The following December, a former factory building on First Avenue was let for this purpose, equipped with what would become the usual array of beds, baths, fumigating agents, and a team of "investigators" to certify the need of applicants. A decade later in 1909, the city opened the first Municipal Lodging House designed specifically for that purpose at 438 East 25th Street. It remained in use until operations were transferred to the East 3rd Street facility on the Bowery in the late 1940s. Well into the 1930s (and, informally, long after that), however, the piers and ferries along the East River would be resorted to in times of unusual need.

Shelter capacity proved chronically unequal to demand. When facilities were full, homeless men took to familiar haunts. During the depression of 1907–1908, they slept in flophouses, in saloons, in vacant cells in the city jail, and in public toilets in city parks. Despite sometimes extraordinary measures taken during depressions (e.g., the city put up six hundred men on Ellis Island during the winter of 1915), varieties of vernacular shelter multiplied. Estimates of those "with no fixed abode and no regular means of subsistence" during the depression of 1914–1915 ran as high as sixty thousand. Thousands slept in the parks. Others sought refuge in churches where

Municipal Lodging House, Department of Public Charities, New York City, circa 1910

they slept sitting up in pews, or on the floors of settlement houses where newspapers were used for sheets. Several hundred slept on benches in city missions. In one nighttime census, over 1,400 were counted asleep in ninety-four bars. The city's Farm Colony on Staten Island opened its doors to overnight lodgers. And, we have it from no less an authority than the Commissioner of Welfare himself, homeless men even shared quarters with the dead at the city morgue.[21]

A Hybrid Institution

In the wake of the depression of 1914–1915, it became painfully clear that the Municipal Lodging House was laboring under an impossible mandate. Try as its administrators might to structure conditions so as to promote the "rehabilitation of the homeless man," the vicissitudes of the market would repeatedly scuttle such ambitions. Intended (in the eyes of reformers) as a "great human repair shop" to treat the deficient man, it found itself pressed into service as the temporary bivouac for the "reserve army" of the new industrial capitalist order.[22]

The crux of the problem was an old one. In 1895, in the second of his "scientific" studies of homeless men, John McCook reversed his earlier judgment that alcoholism was chiefly to blame for vagrancy and concluded that the "average tramp is originally a laborer, and a skilled one." True, the road-hardened tramp tended to be hard drinking and single. But such traits attested not to the cause of his vagrancy but to the practice of laying such men off at the first sign of industry slackening. Leaving his comfortable abode for an "experiment" on the road in 1891, William Wyckoff found not work-shirking drifters, but laborers of all stripes willing to do the most menial of jobs. A review of the records of 2,400 homeless men in the COS's case files in the mid-1890s concluded that "[i]n many cases all that was wanted was work, the very thing that could not be procured." A business failure and fruitless search for substitute employment left Mariner Kent homeless at age fifty. For a year he managed to avoid the usual haunts of the habitual tramp, "join[ing] the boundless concourse of lost men" camping in the parks instead, before finally landing work as a circular distributor. In 1910, the social secretary to the Municipal Lodging House followed up on the employment references submitted by homeless applicants and found that confirmed vagrants were the exception not the rule. Most of the men had held jobs and were, even then, seeking work.[23]

But work substitutes were not easily had. Make-work had its attractions as a moral means test, but the COS's wood yard was closed owing to a sur-

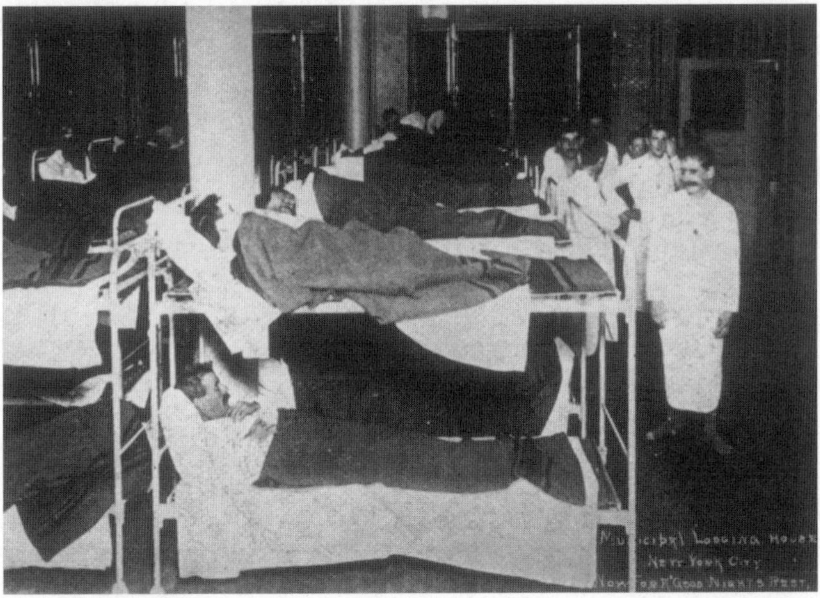

Home for a good night's rest, circa 1910

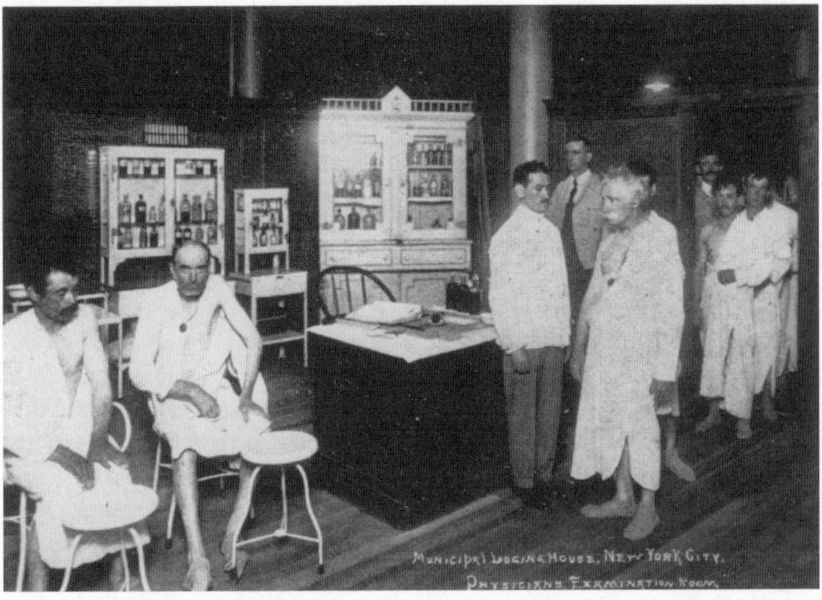

Physicians examination room, circa 1910

plus of wood. Fifteen years earlier, in May 1894, the Wayfarer's Lodge had been all but vacated six months after it opened, when the call went out for unskilled labor to lay a trolley line in Jersey City. The secretary of the Bowery Branch of the YMCA told a state commission in 1911 that his agency saw numerous instances of "intelligent, capable" men who had become "virtually tramps because of their continued search for work, and [because they were] trying to readjust themselves to changed conditions." A study of 1,500 shelter users in 1914 found that half were skilled workmen and another quarter were unskilled laborers ("reserve labor out of place and out of season"); upwards of half arrived at the shelter's door only after having been "crushed by the heel of Commercial Greed." Within a few years, the Municipal Lodging House made it a policy to fill staff vacancies with recruits drawn from the ranks of the lodgers themselves—its most progressive superintendent had once been a guest himself (albeit as an undercover agent for the Commissioner of Welfare).[24]

Stable work, not emergency shelter, was what such men needed. The most the Municipal Lodging House could do was to maintain them in as dignified and decent a manner as possible, and hope that they were not "demoralized" or "broken" by the experience. That proved a formidable challenge. Surplus, redundant men—elderly men, men who practiced obsolete trades, men who had outlived their usefulness but refused to concede that fact, "casual" laborers whose employ turned on the vagaries of season and trade—accumulated on the Bowery and along similar stretches elsewhere in the city, not because misery sought company, but because they had nowhere else to go. Once exposed to lodging house culture, they were subject to a further transformation, becoming "habituated to a life of idleness and uncertainty, so that at last when employment is once more to be had, they are unfit to have continuous labor." Formerly unemployed, they have become "unemployable."[25]

In any event, protective maintenance of the working man had little in common with attention to the service needs of that complement of misfits and infirm, the "continuing problem of social pathology," that made up the "irreducible minimum of patronage for the institution." Nor was it possible to attend to the rehabilitative ideal (whose charge, even then, was compounded by the practice of institutional "dumping") without a significant infusion of resources. But aside from a modest investment in "casework," few such resources, even under the most energetic of stewardships, were ever forthcoming. Attainment of either goal—supportive respite for unemployed workers, rehabilitation for the variously disabled—proved equally unreal in practice. A "hybrid or mongrel institution," the Municipal Lodging House was fated to have its charter written by others, its standards of operation defined by default, and its failure to secure any but the most rudi-

Municipal Lodging House, New York City, circa 1910

mentary approximation of "shelter" for its guests to go for the most part unnoticed.[26]

When it "worked," it was virtually invisible as an institution, a taken-for-granted component of a municipal disposal system for waste men. Among the chief purposes of this system, that is, was to preempt the need for its operations to be subject to deliberate examination and rational design. If "not like us" the ordinary rules of decency need not apply anyway. This, too, is part of the enduring legacy of public shelter.

Shadow Shelter

Before tackling the transformations wrought by the Great Depression, a persisting blind spot should be noted in contemporary analyses. The men who found their way to public shelters—jobless and, temporarily at least, without fallback resources—probably represented only a small fraction of the population out of work. Most such people managed to cope most of the time without calling attention to themselves by a public declaration of need. The ingenuity and improvisations of the unemployed and their extended families that would attract so much documentation in the 1930s were already well-established traditions among the urban poor in the period 1870–1920. Such practices were not exceptional measures instituted in response to acute need, but commonplace means of getting by and making do, "indistinguishable from the larger and more permanent task of coping with being poor." Before the welfare state, these kin-based improvisations "formed the very base of social security and assistance in times of crisis."[27]

Turmoil, loss, unsteady income, relocation, and adaptation to new forms of work were familiar presences in working-class households. And kinship—that "diffuse, enduring solidarity" usually mediated by blood and marriage—provided the indispensable connection to obligated others that enabled people to carry on. Tradition and innovation both played a part, which is to say these were adaptable practices. Local and far-flung members of extended families were recruited at different times depending on the need at hand. Latent (activated only in times of trouble) and active (regularly nurtured, invariably by women) ties required different degrees of cultivation. Networks of kinsfolk extended across communities enabled people to take risks (leaving home, undertaking an apprenticeship, starting a business, taking on new work) and cushioned the shock when such ventures failed. Under such circumstances, the decision to apply for institutional aid—especially when that meant enduring the humiliation of the almshouse, or the seedy, lowering democracy of the police station house or municipal lodging house—was an act of uncommon desperation. For the most part, it was custom and kinship that eased the bite of misfortune, not the interventions of the state. When those failed, and things seemed beyond repair, many single men took to the road. Making themselves officially homeless alleviated the burden at home.[28]

The success of deterrence, then, had less to do with forcing would-be shirkers to look twice at available work than it did with trading on the distinctive working-class practice of treating the home as an asset with multiple utilities—"a *resource* [not a private refuge] that could be used for generating extra income, for paying debts, for staying out of poverty, and for maintaining autonomy in old age."[29] Deterrence worked not because jobs were going begging, but because when pressed many applicants for public shelter could contrive some other alternative to the street. The flexible workings of kinship, not the discipline of the marketplace, was the secret behind its success. Like shadow work, this shadow shelter forms an indispensable part of the abeyance apparatus that checked the recurring threat of mass homelessness. *Shadow work* is distinguished from both subsistence and waged work in being *indirectly* related to livelihood. Essential to the reproduction of market labor, it does not itself produce goods for use or trade. If the prototype of shadow work is modern housework, the prototype of shadow shelter is the routine overcrowding of working-class dwellings in the nineteenth century city. (Boarding, by contrast, produced income for work performed within the home.) Informal and often illegal, shadow shel-

Registering applicants, circa 1910

ter enabled the official apparatus of relief to function by assuming the larger share of the burden of support imposed by periodic unemployment.[30]

Innovations in the Great Depression

The vagrant may have been the critical object lesson that made possible the "discovery of unemployment," but he was not long its representative instance. When distress was widespread, his solitary suffering paled into insignificance next to that of families who had lost breadwinners. Nothing in the American experience drove that home with greater force than the relief experiments of the 1930s. No one date marks the beginning of the Great Depression. There was, Lillian Wald observed, "no sudden avalanche, but a creeping daily change." Evidence of unusual distress began to mount in the early winters. Shantytowns were resurrected, "jobless women" found living in parks, and breadlines began to proliferate.[31]

The Official Response

By 1933–1934, the same dilemma that had confronted lodging house supervisors two decades earlier—how to ensure intensive casework for those who need it while supporting those who lack only work—had resurfaced. As before, administrators proved no more successful in resolving it. Social casework would largely ignore the homeless man for the duration of the Depression. In the early years especially, public shelter simply reverted to form—"an emergency almshouse" premised, at a time when ample evidence ran to the contrary, "on the theory of the bum." The varieties of shelter proliferated as never before. Two huge "annexes" were erected, one on a pier at the foot of East 26th Street and the other at South Ferry, with a combined capacity of nearly four thousand men. One lodging house (the Gold Dust Lodge, a converted mill at the corner of Corlears and Cherry Streets) was restricted for the use of a "better class" of homeless men, unemployed professionals and mechanics, who had more of a say in the day-to-day management of the place. For the first time, too, a separate facility was established for women on West 14th Street. One hotel was designated for elderly and disabled men only; another, on West 124th Street, was opened to accommodate African American men. Two camps were set up outside the city—in Chester, N.Y., and in Bear Mountain Park—where work relief projects were initiated.[32]

For the first time, the federal presence was substantial. Elsewhere, the Federal Transient Program's (FTP) camps may have amounted to little more than "thinly disguised flophouses." But in New York City, an FTP voucher purchased a berth in a private facility or commercial lodging house that was a cut above the accommodations available in the city annexes. Hartford House, an "experimental rehabilitation center" established under federal auspices and located in midtown behind the Ziegfield Theatre, served a select clientele of white-collar homeless men, many of whom had attended college. At its peak in June 1935, the federal caseload included nearly seven thousand "unattached" men and women who lacked the requisite year's residence to qualify as "local homeless." Liquidation of the FTP program later that September proved disastrous, though, as is commonly the case in such matters, documentation is spotty. Thousands of men and women were dropped from the rolls without any formal transfer of relief responsibility. Begging, street encampments, and sleeping in parks, subways, and building hallways all increased. Over two thousand transients were officially counted in a night census of people sleeping rough the following spring. But most were never accounted for. Regarding their fate, Lilian Brandt's surmise is as good as any, and as harrowing for its syntax as it is for the content: They "disposed of their own cases by finding work or committing suicide or marrying or making other arrangements."[33]

Homemade Housing

The "Hoovertown" made infamous in Steinbeck's *Grapes of Wrath* was one of thousands at the time. Such collections of temporary dwellings could be found even in the precious waste spaces of Manhattan. Shantytowns were established in Central and Riverside Parks and along the East River, some with substantial structures in them. One hundred twenty-nine men were counted in a "Hobo City" at the corner of West and Washington Streets in Manhattan; a few even found refuge in an unused sewer pipe. Six hundred people were reported living in a settlement at the foot of Henry and Clinton Streets in Brooklyn. Official tolerance of such colonies seems to have been the rule. When the police raided "Hoover Valley" in the old reservoir bed near the obelisk in Central Park, they "politely arrested" two dozen men. Although solidly built (a few were made of brick) the dwellings lacked water and sanitary facilities. The magistrate suspended sentence on agreement with the men that they would vacate the premises. Such raids were only reluctantly undertaken; more indicative of the social status of such settlements is the fact that the courts granted 175 residents of two colonies the right to vote in local elections.[34]

Homemade housing took a unique turn in the "space hotel" movement. When it formally opened on May 1, 1931, the newly finished but still three-quarters vacant Empire State Building, for all its stark spiring beauty, struck some observers as obscene—its unveiling occurring in the midst of the Depression. Architect Simon Breines had a bold suggestion: Why not turn the building into quarters for homeless men? For that matter, why limit the suggestion to the "Empire State Apartments"? Why not turn all these "tombstones of capitalism . . . with windows" to good account? The notion to "put the skyscrapers to work" caught on, with a "space hotel" movement launched by an architectural firm and championed in its journal *Shelter* (edited by Buckminster Fuller).[35] The premise was simple: any vacant or partially occupied building over six stories and preferably of commercial status (to avoid having to obtain certification from the tenement house authorities) should be

> converted into a shelter where the unemployed will obtain food, clothing and work under a communal basis. The hotels shall, like our naval battleships be self-sufficient, taking on supplies fundamentally in the form of raw materials, and through communal effort on the part of the inhabitants provide food, clothes and shelter for themselves.[36]

Returning veterans from the routed "Bonus March" on Washington successfully renovated a derelict factory into habitable space, demonstrating the viability of what would later be called "sweat equity" programs. Appointments were primitive, but the men had moved in, negotiated for regular supplies of surplus food from a grocery chain, and begun further renovations when the bank, fearful of its liability in the event of a fire, reclaimed the building and turned the men out.[37]

Regulating Demand for Public Shelter

Public shelter never lost its provisional character. Emergency stopgaps were simply allowed to crystallize into accepted modalities of relief, while the logic of shelter militated against permanence. Initially, and for the duration, the operating premise was deterrence. When demand proved unremitting, steps were taken—not to expand capacity further—but to intensify scrutiny of applicants. In the late 1930s this raised the rejection rate to 56 percent, usually because "legally responsible relatives" were determined to be in the area. The dominant architecture remained the warehouse: with its huge scale and batch-processing of residents, it effectively functioned as a storage facility. A "philosophy of temporariness" prevailed throughout the decade, in which it became accepted practice "to lose people in the process of shuttling them from one agency or type of care to another."[38]

For many men, public shelter was more a "supplementary habitat," resorted to when other resources were exhausted, than a crisis residence in emergencies. Foremost among those resources were the dividends of kinship, real and fictive. What "parents, married brother, or other close relative" provided by way of "a common economic household," others found through "a substitute family group."[39] And thank God for them. For, as happened two decades earlier, seasoned observers warned that barracking idle men only reinforced their marginality and threatened to breed "a nomadic tribe, irresponsible in its habits of life, subsisting ultimately as parasites upon society and potentially . . . dangerous."[40] As before, these warnings were routinely ignored and eventually rendered obsolete by the gearing up of the war economy.

Postwar Years

Shelter demand rose in the wake of the demobilization following World War II and appears to have caught the city unawares. In the winter of 1948–1949, from 400 to 900 or more men slept on the floor of the Lodging House Annex on East 3rd Street; as many as 624 men were similarly ill-disposed the following winter. Overt homelessness may well have outlasted that temporary blip, save for the prolonged upturn in the postwar economy and the abeyance effects of the G.I. Bill. Instead, for the next quarter century, homelessness was confined to those grubby niches of central business districts known as "skid rows," of which the Bowery remains the most infamous. So profound was link between habitat and inhabitant that sociologists took to *defining* homelessness—not as the lower end of a housing market spectrum—but as the social condition of "disaffiliation" from the usual ties that bind.[41]

The city continued to lodge up to six hundred men at its East 3rd Street facility until 1964 when the beds were removed and the building converted into a "reception center." (Renamed the "Shelter Care Center for Men," it was still referred to by old-timers as "the Muni" well into the 1980s.) Inventive research was done by the Columbia Bowery Project into some of the more unusual "habitats of homeless men in Manhattan," including illegal occupancies in such spaces as boiler rooms, basements, and sewer pipes. For the most part, though, men whom today would be classified as homeless tended to stick to the immediate Bowery environs. There they were housed in "hotels" (flophouses) and missions, where conditions had changed little since the 1930s. Bowery denizens tended to be elderly white men, roughly a third of whom had chronic drinking problems; most survived on pensions, not charity. The standard inventory of skid row institutions and practices—the bottle gangs, panhandling, windshield wiping, cheap taverns, gospel missions, and barber colleges—were much on display. Tour buses regularly ferried their safely caged sightseers through. Still on the books, vagrancy laws were routinely ignored; and even when enforced, they amounted to inconvenience. Only when forced to preen, as happened during the 1964 World's Fair, did the city vigorously enforce laws against public drunkenness. Sleeping rough was an anomaly, confined in warmer months to a few score men along the Bowery. Containment at arm's length was what the postwar urban niche of skid row was about. The Bowery functioned as the urban equivalent of a reservation.[42]

Economies mutate, kinship's limits are reached, redundancy's meaning and impact get redefined. Programs contract before the need is met or prove unequal to a surge in demand. Abeyance measures break down. The most effective of alternative employments—warfare—is rather awkward as a supplement to planned relief measures. And so the city is periodically confronted with men whose presence represents unneeded labor, a drain on households, an affront to the peaceful enjoyment of civic space. No longer up to the task, the reservation is breached and an old perplexity returns: "Homeless men are a baffling class," one of their more dedicated students wrote in 1915, "and nearly everything that is done for them is done in a haphazard manner."[43] Along with perplexity comes the old dodge: that the deepest truth about such men is that they are fundamentally different (if not unalterably so) from the rest of us. Such a canard has its motivating utilities, and expediency is one of them.

So long as the appearance of unusual numbers of homeless men (in addition to the accepted residuum of "unemployables") can be framed as a temporary aberration, the fiction can be entertained that homelessness signifies nothing other than the deranged mentalities, bad habits, or faulty coping skills of those whom it affects. At the same time, as we have seen, it isn't as though Cassandras have been wanting; as the myth requires, their prophetic powers came at the cost of being ignored. Repeatedly advised by its own administrators and researchers that at the heart of the dispossession *expressed* as homelessness is a core fault built into "flexible" labor markets, the institution of shelter persists in providing a stigmatized corrective, mobilizing for action only under duress and, even then, doing so in a jury-rigged fashion.

Function and Representation

From the outset, the ranks of the visible poor were suspect and official commentary was unsparing in its depiction of these "offenses to the good order of society." Running through the various constructions set out by government agencies, professional reformers, and scientific charity is the notion that the homeless man is different, made of ruder, less durable stuff. The distinctive species of "otherness" ascribed to such men was typically underscored by seeing them as standing outside of, or apart from, our history. They occupied a time warp of their own, one sometimes thought to be of their own making. Whether construed as civilization's exile, its nemesis, or as evidence of its failure, this interpretive taxonomy was built on a prior refusal to recognize him as part of the inclusive world of the observer. That practice, what Johannes Fabian has termed the "denial of coevalness," is one of the traditional ways anthropology has distanced the objects of its study, locking them in an "ethnographic present" of its own. Understand *coevalness* as designating "shared time" and, by extension, equality of stature in occupying that time. Any "discourse employing terms such as primitive, savage (but also tribal, traditional, Third World, or whatever euphemism is current) does not think, observe, or critically study, the 'primitive'; it thinks, observes, studies *in terms of* the primitive."[44]

In depictions of homeless men, this distancing practice found domestic application as well. I examine three versions—the tramp, the moron, and the shelterized man—to illustrate. Two exceptions, the stubbornly out-of-step work of Stuart Rice and Nels Anderson, represent rare voices of opposition.

Standard Fare

Tramp

Popular and official denunciations were echoed, in part, by scholarly lore. John McCook, in what is considered the first "scientific" study of a sample of tramps (1895), invoked the tenuous sway of civilization over its reluctant charges. Like those "converted aborigines" recruited to work on Australian sheep stations, who happily quit their jobs when the "festive" seasons of their "savage life" come round, so too the tramp becomes tuned to the rhythms of a prehistoric time. He discovers that "living and labor are not interchangeable terms" and reverts to a primitive state. Ironically (given the chosen image), what was dangerous about the tramp was not his "otherness" but his familiarity (our repressed Otherness?). The tramp was believed to embody some of the strongest yearnings, regrets, misgivings—however one wants to characterize industrial civilization's discontents—of a working population only newly and imperfectly harnessed to the factory wheel. The point implicit in McCook's analysis (and explicit in more anxious commentators) is that we are all latent tramps by inclination and heritage, and it is an essential part of the work of culture to hold that impulse in check.[45]

Culture houses restive elements as well, and it pays to take a closer look at the fears expressed in these throw-back fantasies. For although most tramps were "wandering workers with homes only part of the time" who, for the most part, retained mainstream values, there was an element of dissent (or, better, a corps of dissenters) in their ranks. Some of these were men who had acquired "a special feeling for life on the tramp . . . who worked to live on the road," and who rejected conventional responsibilities. Some, for a time at least, had simply had enough of subsisting at the pleasure of the industrial machine. Some sought higher wages or more skilled work. Some rebelled against "the demands of the time clock and the bell tower." And some saw the road as the last rite of untrammeled adolescence before the claims of adulthood set in. However it was played out, it was clear that among the working class were many who joined the ranks of tramps "temporarily, for varying periods, because they wished to."[46]

So there was truth to the reformers' and professional charities' suspicions that the tramp was a creature from another time, but it was a recent not a prehistoric one. The more uncomfortable and general truth, however, was this: The rules of work had changed, and what had been thought to be the progeny of vagrancy—unemployment—proved instead its parent. Nor was the tramp unemployment's only issue; he merely announced its presence in the most extreme, visible way.

Moron

The Progressive Era's fondness for eugenics as a prospective remedy for social ills seeped into studies of homelessness as well, and through the most unlikely of vehicles. Charles Barnes was a young researcher engaged by the Russell Sage Foundation to examine the operations of the Municipal Lodging House. He proved an eager apprentice, frequenting the haunts of homeless men, interviewing staff and desk clerks at relief facilities and lodging houses and observing them at work, posing himself as homeless on occasion, and investigating operations in other cities. He fashioned extended "life histories" from dozens of lengthy interviews with homeless men. Apart from the occasional first-person account of life on the road, his was the first serious effort to see this life "from the native's point of view."

Barnes's portrait—especially when set against the shrill moralism of his contemporaries—stands out as a closely documented account of men struggling to cope, not always successfully and not with the finest of tools, with an economy of scarcity. Lack of a work ethic, he argued, was less a problem than its tenacity in men with no option of exercising it. He recognized that modernity was at the root of the problem. The invisible hand of the market has no memory and honors no debts. But how, he wondered, do you explain that to an elderly man who refuses to go to the almshouse because he cannot let go of the notion that he should be doing something useful?

For the first six chapters of *The Homeless Man,* Barnes plays their anthropologist. His reckoning is so informed and incisive, his commitment to grasping the truth of their lives so evident, his analysis so tempered and nuanced, that one reads his concluding chapter in a state of shock. In it, ethnography gives way to unadorned Social Darwinism: were appropriate testing of homeless men to be done, Barnes asserts, the brute fact would emerge that "from 50–60 percent, if not more, are morons." He intends this assertion, overriding everything else that has preceded it, to be scientifically demonstrable. "Feeble-mindedness," an uncorrectable "structural abnormality" of the brain, is what explains both recurrent unemployment among apparently capable men and their inability ever to manage self-sufficiently. The homeless man was a creature of nature's mischief, not culture.[47]

Later that decade, systematic testing of an even larger sample would indeed reveal that half fell into the "feeble-minded" range. These were not homeless men, however; they were army recruits called up during the Great War's mobilization. And if such test results were valid—not without a great deal of trepidation over their implications, they were endorsed by some of the leading figures in American psychometrics—this meant that "we are a nation of half morons."[48] Stigmatized as an exception, the homeless man proves once again the discomforting rule, if only, in this instance, the rule of a misapplied science.

The Shelterized Man

As mentioned earlier, Progressive Era reformers feared that lodging houses would turn into incubators for tramps. Once "habituated to a life of idleness and uncertainty," such men would lose initiative and drive, becoming unfit to work even were jobs available. This fear was formalized by two Chicago sociologists in the 1930s as the "shelterization" thesis. The developmental logic was the same if more elaborate. After an initial period of disorientation, the newly homeless man shrugs off his discomfort and settles into the stuporous regimen of the shelter in the constant company of lost men. A warped rite of passage transpires. As he completes his novitiate and "acquires the customs and traditions of the shelter," he tends "to lose all sense of responsibility for getting out of the shelter; to become insensible to the element of time; to lose ambition, pride, self-respect, and confidence . . . to identify himself with the shelter group."[49] He becomes one of them.

Even during this time of widely shared hardship, a logic of displacement and distancing is apparent. Social work and social research were preoccupied with the "demoralization" of unemployed workers and families, afraid not only that it impeded present-day coping but handicapped future jobholding prospects as well. As "shelterized" men demonstrated in the extreme, the danger lurked in even well-meaning relief efforts. Rehabilitation (however infeasible) became the preferred remedy. What began as a lively debate about the structural roots of unemployment devolved to a fretful concern with the social and psychological needs of "special populations" of the jobless.[50]

The problem with this thesis is less its accuracy—the observation was too common then and is too often repeated by competent researchers today for it to be mere sociological fiction[51]—than its incompleteness. Enforced idleness has its costs and demoralization is surely among them. Full-blown "shelterization" no doubt characterized some men. But for most, the shelters were but one makeshift among many that enabled them to get by. Enforcement of limits of stay provisions meant frequent moves at any rate. An exceptional few, like Mariner Kent early in the century and Tom Kromer in the 1930s, managed to avoid the shelters altogether, surviving not only with their wit and work ethic intact but with the skill and energy to write about it.

More to the point: for a process that was thought to be damnably treatment resistant, shelterization proved no impediment to recruitment for the stepped-up war economies of the late teens and thirties, when the shelters were quickly emptied of all but the elderly and disabled. (In Chicago, the Municipal Lodging House actually closed down in 1918–1919, "because of lack of applicants during wartime prosperity." New York's counterpart employed two staff for every lodger.) Shelterized men had no trouble acquitting themselves as soldiers or factory hands. When exigency demanded, a functional normalcy returned.[52]

Exceptions

Still, there were those who got it right, whose immediate answer to the question posed in the heat of an unemployment crisis or civil unrest was: It's not so simple. The stand-outs in this small crowd were Nels Anderson and Stuart Rice. Applied anthropologists before their time (and, it turns out, civil servants too), their work is distinguished by its empirical rigor, close observation, self-reflectiveness, and long duration, over the course of which it underwent a good deal of revision. What the two had in common was a commitment to "participant observation" (made by dint of circumstance and principle early in their formative years, not as a disciplinary tenet). They spent time with the men about whom they would later write, got to know them, endured the hardships, sussed out the gambits, learned to dodge the cons, and experienced the camaraderie. Anderson would later gently mock the appellation (he wasn't slumming or rucking about with the natives at the behest of his thesis advisor; he was returning home and writing a book to escape it). Both men were avid note-takers and ruminant analysts. Rice's archives are filled with undiscarded jottings and rough memos: key words to a taxonomy taking shape ("Causes of dependency"), a formative idea (the distinction between reason for last job lost and reason for being unemployed), the sketch for a short story—things that would later find their way into a formal analysis or position paper.[53]

In 1914, Rice began work as an undercover investigator for the New York City Commissioner of Welfare, took over as superintendent of the Municipal Lodging House (1916–1918)—where he kept matchless records and published incisive accounts of that facility's operations—and eventually went on to a distinguished career as statistician with the U.S. Census Bureau. In the wake of his minor classic, *The Hobo* (completed as a masters thesis at the University of Chicago), Anderson took a doctorate at New York University (NYU) and hired on as a researcher at the Welfare Council of New York. There he undertook exhaustive studies of homelessness during the Depression years, with Rice (then at University of Pennsylvania) serving on an advisory committee. After a stint with the WPA, a book on Depression-era migration (*Men on the Move*), and a tour with the navy, Anderson worked for the United Nations Refugee Resettlement Program. Late in life, both men returned to the rough-and-tumble scholarship of their early years—Anderson in published autobiographical accounts, Rice in sketches submitted to *The New Yorker* and *Harper's* that never found their way into print.

Their joint contribution to the understanding of American homelessness may be summed up under four ideas: (1) that vagrancy had not one, but any number of developmental logics to it; (2) that social structure—the labor market and kinship in particular—played a critical role in shaping homelessness in a given era; (3) that individual initiative and mettle nonetheless found expression in how men coped with unemployment; and (4) that, if poorly designed, instruments of relief could have disabling iatrogenic effects.

Ethnographers on the home front, Rice and Anderson proved faithful stewards of the documentary credo. In refusing to allow homeless men to be reduced to victims of circumstance or creatures of impulse and bent habit, they reclaimed them as *our kind too,* and for the most familiar of reasons. Available work, its demands and entanglements, is the dominant chord throughout their accounts. In making sense of either the genesis of homelessness or its resolution, labor provided essential leverage. Without it, no matter how strongly surface appearances might suggest otherwise, the portrait was incomplete. Character may explain choice of occupation, but rarely sufficed to explain a fall. If sustained long enough, on the other hand, vagrancy could eat away at character. Programs built on the easy misunderstanding that broken men authored their own disenfranchisement misdirect their resources and injure the intended targets. In place of reassuring simplicities (tramps, feeble-mindedness, shelterization), Anderson and Rice presented unsettling complexities, real lives enmeshed in broken opportunities, hard luck, and unavailing fixes. Measured against such complexities, relief often proved a farce.

New Calcutta or Old New York?

This chapter has dwelt at some length on the development and demise of formal but avowedly makeshift mechanisms of shelter (the police station houses, etc.) because they seem to me the archetype for municipal shelters today.[54] The tendencies for such a proto-institution to have its functions defined by default and to cater in practice to the lowest common denominator of those forced to seek help there have obvious contemporary parallels. So does the habit of allowing conditions to sink to levels below what common decency would demand if it took the trouble to look. Such slippage is typically condoned not as deliberate policy but rather as an inevitable by-product of the clientele served: These places were thought to owe their wretchedness to the company housed. Thus do the twin themes of deviance and deterrence join forces to create the workaday logic of shelter, a logic that—with the notable exception in recent years of judicial relief—has proven all but impervious to criticism.

Except for the occasional "scandal," such facilities usually manage to get away with it, their work being of the messy sort that decent citizens would just as soon *not* contemplate, so long as it occurs out of sight. But the system contains another destabilizing element. The downward slippage of conditions that adds to effective deterrence (convincing would-be applicants that other, usually informal, options would be far preferable) has been known to work only too well, discouraging men who have no alternative but to take up residence in the street. The "spectacle of the degraded pauper" so indelibly engraved in the history of poor relief is a tricky thing. It works best when its display can be contained within carefully bounded theaters, like the Bowery of legend, and not when ordinary citizens encounter it as a constant reminder of the wages of idleness.[55] Vagrancy laws have traditionally been invoked to contain that spectacle, often under imagined circumstances that only added to its terror. In that case, deterring the poor at the door of shelter ran few risks except that of the costs of sheltering them elsewhere. But when police power is checked, its enforcement uneven, or the costs of quartering the indigent elsewhere (whether in asylums or jails) prohibitive, the spectacle is everywhere. Until quite recently in New York,[56] that was the prevailing reality. Whatever its one-time efficiency may have been, the abeyance process embodied in public shelter had begun noticeably to unravel.

As it happens, we hear with growing frequency alarums about the dangerous poor reminiscent of the nineteenth-century city's anxiety over epidemic disease and gang violence. So striking was the reemergence of widespread visible homelessness in the 1980s that some journalists took to referring to the city as the "New Calcutta."[57] But surely the more apt comparison is the old New York, at least with respect to the routine encounters with stark poverty: the burgeoning numbers of beggars, the many replicas of that "boundless concourse of lost men" whose ranks Mariner Kent had joined, the miscellany of street merchants and grifters everywhere apparent. Massive institutions (the city's armories and hospitals) had once again been pressed into service as emergency lodging for the homeless poor; once more, the precise "mandate" of such facilities had become a much-contested matter.[58]

History and theory aside, the best indicator of the reputation of shelter in New York City today may be the protest voiced in a scene from a 1985 film, when a mute homeless man with a peculiar gift for things electronic shows up in a Harlem bar. Night falls, he's still stranded, and someone suggests the obvious, to which the bartender responds: "That man's got talent; you can't send him to the Men's Shelter."[59]

PART II

FIELDWORK AND FRAMEWORK

Introduction: Ethnography in the Annals of Homelessness

Homelessness has long figured as a subject in the documentary tradition of American letters.[1] In fact, participant observation as a method—and ethnography as a genre—may be said to have cut its teeth domestically in the effort to capture the dynamics of rootlessness and mobility apparent in post–Progressive Era America. The University of Chicago's sociology department, in particular, championed urban ethnographic research—of the eight studies W.J. Wilson refers to as evidence of this school's productivity in this period, three dealt exclusively with homeless men.[2] The story is especially well documented for such cities as Chicago and New York, where qualitative accounts complement early survey research.[3] Original and, for the most part, unpublished,[4] studies were done on the Municipal Lodging House (or public shelter) in New York and on the lively reign of "hobohemia" in Chicago.[5] These anticipated, and later Depression-era studies described in great detail, the demoralization (or "shelterization") that could set in among long-term homeless men.[6] Outside the cities, "tramping"—a pattern of migratory work (laying railroad track, cutting timber, working in mines, and harvesting crops), often done in remote areas—flourished in the latter half of the nineteenth century and was periodically revived during economic hard times thereafter.[7] First-person accounts of tramping begin to appear at the turn of the century and full-fledged guides to (or descriptions of) life on the road were published in the 1930s, when the number of "transients" criss-crossing the country in search of work was estimated at two million.[8] But by 1940, seasoned observers argued that "transiency" was no longer a viable occupational niche: The demand for that kind of rough, rootless laborer had dried up.[9] Shortly thereafter, the requirements of war-related production emptied homeless shelters of all but the most elderly or disabled residents. What was once a thriving reservoir of "casual labor" had become "a welfare community"; even the lumberjack had settled down and been "domesticated."[10]

Postwar analyses of the men and "subculture" of skid row may have been far out of proportion with "the relative urgency of homelessness as a social problem,"[11] but its draw on social scientists was unmistakable. Studies were undertaken in Minneapolis, Philadelphia, Chicago, and New York, to cite only the most prominent. In the 1960s, for example, a team of Columbia University sociologists descended on New York's Bowery where, for all intents and purposes, another country—another time—was laid out for inspection. Or so, at first, it seemed. The title of its summary publication neatly captures the disillusionment that followed: These natives turned out to be merely "old men, drunk and sober."[12] Much of the work undertaken in this period seems driven by an interest in documenting "deviant" and seemingly isolated subcultures,[13] often with scant notice paid to the structured frustration built into a culture and an economy of "flexible" labor markets, that simultaneously insisted on unchecked mobility and presented strictly bounded options to those with few skills.[14] Even in an era when pathologizing held sway, however, exceptions did occur.

Without having set out to do so, a few researchers managed to unearth some telling (if "working") misunderstandings of clientele on the part of line staff in the service industry. Careful studies of homeless men in their interactions with the police and alcohol treatment centers, for example, revealed a distinctive "native" perspective on the utilities of such resources that was strikingly at variance with the official view on jail or treatment.[15] James Spradley, an anthropologist who set out to study the nascent culture of a new alcohol treatment center, wound up doing an exposé on the abuse of tramps in the Seattle jail. Others traced much older linkages to marginal labor markets. As late as the early 1970s, it was still possible to find rich dissertation material in the timeworn life ways of "fruit tramps" in the orchards and on the railways of the American northwest.[16] Handbooks for "jumping freights" appeared in the 1970s and 1980s.[17]

But even then, a new variant of homelessness was emerging, one that would define its urban niche—not by work, as the traditional "hobo" had; nor by absence of ties, as was alleged of the skid row man; but by location, fleeting or prolonged as the case may be, in the "interstices" of public space.[18]

In the late 1970s and throughout the 1980s, the ethnographic tradition in the United States was revived for studies of the homeless poor in at least a dozen cities.[19] Its practitioners have participated in larger, multidisciplinary projects as well. Such studies have explored the situation of older Bowery residents;[20] the special problems of the homeless poor with severe psychiatric disorders, both on the street and in innovative outreach, shelter, and housing programs;[21] rural poverty and homelessness;[22] crime and victimization among the urban homeless;[23] the U.S. Census Bureau's attempt to enumerate street and shelter populations in 1990;[24] and a host of emerging methodological issues.[25] Ethnographers have also charted some of the distortions introduced by the dominance of an epidemiological (especially psychiatric) perspective in the published discourse on homelessness,[26] a corrective that has made its way into the psychiatric literature as well.[27]

Finally, with the development of longitudinal studies of homelessness, it has become clear that far from being a terminal status (as was true of skid row men a quarter-century ago), contemporary homelessness is increasingly an episodic or recurrent circumstance. Hence, "residential instability" would appear to be the more encompassing framework,[28] and attention to the routine, everyday strategies of survival practiced in poor neighborhoods essential. Given their overrepresentation in urban homeless populations, members of black households should be of particular interest. Yet, with a number of notable exceptions (see Chapter 6), American ethnographers in the 1980s—like their social scientific counterparts more generally—tended not to delve into the ecology and social capital of African American "ghetto" life, hampering our ability to talk intelligently about patterns of improvised or irregular residence, let alone literal homelessness, among this group.

In the chapters that follow, I tackle a number of dimensions of contemporary homelessness, using situated ethnographic methods. For that reason, too, the four portraits sketched here—the streets and shelters in New York City, marginal work in the Catskills, an airport functioning as alternative shelter, and the 1990 census count of the street-dwelling homeless—are self-consciously fixed in time and place. Rather than rush to "update" the picture in each instance (which, in any event, would have meant redoing the study), I've chosen to present them in much their original form, as time-windows into pieces of a continuing story.

[3]

Streets, Shelters, and Flops: An Ethnographic Study of Homeless Men, 1979–1982

> What you doin' down here, all shiny-eyed? You ain't no tramp.
>
> Homeless man to author, Men's Shelter, winter 1980

This chapter revisits early years of research in the largely unedited words of original fieldnotes and observations. If it reads at times like a portrait of the anthropologist as a young crusader, fueled by equal measures of naiveté and outrage, it also captures something of the fitful bouts of disbelief (fading nervously to acceptance) with which homelessness was met at the time.

By the fall of 1979, when our research got under way, it was apparent that vagrancy was undergoing a sea change in character and numbers, though few observers were reckless enough to hazard any but approximations of either. A rough gauge of the perceived magnitude of the problem may be gleaned from a look both at the numbers that did exist and at the narrative uses of homelessness as a cultural symbol.

Numbers

Any attempt to arrive at an accurate number of homeless people in a given area is subject to a host of difficulties. The estimates that surface from time to time have proven notoriously unreliable, subject to wild discrepancies depending on methods of estimation used, sources relied on, the season of the year, and (it may not be too cynical to suggest) the intended purpose of the count. As Chapter 1 argued, the kinds of living arrangements defining one as "homeless" can vary considerably from one investigator to another, adding a further note of uncertainty and making historical or regional comparisons risky.

When Ellen Baxter and I began the research for what would become *Private Lives/Public Spaces* (1981), nothing approximating the depth or breadth of the Columbia Bowery Project had been undertaken in the interim. A legislative report noted that the Bowery population itself proved relatively stable (at roughly 4,000) from 1969 to 1975. Total numbers of men served at the city shelter had declined slightly in the same period, although the annual number of new arrivals had increased by over 20 percent. But such figures were not only five years old; they were also restricted to an area that homelessness had long since outgrown.[1]

Two documents gave more up-to-date and broad-based estimates. Although by no means unimpeachable, they do suggest the magnitude of the problem as seen within official (or quasi-official) bodies at the time. The first, a 1979 internal memorandum by the State Office of Mental Health, arrived at a total of 30,000 homeless men in the course of a year. Men's Shelter staff had estimated that the 9,000 different men they saw annually amounted to about 30 percent of the total population of homeless men in the city. (The basis for such an estimate was not given.) The second, a report by the Manhattan Bowery Corporation, calculated the total number of homeless women applying for shelter at the women's facility on Lafayette Street over a three-year period (1974–1977) and arrived at a figure of between 6,000 and 6,500 "periodically homeless" women. The sum of these two counts produced what was to become the infamous figure of 36,000 homeless in New York City.[2]

The 1980 census added a "casual count" to its normal "mission count"(or M-night count) of people staying in missions, jails, flophouses, and other transient accommodations charging four dollars a night or less, as well as those in "railroad stations, bus depots, all-night movies and similar places known to have persons staying overnight." The casual count was intended to net "highly transient individuals" who were likely to be missed otherwise; the sites were to include employment offices, pool halls, street corners, welfare offices, and transportation terminals not counted on "M-night." Such counts, especially the aptly named "casual" one, are widely believed to have been less than optimal affairs. The Census Bureau's final numbers for New York City were never released. The only published figure was that for the combined count of the M-night enumeration and casual count for the state as a whole: 9,233. Nationwide, the casual count, restricted as it was to certain census districts, discovered only 23,237 persons.[3]

By the end of the 1970's, increasingly frequent public outcry, press coverage, and a growing advocacy movement signaled that homelessness was an urgent issue demanding attention and redress. Less obtrusively, it was also clear that the image of this most marginal of human conditions had infiltrated mainstream urban culture in curious ways.

Cultural Images of Homelessness

To be homeless is to have suffered a fundamental rupture in the ties that bind. It signifies the breach of that intimate contract that regulates relations between private lives and the public worlds of work, consumption, political participation, and general social intercourse. The alleged offense of the homeless poor (aside from the exhibit forced upon eyes that would prefer not to see) is their "failure" to belong. The "dissolution of bonds without the formation of new ones," and the host of uncertainties about an individual's trustworthiness this gives rise to, explains (in the sociological account) the disreputable status accorded homeless persons.[4]

On the surface, homelessness does violence to another cherished cultural pattern as well. The social value of the home is to ensure that the organization of private life plays its appointed role in the reproduction of a given public order. Street people, in effect, reverse the order of priorities. Their objective, flaunted daily to the distress of proper citizens, is to see that the public order of commerce, space, waste disposal, and casual encounter suffices to sustain their individual lives. The public domain becomes personal theater, site of those private practices and stigmatized bodily functions that are normally carried out in hidden reaches of home.

A brief catalogue of prevailing cultural images of homelessness at the time we undertook our research would include the following:

- *Dispossessed and disaffiliated*: In the reigning sociological position at the time, the homeless man was bereft of social bearings. He observed no rules except the often ill-serving ones of apparent self-interest, was innocent of any sense of responsibility, professed no allegiances, and pursued a rootless and isolated life. The absence of a home—that "minimal possession of civilization"—was seen as symbolic of a larger refusal of the proper roles of adulthood and citizenry. Lacking any real nexus with the social community, the world of work, or the entanglements of kinship, he was the archetypal "stranger in our midst."[5]
- *Victim*: From the earliest days of forced relocation under the Elizabethan Enclosure Acts, through the horrors of the Victorian workhouse, and on to the dockets of social legislation in the welfare state, one undeniable fact was that the homeless were first and crucially poor. Their poverty, in this view, was not the result of indolence or mischief, but a symptom of structural deficiencies in a capitalist economy, abetted by the neglect of

the state. Homelessness represented only the extreme instance of a precariousness to which all are subject in a society geared not to the commonweal but to the profit of the few.[6]

- *Waste products or disease*: Cultures have various ways of stigmatizing waste products in powerfully negative ways. These practices extend not only to inanimate objects and animals, but to people as well. In illustration of "a general principle of social hierarchies that the weak are believed to endanger the strong," the idiom of waste may be used by those with power "to suggest that ill health and misfortune are caused by people they wish to keep at a distance." Waste pollutes; it defiles and corrupts. Press coverage in the 1960s and '70s lapsed frequently into the jargon of "derelicts," "degenerates," "defilement," or "scum." Simultaneously worthless and (it isn't always clear how or why) dangerous, the homeless poor were a menace to be eliminated or contained.[7]
- *Deviant subculture*: Resorting to the language of "outsiders" or "tribal populations," this perspective saw homelessness as a distinctive way of life—as much chosen as conferred—with characteristic sets of beliefs, attitudes, behavior patterns, and institutions. The distinctive traits of this subculture were described as the shadow, or negative, versions of mainstream culture. Still, "culture" seems awfully forced. These venues exist at the pleasure of the dominant social order; their defining ethos is insubordination, their guiding ethic noninterference.[8]
- *Social signifier*: In a number of accounts, the most crucial social fact about homelessness was its symbolic import. In nearly every case, its valence was negative, a condensed version of all that is sick and disordered about the present society. In rare instances, homelessness was seen positively, legitimate heir to the medieval tradition of holy poverty and precursor of the noncompetitive society of the future.[9]

These were not mutually exclusive representations. The folklore of "hobohemia" and the down-and-out literature of the 1930s both managed to combine elements of the victim and outsider images, took pains to distinguish themselves from the noisome figure of the bum, and lent a fleeting heroism to what otherwise looked like simple misery.[10] Assigning a disease label to the urban wino may temper vindictiveness on the part of service providers, but it is far from clear that it leavens the public's distaste for a colony of "derelicts" in their midst. Yet even the more disreputable portraits of the homeless man were not without traces of whimsical envy.[11]

For Howard Bahr, these various images coalesced in the figure of the leper. But by leaving it at that, he failed to do justice to what was arguably the most intriguing aspect of the social response to homelessness: the degree to which it mixed—in changing proportions, according to the circumstances of the times—measures of pity and abhorrence, the impulse to care and the instinct to avoid, acceptance and exile. Further, neither the horror of contagion, nor the "social abhorrence of powerlessness" (the imputed "defectiveness" of the homeless)—nor, for that matter, the bondlessness of their life—suffices to account for the repellent quality homeless men have traditionally had for the society in which they lived.[12] To those elements must be added the assumption that has underwritten social policy toward the poor since Elizabethan times: the refusal to work. It is only by recalling the social ambivalence toward relief in general that the special resentment of the homeless man can be understood.

The images in this inventory were gathered at a time when homeless women and children were relatively rare and before the impact of the depopulation of state mental hospitals. It was a time, too, when cheap lodging was relatively easy to come by. These new factors in the homeless equation would become more apparent as the 1970s drew to a close; by the early 1980s, their effects on cultural representations of homelessness were detectable. No longer mere "bums" or "derelicts," street people had become tokens of a species of alienation peculiar to our times.

Jean-Claude van Itallie's play *Bag Lady,* which opened in 1980 in a theater only a few blocks north of the Men's Shelter, was an early index of this trend. The title character was Clara, self-proclaimed "Empress of New York," a figure of fiercely warring contraries. Dignity alternated with groveling, self-possession with loss of control, rage with longing. Her predicament, confinement at the margins of polite society, was portrayed as one that she had a hand in making. In her refusal to accept her appointed lot in a hospital or nursing home, she is at once heroic and pathetic. That her mind is slipping is at least a partial blessing. Her dreams are untrammeled by age or infirmity; her pride refuses to be cowed by circumstance. She is prey to tricks of a memory no longer always able to distinguish past from present. Easily incensed, she freely hurls insults at those who disdain her requests for a handout. These may be poor substitutes for a life secure in the companionship of others, but they do serve as buffers against further incursions by a hostile world. Constant vigilance not only makes her exile complete, it also enables her to survive. Her life, like her bags, has been reduced to "only essentials."

At the same time, the bizarre uses of homelessness as symbol or trapping counsel against facile readings of its cultural value. The city's fashion moguls, for example, were quick to draw a parallel between the blanket-draped figures on the street and that year's "layered look." Designer "shopping bags" made their appearance. In the spring of 1983, by which time awareness of a mounting homeless problem was commonplace, Bloomingdale's opened a new display in its second-floor boutique, called "Street Couture." It featured clothing designed to mimic the dress of the street-dwelling poor: disheveled, patched, wrinkled, and mismatched. A jacket with artfully torn sleeves listed for $190. An employee explained: "Bag ladies are in," and the "street look" sells.[13]

The press was no less contrary. In the 1970s, its coverage ran the gamut from idle curiosity to sympathy, even indignation at the plight of homeless men and women. Early reports were likely to be marked by the traditional scorn for skid row. A *New York Times* story on those who ride the subways all night depicted them as "the worst of life . . . drunks, vagrants, prostitutes, wild-eyed men with matted hair and beards who may well be insane." Nor were women, when they began to appear on the street in significant numbers, exempt from suspicion. One account told how an enterprising beggar kept her sores from healing the better to elicit sympathy. Other stories depicted the homeless as mysterious, reclusive figures who chose their nomadic lifestyles and were loath to accept any assistance. The most preposterous allegation—that the "shopping bag ladies" carried bankbooks with assets in the thousands of dollars—achieved, with regular reiteration, an almost mythic status. Coverage of the murder of one such eccentric heiress focused exclusively on her singularity, making no mention of the fact that the subway entrance she shared as home was occupied by dozens of companions each night.[14]

Some inhabitants of public space proved voracious readers and were keen critics of stories about their lives. An elderly man once chewed me out for having introduced a reporter to him some days earlier. In her article (spring of 1980), she had attributed a number of ungrammatical remarks to this man (who prided himself on his faultless English) and then compounded this error by describing his shabby (but intact) overcoat as held together by safety pins. A reporter's memory lapse had been repaired by sentiment, negating a man's abiding efforts to maintain a respectable appearance, and he resented it.

A final index of the changing climate of social concern at the outset of our research proved the most consequential. On October 2, 1979, two attorneys for Legal Aid filed a class-action suit in the state supreme court on behalf of homeless men in the city. The three named plaintiffs in *Callahan v. Carey*—Robert Callahan, Clayton Fox, and Thomas Roig—charged that the city and state (as codefendants) had failed to honor their legal responsibility to provide shelter to indigent, homeless men. Much to the amazement of many observers, the judge found for the plaintiffs in early December, ordering the city and state to provide shelter beds sufficient to the need from then on, thus beginning a tortuous process of grudging compliance with, and exacting monitoring of, what would become a slew of court orders.

Methods

For purposes of our research,[15] we defined as "homeless" anyone whose primary nighttime residence was any of the following: publicly or privately operated shelters, park benches, street corners, doorways, subways, train stations, bus and ferry terminals, abandoned buildings, breadlines, or hospital emergency rooms. This working definition had the double advantage of being both relatively easy to apply and congruent with official approaches to enumerating the class. Census Bureau estimates in 1980 included, at least in theory, both a "mission count" of people sleeping in designated shelters and a "casual count" of those on the streets. Even if such counts are scrupulously executed, they underestimate the numbers in irregular or unreliable dwellings. Clearly, too, a single-point-in-time count was unequal to the task of measuring homelessness. Many of the more disabled tenants of SRO hotels, for example, had been on the streets in the past and were likely to wind up there again with any minor upset in their lives.

The original objective in our inquiry was to determine how "street people" survived, and why they "chose" this means of doing so over (presumably) "available" alternatives. Two distinct issues were involved: (1) how people became homeless in the first place and (2) the nature of public provision for their shelter once officially certified as homeless. We would find (as the lawyers in *Callahan* had surmised) that in practice one reason why so many homeless people preferred the street to existing alternatives was the state of those alternatives.

Scope of Work

The environs we investigated took in any space where homeless men and women slept, staked out a domain, or were fed or received services. The bulk of the work was done in Manhattan, although we eventually explored all five boroughs. For comparative purposes, I also visited public and private shelters in Washington, D.C., as well as private facilities in Boston. For two weeks in May 1981, I signed on as a houseman in a Catskills resort hotel where many Bowery men sought seasonal work, and lived in a staff dormitory.

The initial proposal had been to document "quality of life" issues, especially those concerning "maintenance (or survival) needs," for ex-psychiatric patients living in a variety of accommodations in the "community." So we surveyed the deinstitutionalization literature, visited a range of specialized residences, and spoke with tenants, service providers, and clinicians. In the course of these initial forays, we found a large number of ex-patients to be more or less permanent residents of the city's private and public shelters, or living on the streets. From December 1979 onward, we concentrated our efforts on that subpopulation, but decided to also include the homeless class as a whole because our early work had suggested that the common denominator was likely to be disenfranchisement not disability.[16]

Our methods were the time-tested ones of "participant observation," adapted (as such methods invariably are) to the exigencies of fieldwork and the practical objectives of the research endeavor. The motivating puzzle was simple enough to state: In any civilized society of sufficient means, decent shelter should be available to those unable to provide for themselves. What, then, was it about these people, or about the quality of emergency dwelling available to them, that led some to choose to fend for themselves on the street? The practical implications were also clear: If it could be shown that the chief causes of visible homelessness resided in street denizens themselves, then the direction of public policy would be considerably different from that being pursued in the courts. An adequate supply of rudimentary refuge, with certain built-in guarantees of security and dignity, would constitute a sufficient solution to homelessness.

Getting Oriented

To help chart the terrain that we hoped to explore, we met with dozens of informants at various sites with a reputation for trusted service to the homeless. These included the longest running breadline in the city (at St. Francis of Assisi Church); two successful outreach programs (the Manhattan Bowery Project and Goddard-Riverside's Project Reach-Out on the Upper West Side); a well-patronized drop-in center on Manhattan's East Side (The Coffee Pot), which served meals and coffee to between fifty and eighty homeless people and SRO residents each day; and both staff and guests at four privately run shelters (Mary House and Joseph House, two hospitality houses [of fifty and thirty beds respectively] run by Catholic workers within two blocks of the Men's Shelter; The Dwelling Place, a thirteen-bed shelter run by six nuns near the Port Authority Bus Terminal; and Star of the Sea, a newly opened residence for homeless women in Queens). With the exception of Joseph House, none of the small shelters took in men. So we made our way to the Bowery and Water Street Missions (where conditions were virtually unchanged since the 1960s), to the Salvation Army's Booth House, and to the remaining stock of commercial lodging houses.

Three other individuals proved key informants. Robert Hayes not only served as a source of up-to-date information on city policies and plans but also gave me my initial tour of the Bowery and introduced me to *Callahan* plaintiffs. Hayes was the most avid consumer of our research findings and recruited me both as court-appointed observer and as expert witness when the case went to trial in late 1980. Bill Muller was a night watchman by trade, street worker by vocation. Over the nearly two decades he had been at it, Muller had conversed with thousands of men and women living on the street, and had managed to procure documentation, government disability benefits, and hotel placements for scores of them. Ann-Marie Rousseau, a photo-journalist, was completing a study of homeless women (1981) at the time we met, and coached us on how to approach and interview.

In December 1979—on the same day that the initial court order in favor of homeless men was handed down—we began to follow up leads from various contacts and published reports. For several weeks, we surveyed public sites in Manhattan: train stations, bus stations, and ferry terminals; subways and subway stations; public parks, traffic islands, squares, and monuments (especially in the midtown area); hidden refuges (steam tunnels under Park Avenue, abandoned rail tunnels under Riverside Park, loading bays in commercial districts); soup kitchens, breadlines, and drop-in centers. With homeless people serving as our guides, we investigated other sites: waterfront docks, abandoned buildings, select stairwells and hallways in occupied buildings. In addition, I spent a lot of time on the Bowery, in the Men's Shelter and Wards Island annex, in commercial flophouses, and in bars.[17]

Between the two of us, we spoke to hundreds of homeless people and interviewed scores of them in depth. Our interviews were sometimes recorded; for the most part, though, we relied on hastily scribbled notes made at the time of the exchange (or shortly after), which were then reconstructed as formal "fieldnotes" as soon as possible. Over the course of the first two years of our work, we remained in regular contact with two dozen or so homeless men and women. For a while, our office served as impromptu meeting space for a small group of homeless men, whose efforts at refurbishing an abandoned building on the Lower East Side we had supported. On occasion, too, thanks to the willingness of our employers to look the other way, they slept there.

Methods of Approach

A tattered appearance, "inappropriate" public behavior, a cache of belongings assembled in plastic bags or cardboard boxes, swollen ulcerated legs, apparent aimlessness: These were the canonical signs of homelessness as we read them. Display of any of these usually sufficed to distinguish our

ONSES OF THOSE APPROACHED

ary to the image sometimes purveyed in the press of homeless per- eclusive urban hermits, most of those we approached and talked to ling to share their histories and travails with us. Remarkably, to a er at least, social graces were retained on the streets; even fumbling at engagement were met, for the most part, with an unexpected of comity. Offers of food or coffee were accepted or rejected po- quiries as to our respondents' health and welfare were reciprocated; f leave-taking, including some touching face-saving maneuvers, ularly resorted to. Some did rebuff any effort at contact. Others ac- he sandwich, goods, or cash, but communicated—by moving away, g silent, or stating so—that they preferred not to talk.

orm, however unexpected, was the ease with which even an obvi- oubled man, locked in verbal combat with unseen adversaries, spond in a way commensurate with the offer. Adopting, for the mo- least, a poised and self-possessed attitude, he might accept or de- offer of cigarettes or coffee; if the latter, protests of "business to at- reassurances that they had money to buy such things should they or a shy, self-conscious shaking of the head were common. Then me clearly resented the intrusion:

> *ylvania Station*: I approached an elderly, scowling man, lugging several round, who was making his way—with great dispatch and efficiency— one trash bin to the next, sifting through their contents for discarded les or food. He dismissed my offer of coffee with a curt expletive, rhetorically: "Haven't you people done enough damage already?" (Cir- ances seemed less than propitious for inquiring as the identity of "you .") (February 13, 1980)

, as noted earlier, our interest was itself suspect, violating as it did f noninterference and privacy. One woman warned Ellen that vould wonder why she wanted the information, thinking that she vell be from some agency that wants to take them some place they nt to be, like an institution of some kind" (EB fieldnotes, July 14,

s had been approached before and were either bored or fatigued by pect of reciting their story again. One woman, clearly grown cynical epeated entreaties of reporters, asked when my turn came: "What's t? Telling people what it's like won't change anything. They see us. ow what it's like. What difference does it make?" (June 1, 1980). appeared to be a refusal could also prove a missed signal:

subjects from other travelers "rightly" making their way on public thoroughfares. But there were also those who painstakingly managed to maintain a reasonably high standard of appearance, who scrupulously policed their behavior to avoid drawing attention to themselves, and who were thus likely to be overlooked in casual surveys. Their presence in public spaces during post-commuter, post-shopper hours, and especially their repeated presence for days or weeks on end, was sometimes the only telling giveaway. In the early morning hours, the homeless poor of the city were the chief occupants in the waiting rooms of stations and terminals.

We began with prolonged observation and exploration of the physical outlay of the chosen premises, usually making no effort to conceal our presence. Typically, we made offers of food, coffee, cigarettes, or change as a means of initiating conversation. Many of those we approached were used to such offers; even our awkward attempts to follow up with talk were not unprecedented. For reasons of mutual ease, Ellen approached women and I approached men as a general rule.

We made it a practice to identify ourselves as "researchers" in the opening round of exchange, but it soon became clear that this was a role neither recognized nor easily fathomed by many of our prospective informants. After all, we were not "slumming" or seeking to purchase a souvenir photograph, nor were we quite like the cadres of good Samaritans who occasionally made the rounds of the down-and-out, dropping off food and other survival goods. Confusion often ensued, our opening gambit being met by expressions of disbelief, suspicion, incomprehension, or disinterest. So we changed tack, and held off going into the purpose of our inquiry until an opportunity presented itself in the course of the conversation. We took to describing ourselves as "writers"—"reporters" was a common association for our informants—doing a "story" or "project" on homelessness in New York City.

More than a few fleeting contacts were conducted under a veil of mutual bewilderment. But in prolonged contacts, we made a determined effort not to deceive or mislead people who agreed to be interviewed (excepting the rather different conversations that took place when we sought to pass as homeless ourselves, as discussed below). Still, it must be said that it was not always clear that the consent of our informants could be considered "informed."

Cultural prescriptions governing the behavior of strangers were not difficult to circumvent when contrary rules (like those dealing with almsgiving) could be invoked. Trouble arose, however, when there was no appeal (not even tacitly) for assistance, and the individual in question was making an evident effort to "pass." It was not uncommon for people apparently without shelter to deny that they were homeless. Nor was it always easy to tell:

> *Grand Central Station,* shortly after midnight: Spoke for a while with a Swiss émigré, about 50, who's been in the States since 1960. Had been standing at one of the phone banks in the main room, with half dozen or so paper shopping bags arranged around him. Out of work. Stays, he says, at a hotel on the West Side; pays less than $30/week, been there for 20 years. I explained my work as trying to see whether there was a need for more public shelters. He understood, but replied that it was "not a program I need," as he still retained his small hotel room. Spends most of his time outside, he said, because conditions at the hotel are "overcrowded." [A week later, at roughly the same hour, he is there again: same place, same pose.] (March 19, 25, 1981)

Conceivably, here was a man whose dwelling place shuttled between a hovel and the street. Such a predicament was not uncommon. We would meet others on the street who occasionally found a place inside. Interviews with SRO residents in the city at this time likewise revealed a number of variations on this pattern.[18]

Passing

If it wasn't always easy to tell who was homeless, neither was it always obvious that we were not. Indeed, though we made no effort to disguise ourselves as beggars and in the winter wore warm clothing that fit, the regularity with which we were taken to be homeless was a bit unnerving. It was a common experience for both of us to be taken casually under the wing of a more experienced street dweller when we made inquiries, late at night, about a place to stay. He or she would advise us on places to avoid, havens to seek out, the better quality of food that could be had if one knew where to look. I observed similar instances of solicitude extended to older and younger men as well.

There were times when I made a studied effort to pass as homeless myself. I spent a number of evenings, up to the 11 P.M. lights out, in Bowery flophouses, chatting casually with men I met. I slept overnight as a paying customer in a cubicle at one of them (The Palace), later stayed at a mission in Houston (where demand for beds was not so high), and lived for two weeks in a dilapidated staff dormitory at the Concord Hotel in the Catskills. I passed countless late hours and many full nights walking the streets of Manhattan, investigating likely sleeping spots, photographing those I found, and interviewing anyone who was awake.

I made no effort to identify myself as a researcher on these occasions. Conversations were invariably more discursive and less informative about the specifics of an individual's life history. The old Bowery rule

about not inquiring into another's past without g
force. Still, these encounters were instructive in
the rhythms and texture of a way of life—the eve
pass and threat of discovery that one learns to liv
of exposure and vulnerability that only fatigue d
level fear. On a few occasions I tried pacing an o
wine in an abandoned building, or passed the be
drinking unobtrusively in a Bowery tavern. Wha
have been vouchsafed to me at such times were
by the next day's light.

Participant observers who attempt, however br
ably get their comeuppance. I was no exception. I
suring that I was "made" (as was true of "pseud
wards and a *Washington Post* reporter masquerad
by the experts or staff, but by those I had hoped
them. The more obvious pratfalls were of my ow
the early morning muster of housemen with a co
tucked under my arm (every other man was readi
ing a bottle of (really) cheap brandy rather than r
turn to contribute; not going in for an additional s
staff dormitory after a full evening spent in a bar
tler giveaways as well: the use of a brand-name s
cheap generic; a slip of language that drew bem
panions; the lack of scars or wounds on my nude
marched off to a mission bunk; even, to the obse
that began this chapter, a certain untrodden look
larly soused fellow houseman at the hotel, on h
said that I hadn't looked to him like I belonged t
these guys are mental midgets."

In any event, I was confronted directly once o
was working on a story but would use no names.
count are fictitious.) One hotel worker of some
rather circumspect about it—as befitted an old
bought me a beer on my last day of work:

> Jim couldn't figure out what I was doing there at t
> educated" (though the only evidence of that, I th
> the *Times*). "I just couldn't figure out what this guy'
> to asking me outright, but veered off. Several minu
> a story of how a reporter had infiltrated Grossing
> experiences for a local paper, some time ago. He p
> if he could dig one up. (May 24, 1981)

Pennsylvania Station: I walked up to a gray-bearded man rummaging through trash and offered him a cup of coffee. He did not so much as look up to acknowledge my presence, but went on about his business. Having exhausted that bin, he went on the next. On my way out of the station, I was about to pass him again and this time simply handed him the cup of coffee. He saw the cup before he saw me, but once he did, he was happy to talk, if a bit wary about using his name. ("I don't want to get into trouble.") It turns out he's deaf and never heard my first offer. (February 13, 1980)

Many contacts proved to be hopelessly opaque, at least for the opening rounds of conversation. At such times, pointed questioning was fruitless and the would-be ethnographer found himself an unwitting player in what was evidently a running theater of improvisation. In other places, my meager notes read like psychotic brush-offs:

Men's Shelter: I approached a man sitting on the second-floor steps, who had been returned (apparently as unacceptable) by the Keener van [see "The Keener Building" below]. As I walked up, he said: "I know you. You're my son. I'm the father of them all. Rockefeller I." (February 8, 1980)

Grand Central Station: After a brief conversation about where he was staying (at a Bowery flop; comes to the station to panhandle), Chauncey gives this version of how he came to the streets: "After I had watched *Superman* and *Star Trek*, I had an institution . . . and I had just made the sound effects. [A mental institution?] Yes. [Do you know how long you were there?] No, I don't remember. [How long ago was it?] I don't know. I am too busy listening to the radio. This AM/FM. 1600/1700/1900. Monaural and stereo." (October 27, 1980)

And then there were times when it would have been wise to recall Edward Evans-Pritchard's observation that native informants are invariably possessed of a better sense of humor than their interrogators:

Grand Central Station: An older man, fairly rag-tag in his dress, took me up on my offer of coffee. Started off with: "They always get me confused with historical characters." And then launched into a long paean to the heroics of "psychologists"—unbroken save by my futile efforts to ask some rather homespun questions [like: Do you live around here?] which he would answer by yet another comment about these dauntless explorers of the mind—all of which, to my unlettered ear, was virtually incomprehensible. At one point, perhaps a nod in the direction of my obvious bewilderment: "You may agree or disagree. But at least you can give his argument a hearing and go to your front porch and tip your hat." As we parted, spying the load of books I was carrying, he said: "If you run into any Immanuel Kant, read some for me."

On still other occasions, informants with whom I had a fairly long-standing relationship would suddenly lapse into apparent nonsense or hit a narrative furrow from which it proved impossible to extricate them. On reflection, some of these seemed more like childlike attempts at face-saving than deception or pathology. No tale was too preposterous:

> *Horn and Hardart, near Grand Central*: Ken relates, in a hushed conspiratorial tone, how some guy out in southern California has offered him a job as a bouncer in his bar. But bigger things are at stake: the guy is involved in high finance on an international scale—"you know, like Robert Vespo down in the Dominican Islands"—and is in some kind of trouble. He needs to borrow some money from Ken ("250 or 500 thousand") to bail himself out. "'Course, I'd be expectin' a return of 3 or 4 million." He closes with: "I'm just lying out now [in the steam tunnels] while I consider this." (January 1, 1980)

Repeated contacts with the same individuals enabled us to sift through much of what they said, recheck or seek clarification on things that seemed unlikely, and winnow out some fabricated or misremembered information. What we were unable to confirm firsthand, we usually sought to corroborate with other informants. Continuity of contact, of course, was not easy to maintain with a street population whose habitual refuges changed in response to weather conditions, run-ins with the police, or harassment by passersby. Remarkably, some informants were faithful about telephoning or periodically checking in to see how the research progressed. A few volunteered to assist the effort and would take notes or report to us the next day on their observations and experiences.

Some practical considerations should be mentioned as well. We made it a rule not to wake people for purposes of interviewing them. Noise could make a conversation conducted on subways, or at the edges of train tracks or roadways, an uncertain affair. Then, too, it was not uncommon for research interests to be preempted by more pressing concerns:

> Late yesterday morning, while walking around the area of Lexington and 23rd St., I watched a man get expelled from a restaurant and an antique store (into the basement of which he had made his way). In each case, he protested that he lived there. I approached him as he wandered down 23rd St. In addition to his apparent confusion, his right arm was hanging peculiarly and a closer look revealed a badly swollen hand. In response to my repeated questioning about where he lived, he kept insisting (in a West Indian lilt): "I don't know his name. He was the broad-shouldered one. He borrowed the screwdriver—I wasn't using it—and he brought it back." After a fruitless attempt to enlist the aid of two cops, and an hour of repeated failures to explain to him what I was proposing, I led him by his good arm to Bellevue.

Once in the hospital, he suddenly switched into a different mode of functioning. He was able to recall his name and (vaguely) where he was from (either Montego Bay or St. Margaret's Bay in Jamaica). Referred to Psychiatric ER. The examining staff described him as "disoriented, confused, unable to answer questions other than name"—and sent him back to the medical ER. I spoke to a resident there I happened to know and then left, having been assured he would be taken care of.

Next day, I called and found out it had taken a 24-hour wait in the ER before he was admitted to Neurology for a workup. In addition to his evident confusion (the result, the resident guessed, of Wernicke-Korsakoff syndrome, "occult seizure," or meningitis), he was found to have a broken shoulder. (March 19, 1980)

Most interventions were stopgap measures: riding with someone in an ambulance to a hospital; accompanying someone to the shelter who had no notion that one existed; securing a hearing aid; paying for transportation or recovery of belongings from storage lockers; making small loans. We helped some people to negotiate the shoals of bureaucracy in occasionally successful applications for relief. At such times, we justified the time involved as an indispensable part of the story from our informants' point of view. On other occasions, when the usual routes of assistance were too forbidding or demanding for the individual in question, we would make use of personal contacts with physicians to secure medication, an examination, and advice on what to do next. And, if pressed, we would not hesitate to offer counsel on places to sleep or reliable sources of assistance. In a few cases, after talking to some young guy, newly arrived on the Bowery with no idea of what he was getting into, I would offer carfare to a friend's place in lieu of a night in a flophouse.

There were a few dicey moments, when retreat seemed the better part of ethnographic valor. Curiously, these came not during late-night explorations of ill-lit, isolated sites, but during routine visits to common lodgings:

Kenton Hotel: It's early afternoon, and I retire to my assigned bed on the second floor. Throw down my rucksack and start to chat with Terry, the guy in the next cot. Two beds away, a young man in his late twenties is mumbling angrily to himself: "Gave that motherfucker five cigarettes and he ain't paid me the twenty-five cents." Looking my way. No one else on the floor. He pulls out a knife, flicks open a five-inch blade. More mumbling, only snatches of which I catch: ". . . cutting him up . . . just as soon kill you as look at you." I take the opportunity to ask Terry about meal-serving hours at the Muni. He turns to the mumbler and repeats the question, but the kid merely glares at us and keeps muttering to himself. I grab my rucksack, place it between the knife and me, and slowly get up to leave. As I make my way out, he watches me, fingers the knife, and continues the monologue: ". . . like that boy they cut up last night—his muscles were all cut through to the bone, you could see the bone. They cut his ass up good. That's the kid I'd like to get . . ." (October 16, 1980).

Getting There

Routes to homelessness, and the kind of subsistence strategies it entails, have varied across time and place. Historically, the great causes of homelessness have included pilgrimage, war, famine, social upheaval, itinerant labor, alcoholism, and the lure of the open road. In the twentieth century, three forces joined the traditional ones: (1) cyclical unemployment and/or massive job loss; (2) recurring shortages of low-cost housing; and (3) sudden dislocations in government relief or institutional programs—especially (for the period and people of interest here) the depopulation of the state mental hospitals. These factors are worth examining in the light of what we knew then in the early 1980s.

Unemployment. In the United States, widespread unemployment was unheard of before the introduction of wage-labor on a large scale. It appeared in recurring waves in the latter half of the nineteenth century, most disturbingly in the guise of the "tramp problem." Our original research just overlapped with the recession of 1981–1982, but the immediate consequences of that downturn for homelessness in New York were not apparent in columns of the "new poor" (as was alleged, say, in the industrial north central states). Officially, unemployment stood at 8.8 percent midway through our initial fieldwork. If adjusted for part-time work, the inclusion of military personnel, and the exclusion of "discouraged workers" or others who wanted work but were not actively seeking jobs, the figure would have been at least twice that.[20]

Loss of a job had drawn increasing attention as a "stressful life event" in the 1970s, and its relevance to the topic at hand was not limited to those instances where job loss prompts an immediate taking to the road in search of employment elsewhere. The drop in income, disruption of personal support networks, and mounting personal distress all take their cumulative toll in ability to cope. A number of studies had suggested that secondary—often maladaptive—coping behaviors may ensue, including alcoholism. But all such attempts to trace the effects of job loss bristle with difficulties. Suffice it to observe here that, at the very least, loss of a job, or failure ever to secure one, made a man's survival less secure and increased his vulnerability to displacement.[21]

Housing scarcity. Decent low-cost housing sufficient to meet the needs of the poor was in chronically short supply in Manhattan throughout the twentieth century. By the late 1970s, the shortage citywide had reached what would soon be termed crisis levels. Overall vacancy for rental housing stood at 1 percent (5 percent is considered minimal for normal market fluctuations). Nearly 9 percent of the total rental stock was *in rem* (i.e., remitted to city ownership for failure to pay taxes); an additional 33 percent was in imminent danger of becoming so (three or more quarters tax delinquent). Between 1976 and 1979, median household income crept up by only 7 percent, while rents rose by nearly 24 percent and the cost of living by nearly 20 percent. More than half of renter households spent a quarter or more of their gross income on rent and utilities.[22]

Deinstitutionalization. Between 1965 and 1977, New York State released over 126,000 patients from its state hospitals in the New York City area. If one subtracts deaths and readmissions, an estimated 47,000 former patients resided in the city at the time our inquiry got underway. This figure does not include the estimated 8,000 persons who were refused admittance each year under the tightened entry criteria (imminent danger to self or others), and who, in all probability, would have been admitted under the old regime.[23] Psychiatric disorder itself is neither a necessary nor (or only rarely) a sufficient cause of homelessness. The real forces of displacement proved to be the living circumstances confronted by people with diminished coping skills and low tolerance for stress. Especially relevant was the growing scarcity of what had been housing for thousands of ex-patients: the stock of residential hotels. As the supply of SROs fell precipitously in the late 1970s and demand rose, many of those who had escaped the initial rounds of displacement found themselves pressured to move by landlords seeking a more "desirable" clientele.

These factors are of interest chiefly for the extent and depth of vulnerability they hint at. Marginalized individuals, living at the edges of subsistence, routinely subjected to further buffeting by the job market or the apparatus of relief, and occupying what was fast becoming an endangered species of housing, were at enhanced risk of displacement. In the housing climate that existed at the time, people with fixed incomes were finding it increasingly difficult to replace low-cost dwellings, however poor their quality, once lost. Those who could turned first to friends and family; lacking or having exhausted that resource, they next turned to private and public sources of shelter. Neither source was prepared for what became the onslaught of the 1980s.

Triggering Events

A note of caution is in order about the explanatory power of events that are interpreted as "precipitating" homelessness. These factors are never self-contained, and the apparent simplicity they may acquire in the tabulations of survey researchers is largely artifactual. For any valid inferences to be drawn, the events as recounted must be contextualized within ways of life and work, patterns of informal support, and appraisals of individual vulnerability. In our research, it was not always clear what the relative weight of these factors should be and conclusions about their impact should be hedged accordingly.

More to the point: Unless one accepts a strictly linear view of subsistence fortunes, a focus on the threshold events that immediately preceded homelessness is likely to raise as many questions as it answers. If one establishes that 30 percent of new arrivals at a shelter were staying with friends or relatives before applying for shelter, but makes no effort to learn how such makeshift arrangements arose in the first place, what does that tell us about the origins of their homelessness? If it is found that 38 percent of the homeless were "recently evicted," but reasons for eviction go unexamined, what has been learned beyond the almost self-evident fact that many of those without housing were forced out of it at some point in the past? How do the origins of homelessness overlay with dispossessed households who managed to defer applying for emergency assistance by relying on the temporary hospitality of friends? Similarly, to note that the mental status of many newly homeless men is of questionable soundness, or that many have histories of psychiatric hospitalization or incarceration, is to mark probable vulnerability factors for further inquiry but no more.[24]

With such caveats in mind, I turn now to precipitants of homelessness. These should be read, as I hope will be clear, as clues to both the larger forces contributing to homelessness and the adaptive strategies used in order to avoid a public declaration of need.

As recounted by informants, the immediate events that provoked the current round of homelessness ranged from the seemingly trivial to the calamitous. In retrospect, too, there was considerable variation in what I took to be the limits of endurance that a given man had crossed. For some, recourse to the streets or shelters had become habit, to be expected as the vagaries of fate demanded. For others, it was plainly traumatic, the result of a long spiral downward that had left all other avenues of assistance exhausted. For still others, what began as the trauma of displacement had taken on, over time, the look and feel of an avocation, one's adeptness at which was to be prized. For yet others, it was questionable how much they grasped of their present straits; the daily round of events seemed to have a life of its own that carried them with it. For a few, it may even be said that homelessness was a "chosen" course, to be pursued for a while and—if things went according to plan—forsaken when brighter prospects appeared.

Although new forces of displacement had appeared, the older ones persisted. For some men, periodic binge-drinking disrupted whatever residential stability they had and sent them to the streets or shelters; for others, chronic alcoholism precluded any but the most marginal of existences. Cause and effect, of course, are not sealed chambers; matters get complicated when alcoholism is but one of several problems needing attention or when alcohol functions as a coping mechanism—as, for example, when it is used as a form of "self-medication" to quell inner voices and anxieties.[25]

For some men, too, their social isolation, meager pensions, or intermittent patterns of work made stable residence all but impossible. While the ecological niche that had made it possible to survive with two suits of clothes (one worn, the other at the laundry), spot work, and transient hotel lodgings without resort to public relief or skid row institutions[26] had virtually disappeared, some still managed variations on this theme. Independent by conviction, they would on occasion use public facilities when all else failed.

Intolerable conditions in one's prior residence (including deteriorated services, harassment, and the threat of eviction) loomed large in the histories of many men on the street. In listening to some accounts, it wasn't always clear at the time how much of the menace was real and how much imagined. Subsequent reports confirmed a widespread pattern of tenant intimidation by landlords seeking to vacate buildings prior to sale or conversion.[27] A study of over one hundred homeless men and women engaged by an outreach team on Manhattan's Upper West Side in the winter of 1980–1981 offered more direct confirmation: 70 percent of those for whom information on prior residence was obtained had been homeless less than a year; 60 percent of that group said they arrived on the street as a direct result of eviction.[28]

In other cases, where disability was evident and serious, failures of aftercare provisions were at fault. For some, the neglect was long-standing, and displacement was the result of a slow, unarrested pattern of decline. For others, the necessary supports were never put in place:

> *Men's Shelter*: Emmet is back on the street again. Owing to tenacious efforts on the part of the evening psychiatrist on duty at the shelter, he had been hospitalized a few months back, but was released sometime in May (as he recounted to the psychiatrist). He said he's been living in an SRO uptown, but left after his disability check failed to arrive on time. He couldn't get it together himself to go to the welfare office and see what the trouble was. Apparently, no one is following his case outside the hospital. He was told by the clerk here that he was barred from all the hotels because of his record of bad behavior in the past; can't go to the Keener Building [on Wards Island] because

> at some point he tangled with a guard there. In effect, he has nowhere to go but the streets. (July 15, 1980)

More extreme, if less typical instances made it clear that the shelter still functioned (as its predecessor, the municipal lodging house had in the early part of the century) as "the city's dumping ground" for human refuse.[29] A taxi pulls up in front and drops off a man just discharged from the hospital; if the passenger was unable to walk unaided, the cabbie might be paid extra to help him into the shelter. The police show up with a man found wandering around Times Square; he's blind, suffers from epilepsy, and had been recently released from Bellevue. A young man with multiple sclerosis runs out of money while on a trip to the city from an upstate rehabilitation center; some clueless Samaritan directs him to the shelter. An old man never makes it to the door; I find him lying at the corner of the shelter next to his walker, mumbling incoherently, his pants drenched with urine.

The shelter was the last stop; there was no such thing as an absolutely unacceptable arrival. Extraordinary measures could be made—usually, in my experience, owing to the intervention of an outsider or part-time professional staff member—to place a man elsewhere, but they were rare. Circumstances that defied belief, and for which adjectives like Dante-esque were devised, passed without remark, occasioning only a momentary shudder of disgust:

> *Men's Shelter*: While talking with a staff member tonight, I was told about a client who had had a colostomy but was missing the bag. Rafferty is so filthy and smells so bad that he is refused service. When he persists, a staff member will take a plate to the back door and let him eat outside or squatting in a corner by himself. The staff refer to him as "Shitty."
>
> [A week later:] I met Mr. Rafferty tonight on the stairwell around ten o'-clock. He was covered with grime and fecal matter, his clothes were in tatters, and he smelled very bad. He told me that he had his operation in July of either 1977 or 1978; the doctor on duty at the shelter thinks it was probably for a carcinoma. Mr. Rafferty has a single stoma (exit point) in his upper left abdomen. For some time now, he has had no bag for it, which makes it difficult for others to be around him. I checked his 5 by 8 card [in the shelter files] and found that he is first recorded as having applied for lodging on March 21, 1980. There was no indication of any handicap on his record, a curious omission.
>
> The doctor on call and I try to persuade the night supervisor to let him spend the night in the lobby. (Rafferty has been living on the streets.) He agrees on the condition that the doc try to have Rafferty admitted to a hospital the next day. This should present no problems: Rafferty is a veteran, so he should have hospitalization benefits. Rafferty's conversation is disjointed and uncertain, and the doc thinks he is more than a little disturbed. He may be subject to a 2–PC [a two-physician involuntary commitment].

> I called back to speak to a worker with whom I am on good terms just before 1 A.M. Rafferty had disappeared. He was found the next night and admitted to Bellevue on a 2–PC, to be evaluated, cleaned up, and treated. Twenty-four hours later he reappeared at the shelter, with no plans for follow-up treatment. It turns out that he has been fitted with at least six bags, but is unable to keep himself together. (November 6, 13, 20, 1980)

This man continued to make occasional use of the shelter throughout the winter. In March a memorandum went out from the director of social services at the shelter: If Rafferty was found, he was to be brought to the infirmary, cleaned up, and held until a placement can be arranged. Finally, some six months after he was brought to professional attention, a referral to a skilled nursing facility was arranged.

For other men, a sudden breakdown, subsequent hospitalization, and release to an indifferent if not hostile environment left them with few choices other than the shelter. Some were not sure how they wound up there. A former bank worker, who came to the states from Nigeria in 1964, remembered only bits and pieces of his admission and release. He was interviewed at the Keener shelter on Wards Island, wearing only a tattered pair of trousers. He recited what he recalled of his story several times:

> I was told I was crying in my apartment in the night, or something like that, and my neighbor called the police, who forced the door down and found me on the floor. Then they took me down to the hospital . . . They saved my life. . . . Then the department of social services got involved when I was in the hospital. They didn't know who I am, who I belong to . . . so they tried to find out. . . . And after I had the operation [for a ruptured appendix, he thinks] they brought me here, hoping to find a place where I could stay, because they said the place I was staying was taken. . . . And I really can't say, because I really don't know what actually happened to me. (August 12, 1980)

Other men fell through the proverbial cracks in the system. An ex-offender was at the shelter pending approval of his application for home relief. He had been rejected from a Salvation Army program, into which his probation officer had tried hard to get him admitted, because he wasn't an alcoholic. An angry young man from Harlem, a recent graduate of drug and alcohol rehab programs, was staying at the Keener shelter while seeking documentation to apply for relief. Because of his drug use, his family wouldn't take him in. Informed by a welfare office that he lacked proper identification, he was referred to the Men's Shelter for help in obtaining it. He'd been there eighteen months waiting for it. A Vietnam Veterans Outreach Center in Brooklyn reported that 16 percent of its caseload of five hundred were homeless.

The uncertain or intermittent character of family supports meant periodic bouts of homelessness for some men, who otherwise had difficulty making it on their own. An older man, whom I met at the breadline, worked occasionally on a truck crew that picked up grease and fat from restaurants for use in rendering plants. When out of work, he lived with his sons and daughters as long as it was tolerable; when he felt he'd overstayed his welcome, he took to the streets, walking around at night, cat-napping in the day. Family assistance was out of the question for other men, owing to long-standing breaches. A man who'd been staying in the tunnels under Grand Central for several years balked at my suggestion that he try to contact a brother living nearby; he was sure the brother wanted nothing to do with him.

Turnover rates at the Men's Shelter indicate that proportionately few men arrived at the shelter to stay. That fact pointed up a more salient one: The homelessness of a good many men was a sometimes thing, one of the expected costs incurred when living on the margins. Some men managed to stay in hotels for most of the time, repairing to the streets only when their funds ran out—say, for the last week or so each month. Others took to panhandling to make up the difference between income and rent at one of the cheap lodging houses. Still others were resigned to letting other necessities slide, if only they could hold onto a prized hotel room as a paying customer. For one elderly gentleman, this was a point of pride. He would take no "government money," but carefully husbanded his small pension. He showed off a decent overcoat he had recently acquired for five dollars at a second-hand store on the Bowery. His meals consisted of soup, sandwiches, and hard-boiled eggs. He maintained a cubicle on the Bowery, but spent days and evenings in Pennsylvania Station—his "home away from home."

Among the younger men, other patterns were discernible. Leroy, a muscular quick-witted man in his late twenties, was arrested with two companions on a rape charge—"it was all a mistake; we were just fooling around"—and was thrown out by his mother. He and his twin brother have been on the Bowery for a year, working intermittently and drinking regularly. Leroy saw their tenure as "strictly temporary . . . I don't belong here." Others may have begun that way, but have settled into what has become a standing routine. Robertson, an ex-marine with a burn-scarred face, had been staying at The Kenton for about a year, after splitting up with his wife. When I first met him, he was working at a foam rubber plant across the river in New Jersey; the plant sent a van over each morning to pick up him and a number of other workers. Four months later, a strike idled the plant and Robertson was reduced to spot work assigned by an agency on Great Jones Street.

During lean times (he was hospitalized for eight weeks with pneumonia that spring) or while drinking heavily, he'd show up for a ticket at the Muni. Otherwise he fended for himself.

These are not, in general, reclusive men, and barracks-style banter commonly pervades the lodging houses with long-term residents. But it can be a curiously circumspect camaraderie. One night I returned from an ambulance ride to Bellevue's emergency room, having accompanied a young guy found unconscious on the sidewalk in front of the shelter. Still trying to find out who he was, I asked Leroy to introduce me to one of the injured man's friends. He tracked down Tiny, a towering man of considerable heft, who met me at the corner gas station later that night. He described how the man had been beaten by three others, but wasn't much help with respect to his identity: "We hang out together, we drink wine together, we smoke reefer together, we shoot dope together, but I don't know his name." All anyone knew, so far as I could learn, was his nickname: "Chicago."

While not fitting the classic picture of "disaffiliated" men, some had made conscious efforts to cut ties. Two young guys, who tended to stick together on the Bowery, sleeping in flops or on the subways, claimed still to have friends in the Bronx who would take them in. But, as one of them put it, he didn't want to bother them or have them see him in that state: "It's my own fault I fucked up, nobody else's." He felt that the responsibility for managing his straitened circumstances was his alone.

Often, however, those who avoided the shelter and the flops could, when desperate, appeal to friends or family for respite. One hapless peddler of junk items who slept in a closet in an abandoned building just off the Bowery could, he assured me, go to his sister's place in Brooklyn when things got too rough. Even those with manifest, crippling disorders were able to negotiate occasional use of familial resources:

> *Penn Station*: I had a long talk with Ed, a young man of 23, with grizzled beard and sunglasses. He was quite disturbed, tearful at times, about his situation. In the rambling, sometimes incoherent excuse for a conversation we had, I felt like someone eavesdropping on another talking to himself. Among the snatches I caught: ". . . the Lamb of God, because God wants it that way. It was so much better when I had my apartment. I would listen to the radio, have a Marlboro, cup of coffee . . . I always knew I would be someone special, but I never expected this."
>
> We talked in a windswept stairwell, Ed refusing my repeated suggestion that we move somewhere warmer. Wolfed down a bagel and a carton of milk, but refused coffee because it made him jittery. Rapid shifts in conversation and mood. "Do you believe in war?" he asked me. At my negative response, he turned away, then shouted "Armageddon!" and went on to mumble something about his arm. He slept last night in a warehouse, but can always—when really

hard up—return to his father's house in Brooklyn for food and clothing. (March 12, 1980)

It was these anomalous cases—part-time workers who were occasional clients of the Men's Shelter; men who for the most part managed to hold on to lodgings and who trusted to their wits when that failed; men who mixed periodic stays at public facilities with reliance on families; men who, for purposes of my research, tended inconveniently to disappear after initial contacts—that led eventually to our rethinking of public homelessness as part of a much larger class of subsistence patterns common among the urban poor.[30] But at the time, I saw such periods of self-sufficiency or unexpected respite as departures from what I took to be the more enduring norm of homelessness.

Some cases stubbornly resisted categorization. Take Albert, for instance. He received supplemental security income (SSI) and, when he held onto his rent allotment, alternated his lodgings between two residences with on-site support staff and a less reputable downtown SRO. The trouble was Albert's affection for things electronic. His inventory of portable stereos would have been truly impressive had it not been regularly depleted by theft. To replenish stolen items or upgrade his current stock, Albert would dip into the nondiscretionary portion of his government check, a practice that resulted in his periodic ejection from wherever he happened to be staying at the time. On occasion this meant that he would be on the street for a while; he avoided the shelter at all costs. But Albert had a convincing psychiatric history and, more to the point, had mastered the art of emergency admittance: He simply told the examining psychiatrist in the ER that the statues in Central Park were threatening to kill him. It was nearly always good for a week's stay.

I was stumped when it came to fitting such cases into a contemporary "classification" scheme of "homeless types." The difficulty proved more telling than I first appreciated; in fact, it proved to be one that extended to the survival strategies of homeless men as a whole. What I was hearing and trying lamely to organize into some coherent picture were dozens of variations on basic problem-solving techniques. The trick, as some commentators recognized at the time, was not to confuse categories of problems with typologies of persons. It was practices not personalities that needed to be understood.[31]

In moving to a discussion of what is often seen as the most basic of survival problems—shelter for the night—I want to underscore this point. Stylistic considerations may sometimes produce phrases like "shelter men" or "street dwellers," but these are idioms of convenience not kinds of men. It may say more about the namers than the named that the most common appellate for the visibly homeless poor at the time was "shopping bag" people.

Varieties of Shelter

I begin this section with a description of public shelters because decisions about where to seek a bed for the night were foremost on the minds of the men with whom I spoke and because "shelter" was central in the public debate on the proper response to homelessness. Shelter is so basic a need that its satisfaction, in formal (institutional) settings at least, often entailed the solutions to allied problems of food, income assistance, and clinical attention. Even in informal (improvised) settings, decisions about shelter tended to limit or bias one's options regarding those other needs.

The Men's Shelter

At the outset of the study, the one truly city-run shelter was Camp La-Guardia. The camp was a twenty-four–hour facility at which older men tended to stay for extended periods of time; a "voluntary total institution" was one analyst's characterization of the place.[32] When men referred to the "Men's Shelter," they meant the East 3rd Street facility, which at that time—apart from a specialized detox facility on one floor—functioned chiefly as a processing and referral center.

Until July 1964, up to six hundred men had actually slept in the building. Since then, the shelter had contracted out for beds with Bowery lodging houses. Vouchers good for variable lengths of stay at one of six such hotels were issued to applicants by intake workers in the "5 by 8" room, so-named for the size of the cards on which men's records were kept. Men received meal tickets as well, and up to fifteen hundred were served each day in the basement dining room. Caseworkers were assigned to new applicants within a week of their arrival and were occasionally successful in securing public assistance or disability benefits for clients.[33] In 1980, a Community Support System team was assigned to the shelter to assist men with chronic psychiatric disorders and extensive inpatient histories in finding alternative residences. For the duration of our study, the success of the team in this endeavor was modest at best.

Intake workers were separated from applicants by a chest-high counter and a Plexiglas divider, much like bank tellers. Documents were exchanged as necessary through slots in the divider where it met the counter top. Up to five intake workers could be processing parallel queues of applicants at the same time. Interrogation was typically brisk, perfunctory, and not uncommonly harsh; on rare occasions, especially with the obviously disabled, it could be disarmingly kind. Infrequently, a man would be ejected because he was unable to convince a worker that he was indeed "destitute and needy." But for the most part, to cross the threshold of the shelter was to have passed a de facto means test: It was rightly assumed that only the desperate (or the clueless—who would soon leave) would willingly undergo the ordeal.

For two months after the initial court order (in December 1979), which recognized a provisional right to shelter on the part of homeless men, latecomers to the shelter, sometimes scores of them, would be herded into the Big Room off the main lobby of the East 3rd Street facility, there to spend the night. In February 1980, this practice was discontinued, only to be renewed a year later as available bed supply gave out. For a time in the fall of 1981, cots were set up in the offices, dining and recreation areas, and main lobby of the Men's Shelter, but that stopgap measure too was soon outlawed by the court.

Repeated intercession by the court would result in a burgeoning shelter system in the early 1980s. As many as 169 men would be put up in the newly opened Keener Building on Wards Island by the end of 1979; more city-operated beds would soon follow. But for the majority of men seeking shelter in the late 1970s, and for a thousand homeless men each night throughout the 1980s, a successful application meant a berth in a flophouse.

Bowery Flophouses

By the late 1970s, the Bowery was already a neighborhood of striking contrasts, and getting more so each year.[34] Some of the traditional institutions of skid row were still in evidence (the flophouses, cheap taverns, second-hand stores, and missions); others (the blood banks and barber colleges) were already gone. Hookers may have still plied their trade on the corner of Delancey and Bowery, but brownstones with sturdy gates now shared the block with the Men's Shelter and a Salvation Army halfway house. Vacant lots stood next to abandoned shop-floors in buildings whose upper levels had already been converted into residential lofts. Instead of equipment or warehouse workers, newly restored industrial elevators now carried tenants in three-piece suits.

Nor were the regularly trundling tour buses the only sign of intrusions from the outside. Come weekends, upscale professionals descended on the area to purchase lighting and kitchen equipment from wholesale outlets.

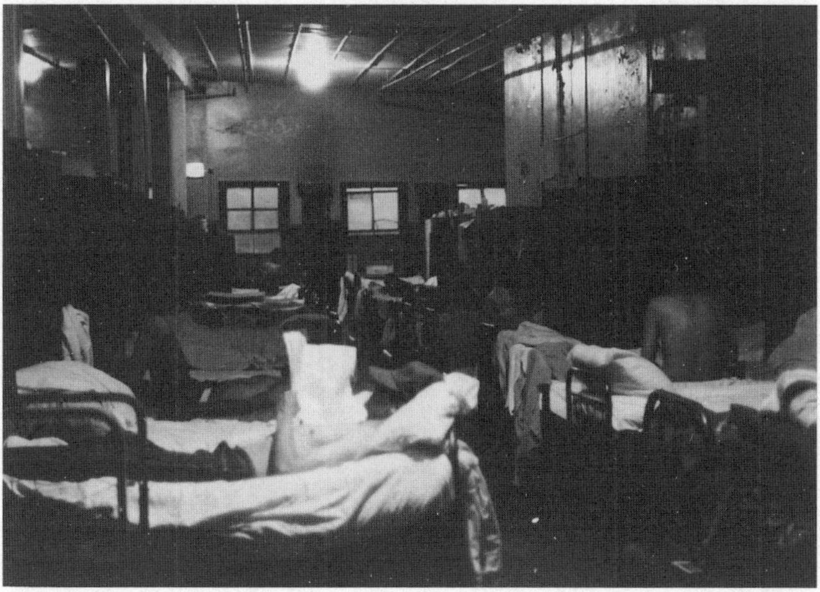

Kenton Hotel, August 1982

Suburban kids from Jersey and Long Island rubbed shoulders with elderly alcoholics—the former heading for two of the hottest punk-rock clubs at the time (CBGB's and Great Gildersleeves); the latter, for one of the two flophouses (The Palace and The Kenton) occupying the upper floors of the same buildings that housed the clubs. The steady thrum of rock could be heard well into morning hours (in places that had been used by the city to house homeless men since the 1930s). Well-heeled aficionados of jazz patronized the Tin Palace on Bond and Bowery; a good ear could identify the tune from the shooting gallery in the vacant lot behind.

Within shouting distance of one another could be found a Hell's Angels garage and headquarters, the newly renovated home of a repertory opera company, the *dojo* (practice room) of an *aikido* chapter, a counter restaurant serving the best Ukranian borscht and black bread around, the dance studios of New York University's terpsichorean annex, and two Catholic Worker hospitality houses. At one end, drinking establishments had neon "Bar" signs hung out front; at the other, "Phoebe's" was lettered on the wall next to a posh sidewalk cafe. Glitter countered dross on nearly every block. The effect was a neighborhood of warring contrasts and accommodating tendencies.

At the time, rooms and dormitory beds in the flophouses under contract with the Men's Shelter were available to paying customers as well, so it was

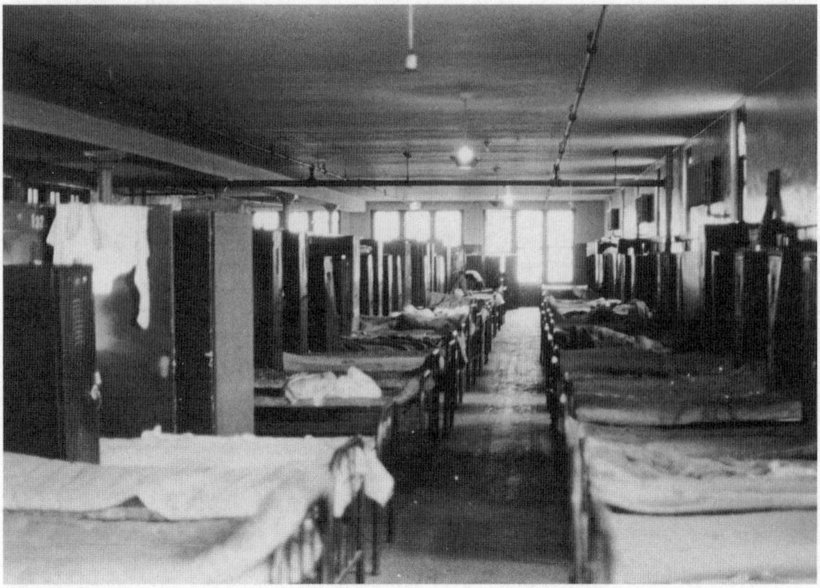

Palace Hotel, October 1980

possible to gain a firsthand view of conditions in these hotels. The largest of these, and the most notorious, was The Palace:

> *The Palace:* I got the last room available, paid $3.33 for it. It was a 5-by-7-foot cubicle with a locker, a bed with fairly clean sheets, no lice, and only a few roaches. Overhead was a chicken-wire ceiling, covered with cloth. Partitions between rooms were of wainscoting; whole place looked like a tinderbox. The room, along with perhaps two dozen others, was situated on the building's third floor, near the desk at the head of the two flights of tiled stairs. There was no dormitory on this floor. All the rooms were singles.
>
> I stayed in the TV room, along with maybe 150 other men, watching [bad idea] *The Towering Inferno* until 11 P.M. Cigarettes seemed a scarce item: A number of men were hawking them at ten cents apiece; others passed out one or two each time they lit up. Some of the men appeared decidedly disturbed, carrying on highly animated conversations with themselves (the guy next to me, in what sounded like Russian). They are ignored by the others. A fair amount of open drinking is tolerated, but arguments and fights are not. Even a brief outburst, if loud enough, is met by an order to hush up by a well-built desk clerk.
>
> In general, good spirits pervade the room. No real fights or unpleasantness. It's a mixed crowd: one dashingly attired artist (turned out in beret, black turtleneck, and a beige wool coat trimmed in black velvet) sketches on a large pad, carried in a portfolio; some young guys in their twenties share the space

with some old, weather-beaten faces. Most are dressed for the season. Other than the disturbed men, there are no apparent wounds or debilities. The disturbed men, poorly dressed with matted hair, were unable to sit still through the film. They gestured in repetitive patterns and grubbed butts off the floor. The state of disrepair of their shoes was nearly always a dead giveaway [of their disturbed state].

As men prepare for bed, it is clear that many on the floor are regulars. The tiny rooms are cluttered with possessions (radios and mementos), their walls lined with pictures in cheap frames, clothes hung from makeshift closet rods. These are paying customers, not referrals from the shelter. A friendly, bunkhouse repartee peppers the air as the men retire; an oddly unfrightening place from this safe vantage. (February 18, 1980)

For the "ticket men" referred by the shelter staff, conditions were less hospitable. The dormitories occupied two floors of The Palace. Bed assignments tended to be racially segregated so far as practical. Approximately 120 beds were crammed into a room perhaps eighty feet by forty feet; another twenty cubicles were built into the north wall. Beds were arranged in four long rows, each stretching the length of the room. Each bed was separated from its neighbor by a metal locker, many of which were sprung (making useless the key paying lodgers received at the desk). A few of the beds had no mattresses, the bare metal springs covered instead with an old rug, a sheet of corrugated cardboard, or nothing at all. Without exception, the mattresses were blackened with dirt and grime, pockmarked with the burns of innumerable cigarettes, and tufted with protruding stuffing. A visit in October 1980 revealed that perhaps a dozen beds had sheets or blankets. Inquiring at the desk, I was told that no more were available. The illumination from four bare bulbs was insufficient to see whether the bedding was louse-infested.

It's early evening. Most men are either at dinner or downstairs in the TV room. Those in the dormitory are mostly elderly. Men lie in beds, smoking and staring at the ceiling. A few manage some privacy by pulling covers or coats over their heads. A racking cough, the sound of incessant scratching, someone singing softly to himself, sporadic conversation—apart from these, the room is still. (October 14, 1980)

The Palace was the worst of the six hotels, although the neighboring Kenton ran a close second. Dormitory beds were better appointed, surroundings less grim, and lockers occasionally locked in the less populous hotels (the Comet, Sunshine, and Union). Ticket men were generally required to be out of the hotel by 7 A.M. or so, and were not allowed back in until afternoon. Moreover, they were often banned from using such common space as

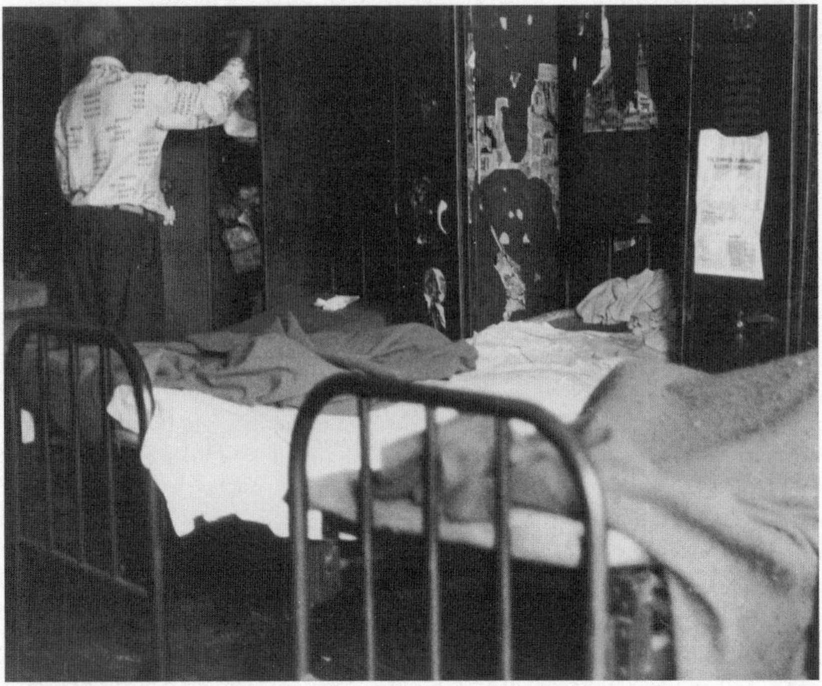

Kenton Hotel, October 1980

the TV room. Such privileges could, of course, be extended to ticket men who managed to slip the desk clerks a tip from time to time.

My impression of these places, formed after repeated visits at all hours, was of almost unrelieved grimness. Part of it was the air of neglect that pervaded the places. John, a 35-year-old interviewed at the Keener shelter on Wards Island, explained why he preferred even that isolated spot to the flophouses:

> At the hotel, you got maybe two hundred guys sleeping in the dormitory. They don't give you no clean sheets; they got all kinds of lice on them, crabs on them. They don't give you no type of stuff to take care of your personal hygiene. . . . Plus they have ex-mental patients down there. They babble and talk to themselves. They don't give them no type of assistance. Plus they have security guards down there, hitting people on the heads with sticks. And this is the Department of Social Services . . . they got to know this is happening. (August 12, 1980)

Part of it was the ever-present threat of assault. Older men especially found the flophouses fearsome. Many of the elderly men I spoke with in the

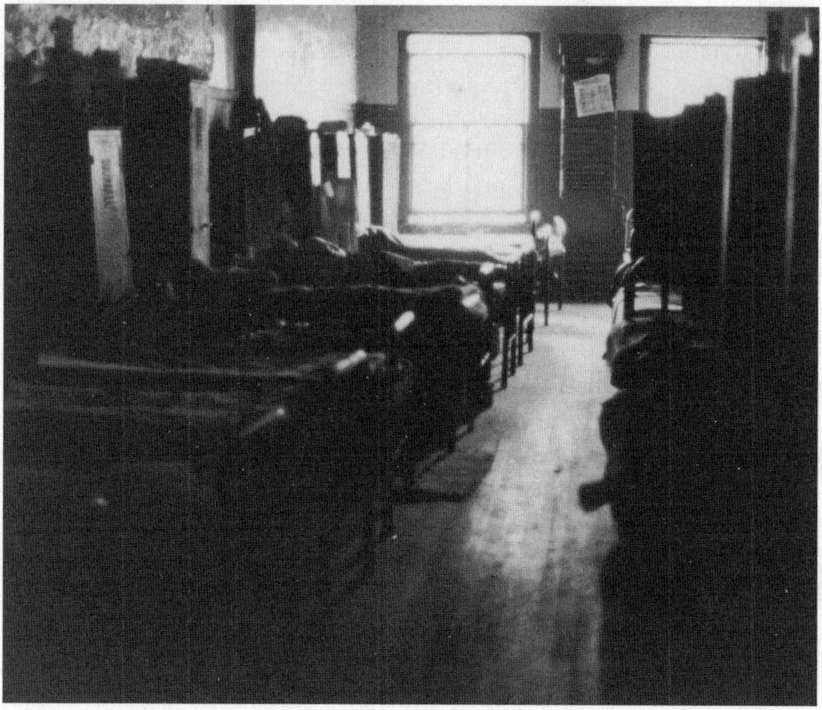

Kenton Hotel, October 1980

midtown bus and train stations had assigned beds in the flops, but avoided them until bedtime. The "hawks" or "jackrollers," they explained, weren't stupid: Older men were more likely to be on pensions or receiving VA checks, and were sure to put up less of a fight.[35] After being robbed repeatedly themselves and witnessing it frequently—a favored method was slitting the trousers of a sleeping figure and removing the pockets intact—these men cultivated an unobtrusive presence elsewhere.

And part of it, more difficult to document directly, was the lowering effect, the seeping demoralization that had so impressed turn-of-the-century commentators. To be a steady tenant of one of these flophouses was to be faced daily with the evidence of having joined the ranks of the lost.

The Keener Building

The only alternative to the flops for almost two years following the December 1979 court order was the Keener Building on Wards Island. Set up in a refurbished hospital building and abutting the grounds of a state psychiatric center, Keener was physically isolated and difficult to reach. Apart from the official vans carrying men from East 3rd Street, transportation to the island was cumbersome, requiring lengthy rides that combined bus and subway, or a long walk over the "Night Train Express" bridge linking the island to Manhattan at 103rd Street When first opened, the shelter shared quarters with a small colony of artists, some of whom had arranged to run classes for the men in exchange for continued use of work studios. Demand for bed space soon forced the artists out.

Aside from the short-lived presence of the artists, Keener was a paragon of institutional thrift. It was run by a limited and overworked staff. Bedding was rudimentary: light mattresses on metal frames. Walls were bereft of any ornament but graffiti. The one concession to relief of tedium was a new mess hall, open only during mealtimes. Few of the televisions in the common rooms worked reliably; newspapers were days, even weeks old by the time residents had them in hand; magazines were nowhere to be seen.

Men lounged around in various states of undress, in contact with an assortment of realities. Recycling institutional space once the original occupants have moved on was nothing new,[36] but a certain irony obtained in this instance. Some of the ex-patients among these men had come full circle back to the institution that had originally discharged them—this time as shelter clients, not hospital patients. Even when certified as in need of treatment, appropriate placement proved difficult to secure. A team of psychiatrists determined in May 1980 that 16 of the 250 men examined were in need of immediate hospitalization. But it was two weeks before half of them could be placed in state hospitals; the rest seemed to have disappeared in the interim. The nearest such hospital was less than a quarter mile away.

Keener was originally intended as a nighttime residence only. A limited number of subway and bus tokens were made available to men wishing to go back to Manhattan; they returned in the evening by foot or via the van operating out of the Men's Shelter on East 3rd Street. But many men left the island only infrequently. In the main, they languished in nearly unbroken torpor, confined to the building through the day but for an occasional supervised walk, inmates in all but name.

So bad did matters become in the spring of 1980 that a second lawsuit, this one protesting the conditions at Keener, was prepared in May by the lawyers who had filed the original lawsuit. The complaint alleged that owing to the isolation of the facility, limited transportation, and absence of appropriate services, "the mental and physical condition of class members [Keener residents] have deteriorated and will continue to deteriorate." Again, judicial relief was sought in advance of a trial. This time preliminary relief was denied, but the judge ordered an immediate trial because, in his words, the "health of the City's homeless men should not suffer because of judicial delay." Extensive negotiations with city officials followed and, on the eve of trial in August 1980, the lawsuit was dropped. The city agreed to triple funding for the shelter and to strengthen on-site medical and psychiatric resources at the facility. By January 1981, with *Callahan* just entering the initial phases of what promised to be a lengthy trial, over 600 men were quartered in Keener each night. The original "Memorandum of Understanding" between the state (which owned the building) and the city (which contracted with the Volunteers of America to run the shelter) had set capacity at 180.[37]

Why Men Didn't Use the Public Shelter

Ray Monroe spent two months living in the subway system in the late summer of 1980; he was, according to Bill Muller (the night watchman who made rounds on the street) who happened upon him, lying in his own excrement and urine. He had trouble with his legs and great difficulty moving around. Muller succeeded in finding a cabbie who would take him to Columbia Presbyterian Hospital. He was treated and later released; a cab was called to transport him to the Men's Shelter. The taxi never made it; having been paid, the driver dropped him off along the way. Some compassionate soul found him and paid another cabbie to take him to the shelter. On arrival, he still couldn't move his legs and was sent to the infirmary. After a week there, he called Muller, who came down and had him taken by ambulance to Bellevue. There he was diagnosed as having a tumor on his spine.

Mr. Monroe had spent time in the flophouses and at the Men's Shelter and had vowed never to return. His list of grievances was lengthy: the shelter and flops were lousy, unsafe, dirty places, where brutality was common. Your clothes were stolen and your life threatened. Maintaining your respectability or cleanliness was impossible in such a setting. Sure, the streets were rough, especially for a man who was all but immobile, but you could keep your "dignity" there. The alternative, a night in a flop or the Big Room (the overflow space at the Men's Shelter), was "worse than the zoo—at least the animals are safe in their cages" (December 30, 1980).

Although he was able to articulate them with an unusual degree of detail and scope, Monroe's sentiments were widespread among the men I interviewed on the street. For most of them, mention of the Men's Shelter conjured up images of easily acquired wine, lots of "sick people—you know, psychos," degrading treatment and vile settings, and the ever-present threat of assault. The violence was the strongest deterrent to men who refused to make use of the shelter. This pertained not only to sleeping but to eating there as well: Older men especially feared the long wait, in close quarters and a dark stairwell, for a seat in the dining room.

Excerpts from a single evening's notes, taken on my initial visit as a court-appointed observer, capture something of the prevailing atmosphere:

> *Men's Shelter*: I arrive at 5 P.M. in time to witness an argument become a scuffle as two younger men wrestle an older man to the ground and begin to go through his pockets. The older man's efforts at fending off his assailants are feeble and ineffective. The noise quickly draws three cops from the shelter, the entrance to which is maybe twenty feet away. On their arrival, the two younger men take off and the older man, bleeding from the lip, is helped into the shelter. One cop, in apparent disgust, yells after the retreating pair: "You should have known he'd have nothing worth taking." What little the old man did have in his pockets lies strewn about on the sidewalk: packets of sugar, some twine, a belt. The next man coming along carefully sifts through them. . . .
>
> After dinner, outside the shelter: Four men, at least two of whom appear quite drunk, stand in a bunch a short ways from the entrance. One of them repeatedly assures the others that they are his friends, while brandishing a revolver. There is the clear, unmistakable "click" of a hammer hitting an empty chamber as I walk by. A large man yells across the street to a young woman mounting the steps to her house: "Hey blondie, it's snowing, blondie!" Here and there along the block, knots of three or four men huddle in doorways, passing a bottle.
>
> Around 7 P.M., I came upon a resident from one of the apartment buildings across the street who had stumbled on an older man who lay crumpled up on the sidewalk next to his stoop. The man is bleeding from cuts on his forehead and mumbling. . . . I helped him across the street and into the shelter, and tried to clean him up a bit while the sergeant on duty called for an ambulance. After making the call, the sergeant comes out to tell me: "It happens all the time . . . young guys rolling the old drunks . . . for fifty cents or whatever." As we wait for the ambulance, I got this story from Fred, a 57-year-old World War II veteran, who's been around the shelter since 1948. He believes (and sticks to the story for the rest of the evening, except when a fatigued "I don't know" momentarily substitutes) that he was hit from behind and knocked to the sidewalk. Didn't see his assailant; not sure whether he blacked out or not, but doesn't think so. . . . He lay there for a few minutes or so; blood had already caked on his head when I arrived.
>
> That he was mugged and didn't just fall, as the attendants at the St. Vincent's ER later suspect, is strongly suggested by his left trouser leg, ripped at the pocket seam, exposing the white pajamas Fred had on underneath. It's unlikely that this happened very long ago since the under-pair was remarkably clean, in contrast to the grubby, grime-stained pair of outer pants, along the length of the tear. Fred said they'd taken a small suitcase, and then, after searching his pockets, discovered that they'd lifted his identification cards (meal ticket and hotel voucher) as well. He didn't know where he'd stay that

night and half-hoped, I suspect, that he'd be admitted to St. Vincent's. . . . [We returned from the ER four hours later. Fred's head wounds have been cleaned and his skull x-rays came back negative. He wound up spending the night in the Big Room, as all the Bowery hotels were full. The sergeant on duty assured him "it's more secure, anyway."]

Shortly after midnight, as I'm leaving, a ruckus breaks out in the Big Room. [Men were being loaded into the van to be transported to Wards Island.] When the staff member supervising the loading turned to talk to me, one man in the line bolted for the bathroom. He was chased out by a staff member wielding a night stick, with which he had already struck one straggler to hurry him onto the van. The man ran into the Big Room [adjoining the lobby]. He was a large, fleshy young man, wearing a dirty sweater and loose pants; he was barefoot and looked frightened. When I got to the Big Room (along with a number of the guards), he was being pinned against the wall by two staff members, using a row of the plastic chairs as a prod. The tall man with the nightstick was standing over him, yelling and threatening to use the stick. The young man crawling around the floor for cover was crying: "Don't hit me, don't hit me."

Things quieted down considerably when the sergeant arrived, persuaded the man with the stick to return to the front desk, and ordered other staff members to pick the man up. He was then walked to the front door. The cop standing next to me remarked: "He belongs in a hospital. He lives in the streets, eating from garbage cans, and sleeps in the bathroom (in the shelter)." As I was leaving, the young man was tearing up pieces of paper and throwing them in the door of the shelter. I don't know whether he spent the night on the street or in the shelter. He did not make the last bus for Wards Island. (January 25, 1980)

Similar incidents occurred with some frequency and regularly punctuated the reports of court observers. Accounts of harsh, even brutal treatment at the Men's Shelter were readily elicited from men on the street when I asked their reasons for refusing to use the shelter. In the minds of most informants, the staff were party to the general air of intimidation and threat that clung to the place. Relations between staff and applicants for shelter were usually brusque; more often than not, they were abrasive and, not uncommonly, combative.

The workers at the shelter, it must be noted, were in a peculiar bind, at once agents and victims of a singularly desolate set of circumstances. Conditions were harsh, duties demanding, pay modest, and performance thankless. More than a few admitted to the demoralization that came from knowing that the problems they were expected to deal with ran far deeper than their own puny efforts could reach. Complacent, uncaring, even cruel instances of staff behavior could always be cited. But the norm, in my experience, were workers who had trouble justifying to themselves the treatment accorded clients. Denied channels to voice their own dissatisfaction effectively, lacking power to alter significantly the conditions under which they worked, and keenly aware that in the eyes of the city welfare's bureaucracy their assignment was equivalent to the Siberia of civil service, workers not surprisingly found clients convenient targets for their own anger and frustration.

Almost without exception, staff members were fearful, not only of falling victim to some random act of violence by a client but also of catching some dread disease from the men and bringing it home to their families. While exaggerated, such fears were not unfounded. Lice, tuberculosis, hepatitis, and a variety of respiratory ailments were common among the men. Nor were apparently inexplicable instances of "berserk" behavior unknown: One supervisor recounted how he spent six months in bed after being beaten by a client; in the fall of 1980, a patrolman was blinded in one eye after a client threw lye in his face. Although isolated occurrences, repeated retelling of these and similar incidents tended to create an institutional mythos of the clients as dangerous and unpredictable. Given an already taxing work situation, this added burden of vigilance made for an all but intolerable situation.

Most of the staff on the floor conducted themselves defensively when in close contact with the men. They carefully maintained their distance and affected at least a semblance of control by the use of sticks (to avoid direct contact), rough language, and barked orders. Most tended to hold the younger clients in particular at least partially responsible for their plight. Many were on the lookout for double-dippers and frauds and would on occasion subject an applicant, whose sobriety or sanity was openly in question, to tough interrogation.

Aside from grossly insubordinate behavior, the power of this client population to retaliate was limited. With a little imagination and diligence, however, even a sorry crew of defeated men could make the effort:

> *Men's Shelter*: At 11:30 tonight, a general clean-up commences. All those men not able to give a clear and immediate answer to the question: "Do you want to go to Keener?" are told to leave. Four men are bodily ejected down the stairs and out into the street; two of them are noticeably drunk. One of them promptly lets the air out of the tires of what he hopes is a guard's car parked out front.
>
> It is a bitterly cold night to spend on the street. Most of the half dozen men standing outside the Shelter will spend snatches of the night on the stairwell, warming themselves until once again kicked out. (February 18, 1980)

Instances of rank brutality were unlikely to go on unimpeded in the presence of court observers. As recounted by coworkers, however, staff hostility in the absence of outside witnesses could be severe:

> *Men's Shelter*: A little over a month ago [James, an intake worker, informs me], one of the clients was badly beaten by a staff on security rounds. The attack, on his account, was entirely unprovoked. The assailant was a staff member of some eight years' standing. No attempt was made to break it up, either by other staff or by the security force, until blood began to pool around the man's head, as the staff member smashed it repeatedly on the floor. The cops, it should be noted, do not intervene unless called upon to do so by one of the staff; no such request was made. [I checked the logbook.] A whitewash report has been logged in the record. It notes only that an "altercation" had occurred, in which a staff member claimed that a client "took a swing at him and he retaliated." (May 26, 1980)

Other, less dramatic instances passed literally unnoticed, fading into the expected backdrop of everyday life at the Men's Shelter. In my presence, clients were regularly shouted at in harsh and threatening tones, were pushed and prodded with nightsticks, and, not infrequently, were thrown out for failure to observe some actual or ad hoc rule. Striking only to the new arrival, such practices went unremarked by anyone familiar with the institutional routine.

One night I split a pint of brandy with a man about my age who was proving an able source of material on the Bowery. The two of us returned to the shelter, he to await a hotel voucher, me to resume my station as a court observer. After a while, he came over and pulled me aside:

> "Do you really want to see how they treat the group down here?" When I nodded, he told me to go into the bathroom, where I found a man cleaning the floor. The man's shirt was stiff with dried blood from, it turned out, two stab wounds he had received the night before. Both wounds were open, though the bleeding had stopped. He was mopping up the floor at the staff's instruction, and there was no way he could have received his assignment and gotten his mop and bucket out of the closet without having passed in close view of a number of staff members. (February 1, 1980)

Reports commonly came my way, from both staff and clients, of workers exacting sexual favors from younger men, presumably in exchange for a promise of preferential treatment. At the Keener Building, where security guards and "institutional aides" had, in effect, unsupervised run of the place, such behavior was thought to take place on the premises. "Guys walking up and down talkin' to themselves," John complained to me, "and all the guards do is be back there playing with the homosexuals." Pointing to an obviously disturbed young man rocking in his bed, John added: "They give them more 'treatment' than they give this man here" (August 12, 1980).

Supervisory staff could be candid about their inability to ensure the safety of men staying at the Men's Shelter. When a young man with multiple sclerosis was brought in by the police one February night, to be boarded only until the next morning when the rehabilitation center could be contacted, the night supervisor objected strongly: "He can't stay here. He'll be taken advantage of physically, mentally, sexually—any way they can." He was left at the shelter.

Another, subtler kind of violence, a violence that preyed on one's spirit and sense of identity, was even more pervasive. The whole routine at the Men's Shelter—from the impersonal, often hostile, intake interview; to the casual indifference shown by staff to the comfort and security of the men under their charge; to the abominable state that toilet facilities were regularly allowed to lapse into; to the anonymous, batch-processed way in which one's most intimate needs were expected to be satisfied; to the constant threat posed by one's keepers and companions in misery alike—operated as though it had been designed to break rather than salvage any man fool enough to venture there for help. It was one unremitting degradation ceremonial.

This order of violence, this species of harm, proved an elusive thing to document. Informants, in my experience, rarely protested that their "dignity" or "self-respect" was under assault at the shelter. It was not uncommon, on the other hand, for men living on the street to cite dignity and self-respect among the traits they hoped to preserve on the street. Men in the shelter did not ask me to help them file formal grievances at the discourtesy shown them. But a number of them did echo the 35-year-old at Keener, bitter at what he felt to be the institutional betrayal of his own efforts to kick a drug and alcohol habit, who blurted out: "It makes a man, you know, want to do something illegal."

Nor was it simply the fact that the shelter was synonymous with abuse in the minds of many men. To be lodged courtesy of the city entailed submission to a discipline and authority that many men found intolerable: It was an insult, an affront to one's adulthood to be ordered about in this fashion. A younger man, who elected to live in an abandoned building rather than go back to the shelter on Wards Island, put it plainly: "I don't want the aggravation of the cops or security guards at Keener Building. They treat you like boys there; and I'm not a boy, I'm a man."

Finally, and admittedly inferential on my part, one must reckon with the symbolic cost to one's sense of self. The simple fact of being—and, it tended to follow, *belonging*—there, was a formidable statement about one's self-worth. However much the homeless population had changed, the shelter itself retained a kind of time-warped fidelity to the old skid row. In its institutional stance and practice, it perpetuated that legacy and was party to the stain of disrepute and failure that still marred the Bowery. For some men, at least, using the shelter meant confronting the message engraved in every institutional surface: "Bums welcomed here." To accept the city's offer of shelter on its terms was to acquiesce in its attitude toward the lowlifes the system was set up to serve.

The root attitudes of staff members were no less difficult to elicit. Some insisted it was just a job, one that allowed regular and well-paid overtime, and denied thinking twice about the clients. Others, especially (it was my impression) those who had been there as clients themselves, held them in open contempt. Few volunteered that they viewed their charges as subhuman. But when a young worker showed me around the new shelter built near the Keener Building in the spring of 1982, he proudly displayed the orderly way in which "we cattle them" into the showers; he referred to the turnstile controlling entry into the intake area as "the cattle-gate, so to speak." Such an attitude did not go unnoticed by the men themselves: A man who fell asleep in the lobby while waiting for the van to Keener was tipped out of his chair by a staff member, kicked, and then thrown out of the shelter. The fellow behind him protested: "Hey, man—the man's no dog. You don't have to kick him." He, too, was summarily ejected (July 19, 1982; August 12, 1981).

At the outset of my inquiries, I had little appreciation of how easily a will-o'-the-wisp quality could be imputed to such notions as dignity. I was soon disabused of naiveté. In repeated meetings with city officials, court observers were assured that complaints they had presented about the "disrespect" routinely shown the men had never been voiced by clients themselves. If this was so important a point, the officials wondered aloud, why was it that no client had ever brought it to their attention before? Leave aside for the moment questions of access between inmates, their keepers, and their keepers' masters. Reducing the charge to farcical dimensions sufficed to defuse it: HRA (Human Resources Administration, the city's welfare bureaucracy) officials would agree to issue a directive to the effect that shelter staff were not to use profanity in dealing with clients.

Above all else, it was this studied disinterest in any but the most rudimentary—and court-enforced—elements of refuge that governed conditions at the Men's Shelter. The rule was to offer as little as possible and so force as many as could to seek shelter elsewhere. Under such circumstances, the inappropriate presence of some men—men with snot-smeared beards and matted hair, standing mute and unmoving in the intake line, ignored by staff—effectively became part of the institution's repellent quality for others. Late at night, when anyone who had even a desperate alternative to the shelter had exercised it, the scene could be read as emblematic of the "safety net" strung below the institutional gaps:

Men's Shelter: It's 11 P.M. and there are 85 men still in the lobby waiting to be assigned a bed. [Many would end up staying there all night.] An old man is slumped in a chair, alternately dozing and starting awake; he stirs occasionally to demand "What is the law?," then spits on the floor. A young bearded black man incessantly moves his lower jaw back and forth, his eyes wide open. A man with 3-D glasses chugs from a bottle of Thunderbird. Another man makes repetitive movements as though winding and unwinding a scarf around his neck. Still another rocks continually in his seat, a look of mild—even ironic—concern on his face; eventually, he gets up, holding what looks like a textbook on physics. One man, the hospital bracelet still on his wrist, tells me he had just been released from Beth-Israel, where he'd been hospitalized five days for seizures. (January 21, 1981)

Sleeping Rough

At the outset of our study in 1979, strict limits governed the capacity of public shelter: once the Bowery hotel beds were exhausted and the Big Room crammed full, there was nothing else available. Further, the danger and degradation widely associated with public shelter effectively deterred many men from using it. Litigation would eventually increase the number of beds and improve conditions. But it is fair to say that for the duration of our original research (1979–1982), except for fitful efforts to add beds and clean up conditions, the avowed principle of "less eligibility" remained in force.

Under such circumstances, expressed demand for shelter could not be taken as an accurate indicator of the extent of need. Not only were many otherwise shelterless men making do with jury-rigged quarters in the homes of friends and family; there was also the undeniable evidence of men living in the streets and public spaces. No one knew their numbers. For reasons discussed earlier (under "Numbers"), the feasibility of any effort to take an accurate count was questionable. But there were indications, even to casual observers, that the numbers were considerable. On a few occasions, I ventured to get limited counts in circumscribed areas. In the summer of 1980, a local news station reported that certain areas of the city "had an unaccustomed shine to them" and that officials were in the process of "weeding the Garden" in preparation for the upcoming Democratic Nominating Convention. It noted that this would mean removing "the homeless, derelicts, and bag people to whom Madison Square Garden is home." Six weeks earlier, I had made several counts at daybreak of people sleeping in and around that area: On the outside plaza of the Garden alone, it was not unusual to find 75 men and women sleeping there at dawn.[38]

Another quick count, made between 5:30 and 6:00 on a summer morning

Midtown Manhattan, July 1982, 1:00 A.M.

in 1982, revealed 62 men and women sleeping along the southern perimeter of Central Park. The outreach team serving homeless people in the park reported that there were at least a hundred living there on a relatively permanent basis. The director of security for Amtrak at Penn Station estimated that at the time about 150 homeless people "consider[ed] the station home." In a single month, mid-January to mid-February 1984, the outreach team serving the Port Authority Bus Terminal made 2,400 contacts (including, no doubt, many duplications) with homeless people in the station.[39]

In many areas of Manhattan (the region I explored most intensively), men could be found sleeping wherever haven, however tentative, presented itself: in the steam tunnels that ran under Park Avenue, alongside the railroad tracks and service yards; in vest-pocket parks, recessed doorways, and storefronts along major thoroughfares; in abandoned buildings and deserted subway stations; in the loading bays of manufacturing firms; in storage bunkers below the entrance ramps to highways; in the lower stairwells and basements of unlocked tenements; under bridges and in parking lots; and in makeshift camps along unused rail lines, closed highways, and derelict freight yards. In the early morning hours, some public places resembled nomadic encampments, with linked cardboard boxes serving as individual sleeping quarters. Some settlements were congregate, small numbers of men improvising quarters together; male–female couples, rare in

Perimeter of Central Park, August 1981, just before dawn

my experience, were not unheard of. The pluck, ingenuity, and resilience of these men—in the face of hostile elements, police surveillance, and the indifference of passersby—impressed me.

Things had changed on the street since the days of skid row, and the changes were apparent to anyone who had spent time there:

> *42nd Street at Park Avenue*: It's 2:00 A.M. on a very cold night. A black man on crutches hobbles about the entranceway to a subway station at Grand Central. He was among those who had been ejected at 1:30 as the terminal was closed. Now he looks around and keeps repeating, a tone of wonderment in his voice: "All these people with no place to go—and they're white, too. No place to go, and white too." Most of the tattered figures were reclined up against the walls of the subway station entrance, immobile and awake. Others wandered around cadging cigarettes or talking to themselves. A few slept in ragged heaps on the floor. (January 24, 1980)

Long periods of uninterrupted sleep on the street were difficult to come by. The most effective means of ensuring this was to find a berth in some hidden spot, off the track of patrolling cops, maintenance workers, or passersby. Clandestine refuge came at the cost, however, of greater vulnerability to robbery and assault. Surviving on the street meant a continuing ef-

6th Avenue office building, fall 1981

fort to weigh the privacy of unprotected sanctuary against the security (and likely harassment) of open public spaces.

The Steam Tunnels

Among the more imaginative resorts devised by homeless men, one that had been long used for the purpose, were the tunnels housing the steam lines and railroad repair yards that extend north from Grand Central Station below Park Avenue. The tunnels first came to public attention through feature stories in the press about a "hobo colony" living there.[40] But to judge from the graffiti on the walls and the recollections of men interviewed there, the place has been part of the lore of the streets for several decades.

The tunnels and repair yards make for a vast subterranean network, extending for many miles and acres underground. One notices the smell of ozone immediately. And it's hot: Along some stretches, abetted by steam, it can reach punishing levels. Besides housing an array of pipes and electrical conduits, the tunnels connect a warren of storage rooms, juncture points, repair pits, toilet and locker rooms, and emergency access stairways. At one point, they open onto the freight elevator that Franklin Roosevelt used to get from the train station to the Waldorf Astoria. Train crews make frequent

Near Penn Station, August 1981

rounds throughout the system at all hours. But for the most part, its denizens reported, they were undisturbed.

There are a number of entrances to the tunnels, ranging from an ornate bronze door at the side of the Waldorf Astoria, to various emergency exits from the commuter platforms underground. I ventured down for the first time on a winter morning in 1979, having just been informed by a train worker that the tunnels had been sealed up. After walking to the end of a boarding platform, I entered a hole in the wall just north of a chalked sign that read "Rat's Nest." A climb down a twelve-foot fixed ladder brought me into the main tunnel. It was a dimly lit space, perhaps twenty feet high and twelve feet wide at its broadest point; the temperature was at least eighty degrees.

After wandering around for a while, I came upon a man seated on an upturned milk carton at the juncture of three tunnels. He wore only a pair of pants; a long-sleeved shirt hung on a line nearby. He was sipping a cup of tea (purloined, it turned out, from one of the trains parked in the terminal). I walked up, introduced myself, and described my work. Ken agreed to be interviewed, and we spent the next hour and a half talking. Over the next

South end, Central Park, July 1982, 1:30 A.M.

few months, I visited him frequently in the tunnels. At one point, after explaining the litigation in progress, I recruited him as an additional named plaintiff in the *Callahan* case. For several years thereafter we would meet in the tunnels and elsewhere at odd intervals for coffee, a meal, or an extended walk.

Ken had a regular housekeeping routine in the tunnel segment where he made his camp:

> Ken sleeps on a neat and frequently changed bed of newspapers, which he has laid over a few thicknesses of corrugated cardboard. He says he's been "on the bum" for some twenty years, and in the tunnels off and on for 5 or 6 years. [Indeed, he matches the description of one of the men interviewed in the original news story.] The immediate surroundings appear to provide for most of his necessities. After rush hour, the idle trains can be raided for tea, soft drinks, wine, newspapers, and magazines. The employee who works the late shift in the commissary that stocks the trains will also hand out leftovers—cereal, soups, cake, and soda—to the tunnel men at night. Nearby water lines can be tapped for hot water and, with a little ingenuity, rigged up for a shower. (If one is careful about it, one can also sneak into the locker and shower rooms used by the maintenance crews; the toilets there are easily accessible.) Water and food can be warmed on the larger steam pipes in spots where the insulation has been stripped away—Ken usually had a pot of coffee simmering. Light

Columbus Circle, July 1982

> bulbs can be pilfered from other areas of the tunnels to increase the illumination around one's camp; this allows for reading and keeps the rats at a distance. Sinks nearby make washing clothes easy, and they dry quickly in the heat of the tunnels. Train crews don't bother regular inhabitants, and one can avoid the station police by using out-of-the-way passages for coming and going. (December 6, 1979)

But even this rough haven could be undone by the glare of publicity. By happenstance, in the same winter as my initial forays (1979), the tunnels were visited by reporters and cameramen from two national newspapers, a camera crew from a local TV station, and the odd freelancer or two. After steady visits spanning four months, I returned one night to find that the predictable had occurred: The tunnels had been purged. The two safe entrances that had allowed the men undetected access had been welded shut. A locked gate had been installed in a section that had formerly provided a large sleeping area. Spigots had been removed from the faucets tapping hot water lines. Signs had been posted warning that the premises were now patrolled by Conrail police and attack dogs. Most traces of the men's camps had been removed and their former inhabitants were nowhere to be found. A pair of shoes, some discarded containers, and a few cigarette butts were all that were left.[41]

Aside from such periodic sweeps, the routine surveillance of the station police was the most frequent hazard with which the men in the tunnels had to contend. One afternoon, Ken accompanied me on a lengthy tour of the tunnels and other hidden recesses in the area. In one of them, a hollow concrete bulwark separating two lines of track, I found a teenager, left him a hamburger, and promised to return later to talk. I never made it. That evening, Ken and I were making our way across the lower level of Grand Station en route to retracing our steps of the afternoon.

> Just before entering the boarding platforms, we spotted what we thought were two railroad workers and hesitated, stopping to admire the architecture. "OK fellas, we're cops. Get up against the wall." Docilely, we complied and were frisked by one cop while the other radioed in our location. One thought he recognized Ken: "He's the one who had his picture in the *Times*, the one who hit Donnelly about ten years ago. . . . He set fire to a [train] car a couple of months ago."
>
> Within moments—the police station wasn't far away—two other cops descended upon us and we were frisked a second time. One riffled through the contents of my wallet and pockets; another interrogated Ken about the pocketknife he carried.
>
> "You fucking bastard, what do you need this for?" "Whittlin'," Ken replied quietly. The cop swatted Ken on his head and jammed the closed knife into his throat: "You talk to me like that, I'll take you apart." Then he turned to me.
>
> "How long have you known this guy?"
>
> "About two months." [I lied.]
>
> "You sleeping in the tunnels with him?"
>
> "No."
>
> "You know this guy—you know what he'll do? He'll fuck you in the ass and then rob you. You know that? Huh? Unless you like that . . ."
>
> The cops told Ken that if they caught him around there again, he'd be broken in two. Then they let us both go. Ken punched the telephone booth on the way down the street: "He took my fuckin' protection. They always do that." (December 16, 1979)

In contrast to most street refuges, such basic survival issues as food, toilet facilities, warmth, privacy, and cleanliness were not pressing ones for men in the tunnels. Many resources could be tapped there in the underground area. Just above was located one of the most favorable panhandling spots in the city: One man told me he never actually had to ask for handouts—people just saw him looking "down and out" and made unsolicited offers of money, coffee, and sandwiches.

Despite its advantages, life in the tunnels was far from ideal. Even if one avoided harassment by the police, the isolation and loneliness could be wearing. The men (and, on one occasion, a woman) tended to know and

Under the Brooklyn Bridge, July 1984

look out for one another. But there was little evidence of real companionship. Asked what he found most difficult about life in the tunnels, an older man (David) responded: "The loneliness. You get used to it, you know, but it's not good. . . . You get funny without people to talk to." He added that talking to me was the first extended conversation he'd had "with a regular person" for about a year; the last one had been with a news photographer.

David had trouble getting around. But he had friends, or at least people who knew him, who kept an eye out for him. One of the sextons at St. Patrick's Cathedral (a short distance away, as the tunnels run) would welcome him in for extended visits from time to time. In the tunnels, Ken regularly checked in on him, and shared whatever he was able to forage (cereal, potato chips, coffee) from the commissary or parked commuter trains.

Variants of Work

For many men with whom I spoke, the casual charity of strangers was a steady source of income and food. Some stationed themselves in the same spot along commuter routes day after day, and were rewarded for their steadfastness by regular handouts from travelers who came to recognize and look for them. Some merchants could always be counted on for a meal or coffee. On some occasions, the proffered assistance went well beyond the ordinary:

> *Grand Central Station*: Ford [who had been ejected from the station] and I had been standing around in the subway entrance since about 1:00 A.M., shivering every time someone came in off the streets. Around 2:00 A.M., an acquaintance of his arrives, a neatly dressed man of 40 or so. Apparently, he lives nearby, has a job and steady income. He gives Ford half a loaf of rye bread and a canister of butter. In exchange, Ford gives him a few plastic disposable razors that he had acquired earlier in the day when the lockers in the station had been cleaned out. The man made idle chatter for a few minutes, then walked over to stand by himself in the drafty corridor. Ford tells me he often comes down with something to eat. (January 24, 1980)

Other men turned to various forms of scavenging. A new law made it profitable to collect and redeem discarded cans and bottles. Phone booths were reflexively checked for change. Other men found work off the books—doing cleanup at businesses, running errands—in exchange for cash or in-kind payment. Others struck deals with building superintendents to trade occasional work for a bed in the basement.

A few men turned to the one commodity, besides their labor, they had to peddle. The earliest studies of tramps make circumspect reference to homosexual relations between older men and young "punks." Nels Anderson and his informants discussed the matter openly.[42] Tom Kromer related in some detail how he allowed himself to be picked up by an old "queen" in exchange for money.[43] On rare occasion a man told me directly that he engaged in prostitution. Others obliquely referred to what I took to be the fact:

> *Grand Central Tunnels*: Mack mentioned a "friend" of five or six years' standing, though he didn't recall his name. He lives in Queens, in an apartment on the beach at Far Rockaway. Earlier today, Mack had met him in Times Square. Curious, I asked him what they did. And, with disarming innocence, he replied: "We'd go up to his hotel room, you know, get buddy-buddy." (January 1, 1980)

As mentioned earlier, some men on the Bowery found frequent spot work, either on their own or through one of several employment agencies in the area. In the course of one afternoon in a bar, I gathered two leads on jobs, including the name to ask for and a new acquaintance's offer to serve as a reference. Much of the spot labor was sporadic and short-lived in nature. Unloading trucks was a common assignment. There were stories as well of more exploitative labor arrangements, of men being transported under dubious arrangements to job sites where they had no option but to work, at least until they earned enough to pay for transportation back.

Two locations in particular were frequently mentioned in connection with this practice: seasonal farm work in eastern Long Island and along the eastern seaboard, and maintenance and kitchen work in the resort hotels in the Catskills. The latter jobs were said to draw especially on men staying at Camp LaGuardia, located in the foothills of that region, although vans were reported to cruise the Bowery from time to time looking for help. After some initial inquiry, which disclosed the rather hefty fees charged by employment agencies in the city for a job placement in the hotel district (a flat $72, plus $12 for transportation, to be garnished from one's first paycheck), I decided to seek employment in the Catskills on my own.

Hotel Work

I arrived at Monticello, a small town in Sullivan County, in May 1981 by bus, then hiked the three miles or so to the Concord Hotel. The Concord was the largest of the Catskill hotels, with some twelve hundred rooms accommodating up to three thousand guests. It was a huge place occupying thousands of acres, complete with golf courses, tennis courts, swimming pools, and skeet range. Word on the street had it that the Concord was always hiring. (They had better be: I was stuck otherwise, with $20 in my pocket.) By evening I had landed a job on the housekeeping staff.

I was assigned a room at the "Jacobson Building," a ramshackle three-story wood-frame house, located 150 yards from the back entrance to the hotel. In the eight by ten room were a bed, two night tables, a chair, and the wreckage of what appeared to be an old radiator. The set of bed linens I was given was fresh, and hot water was regularly available. Such, along with its convenient location, were the amenities. There was no heat (and on May nights, the temperature still dipped into the thirties). The roof leaked. Dozens of cats shared the premises, and the floors bore the permanent sign of their presence. The ceiling plaster had been torn away in the bathrooms; a variety of fungi flourished on the exposed beams overhead. Little wonder that among some staff the place was known as the "snake pit."

For this, workers were charged $3 a day; meals were an additional $4.50. Both were automatically deducted from one's pay. When I voiced a complaint about the costs at dinner one evening, a young black man (no doubt incredulous at my cluelessness) remarked: "I've worked here ten years. These people don't care about their staff. They don't give a shit."

To hear tell, however, the Concord's quarters were by no means the worst in the region. An older worker told me of sharing an attic room with five other men ten years ago at Teacher's (another hotel). With the bathroom located several stories below, they made routine use of a chamber pot. Men who had worked elsewhere concurred.

The only area in the hotel proper open to the staff in off-duty hours was a back room, perhaps twenty-five feet square. It held a dozen dilapidated chairs, a rough bench, and a television. I spent one thoroughly depressing evening in that room watching *Roots.* In fine institutional form, the TV was in one corner, and the eighteen men watching it were lined up against the walls in their plastic chairs.

The morning after my arrival, the supervisor of the housemen showed me my assignment and explained my duties. I was to police the roughly hundred yards of corridors on the "F" floor of the 200 wing. On checkout days, I was also to follow the maids, vacuuming, dusting, and rearranging furniture in the vacated rooms. Rules of conduct were simple: "No drinking, marijuana, or LSD on the job. Don't make yourself conspicuous around the hotel. Don't make a name for yourself. And no patronizing [*sic*] with guests." As 90 percent of the staff were "transient," the supervisor said he didn't expect any advance notice about my leaving, but would appreciate a few days warning if I could give it.

I spent the days vacuuming hallways and rooms, cleaning stairways, emptying ashtrays, and washing doors. Except for coffee breaks, lunch, and sporadic encounters with the two Spanish-speaking maids on the floor, the hours were almost totally void of human contact. Hotel guests hardly noticed the help. Should something catch their eye—a vague resemblance to someone they knew—they would remark on it to a third person as though the staff member in question were absent or deaf. Nor were the other hotel workers much more approachable. (After a few futile efforts at conversation, I learned from a fellow houseman that our ranks were uniformly viewed by guests and staff alike as "alkies." In the first week of my employment, there was a 33 percent turnover in the corps of twenty-one housemen.) My allotted chores took about three hours to complete. After that, the tedium and isolation began to wear. By day's end, I lay ambush in the hallway for guests, ready to pounce on the dropped cigarette butt or discarded wrapping.

I found it an awkward thing to master, this discipline of the appearance of work.[44] As long as one was not sitting down and was at one's "station" (anywhere in the hundred yards of assigned corridors and rooms), one was technically working, even if this meant prowling the area for something to do. Aside from the hectic schedule of checkout days, there was no pace or end point to the work; it was impossible to be "done" before the day was over. Accordingly, process took precedence over product. Spot inspections looked for apparent busyness, and the same job could be done over again in a pinch because the difference made by any one effort was so slight. Aside from the obvious—trash in the hallways, doors to rooms left open for vacuuming, ashtrays full of butts and discarded containers, a wad of gum ground into the rug—the effect of the work performed was nearly invisible. But for telltale tracks in the nap of the rug, it was difficult to tell whether the floor had been vacuumed two minutes, two days, or two weeks ago. The semblance of laboring was everything; it was just too hard otherwise to say whether a specific task had actually been done or how well.

With the notable exception of supervisory and "front" staff—desk clerks, bellmen, waiters, and recreation workers—most of the Concord's workers were black or Hispanic. Origins were quite diverse: Many hailed from the Caribbean Basin (Cuba, Puerto Rico, Haiti, and Jamaica); a growing number of the Spanish-speaking maids came from South America, with a large contingent from Colombia. Ethnic divisions tended to be reproduced in work and residence assignments: with a few exceptions, the housemen were white, kitchen staff were black, and grounds crews were Hispanic. Black and white workers were housed in separate buildings. Despite their comparatively brief tenure in the country, Hispanic workers were more likely to be local residents, having immigrated to the Catskill region to work and live.

Some of the men with whom I worked came directly from New York City, typically by way of "Louie's" employment agency. Others came from as far away as Key West and Atlanta, traveling what appeared to be a regular circuit. No man with whom I spoke had been recruited off the streets on the Bowery, although there were frequent comments (in town and in the hotel) about the practice. Rather, in the midst of what was proving the most severe postwar recession the country had experienced, hotel work was apparently attractive enough an employment opportunity on its own.

Studious efforts were made to avoid what were referred to as "racial tensions" within the staff. According to veteran workers, the Spanish maids distrusted black housemen, believing them to pick up tips meant for the maids. When two desperately needed black housemen were hired nine days after my arrival, they were assigned to floors with a black and a white maid respectively. Similarly, within the kitchen, preparation and cleanup were entirely within black hands, while the tasks of taking orders, chatting up guests, and transferring dishes and food were entrusted to young white college students.

Finally, of all the sites I visited in the course of my research, only Camp LaGuardia came closer to replicating the picture of the old skid row.[45] It was my distinct impression that the houseman's reputation as a drinker of heroic proportions was hard earned. Indeed, if one accepts the need for some diversion and respite from the deadening tedium of the workday, alcohol was all but unavoidable. Taverns were everywhere (five within walking distance of staff quarters), as was evidence of their custom and consequences.

Within the space of a week, one houseman had been taken off to detox, another was suspended for drinking while on the job, and three more were fired for failing to show up after a bout of drinking the night before.

Aside from simple dereliction of duty (failing to be at one's station during working hours or goofing off while there), drinking on the job seemed to be the most frequent reason for dismissal. It was not uncommon for some men to drink their lunch at a bar located a stone's throw from the rear entrance to the hotel. Others kept a stash hidden at their station, replenished at regular intervals by the remains that guests left behind. (One day, a fellow houseman on an unauthorized break made his way furtively to my floor with a valued gift: a third of a tumbler of Dewar's.) Whatever their habits during the workday, most housemen residing on the hotel grounds repaired to one of the bars nearby as soon as they clocked out or grabbed a six-pack and headed back to Jacobson.

Regular patrons ran tabs at the taverns, a practice encouraged by their keepers and one that made for a common postwork routine. After several hours of steady drinking, and having missed what was in all likelihood a forgettable meal in the staff dining hall, a number of us would head for town to eat a late supper. Drinking would then resume at one of several bars (also largely segregated by race) frequented by townsfolk as well as hotel workers. Around midnight, we would head back to the hotel, usually with an additional six-pack in hand. As noted earlier, one of my recurring missteps was my inability to keep stride with this pace.

Drinking in the bars, in my experience, was curiously impersonal. Round after round would be set up and disposed of with barely a word of conversation being exchanged. A kind of mesmerism would set in, the joint effect of whatever happened to be playing on the television and the residual enervation of the day's work, which defeated most of my efforts at engaging coworkers in talk. Meals in town proved more conducive and much of what I learned about how men wound up working at the hotel (aside from the gossip that made the rounds when a man was let go) was gleaned during these conversations.

The constant drain on income this routine involved—the costs of liquor, off-premise meals, and cab fares back and forth to town—together with deductions for room and board and personal necessities, meant that very little of one's wages was saved.[46] For these men, the resort circuit was valued less as a source of income than as a viable avenue of escape. The classic earmarks of the skid row habitat—low-waged, low-demand work; group quarters in an all-male environment; few if any social obligations; little concern for the future—were firmly in place.

The two workers I came to know best were both men in their mid-thirties to early forties, with education, skills, and decent work histories behind them. Each had left family, debt, and a string of recent job failures behind, in exchange for the time-limited anonymity of the mountains. Each was fighting a losing battle with the bottle, and at least one of them (a certified social worker and former alcoholism counselor) knew it. Neither had clear plans for season's end. One day, observing the near-evangelical fervor with which the housekeeping supervisor hectored the housemen on our personal appearance and quality of work prior to dispatching us to our stations, one of them remarked: "Look at him: thinks he's got an important job—in charge of a bunch of guys who don't want anything out of life."

Reprise

The field study provided a better understanding of the "habitats" of homeless people, both at the microlevel of their day-to-day survival on the streets and in the shelters. One finding especially proved of practical import. It was the oft-repeated complaint of service providers at the time that the problem with the street dwellers was their unwillingness to accept assistance. This unwillingness was variously attributed to their impaired judgment or eccentric outlook. Either way, it was alleged, pathology trumped need. Neither the overture of assistance nor the terms and conditions attached to the offer of shelter—nor, indeed, the meaning of "refusal" to those who rejected such offers—was ever questioned in such pronouncements.[47] Our experience suggested a contrary reading of this commonly reported observation. Given the nature of the public shelter available—the dirt, the ever-present danger, and the degrading treatment routinely meted out to applicants; the continuing association of shelter facilities with the Bowery environment; and the corrosive effect on one's dignity and self-respect that an extended stay in such settings was bound to have—the city's offer of refuge was a tarnished one. Public shelter, as Matthew Jacobson had observed the last time that available facilities had been overwhelmed (in 1932), was still "premised on the theory of the bum." Under such circumstances, it was easier to understand the decision of many homeless men to fend for themselves on the streets.

A corollary also proved to be the case. Aside from the missions, which tended to have their own crews of regulars, the few alternatives to the public shelters were typically small-scale operations, run by not-for-profit groups barely subsisting on shoestring budgets. (The Catholic Worker "hospitality houses" were prototypical.) Whenever decent, humane shelter had been made available, it had never gone wanting for willing recipients. Indeed, so constant was the demand that a few such shelters had been forced to impose limits-of-stay restrictions, rotating available beds to distribute a scarce resource.

In light of such considerations, the presumption of incompetence on the part of the homeless poor may be said to have been more a self-fulfilling prophecy than a faithful reading of their experience. Contrary to the received wisdom of the day, the "inability" or "unwillingness" of many to accept help was a deliberate decision to seek relief on their own terms. Moreover, so long as present circumstances continued, one should expect the same patterns to persist, furnishing more "evidence" of the hostility of the homeless to beneficent efforts on their behalf.

In a word, once the *niche* of homelessness was understood, the allegation that the irrationality of its inhabitants was the key to their homelessness lost some of its force. At the same time, the ethnographic picture reconfirmed the "complicated meanness" that survival on the streets entails.[48] The daily round of handouts and soup lines, the fruitless efforts at seeking documentation and income assistance, the high-handed attitude of those to whom one turned for help, the scorn and occasional mischief of passersby—the whole bloody ordeal of subsistence—were plain to see. To prize the ingenuity and resourcefulness of those who managed despite the odds was not to condone the circumstances that required that craft be made of such necessity.

Contrary to expectations—another dispatch filed, shelved, and forgotten—the original report, *Private Lives/Public Spaces* (1981), focused public attention on a scandal of major proportions. In as artless and jargonless a form as possible, we had compiled a detailed bill of indictment of the public agencies charged with the care of the homeless poor. But exposés of this sort are commonplace in a city like New York, and the considerable media attention the report received was a surprise. The least reliable item in the entire study, a crude estimate of the total number of homeless men and women culled from unpublished documents, quickly became part of the public lore of homelessness. French and Dutch publications ran details of the story. The Soviet paper *Isvestia* seized on the findings as indicative of the decay of late capitalist society and of the heartlessness of city administrators, a charge Mayor Koch characteristically took as a compliment.

In the wake of the report's appearance, Ellen and I made scores of appearances on television and radio news shows, often debating city officials. Predictably, they attempted to dismiss its findings as myopic and biased. In part, this was the reflexive response of bureaucrats to outside criticism. In part, it was a refusal to admit that the dimensions of homelessness had qualitatively changed and that city policy should be overhauled accordingly. And in part, it was a political choice to deny that the growing shortage of low-income housing had anything to do with the burgeoning ranks of the homeless, so as to forestall the day the city would have to confront a residential neighborhood (not one on the Bowery or on an island) with the news that a shelter was coming.[49]

The *Times'* coverage legitimized the issue as one of public policy.[50] But the correctives envisioned—and thus the terms of the debate—were limited to emergency relief. What impressed the editors was the fact that decent shelter, humanely delivered, was possible on a large scale; they cited our description of the Pine Street Inn in Boston as living proof. Thus, a few months later, when the *Times* proclaimed that the city faced a "'crisis' on vagrants," it was the refusal of communities to accept proposed shelters in their neighborhoods that was seen as the core of the problem.[51] Such were the working premises of a progressive approach, circa 1982: retain the warehouse model but humanize its operation; distribute the burden more equitably; prepare to ride out what should prove a transient crisis. Not seen as part of the problem, housing had no place in the remedy. Twenty years later, a statewide coalition of service and housing providers announced a plan "to end city homelessness"—in another ten years.[52]

[4]

The Airport as Home

> Some establishments, like Grand Central Station, are open to anyone who is decently behaved . . .
>
> Erving Goffman, *Asylums*

No theme has so dominated and distorted contemporary discussion of homelessness as that of disability. In some quarters, the notion that most homeless people are badly damaged and that this damage is what best explains their homelessness has become something of a talisman, the hidden key to the otherwise vexing mystery of enduring street poverty. Severe mental illness and chronic substance abuse are the usual impairments cited. Evidence to the contrary—that although many homeless people suffer from severe psychosis and/or addictions, this does not constitute a majority; nor does the disability of those afflicted alone account for their homelessness—is substantial and growing.[1] But fed by a steady stream of opinion pieces and press accounts, the idea that "the street" is simply a compressed symbol for the strange and disturbed has fast assumed the trappings of common sense.

Written as part of a running argument with the impaired-capacity model of homelessness on historical, ethnographic, and conceptual grounds, this chapter examines a rather specialized niche that emerged early on as an unlikely redoubt for the contemporary homeless poor: the airport. It was there, in fact, that the tag "crazy," a term that today courts the status of a self-evident truth, was first applied to the new homeless. But the chapter owes its origin to a pragmatic question: Should we be trying to reach and relocate such people?

Background

In the early 1960s, as the first phase of deinstitutionalization was hitting stride, the occasional article would appear in psychiatric journals that chronicled the antics of deranged former patients who had made their way to airports en route to some delusional destination. For twenty years, such accounts remained psychiatric curiosities. But in the mid-1980s, reports began to accumulate of the growing presence of such individuals at airports throughout the country and of the usually feckless efforts of social service agencies to reach and resettle them. Early in 1988, I was approached by the Red Cross and asked to render, in short order, an assessment of the feasibility of mounting an aggressive outreach effort at one airport.

For six months, I conducted field interviews and logged extended periods of observation at "Metropolitan Airport," one of five serving the New York area, in order to acquire a sense of how homeless people had redefined this particular space to serve as an informal shelter. This was an exploratory study and the interviews—with homeless men and women, airport authorities, and concession workers—were largely unstructured. For the most part, I worked in the late night hours, after normal airport traffic had dispersed, or in the early morning before it began. When approaching homeless informants, I made offers of food and coffee; I spoke with some for hours at a time, with others only a few minutes, always making it clear that I was interested in why people preferred the airport to the public shelter and how they managed to survive. In a few instances of obviously disoriented, badly deteriorated, and hapless folks, I was able to engineer placements with agencies in the city (by having the director of a mental health outreach team accompany me and make the appropriate referrals). But for the most part, I sought simply "the native's point of view" on this unusual habitat.

The practical aim was to determine the need for and advisability of further outreach efforts at that site. But there was another, historically particular, point to the inquiry, one that situated this space and its inhabitants in a larger story of discharged mental patients and contested public places. By the late 1960s in England and early '70s in the United States, it was evident that badly planned and poorly implemented deinstitutionalization policies effectively meant that some former hospital inmates had nowhere to go. British researchers took to referring to this development as one that transformed "patients" into "vagrants." By the late 1970s, it was common knowledge that psychiatrically disturbed residents were to be found among New York's shelter population in substantial numbers.[2] And yet, the metropolitan airport—not skid row—was where complaints about the wandering deranged first arose.

This chapter describes the background to, the psychiatric interpretation of, and an alternative approach to understanding the anomalous presence of obvious psychiatric disorder in the well-ordered environment of the airport. It then seeks to reinterpret this somewhat marginal phenomenon, but not in order to register yet another indictment in the continuing trial of deinstitutionalization—that literature is vast and variegated enough.[3] Rather, it seeks to show how thin is the explanatory power of pathology as a cause of homelessness. It offers instead a "common sense" perspective that, while not neglecting clinical factors, is shaped by the results of the brief ethnographic study undertaken and is more in line with both classical ethnographic accounts and recent street-level studies.[4]

Alternative Utilities of Public Space

It was not until 1939 that the first commercial airport (LaGuardia) opened in the metropolitan New York area. But nearly three decades would pass before that facility, and others like it, would play host to homeless people—owing, one assumes, to the expense of air travel. Parks (or, tellingly, "the commons") may be the oldest and most obvious example of a public area being put to private use, but bus terminals, subway and train stations, and ferry depots have also long been used by unauthorized squatters. Accounts documenting a homeless presence in such spots in New York can be found at least as far back as the 1920s.[5] In the postwar years, when the numbers of those without shelter reached their lowest point in thirty years, homelessness was essentially synonymous with its geographical locus, skid row. By the mid-1960s, the only place one might see men sleeping on the street in New York was on the Bowery, and even there the numbers rarely surpassed a few dozen. But in the late 1960s, to judge by journalistic accounts, homeless men (and some women) again began frequenting the streets and subways at night, prompting indignant citizens to call for intensified enforcement of vagrancy laws. Such calls were not without effect. In the summer of 1973, the Penn Central Railroad initiated a new policy at Grand Central Station, closing the premises from 1:30 A.M. to 5:30 A.M., arguing that the station had become the impromptu shelter of dozens of street dwellers each night. The policy was designed to rid the station of such "undesirables" and make it easier to clean. Fifteen years later, the Port Authority Bus Terminal in midtown Manhattan would follow suit, for the same reasons.[6]

Lost Souls and Airports

Nearly forty years ago, two researchers reported on 49 patients who had been picked up at the airport and admitted to the psychiatric ward of San Francisco General Hospital over a seven-year period. None of this group was literally homeless, although some were in transit. Roughly half were diagnosed as schizophrenic, but, unlike some reports in the literature, their psychiatric troubles were found to be unrelated to the stresses of flight. Rather, air travel was instrumental to some grander, often ill-formulated scheme. Half of them either had no travel plans at all or were just beginning journeys. None had taken up residence at the airport; one had managed to procure a room at a nearby hotel. Clinicians identified a distinctive "syndrome" in these "perigrinating paranoids": their intent to use commercial airlines to maintain interpersonal distance, to achieve immediate closeness, to vary the environment, or to act out a delusional system on a grand scale.[7]

In the next five years (1968–1973), 359 of the psychiatric patients admitted to Queens Hospital Center would come from John F. Kennedy International Airport (JFK). The vast majority of these (79 percent) were local residents; 82 percent had been picked up in the midst of a psychotic episode and had none but the most fantastic travel plans. Three-quarters of these patients were diagnosed as schizophrenic, and the airport was found to figure prominently in their delusional system, chiefly as a "symbolic representation of connection with the family." Manifestly disorganized and driven by unusual ideas of separation and reunion, these people had nonetheless been able to negotiate a rather complicated transportation system to reach the airport. Once there, they had apparently wasted little time in bringing their idiosyncratic presence to the attention of airport authorities: only 12 percent resided at the airport undetected (or at least unreported) for longer than two days; "several" reported living in the terminal for a week. And some of these same individuals had apparently been through the same routine before, making their way to the airport during times of acute "decompensation."[8]

The Airport as Symbol and Symptom

None of these persons had taken up permanent (or even temporary) residence in the airport as an alternative to emergency shelter elsewhere. The airport was chosen on symbolic rather than utilitarian grounds, the act not of a will determined to preserve its independence but of an imagination lost in the throes of disorder. "The airport," observed the researcher at JFK,

> had apparently come to represent concretely the focus from which time and space would somehow be bridged and the safety, security and reassurance of reattachment to loved ones might be established.[9]

A pair of British researchers argued that the airport exerted a "special fascination" for the mentally imbalanced, not so much because of its symbolic value as transit and reunion but rather because it was a logical terminus for the "wandering propensities" that certain psychoses exhibited. Although they represented only 13 percent of those referred from Heathrow Airport for psychiatric care over a three-year period, these individuals were three times as likely to be diagnosed as schizophrenic as patients from the surrounding catchment area. Part of this overrepresentation of severe psychoses, the authors point out, may be traced to a "detection bias": peculiarly behaving individuals are more likely to cause a disturbance if they disport themselves on the grounds of Buckingham Palace (or Heathrow Airport) than if they restrict their antics to the crowded London streets. But the peculiar lure of the airport could not be reduced to the impulsive push of disease processes (whether delusional ideational systems or deranged biochemistries) that made wandering irresistible. These researchers concluded that other, social circumstances had to be considered—like the desire to spice up an otherwise "lonely, unstructured life" by a visit to a public landmark.[10]

Their American counterparts saw only pathology. The title of one study, "Airport wandering as a psychiatric symptom,"[11] says it all. Nor is it one restricted to homeless denizens of airports. A "tendency to drift" afflicts many of the chronically mentally ill who show up in the ranks of the homeless, some argued. They drift

> to outrun their problems, their symptoms, and their failures . . . [because of] difficulty in achieving closeness and intimacy . . . in search of autonomy, as a way of denying their dependency, and out of desire for an isolated life-style.[12]

The emphasis is on the pathological impulse, the irrationality and lack of goal-directedness. It seems not to have occurred to these researchers that the choice of an unusual abode may have been forced, or that the selection of an out-of-the-way refuge owed something to ingenuity and resourcefulness. Rather, the argument is that residence on the streets or in public spaces should be taken as ipso facto evidence of mental disability.

The Terminal as Haven

In marked contrast to the 1960s, the phenomenon of airport dwellers was widespread by the late 1980s. In a nationwide 1988 survey, over 75 percent of major metropolitan airports contacted reported having had homeless people "living" on their premises; in 60 percent of these, the problem was a current one. Anecdotal evidence suggests both that the problem has grown since then and that repressive measures have been stepped up. Until late in the 1980s, Chicago's O'Hare served as home to several hundred homeless people, according to counts done by the local Coalition for the Homeless. By late 1989, public officials had planned to police the premises and build a shelter nearby to house the displaced homeless; by March 1991, there were virtually no homeless people living at the airport, though the new shelter accommodated only a portion of those displaced. Over 50 people were living at one terminal of Newark Airport in the winter of 1988. The removal of all seats and benches in the terminal beginning in the fall of 1989 effectively eliminated the problem. In the summer of 1987, Port Authority officials estimated that there were 120 people living in New York's three major airports; three and a half years later, more than that number were thought to live at JFK alone. During the winter of 1987–1988, outreach teams from New York City's Human Resources Administration (HRA) recorded 125 contacts with homeless men and women living at JFK and LaGuardia airports; only 15 of of these accepted HRA's offer to be transported to a public shelter.[13] The reason was no mystery: Homeless life at the airport was "like a stay at the Concord [Hotel] compared to the city shelter system."[14]

Dimensions of the Problem

A working knowledge of the dimensions of homelessness at Metropolitan Airport in late 1988 may be had by considering the numbers, demographics, health problems, and local culture of those who make the terminal *home*.

Numbers: In January 1988, the Port Authority's executive director estimated that a total of a thousand homeless people could regularly be found scattered throughout the transportation under his jurisdiction; over two hundred individuals and "a few families" were thought to be living at the three largest airports.[15] At Metropolitan Airport, the population appears to range from two to four dozen at any one time.

How many different homeless people take up residence at the terminal over the course of a year is difficult to say. A provisional breakdown might distinguish between transient, permanent, and seasonal residents. *Transient residents* refer to those who sleep at the terminal from a few days to a few weeks before finding alternative accommodations elsewhere. *Permanent residents* refer to those—some of whose tenancy at the time of the study was running three years or longer—who have no intention of leaving the terminal in the near future and, indeed, may well consider the terminal as home. *Seasonal residents* refer to those who make use of the terminal in the winter and make other arrangements—usually, sleeping rough—in the summer.[16] Permanent residents constitute a core group of about a dozen.

Demographics: Men outnumber women at the airport, although not to the same extent (roughly 9 to 1) as is true among residents of the public shelter system. Rather, among permanent residents at least, the ratio is roughly 3 or 4 men to 1 woman. African Americans, Hispanics, and whites were all observed living at the terminal, although in a marked departure from the trend in the shelters, whites appear to outnumber minority groups significantly. All but two of those observed or interviewed were by themselves; the exception was a quarrelsome couple who had been living at the terminal for some time. Last, the terminal's homeless poor appear to be much older than the shelter population.

Health problems: Edema and related circulatory problems (e.g., cellulitis) were fairly common, as is often the case with homeless people who go for long periods without elevating their feet. Some open sores were seen, several chronic ailments were reported, and a few cases of lice infestation were observed. Although clearly the exception, several people did exhibit signs of psychiatric disorder. In one woman who recited the names of a string of psychotropic medications, the ticlike movements of her tongue and lips suggested tardive dyskinesia, a neurological disorder seen among long-term users of antipsychotic drugs.

Local culture: Given the brief period of study and the lack of sustained rapport, it is impossible to say how fleeting, circumstantial, or even feigned some of the observed peculiarities of behavior might be. It is at least plausible, to take one instance, that the evasive and suspicious responses of one woman to a gentle line of questioning owed as much to the oddity of a stranger initiating a conversation at midnight, or to less than satisfactory encounters with outreach workers in the past, or to a street-honed sense of self-protection as they did to any resident disorder. Then, too, standards of behavior are considerably more flexible in this setting. Indeed, the most striking cultural distinction of the airport is the degree to which some accepted canons of social behavior—especially those having to do with the segregation of private and public spheres of life—are conditionally suspended. In this rather limited sense, the airport (especially as flights have become more affordable) may be seen as a kind of "liminal" space, where public behavior is governed by a set of rules notable chiefly for their elasticity (excepting, of course, security). In this self-contained space of happenstance and strangers, a casual and improvised attitude toward the presentation of self (not unlike that seen in recreational camping areas) seems to obtain.

For a few of those encountered at the terminal, the symbolic value of this transitional space, so central to the analysis of earlier researchers, was clear. There was a German student who, having flunked out of the university and undecided about an alternative career, had faced what he felt to be a Hobson's choice in his life. Rather than choose, he ran, and to keep from arriving anywhere, he stopped running in midstride, taking up residence in the limbo-world of the international traveler on a stopover in Metropolitan Airport. With assistance from a local outreach program, he was eventually returned home to his family in Munich.

A final note on the self-perception of (at least some of) the people living at Metropolitan Airport. An airport cop referred in conversation to the "better class of homeless people" he found at the airport. He meant that a good number of them have regular sources of income (from pensions, family, or work) and take great pains to maintain a presentable appearance. That distinction is not lost on airport residents themselves. One former resident remarked that living at the terminal allows one to sustain the impression that "you are different from the other homeless people that walk the streets."[17] On two occasions, men whom I was interviewing made oblique reference to their own discomfort or embarrassment at finding themselves sharing quarters with "all these homeless" people. One, a veteran who received over five hundred dollars a month in pension and social security payments, had been living at the terminal for three years.

Aspects of a Survival Niche

As local havens for the homeless go, Metropolitan Airport is unparalleled in the amenities it offers. To list only the most obvious:

1. *Toilet and sanitary facilities,* designed to accommodate the peak demand of thousands of air travelers, are all but vacant in the off-hours. When distributed among the few dozen homeless folks to be found there at any one time, this represents the highest ratio of public restrooms to homeless users anywhere in the city. Moreover, unlike many public accommodations, these toilets and sinks are clean, well-maintained, generously supplied with soap and paper towels, and offer the almost unheard-of luxury of privacy.
2. *Snack bars and cafeterias* offer ample opportunities for purchasing or scavenging meals. An informal charity network among food workers supplements this resource. Some of the homeless are reliably reported to have regular sources of income and are able to purchase their meals. Travelers on the run often leave portions of meals uneaten, and, in the

interval between their finishing and the table being bused, a skillful scavenger can pick through leftovers in a way that attracts little attention. For the proud but penniless, condiments offer a questionable source of nutrition. The less scrupulous can take advantage of the poorly monitored cafeteria line, so long as one cadges items at the end farthest from the cashier.

3. By far the most prized asset of the terminals are the matchless *sleeping accommodations*: air-conditioned in the summer, heated in the winter, reliably patrolled the year round, well-lighted, and clean. Nor do security guards object to the occasional bag or cart of belongings that may be parked alongside a sleeping form.

Such practical amenities[18] alone make the airport one of the best-kept secrets in the annals of alternative shelter. But two additional, call them "cultural," elements apply as well. As noted above, airports occupy a singular place in the American night: Nowhere else may one observe, as accepted practice, ordinary citizens—some in quite casual attire, many with bags, and most looking a little worse for the wear—bedding down for the night in full public view. A reasonably clean and decently dressed homeless person has no trouble fitting in with the impromptu sleepers scattered about. Then, too, behavior that would normally be considered inappropriate—such as unpacking, sorting through, and repacking a bundle of clothing in a public thoroughfare—goes unremarked in a setting where the improvisations of harried travelers can make short work of established convention.

Second, and possibly most valuable, was the attitude of the airport line workers, those in daily contact with them. Almost without exception, it was one of benign, even concerned, accommodation. Some regularly went well beyond the scope of their official duties in assisting the homeless they encountered. Their posture was less one of grudging tolerance than a kind of enlightened (if somewhat baffled) resignation: They understood that given the range of existing alternatives the terminal might be the last best hope for many of these souls. One is not surprised to learn that on occasion a laid-off baggage worker or an Ogden Allied Fuel employee suddenly pitched out by a spouse will find himself at least temporarily among those who live, as well as work, at the airport.

Getting By

Given this impressive array of resources, two patterns of managing a presence can be distinguished. On the one hand are those who cultivate a deliberate unobtrusiveness; on the other are those who indifferently, even defiantly, stand out. The former—the majority of those in residence at Metropolitan Airport—endeavor "to pass" (as Goffman called the artful self-concealment practiced by stigmatized groups) by taking care in their appearance, limiting the time spent in public view at the terminal, and exercising discretion in their income-generating or food-gathering activities. They are disciplined survivors, well-versed in the bounds of appropriate behavior. The measure of their success in invisibility: as one policeman at the terminal put it, "You hardly notice them. . . . Most of them don't panhandle, they don't beg. They just sleep here." The logic of "passing" is to minimize what marks one as distinctive. Except for their extended stays, many of the homeless people who adopted this strategy could be mistaken for stranded travelers.[19]

The smaller but far more obvious group tends to fit the stereotypical picture of street dwellers. At one extreme, their clothing may be disheveled or filthy, their hair matted and louse-ridden; they may smell badly and sit virtually motionless for hours at a stretch; they may accost strangers with importunings for change or fantastic tales of wrongdoing. If they steal food from the cafeteria, they do so in ways seemingly oblivious to the danger of being caught; asked to move on by a police officer, they may loudly try to provoke a fight or contest the order. (Incidents of property destruction or defacement, however, were uncommon.) Such individuals soon overstep even the generous bounds of acceptable behavior in force at Metropolitan Airport and are referred elsewhere. Among the permanent residents of the terminal, only one man was a recurrent source of disruptive behavior, and his offenses were mild (using the men's room reserved for first-class passengers and loudly talking to himself). The only offense given by the enterprising, quarrelsome couple mentioned earlier is that their disagreements tend invariably to be aired publicly, in tones and at a volume usually kept behind closed doors. One young man I recognized as a client of the city's Men's Shelter from a decade before, where he had been a boisterous, entertaining clown. His antics at the airport were no wilder than a silent, pantomimed game of basketball in one of the hallways.

At no time did I notice half-eaten food or discarded wrappers scattered near any of the homeless residents; only once, on the floor in front of a sleeping woman, was an untended cup of coffee spilled. Indeed, the most telling indicator of the "threat" posed by these people was the complaint voiced by one Port Authority administrator. Pressed to specify what he meant by the acts of "vandalism" he charged had been committed, he paused and pointed to a large, rotating advertising display, one that was supposed to be illuminated. Someone, allegedly one of the homeless residents, had switched off the light.

Conclusion

The problem of misplaced people isn't exhausted (let alone refuted) by a recitation of their largely unproblematic behaviors, as the subsequent history of this exceptional haven shows. With the exception of the food franchise operators' charges of pilfering, most complaints about homeless people at Metropolitan Airport came from the airlines leasing space at the terminal. In the main, these complaints had little to do with direct confrontations with customers or staff, or with disorderly or unseemly conduct. The occasional incident of panhandling aside, the nature of their offense was aesthetic. The problem with the homeless poor was their visibility; they were an eyesore. Like the poverty of mid-nineteenth century New York, theirs was an alien, embarrassing, disturbing presence; a species, as one commentator put it, of human "litter." They were a commercial liability, clearly unwelcome in the sanitized space of duty-free shopping.

Port Authority officials, too, tended to link the problem of homelessness at the airport to considerations of "image." Practically, it is difficult to see how they could complain on other grounds: the numbers were, at that time at least, within tolerable limits; incidents of vandalism were trivial for the most part; actual interference with commercial activity or patrons was uncommon; and the population on the whole was well behaved. But the more than half million people who daily make use of Port Authority facilities "suffer," former Executive Director Stephen Berger explained, when confronted with "the graphic human results of the failure of society to address the problem of the homeless." One airport official added that the Port Authority has "an image to protect . . . of our country and everything else."[20]

Self-interest wasn't the only motivating force behind the concern of Port Authority or airport personnel. Officials were not unaware of the genuine service they were providing to the otherwise homeless. A sense of responsibility could be discerned, an impulse to do more than provide rough shelter and security for those who have neither. Warring with this were fears of attracting more people than the airport could handle. The amenities that distinguish it as a haven depended on it remaining a relatively well-kept secret. The tolerance so evident in the terminals and the relatively hospitable attitude assumed toward its homeless guests were both contingent on there being only a small number of people who find their way there. It was not difficult to foresee a more hostile response and a less accommodating environment were the numbers to rise significantly. As income-generating possibilities expanded (the baggage cart rental franchise in particular) at the airport, and safe accessible public space became harder to come by elsewhere, the perceived advantages of the terminal (even given its distance from downtown) would likely mount.

At the same time, it was clear that for all its assets, the then-tolerant posture had evolved in haphazard fashion, with little conscious design. Prudence demanded that a coherent policy be formulated before the problem reached crisis proportions. The dilemma for the authorities was simple: how to intervene effectively without adding to the lure that the airport already exerted or resorting to frankly repressive measures.

The practical issues were two: First, given the unusual security and sanitation arrangements, the small number of homeless people, and the special efforts made on their behalf, outreach workers equipped with no better offer than the city shelter system were peddling noncompetitive goods. In early 1988, the city's outreach van ceased operations at the airport; the return on invested time was simply too small to warrant the effort. And second, the threshold effect alluded to above—that the refuge works only so long as the secret is kept—was itself hostage to circumstance. So long as the numbers remained small; so long as news of this haven traveled a restricted circuit; so long as the more predatory elements among the homeless poor preferred the thickets of central business districts to the isolation of outlying self-contained "villages"—so long as those contingencies prevailed, this niche survived. But the peculiar circumstances that created and sustained it proved vulnerable to forces that have nothing to do with homelessness or with poverty at large.

Intensified air traffic and worsening commuter snarls have prompted planners to rethink the layout of the airport. Major construction began in the early 1990s. By decade's end, it was apparent that a cultural shift in attitude toward the liminal space of airports was under way. In an article featuring the installation of galleries and exhibitions planned for the new JFK airport, a consultant to public arts projects opined: "An airport isn't 'no place' anymore . . ."[21]

It would be misleading to leave the impression that pre-1990s survival in the terminal was uncomplicated or without personal costs. Even in this comparatively resource-rich environment, some constants of homelessness applied. If recognized, a homeless person was rarely openly welcomed; the justly praised hospitality of airport personnel was for the most part a surreptitious, unofficial affair. For all its amenities, the terminal was no solution to homelessness—indeed, it may be argued that the main reason it looked so good as a short-term makeshift was that the public shelters were so unnervingly bad. And even among those who succeed in "passing," the suspicion that one really doesn't belong was never far from consciousness. One elderly man, with friends in nearby Forest Hills who collected his mail and provided him with an occasional shower and change of clothes, took a "G.I. bath" in the sinks each morning and maintained a decent appearance. Still, he could not escape the feeling that "people are rejecting you because you're dirty, you don't shave, your clothes are dirty."

Postscript: Another Ethnographic Dilemma

Ethical quandaries are all too common among ethnographers working on the home front. The study recounted above raised one such dilemma, albeit a modest one: by publicizing the relatively happy state of accommodation that prevailed at the airport, I would be jeopardizing the very condition—that it was little known—that made it possible. (This had happened earlier with the Grand Central steam tunnels, and would happen again with the razing of Manhattan shantytowns in the early 1990s.) Concern that an article might do so is what prompted me to slip the cloak of pseudonymity, "Metropolitan Airport," on the site's identity. Even though the relatively obscure anthropological journal in which the original report appeared made it unlikely that any but a dedicated graduate student would come upon it, the dilemma it potentially raised should not go unremarked these days, when "contract anthropology" accounts for so much of the applied work being done.[22]

Such work raises fresh ethical problems. In the course of his examination of *Forbidden Knowledge,* Roger Shattuck distinguishes a species of knowing that is not so much proscribed as it is awkward, even (his term) "delicate." By this he means objects of knowing that may be harmed, damaged, or contaminated by the act of knowing or, to take it a step further, by the act of disclosing. These are practices, beliefs, or messages that can only thrive, and serve their appointed keepers and intended audiences faithfully, if they remain veiled.[23] (*Samizdat* literature is a contemporary example.) Anthropologists have long dealt with the issue of rendering naked to profane inspection that which indigenous people hold sacred and have, on those occasions when conscience gnawed, devised various means of circumventing the danger. For much of its history, too, the discipline could fall back on the sheer incommensurability of its vehicle (writing) when placed next to its subject (preliterate peoples). But the dilemmas arising today are far less arcane, not when so many of our "subjects" turn out to be our "readers" as well or when they lay claim to physical or intellectual/cultural properties "unearthed" in the course of our investigations. Here the difficulty is not so much the sacred as it is the surreptitious, especially when the practices at stake constitute "hidden transcripts of resistance." The difficulty is compounded for us in applied work, for while relevance demands specificity and local contingencies invariably restrict the range of applicability of whatever "findings" emerge, effective camouflage demands a more artful pseudonym than "Middletown."[24]

Yes, "bearing witness" is an essential part of our discipline's charter.[25] But the act is more easily urged than accomplished. Exposé is not an unalloyed moral good, and its reception no sure thing. The urge to correct or alleviate is hardly the only response provoked by suffering persuasively documented. There are also, depending on the reader and the interests at stake, less noble urges that seek to dissemble, dispute, dismiss, or discount otherwise unassimilable facts. One may retort that in that event, recourse to subterfuge is in order. But if ethnography is true to its job, can "thick description" ever be adequately disguised? Isn't the risk of inadvertent betrayal a constant one?

The limits of moral witness under circumstances of duress or captivity, the subject of the concluding chapter of this book, is an issue that has been with anthropology for a while and promises to endure.[26] The same is surely true of the uses to which our findings are put, only the old rules of caution would seem to apply as never before. It would be nice to suppose that ethnographers could learn to write, as Clement of Alexandria did, "so that the heretics will not understand." But that seems unlikely. The wiser course is to assume that so long as opportunities for misuse vastly outnumber those for appropriate application, the day belongs to the heretics. Prudence, therefore, dictates that we write so as to limit the opportunities for misreading and reveal as little as possible of threatened habitats or practices. How to do that *and* salvage the eccentric authority of the devoted outsider, immersed in the detailed particulars of time and place that are the grist of anthropology's mills, is not so easily resolved.

[5]

Out for the Count: The Census Bureau's 1990 S-Night Enumeration

> . . . if statistical identification facilitates political consciousness among some resource-poor groups, these same statistics make invisible to the policy process other groups at the margins of social and economic life, where measurement often fails—the undocumented workers, the illegal aliens, and the vagrant, homeless populations.
>
> Kenneth Prewitt, Census Bureau director, 1998–2001

The Constitution provides for a decennial enumeration of all the country's residents and, as a court might put it, "all means all." The Census Bureau's interest in the numbers and demographics of homeless persons, and in the institutions catering to them, dates at least from the time of a special enumeration of New York's Bowery men in April 1930. With the exception of a few research projects, so targeted an effort lapsed in the intervening years. But in the late 1980s, the Bureau stimulated renewed interest in the problems of enumerating such populations by funding several pilot studies prior to the 1990 census. It followed up with a set of contracted assessments of the 1990 street and shelter enumeration effort (better known as S-Night) in sections of Chicago, Los Angeles, New Orleans, New York, and Phoenix. Several Census Bureau–funded companion studies were undertaken as part of the New York effort. This chapter reports on a brief ethnographic inquiry into nighttime habitats of the street-dwelling homeless undertaken as part of one of those studies.[1]

The Ethnographic Corrective in Studies of Homelessness

The earliest and still most distinctive feature of the ethnographic approach to homelessness is the reconstruction, "from the native's point of view," of what is often a highly charged and badly misunderstood cultural niche. James P. Spradley and Jacqueline Wiseman both mounted careful studies of homeless men and their interactions with agencies of social control (the police and alcohol treatment centers, respectively), crafting a distinctive view that was in each case at striking variance with the official perspective on jail or treatment. Competing perspectives on the utilities of public shelter and, earlier, the almshouse can be documented as well. Closely allied with the shift in vantage point is the attempt to situate particular practices or beliefs within a larger context—difficult as it may be to determine the proper boundaries of that whole.

Other features of the ethnographic turn have only recently appeared in studies of contemporary homelessness: a commitment to the rigors of sustained fieldwork and to the seasoned version of street-lore that only the long view can offer; an insistence that, rich as the heuristic value of the "adaptation" premise has been, it is also essential to assess its limitations and to show how patterns of accommodation change over time and across contexts; and closer attention to the perils as well as the benefits of participant observation. Finally, a comparative perspective has begun to take shape, as in the question of how distinctive a group within the homeless the habitually street-dwelling may constitute.[2]

Description of Study

It was this domain of the street-dwelling homeless we undertook to study in a New York State Office of Mental Health research project. Seeking to reap the strengths of the ethnographic method—close documentation and extended periods of observation and interviewing—but working under stringent time constraints, we designed a "brief ethnographic" inquiry into some of the informal shelter devised or appropriated by the homeless poor in public spaces. On five successive nights, participant observers were dispatched to seven assigned sites, there to pass the night as if homeless themselves. The research group was made up of graduate students in sociology and anthropology from the New School for Social Research and Rutgers University, a number of whom were international students; a physician's assistant; an out-of-work musician; a graphics artist; two shelter workers; and two homeless women who received special permission from a city shelter director to participate in the study. Their charge was to describe the nighttime use of public spaces by homeless individuals as well as any competing uses of those spaces.[3] Our aim was twofold: first to "disaggregate the street"—to document with as much precision and local color as we could muster the differences in numbers of apparent homeless people, mobility, rules of conduct, and textures of life in these half-forgotten byways; and, second, to derive implications for the assessment of attempts to enumerate the street-dwelling homeless population.

Study Design

The seven sites were chosen to yield a mix with respect to size, stability of population, and location (indoor versus outdoor). To minimize the intrusiveness of our observers, all the sites but two were in the moderate (at least 21) or large (51 plus) size range. The exceptions were both outdoor sites: a plaza with (it turned out) few occupants and a small cardboard box, tarp, and sleeping bag "settlement" with between 15 and 20 occupants. The other sites included two large transportation terminals (one of which was a conglomeration of distinctive subsites) and three subway stations.

Participant observers typically arrived on site around midnight and stayed until 6:00 A.M. or morning wake-up. Several teams found it useful to vary their routine, sometimes arriving earlier, sometimes staying later, in order to observe and interact with residents as they bedded down for the night or awoke in the morning. At sites where occupants were frequently awake throughout the night, observers made efforts to speak with them. Fieldnotes were kept surreptitiously—hastily scrawled during trips to the bathroom, or concealed by a blanket or piece of cardboard—and were formalized as soon as possible after observers left site each morning.

Trick Description

As the scope of work grew progressively more detailed and the demands on observers mounted, the research team found itself beset by a host of doubts about the quality of the data likely to be obtained using brief ethnographic methods. Most of these misgivings turned out to be unfounded. The fundamental problem was not, as I had anticipated, the provisional character or "ethnographic validity" of the observations and reports we were compiling. Enough rough corroboration was obtained from the various observers, who logged and documented uninterrupted hours in diverse but kindred settings, to permit some preliminary judgments about what was idiosyncratic and what characteristic about the street sites. Nor did the problem arise from restricted access. Indeed, project participants were uniformly of the opinion that the degree of access they were accorded would have been difficult to achieve in any other way, especially in so compressed a time period. Rather, it had to do with the terms and conditions under which such access was obtained.

Although strictly instructed to respond to direct inquiries about their purpose with an accurate thumbnail sketch of the study ("I'm part of a study of the nighttime use of public space in the city"), *without exception* the participant observers found themselves unable to drop the pretense of homelessness. Each of them, even those confronted by (sometimes surly) accusations of fraud, maintained the fiction of being homeless. On occasion, this meant going to great lengths to devise intricate narratives as to how they had arrived on the street. Throughout most of the study, this spontaneous strategy proved unproblematic; on the contrary, it became a matter of pride for some to be able to carry off the impersonation successfully. Toward the end, however, a different response began to surface, one that would dominate postproject discussions on the ethics of field technique.

Put simply, most participants came to feel that the artifice was unjustified, that whatever might be learned about the gritty particulars (or even the unexpected grace notes) of street life would be tainted by the method of acquisition. Not surprisingly, the active deception required in direct personal interaction proved more troublesome than the passive version exercised in on-site observation. There may be no better way of documenting spontaneous offers of aid on the street than to be a recipient of such aid oneself, for example, but that doesn't rid one of the sense of having cheapened the gift by virtue of the counterfeit appeal. Moments of shared intimacy, of personal revelation—even when they had been honestly reciprocated by research workers drawing on their own personal histories—were especially likely to provoke guilt and discomfort. Several study participants were nagged by the sense of having tricked people out of what was, for many of them, among their few remaining possessions: their capacity for connecting with another in distress.

We dealt with these issues in an improvised, after-the-fact manner: lengthy group discussions, seminar dissections, and one-on-one consultations. Clearly, much of the problem could have been prevented had I regularly debriefed each participant as she or he left "the field setting" each morning. But time and budget constraints meant that I was running data-gathering efforts in three separate studies simultaneously, and such close oversight was infeasible. In retrospect, that management structure was a mistake. Students and hired hands paid the price, and an outcast trust was betrayed.

The ethics of "disguised observation" in social research have been debated for some time. Classic polar positions were laid out by Kai Erikson and Norman Denzin,[4] but the issues remain far from settled. Anthropological fieldwork that attempts to "study up" or to investigate disavowed cultural beliefs and practices poses the quandary in bold face. This project had hoped to avoid the more troubling of such dilemmas—active deception, as opposed to unobtrusive observation or eavesdropping in consensually defined public settings—by directing the research team to respond honestly to any query about his/her presence there. In the press of the situation, that direction gave way to a determined effort to be as honest as possible without blowing one's cover.[5]

Findings

Much attention has been paid in the press to the deficiencies of the "homeless count" that took place on "S-Night" (March 20–21, 1990). Critics have complained of inadequate coverage of homeless "congregating sites," the erratic performance of street enumerators, and the sometimes surreal presence of the media monitoring the event. Journalistic accounts of the process suggest a great deal of latitude in the frontline interpretations of Census Bureau enumeration instructions. This brief ethnographic study offers an instructive complement to the harried formal count. As efforts have intensified to displace street dwellers from their traditional redoubts, close observation studies, even on the limited scale mounted here, provide data that could inform policy debates on alternatives to the street and enhance efforts to enumerate this population.

Transience and Stability at the Sites

Not only did the ethnographers prove of variable reliability in assessing relative proportions of stable and transient residents at the sites, but the ecology of the sites themselves was quite uneven in permitting such assessments to be made. Sheer visibility of occupants, and the ensuing difficulties of establishing an individual's identity and tracking his/her presence from night to night, was the most frequently encountered problem. Although some ethnographers managed to do it, making the rounds of the premises from time to time to count occupants was out of the question for others.[6] A further problem was the size of a few sites and their resident homeless populations: where we expected large numbers, we divided the site into "zones" and assigned ethnographers to what were, in effect, specific areas of the larger site. Obviously, this introduces difficulties in tracking any individual who may move around within a site from hour to hour or night to night, but who remains "on site" for the duration. Duplication in some instances was unavoidable, and estimates of transience and stability are at best rough measures. With such caveats in mind, in all but one of the nine sites/zones (two sites were divided into two zones) covered, at least 60 percent of an average night's occupants were rated "regulars," present for the great majority of the time our ethnographers were observing that week.

The Order of the Street

Notwithstanding the differences observed from site to site, the most salient lesson to be drawn from this brief study can be put simply: "The street" is not now, if it ever was, synonymous with anarchy. Even here, distinctive rules and routines prevail. Much as the cadre of street dwellers impressed the observers as distinctly "other"—the classic subject of fieldwork—they also met and, in the compressed space of five nights, came to know people who could pass for kin or acquaintances. At several indoor sites, one or two of the "regulars" actively checked out our positioned newcomers and, finding them no threat, offered brief tutorials in the lore of street life. They recounted (at times in painstaking detail) the working "rules" of that space, the schedules and addresses of local soup kitchens, the locations of prized out-of-the-way havens, the names of potential sources of aid. At a train station, a small group of the homeless residents was observed to come to the aid of a commuter suffering an epileptic seizure, while "respectable" passersby passed her by. Beat cops, security guards, and token-booth clerks at certain sites awakened occupants in time for work each day. In places where conviviality stretched well into the night, the observers talked to surprisingly well-read conversationalists and found themselves arguing the relative merits of city shelter and housing policies, debating the value of the census, and bemoaning the state of the job market. Two observers shared the bounty when restaurant workers dropped off leftover baked goods on their way home; two others watched as two members of a wedding party, still in formal attire, made their way into a midtown subway station late one night to offer residents the remnants of the cake.

In contrast to other reports, direct questions of a personal nature—Are you homeless? How did it happen?—were frequently asked of our observers in conversation with other site occupants. Even fragments of family history commonly found their way into casual talk. Whether this had to do with changing norms of interaction on the street, a diminished stigma attached to the condition itself, or specific variations from site to site, we cannot say. Clearly, as journalistic and ethnographic accounts of shantytown dwellers in New York also attest, such a picture contrasts starkly with the received and still prevalent image of homeless individuals as "disaffiliated."[7]

The observations of spontaneous aid and companionship offered by people so obviously needy themselves, so grossly at odds with the predatory picture of homelessness popularly portrayed, merit greater attention. It is worth remarking here that these varied types of assistance were tendered even when the veteran street dweller was suspicious about the reality of the homelessness our researchers professed. There were a few exceptions, as when a snort of dismissal or expression of hostility followed the realization that what one had taken for the genuine article was a poseur instead. Pressed for money by a young man panhandling at the southwest corner of Central Park at 2:30 A.M., a woman researcher offered a spare set of gloves instead—something, apparently, very few homeless persons are in a position to do. The response: "His eyes became hard and he said in a low, vicious voice, 'Get out of here. Get out of here fast. Just get out.'" The ethnographer further comments: "It's as if the truth were written in neon on my face . . . I am clearly a charade—a person privileged enough to play at being homeless . . . A truly homeless person might, understandably, be furious . . ."[8]

In greater detail, significant variation was found from site to site with respect to the following:

- *Norms of behavior and the division of public space*: The dominant site "themes" were three: all-night emporium, stable refuge, party-spot. In larger sites, two or more could coexist in distinct "zones"—as, for example, a clear "no smoking" (of crack) section in one transportation depot. Some areas had specific functional demarcations: a cardboard box was the locus for a brisk trade in drugs throughout the night; a designated track platform where sex could be traded for drugs or money; a section of a waiting room where it was understood that marathon drinking/conversing could take place; an entire subway station where even the insomniacs kept their voices down so as not to disturb the sleep of their compatriots. There were sites (or zones) where quiet was unattained before four in the morning and, in the event, lasted a mere two hours; others where straight (i.e., nonhomeless) traffic continued all night. There were indoor places where great value was attached to a few hours of uninterrupted sleep. "This place is like a dormitory," remarked one observer of a midtown subway station. In the financial district: "This is really a very peaceful station. The regulars keep to themselves and sleep most of the time." An outdoor encampment was remarkable mainly for the mute witness to homelessness given by the cardboard boxes arranged there.[9]
- *Support of companions*: Regardless of the prevailing site ethos, many acts of mutual support were observed, from the simple act of throwing a blan-

ket over a companion who has just passed out, to the more risky business of breaking up fights so as not to attract the attention of police, to the common courtesy of "watch[ing] my things" while someone ran an errand or used the bathroom. At times, it was an articulated ethic of "we take care of [or look out for] each other." More often, it seemed to be a tacit rule of survival. Most perishable foods were readily shared. When midnight soup-runs (delivered by a suburban church) arrived, it was understood that a general reveille would be sounded. Snacks and alcohol especially, but also money and cigarettes,[10] were the most commonly shared items. Even panhandling's yield was at times brought back for collective consumption. Getting sufficient food appeared not to be a problem on the street, given the host of organized and spontaneous charitable sources. Other necessities, less often remarked, remained in scarce supply. For women, for example, menstrual pads or tampons were difficult to obtain and costly, normally available only in the shelters.

- *Ethnicity*: The ethnic mix was pronounced in some sites—a subway station near Wall Street, for example, counted white, African American, Jamaican, Hispanic, and Indian residents one night—and much less so in others. No clear pattern was observed by geography or type of site. Although casually racist slurs (usually by elderly white men about younger black men) were overheard, they were generally not made in the presence of members of the offended group. In the few instances of overt fighting observed, participants appeared to be of the same ethnicity.
- *Gender*: Women constituted a minority on the street, but their relative numbers varied from site to site. Safety and privacy were clearly uppermost in the minds of women residents especially. A number of them sleeping indoors in a transportation terminal were observed carefully fashioning their belongings into the shape of a sleeping figure which they then arranged next to themselves; three elderly Jamaican women assumed regular spots in adjoining toilet stalls in the women's restroom at one terminal and stayed in verbal contact throughout the night. Others, covered with blankets, shawls, sweatshirts, or overcoats, were rendered genderless in the eyes of potentially predatory observers.

Sex was openly traded for money or drugs at a few sites. Impressions are sketchy, but, for the most part, this appeared to be either within group—"You got the wine, you get a ride"—or between residents and their usual suppliers. There were instances (related or observed) when the transaction was clearly commercial.[11] More generally, homeless women appeared to be fair game to all manner of abuse on the street. In five nights, four women on our team were approached by *nonhomeless* men seeking cheap sexual labor. Three were promised room and board in return; a mere cup of coffee was offered the fourth. In each instance, the approach was insistent, so much so in one case that a male homeless companion intervened on the woman's behalf.

- *Responsibility for shared space*: The practice of cleaning up after oneself, removing and storing the traces of bedding in particular, was especially strong in public places given over to alternative use during the daytime. Regulars said that such a practice both ensured continued access and protected their belongings from being thrown away. Clear understandings were in effect in most settings regarding provisions for personal hygiene: public toilets were used (one was kept open by subway maintenance specifically for the purpose); individual containers were filled and discretely emptied into a floor-drain or the street; sections of a space were given over to the purpose (and would-be violators loudly advised of the rule). In only one site, a large outdoor traffic circle/plaza, where residency frequently changed from night to night, was there ambiguity about which areas were to be used for relieving oneself.

The issue of personal space and respect for individual territory is more complex, ranging from the simple gesture of not stepping on another's strip of cardboard in a transportation terminal to familiar rituals of "knocking" on another's makeshift house in more elaborate settings.

- *Support and complicity of cops, clerks, and security guards*: Standing arrangements were observed in two sites where both token-booth clerks and beat cops awakened a few residents for work in the morning. It was apparently common practice to ignore the token drops at turnstiles in subway or ferry stations, and residents were not harassed for the infraction. In at least one site, residents were on a first-name basis with a policeman who took it upon himself to ask paying passengers to move on when they verbally harassed the homeless. (On one such occasion, his partner later distributed muffins, obtained at her expense, to those still awake.)
- *Architecture of improvised shelter*: Homemade housing varied in form and materials used: bedrolls and tarps; cardboard, plastic, and lathing creations; overturned postal carts; mini-hovels—one fashioned from stacked plastic milk bottle carts (filled with magazines for stability) across which boards were laid and under which two canvas postal carts were parked; and substantial structures erected using waste building material, complete with electricity and wood stoves, which did not, to our knowledge, appear on the submitted lists of "addresses" to be covered by the standard census. Our observers also noted what has since been recog-

nized as the widespread practice of homeless people camping out in the locked areas housing automated teller machines in the city's numerous banks.

Violence

Even an observer attuned to the apparent orderliness of much of the nighttime use of public space, however, could not ignore the rough and seamy side of the street. Time and again, the research team found evidence of the traditional scourges of street life.

Trafficking in outlawed substances was commonplace, sometimes done openly and sometimes behind cover. All-night carousing was the norm at a few sites, where the varieties of substance abuse ran the gamut from teenaged "crackheads" to twenty-year veterans of the bottle. The brief bursts of violence (usually clumsy scuffling, though knives and clubs were used on occasion) and staccato rhythms, activity, and talk characteristic of some sites were thought by our observers and some of their homeless companions to be directly related to the consumption of drugs or alcohol.

Random acts of violence made things dicey at times: Two of our observers were dozing on a subway platform not thirty feet from the stairway where another resident's throat was cut early one morning. They learned of it only when signaled by the commotion attending the arrival of an ambulance.[12]

The routine indignities of street life were readily apparent: the precarious status of most makeshift arrangements; the scarcity of common amenities (toilets and places to wash up, the haven of a private spot, tampons for women); the capricious enforcement of antiloitering laws (e.g., forbidding someone to sit on a bench or ridding a subway station of all nighttime occupants); the scorn and verbal abuse of passersby (whether outright harassment or the refusal of a fellow subway rider to acknowledge a polite request for the time of day); the constant vigilance required of an unattached woman. For the most part, these were not articulated complaints, but rather part of the expected costs of life on the street. On occasion, with more regret than bitterness, it was voiced: "You get no respect; [either] people look right through you or they're afraid."[13]

How the Outside World Breaks In

Perhaps most telling—because most unexpected—were the ways in which the outside world, as live presence or memory, intruded. Such intrusions could be either negative (e.g., harassment) or positive (e.g., charity). And sometimes they were just wearying.

In preparing the observers, we had made a point of stressing that such research was not without its peculiar hazards, but had anticipated that the threat (whatever form it might assume) would come from within the sometimes congested ranks of the street dwellers themselves. We had not foreseen that the more vicious and common sources of danger would come from without.

The most frequent disruption was that posed by routine maintenance, often led and bolstered by security. Would-be sleepers in several sites were awakened at odd times during the night and told to move on, so that the space could be hosed down, swept, or otherwise cleaned up. At three indoor sites, accommodations had been reached with the residents: at one, they made their way onto subway trains for the duration of the maintenance; at the two others, the groups moved en masse to sections of the site that had already been cleaned and back again when maintenance was completed. Some residents regularly took part in awakening others and advising them of the impending "time to move"—the same ones, incidentally, who tended to assume the responsibility of notifying others of the arrival of midnight food deliveries.

Less common were instances of police and/or "spree" harassment. With respect to the first: Several instances were reported of police or security guards awakening, forcing sitting persons to stand, or "evicting" residents for no apparent reason other than reminding them that their continued presence there was by no means assured. At times, too, enhanced police presence appeared to be intended to reduce use of this particular site. With respect to the second: On several occasions, packs of young males ran through the sites where our observers were stationed. One group professed loudly to be conducting a "census count"; another yelled and stomped to awaken people in a hallway; a third ran through an open square on the Upper West Side; members of a fourth group confronted individual homeless men and women trying to sleep on the floor of a train station. One of our ethnographers, Dorinda Welle, described the scene:

> At 4:00 A.M., a group of four white teens came through our area, kicking old people, telling them to get a place to live, "get a job," "get a home," "wake up, grandpa," "hey, assholes," "you garbage people," etc. One stole the single roses wrapped tightly in plastic that one sleeping man sells during the day for a dollar each. The teen gave the roses to young women standing by, watching. Then these guys came over to us, looking at me (lying down, but awake and paying attention to their movement). One guy stood at the foot of our blanket and stared down at me. I stared back. D. [a young, African American regular at this

> site] woke up, put his hand on his switchblade in his pocket, but didn't take it out. He looked at me from under his cap brim, signaling me to be cool, be still. I really thought these kids were going to beat us up. Looking the one in the face, I couldn't determine the reason for the hate I saw there—Was it for being homeless? Being female? Being white and homeless? Being white and hanging out with blacks? Finally, I looked at D. again; he seemed to say "Do something . . ." and I said really loudly (but not shouting) so perhaps the cop nearby could hear me: "Get the hell out of my face!" The guy said "bitch," kicking my foot before he slinked off to his friends. D. said: "Good to say it loud. The cops don't want to see anybody get hurt too bad here."[14]

Interactions with outsiders could also be positive, as already alluded to in the citations of assistance and succor extended across the homeless divide. In one subway station, a security guard always addressed the sleeping men there as "gentlemen" when he awoke them so that the night's cleaning could take place. As remarked earlier, token-booth clerks routinely turned a blind eye to homeless patrons passing through turnstiles without paying. The solicitousness of cops toward regular residents was far more impressive than the occasional acts of petty harassment.

The sort of unexpected kinship that could arise between the homeless and nonhomeless is illustrated in an incident involving D. (the same D. mentioned earlier). A young West Indian woman, not homeless herself but new to the city, was visibly distressed at the sight of "all these [homeless] black folks here." D. tried to console her. After establishing that he also had family in St. Thomas, D. gently explained:

> . . . as much as it breaks my heart to be homeless, it really breaks my heart that you have to experience this shock. Let me tell you that nobody wants to be here, but here is where we're safest for now. . . . It's a terrible thing, but you have to understand that we survive, we take care of each other. You have to understand that this is a condition, this homelessness; it's not who we are.[15]

Finally and somewhat more tentatively, the presence of the "outside" world was felt in the tug of memory and in the shape of things hoped for. Anyone who has spent any time talking with street dwellers will know of the loneliness of the street. Nonetheless, our observers were unprepared for encounters with men and women (not much older than they) who told of yearning for intimacy and the privacy to practice it. We hadn't anticipated how much of a "former" life would continue to shadow, even haunt, the survival necessities of street life. "You can't have a relationship when you have no self-respect, no home, no money. You have to take care of yourself, and it'd just drag you down."

Couples were rare in open street sites (not the shanties) and were seen as vulnerable to the manifold threats of the street—male partners were repeatedly warned to keep a close eye on "their" women. One street veteran confided to a mixed-sex pair of observers the location of "a safe spot" in an abandoned bus, hidden in a little-used area of Central Park, where a few hours of uninterrupted privacy might be had.[16]

Implications for Enumeration

The findings of this brief ethnographic study suggest that several modifications are in order if a more accurate estimate of the number of individuals in "selected components of the homeless population" (as the Census Bureau described the objective of S-Night) is to be obtained.

First, as has repeatedly been illustrated in the foregoing account, there are immense logistical difficulties presented when a street "site" is analogized to an "address" and enumerators are dispatched accordingly to do their counting. Descriptive ambiguities abound with respect to the following: the precise location and identifying markers of sites; the boundaries of the area designated by a single site, especially where two or more may be contiguous; the contingencies of access to sites over time; and the still mysterious processes by which congregating sites take shape, are occupied, and the terms of staying or leaving are negotiated with those who have control over such sites. Additional difficulties are introduced by the mobility of site occupants, as evidenced even during the relatively small time window allotted for our study. Further problems arise from the sheer complexity of the site ecologies—such as barriers that may render an occupant "invisible" to an enumerator unfamiliar with the details of the site layout or unwilling to explore its further reaches.

Many, if not most, of these difficulties could be resolved by appropriate use of sampling methodologies and the elimination of the notion of full enumeration. One possibility would be a two-stage process composed of an inventory followed by local counting of sampled sites. A team of research workers would first establish the universe of sites at a time close to that of the subsequent count, preferably stratified by likely numbers of occupants. Statistical techniques analogous to those designed to estimate the number of species in a region would be used to estimate the number of unlocated sites. The field staff would then draw up detailed maps of those sites to be visited, and the same team would be deployed in the actual count or estimation of a sample of the sites identified in the first stage. The results of our brief ethnographic study, combined with those in a companion report, argue strongly for utilizing such statistical approaches to the estimation of the size of fugitive populations rather than raw enumeration with its implied (but spurious) greater precision. The significant progress made in the theory of estimating animal abundance and species suggests that, in combination with statistical techniques specifically designed for the problem at hand, viable alternatives to head counts exist that would be both cost-effective and accurate.[17]

Second, whatever method—enumeration or statistical estimation—is chosen, if sites are to remain the unit of observation, it is essential that the list used be previewed, corrected for inaccuracies, carefully explored to establish the individual areas and boundaries of sites, and that workers be intimately familiar with such areas before the count.

Third, with respect to the problem presented by residents in "shantytowns" who, although present, were "invisible" to enumerators on the night of the count: One immediately practical option would be to add such sites to the list of "addresses" in the "List/enumerate" category to be visited by Census Bureau employees during normal working hours, thus ensuring their coverage.

Fourth, with respect to the Bureau's insistence that only "selected components of the homeless population" would be enumerated: Given the evidence of significant "contamination" by nonhomeless occupants in some sites of what would conventionally be considered a homeless street population, indications that the homeless poor themselves were generally cooperative, and the willingness overall of those approached to admit to being homeless, we would recommend that the Bureau consider using a screening question to establish homeless status, at least in areas where this may be in doubt. The outstanding issue that bulks so large in the enumeration problems presented by poor city residents—What is the incentive to cooperate with a venture from which few benefits appear to derive and to which much suspicion is attached?—did not appear to be a salient feature of 1990 S-Night experiences.[18] Still, how benign can a "dead-of-night" interview be made to appear?

Fifth, one alternative to dead-of-night enumeration is to engage homeless individuals in places where concrete services are offered, under circumstances that are at least more conventional than 3:00 A.M. encounters on the street. Established facilities such as soup kitchens and drop-in centers would be logical choices; however, in places like New York, substantial growth has occurred in mobile services to street populations (food and clothing distribution in particular). Ironically, this may mean that the utility of day service centers as proxy sites for drawing samples of the street-dwelling homeless is compromised in some settings. They are especially questionable for the more disabled and shelter-avoiding individuals of the street population.

Finally, what may be the case with respect to "sites" six months before the count is by no means assured of being so at the time of actual enumeration. A vast array of informal accommodations make for the configuration of street sites at any given point, and the assumption of continuity that underlies the current method of "pre-designated sites" is a risky one.

Impact

Like "the heath" in Shakespeare's time, "the street" in our own has come to signify a kind of close repository of things evil and alien, and that is a badly damaging misrepresentation. For every sidewalk Lear—that reckless, ruined king—for whom the street is a public stage for private demons, there are dozens of others for whom it means a rather complicated way of extracting a livelihood from the waste spaces and discarded resources of the city.[19]

The most direct implication this fact has for enumeration efforts is the obvious one: Any exposure perceived to compromise an already uncertain existence will likely be resisted. Likewise, the incentive to cooperate with an apparently benign procedure (like a well-publicized census) will be enhanced by provision of resources that ease, at least for the moment, the exigencies of street survival. Hence, the prudence of alternatives to wildlife counts that can be linked to desired services and goods.

In response to these and other research-based criticisms (some by the Bureau's own staff, others channeled through the Secretary's Advisory Committee on the Census), the Bureau substantially revised its procedures for Census 2000. There was to be no separate "homeless count." Instead, efforts were redoubled to include all those living in unconventional housing who were likely to be missed in household enumerations. Although the shelter count was retained, an all-out effort to enumerate persons on the street was dropped in favor of two, more focused approaches: (1) a "service-based enumeration" (SBE) visiting soup kitchens, mobile food vans, drop-in centers, and other street-level agencies, and (2) a count of prescouted "targeted, non-shelter outdoor locations" (TNSOL).

The yield of the SBE, in particular, was expected to be mixed: netting nonhomeless users stretching their food budgets and missing homeless patrons who happened not to be there that day. To correct for the former, "usual home elsewhere" was asked for, allowing for unduplication when matched against household rosters compiled during the regular census. To correct for the latter, a modification of a statistical technique ("multiplicity estimation"), developed to gauge total service use from a one-time count, was to be tested. (If the habits of present-time users are known—number of times this and other sites are visited in the course of a week—the total universe of users can be estimated.) If successful, this innovative estimation technique would have gone some way to adjusting for the long-criticized deficiencies of a one-shot count.

In practice, the multiplicity estimation proved a bust. Part of the problem (to judge from an admittedly limited sample in New York City[20]) was due to uneven preparation on the ground. (Operational logistics for tracking a mobile food service, for example, were a shambles.) Part doubtless reflected local officialdom. (New York's largest public shelters, for example, were counted by assembling administrative data *in advance* of the census.) But the chief culprit may turn out to be long-standing suspicion of the purpose behind any unexpected government question. This may be why a quarter of the use-pattern questions on the specialized Census 2000 forms for the SBE were left blank. Those who did respond, especially in the shelters, either misunderstood the question or mistrusted its intent: three-quarters reported using a shelter only one night a week, a figure markedly at odds with other studies on shelter use.[21]

Predictably, too, an aggregate figure for the updated "homeless count" was released, up 23 percent from the 1990 figure. But to the distress of some localities, the Bureau initially refused to provide figures for "homeless populations" by city and state.[22] Eventually, the figures for emergency and transitional shelter counts (but not SBE) were released by locality—along with this caveat: ". . . these figures do not constitute and should not be construed as a count of people without conventional housing."[23] The shelter number (170,706) amounted to 61 percent of the previously reported total. Where the others resided, and under what auspices, is anyone's guess.

[6]

Homelessness and African American Men

> The question of Blacks and Skid Row has been a blind spot for social investigators.
>
> Leonard Blumberg, Thomas Shipley, and Stephen Barsky, *Liquor and Poverty*

Thirty-five years ago, Elliot Liebow drew an unforgettable portrait of a group of African American men in Washington, D.C., who congregated at a carryout shop in a poor section of town. The men of "Tally's corner" were largely unskilled or low-skilled workers, intermittently employed at "hard, dirty, uninteresting and underpaid" jobs. It was the quietly corrosive effects of such marginal work that most interested Liebow. For one of these men to contemplate the job, he surmised, was "to see himself as others see him, to remind him of just where he stands in this society." Over time, the damage done was apparent in the men's scuttled hopes, cramped ambitions, and diminished sense of self. Its recoil was felt in family and neighborhood life as well, where impulsive action, explosive rages, and ragged relations with women were the rule. By the standards of the dominant culture, theirs was an irregular way of life. But it was one with a hidden surety. Uncertainty may have harried their patterns of formal affiliations and modes of work, but these men did not want for necessities. Despite the "fluidity and change" that marked social relationships in the street-corner world, despite the often ephemeral ties of friendships, despite the apparent haphazardness of household composition, despite these myriad tokens of what might strike a casual observer as "disorder," these informal networks were of proven resiliency. The men who gathered on Tally's corner were rarely homeless.[1]

Although traces of the "effortless sociability" that characterized the daily round at Tally's corner can still be found, both the larger economy and black folk culture have become less hospitable to the men—the young men, especially—who once idled in such companies, secure in the knowledge of backup resources of extended kin and friends. The casual labor pools and pick-up employments that had once sustained street-corner men are all but depleted, and, in some places at least, their families are less likely to tolerate mischief making, drug dealing, criminal enterprise, and other types of "messing up."[2] Today, it is "the street" as much the "corner" where young black males with time on their hands are likely to be found. At no time in American history have so many of them been homeless.

Framing the Discussion

Anthropologists search out signature traces of meaning, utility, and power in cultural beliefs and behavior. The discipline's cardinal article of faith is that the intelligibility of practice can only be grasped in relation to context—its "local moral world," as some have taken to characterizing "culture." Values, customs, and daily routines must not only be carefully documented but also situated. Context not only lends color and particularity, it also provides the necessary field of boundaries and contingencies, framing constraints, and insistent pressures within which lives, hopes, choices, and identities take shape.[3]

Placing overt homelessness in context means examining the larger transformation of American cities over the past three decades, a transformation that makes for the distinctive marginality of young African American men. I refer not only to the consolidation of a service-based labor market with its polarized wage structure, the persistent rise of female-headed households, and the new strains on extended kin, but also to the restructuring of urban space into increasingly segregated residential zones, contested public places, ever more costly housing stock. Global forces are reshaping local markets and habitats, creating new spaces and amalgamations where the usual categories of distinction no longer apply.[4]

Because this chapter focuses on African American homeless men, the discussion must also be placed within the enduring legacy of racism in this country. And here we encounter the first of what will prove a number of *sub*marginalizations in this account. Over the past two decades, coming to terms with black homelessness has been relegated to a minor sideshow of the larger (and largely segregated) debates about "the underclass." As Jennifer Hochschild notes, these debates are "usually disguised battles about race"; they are also tacit expressions of the subordination of poverty to color.

The consignment of the bulk of discussion of single black male poverty to the underclass heading illustrates what happens when perceived menace gets the better of pathos.[5]

As an anthropologist, I should take special note of limitations in the ethnographic record that bear on African American homelessness. Longitudinal studies have shown contemporary homelessness to be largely transient or episodic.[6] If "residential instability" is the proper frame, attention to the routine, everyday strategies of survival practiced in poor neighborhoods would seem to be de rigueur. Given their overrepresentation in urban homeless populations,[7] members of black households should be of special interest. Yet, with a handful of notable exceptions,[8] urban ethnographers in the 1980s and early 1990s ignored the community and kinship contexts of African American "ghetto" life—its formations and flows under circumstances of concentrated poverty and residential segregation. Our understanding of recurring patterns of improvised or "doubled-up" residence among this group is sparse.[9] This account of the dynamics of homelessness among black American males is poorer in consequence.

The Historical Record

The decisive features of vagrancy that catapult it onto the stage of public attention are scale and visibility. Once afoot in sufficient numbers, homeless men have customarily been treated as a threat to be contained—whether because they openly challenged the work ethic, implicitly mocked the family and the claims of kinship, or were read as portents of more insidious social disorder. Vagrancy typically becomes a social problem when too many footloose men, unable to "give good account" of themselves, make nuisances of themselves instead, either through the sheer spectacle of their presence or the insistence of their begging.

For black men on the road, scale and visibility presented additional difficulties, among them rank discrimination by both police and proprietors catering to homeless men. Thus, concealment was among the necessary skills of those who did take to the road. This fact is unfortunate for attempts to reconstruct that ill-recorded history. But this is only the first of two kinds of invisibility, an empirical absence that lasts roughly from the Reconstruction Era (late 1860s) to the 1970s. In police station and shelter records, in tables assembled by research studies, and in memoirs of road life, when black men are mentioned at all, they are a tiny (if distinctive) minority. But the absence isn't uniform, or else this account would be very brief. Striking exceptions do appear, as during the Great Depression. More curious, a postwar skid row literature professed to find black homelessness extremely rare, even when its own empirical accounts told a different story. This second kind of invisibility, from the 1970s to the present, is plainly ideological. In this period, while the numbers of black men on the road, in the shelters, and on the streets have steadily grown, their representation in the public discourse of homelessness remains erratic at best, a passing mention as a rule.[10]

Early History

The earliest link between African Americans and homelessness was forged by punishment, not poverty. Colonial poor laws treated the wandering poor as suspect, possibly dangerous, a potential drain on local funds. They shared a symbolic kinship with the slave because "both were perceived as set apart from the rest of society and unlikely to labor unless they were forced to do so." Vagrancy codes frequently targeted "recalcitrant or runaway servants or slaves." Hence, the original New York City "House of Correction, Workhouse and Poorhouse" (1734) was not only a place where the terminally ill were nursed, deserted children put up, and the luckless and friendless quartered; it was also where runaway slaves were jailed.[11] That symbolic kinship persisted into the early 1800s. When street begging became a growing nuisance, the city charged four officers with detaining "for examination all vagrants, Negroes, common prostitutes, and other persons whom they suspect have not gained a legal settlement."[12]

For the most part, though, African American men are conspicuous by their absence in standard accounts of American homelessness. In the antebellum period, only in major urban areas such as Philadelphia, where blacks accounted for as much as half of the arrested vagrants, was their presence notable. Even in the surge of tramping that followed the Civil War, in most regions they appear to have been rare. Black men constituted less than 1 percent of the "tramp census" conducted by John McCook in the late nineteenth century, made up only 2 percent of turn-of-the-century tramp cohorts in Chicago and Minneapolis, and were all but invisible in Progressive era accounts of lodging houses and road life.[13]

This "absence," however, turns out to be more apparent than real. Given the numbers involved, the exceptions found in the historical record may well attest to a substantial and widely distributed presence. To understand how such a conclusion follows, a brief word about "tramping"—the style of homelessness that prevailed from the 1870s to the 1920s—is necessary.

Tramping was a way of paying tribute to the necessity of work while doing so (at least in part) on one's own terms. For all but the dissolute, it was a young man's game, and a risky one at that. One survived on the road by one's wits, trusting to the hospitality of strangers, scavenging when necessary, dodging the police, hoping for a stint of (usually dirty) work at the end. Black men were at a decided disadvantage on all four counts. Not surprisingly, much of the little we know of African Americans on the road in the late nineteenth and early twentieth centuries comes from police records. W.E.B. Du Bois noted in *The Philadelphia Negro* (1899) that blacks were overrepresented in that city's vagrancy arrest rolls after a long period of intense prejudice. Over 10 percent of Washington, D.C.'s police station house lodgers from 1891–1895 appear to have been black ("nonwhite"). The same is true of vagrancy arrests in Omaha from 1887–1913 and charity lodging house occupants in Philadelphia in 1905. A third of Kansas City's transients in that era were reportedly black.[14]

The black presence was larger among tramps in the south, although never in fractions larger than their representation in the local population. Edward Franklin Frazier devoted a chapter of *The Negro Family in the United States* (1939) to the lifeways of those "roving men and homeless women" who took to the road following emancipation and whose ranks had increased significantly in the 1920s.[15] After reviewing an impressive range of records, memoirs, and reports, Kenneth Kusmer concludes not only that blacks were well represented among tramping workers in the post–Civil War period but also that the "egalitarian nature of the [tramping] culture" made road life especially attractive to them.[16] But if the racial divide was relaxed among (at least some) homeless men on the road, the same cannot be said of the establishments catering to them, where strict discrimination remained the rule. Even in Chicago, mecca of the black migration north, homeless black men were restricted to segregated "colored men's hotels" in the city's free-wheeling "hobohemia" or were summarily referred to the Urban League.[17]

The Great Depression

During the Great Depression of the 1930s, black homelessness assumed dimensions that could not be ignored. By the winter of 1932–1933, nearly 25 percent of the "homeless transients" served in Philadelphia were black, as were 10 percent of Chicago's shelter men. Across the country, between 7 and 12 percent of the local caseloads of "unattached" men (the contemporary equivalent of homeless) assisted through the federal Transient Relief Program were black. Such numbers are misleading, for black men on the move during the Depression took pains to avoid relief centers because of what they experienced as the thin line between transience (a social status) and vagrancy (a civil offense punishable by a term in jail or the workhouse).

One black migrant worker recalled being "in jail two-thirds of the time" while hoboing. And although some report that the color line tended to fade among men sharing the road, a memoir of that time raises questions about the extent to which wandering men shed their prejudices.[18]

The documentation for Depression-era New York City is especially revealing. Compared to their white counterparts, black homeless men were nearly a decade younger on average, were more mobile, left home earlier, had less schooling, had been unemployed longer, and were in better health (probably reflecting their age). Black homeless men were also more likely to be married and less likely to be native New Yorkers. Although they comprised only 5 percent of the adult male population in the city, they made up 15 percent of the public shelter clientele in June 1931, owing in part to the scarcity of private facilities for black homeless men.[19] Of 125 men arrested on vagrancy charges over a thirty-day period and referred for casework to a new "Mendicancy Project" at the workhouse on Welfare Island, 9 percent were black. In western New York State, blacks made up fully a fifth of "landsmen [i.e., nonseamen] transients" in Buffalo and outnumbered whites among native-born homeless men in Lackawanna. Black men were similarly overrepresented in Pittsburgh, though not in Washington, D.C., or Houston. For the most part, an unpublished report by Nels Anderson concluded, such men "were generally left to their own devices to seek shelter in private homes or to sleep out."[20]

Another unpublished report offers a glimpse of how such men fared at the time:

> The Negro drifter on New York City is not given to living in "jungle" [i.e., hobo] camps. He prefers to get his food by "sponging" from friends, begging, or doing odd chores of a few hours' duration. For sleeping quarters during warm weather he finds shelter on the docks of the East River, on the Harlem River water-front between 126 Street and 150 Street, in empty rooms, lofts and basements in Harlem, in the subway stations along the Lenox Avenue line, or perhaps he rides the subway or elevated trains a few hours. During the winter of 1930–31 some of them live in an improvised shelter in a wreckage pile on Park Avenue between 133 Street and 134 Street. In colder months of the year they often prevail upon friends or acquaintances to let them sleep in an unoccupied basement or loft. Charity organizations in Harlem take care of a daily average of about 130. . . . On even the coldest nights some can be found sleeping on the benches . . . [21]

Relief rolls and case registers are thus unreliable gauges with which to take the measure of African American homelessness during the Depression. For in addition to these official "transients" were "many more highly mobile solitary men and women [who] without the aid of relief ma[d]e their living by both lawful and unlawful means . . .".[22]

The Postwar Period

War has few peers when it comes to full employment programs, particularly for men whom the market has little use for. Black homeless men were part of the exodus from relief rolls that the wartime economy spurred in the early 1940s, an exodus that effectively transformed "hobohemia" from a reservoir of casual labor into "a place where the impoverished, the disesteemed, and the powerless [could] take refuge and find comfort." Oddly, postwar scholarship on "skid row" paid scant heed to African American men—because, so the occasional commentary would have it, they weren't there. This absence was commonly attributed to the combined effects of discrimination in commercial lodging houses and the accommodating tendencies of black communities.[23] The latter point, though overdrawn, merits emphasis. Despite their poverty and recurrent joblessness, black men did *not* show up in great numbers on skid row thanks largely to timeworn, informal kin- and neighborhood-based networks of support that sustained newly migrating refugees from the American south.[24] Not only were the bonds of extended kinship resilient, but its boundaries elastic as well. It was not unusual for boarders, for example, to be included as family; "adopted relatives" were common. Outside the family proper, mutual aid societies, storefront churches, and "improvement associations" played crucial roles.[25] The redundancy of such "backup" resources proved vital to the self-sufficiency of newly transplanted communities (a fact noted as early as Reconstruction), and largely explains why, in the face of substantial and persisting need, migrating African Americans maintained a lower profile than northern-born blacks in the postwar welfare rolls.[26]

Close studies did reveal a stubborn African American presence in those urban "zones of discard" that skid rows occupied, and in numbers that could rival Depression figures. Nearly 20 percent of incarcerated inebriates in Rochester, New York, were black in the mid-1950s. Black men made up 22.3 percent of the "skid row case load" in New York City in 1955, a percentage thought to be increasing in the early 1960s, when the city's "nonwhite" population stood at 14.7 percent of the total. (An unpublished report estimated that the percentage of blacks among new "entrants" to the Bowery more than doubled between 1955 and 1964, from 18 to 39 percent.)[27] Nor was New York exceptional: In the late 1950s, one-ninth of Chicago's estimated twelve thousand skid row men were black, most residing in segregated districts or facilities; two-fifths of the men showing up for a free breakfast at a Philadelphia church hostel in 1964 were black; half of them had some housing, but 39 percent had just come from sleeping in all-night theaters.[28]

Most relevant here, in the mid-1960s, researchers from Columbia University's Bureau of Applied Social Science consistently found that a substantial minority (29 percent) of Bowery men were black and that some traditional skid row institutions catered to them. Estimates by key informants (lodging house clerks) and actual dead-of-night enumerations put the proportion of blacks among men along the Bowery proper at about a quarter. Two (out of nineteen) Bowery bars catered almost exclusively to a black clientele. "Spot labor" employment agencies served black as well as white men. A fifth of the homeless men in local hospitals were black ("nonwhite") and 25 percent of Camp LaGuardia inmates (a city shelter located sixty miles north) were black.[29] Four years later, the same research group estimated that black men (younger on average than their white counterparts) accounted for nearly a third of the Bowery population, more than twice what it had represented a decade earlier. Such findings, novel enough to catch the attention of the local press, were ignored by their scholar–authors.[30] The only notice given in the definitive volume on the Columbia project was the near-throwaway comment that the Bowery was "probably 'darker' than most skid rows in northern cities."[31]

At that time, too, "the remnant of a skid row" could still be discerned along 125th Street in upper Manhattan. More interesting for our purposes is the report by a graduate student on the Columbia project that makeshift accommodations (such as the practice of men living in basements as building superintendent "helpers") were commonplace in Harlem at that time.[32] This observation and others like it convinced some analysts that the relative invisibility of black men on postwar skid rows was due to misclassification and not missing men.

Missing Men or Hidden Homeless?

Such analysts argued that searching for black "skid rows" was a misguided venture, premised on an ecological fallacy that identified homelessness with distinct neighborhoods. Investigators would be better served, they said, by searching instead for "skid row–like men" among the "ranks of the more amorphous destitute residents of the slums."[33] Simply taking inventory of the signature feature of "skid-rowness" (addiction coupled with extreme poverty), they argued, would reveal the category error that concealed the extent of this problem in African American communities. Such suspicions proved correct: Drug and alcohol abuse alongside a hand-to-mouth existence were common enough. But this obscures the more instructive point. The differences between makeshift residential arrangements found in the black community and formal institutionalized homelessness are as profound as the similarities.

In the early 1970s on the South Side of Chicago, for example, "skid row–like" men (dirt poor, out of work, heavy drinkers) could regularly be found hanging out on street corners. Practices like panhandling and "bottle gang" drinking further confirmed that kinship and distinguished them from other "respectable" men—men who could claim some "visible means of support"—with whom they shared the corner. For "wineheads," food and shelter paled in urgency next to the necessity of procuring another "taste." When "backup" resources gave out, such men would walk the streets all night or snatch brief periods of sleep in parked cars. Some did seasonal work; others traded sex for room and board. Still, relatively few black men showed up on Chicago's skid row.[34]

Similar observations were made about unattached black men living in New York City's SRO hotels in the late 1960s and early 1970s, just before that stock began its precipitous decline. Despite sharing some distinctive afflictions (poverty and addiction) and practices (gang-drinking), the men living in such dwellings were described by their chroniclers and their contemporaries as different from ("a social cut above") their counterparts on the Bowery. The SRO was an "alternative" to skid row, a place where on occasion truly "homeless people . . . wander[ed] [to] use the hotel bathrooms, especially the bathtubs, to sleep in."[35]

If we aim to understand the unprecedented rise of black homelessness in the mid-1970s, there is a difference worth preserving between a mode of subsistence that manages exigency through careful husbanding—or, for that matter, reckless exploitation—of indigenous resources and one that is forced to petition the bounty of the state. These are not mutually exclusive ways of life, of course; people commonly arrive at shelters after having exhausted the resources of kin and family. The issue (one that holds for much homelessness research in general) isn't troubled people or desperate circumstances, but rather how the risk gets buffered, the hardship distributed, or, failing that, how the bureaucracy of relief enters the picture.[36] It's not vagrants or shelters alone, but the prior configurations of livelihoods and households—means and connectedness—and how they unravel and repair, off-load and disown, get betrayed and wear down, or never solidify in the first place. Because it speaks to practices, the stuff of culture, the distinction between an invisibly struggling poor and an officially recognized homeless is useful, not an error of geography.

As the twentieth century ended, racial discrimination remained the rule in many flophouses. "Old Bowery men" were still predominantly white. But a different picture prevailed in the public shelters and missions.[37] A sea change had occurred. As the grubby haunt of elderly white men, the Bowery was already in decline by the early 1970s. By that decade's end, new recruits would transform the place.

African Americans among the Homeless Poor of the 1990s

By the mid-1970s, it was clear to shelter workers in New York City that both the decades-old demography of the Bowery and the dynamics of homelessness were in flux. Between 1966 and 1976, the proportion of the annual caseload at the Men's Shelter made up of first-time users rose from 28 to 48 percent. The new arrivals were much younger than their predecessors, half were black, and most left within months of their arrival (skid row men had typically left in a coffin). By the early 1980s, at least two-thirds of regular shelter users were African American.[38]

Nor was New York exceptional. Throughout the 1980s, researchers consistently found that black males (and especially young black men) were overrepresented among local homeless populations. Fully 41 percent of the 1990 Census Bureau "S-Night" count of residents in shelters were African American, as were 39 percent of those on the streets and in abandoned buildings. The proportion of blacks among *homeless* Vietnam-era veterans is three times that among general Vietnam-era veterans. A review of sixty studies conducted during the 1980s found that, on average, 44 percent of the researched homeless populations were black.[39]

As skid row's populace changed, so did its institutions, especially the public shelters. Formerly seedy retirement communities for men without means or family, shelters came to perform a dual service: seeing to the immediate needs of those who show up at their doors and providing respite to families who would otherwise shoulder their support. Urban shelters effectively took over functions formerly assumed by extended kin. In some poor, minority neighborhoods of New York City, they served as "community bedrooms," especially for difficult household members.[40]

Long-term studies revealed a developmental logic to this practice. In a twenty-year study in Boston, Peter Hainer describes how "transience" is accommodated in an African American folk model of kinship. Periods of residential instability are understandably common among young black men. Owing to what are perceived as their "naturally" disruptive tendencies, even flexibly configured and generous households find it difficult to extend to them the hospitality normally accorded kin. And so, for a while, they

> live a kind of vagabonding existence with age mates . . . [who] support and help each other, as they live "on the street," often as "homeless" people in abandoned buildings, in low rent apartments with their "brothers," or moving in and out of various family apartments.[41]

They learn to shift for themselves while their families practice an economy of makeshifts, ejecting (or passing on) these men in the interest of household stability and peace.

At the same time, public shelters were beginning to function not only as places of rough sanctuary but as flourishing nodes of informal exchange—as institutions of trade, sustenance, and even transient community for the sometimes working poor. Such places were readily incorporated into the "vagabonding existence" of young black men on the move.[42]

Making Sense of Homelessness among African American Men

The factors that account for the rise of homelessness among black males are the same ones that explain persisting poverty in that population—and then some. Poverty in 1990s America was still distinctively weighted by color: The proportion of blacks living under the official poverty line[43] was three times that of whites (28 versus 8.8 percent); nearly half of all black children resided in poor households, a figure four times that for white children. More seriously, 38 percent of black children remained poor for at least six years, a rate more than seven times that of white children. Among African Americans, too, income divisions had widened. Residential segregation, long a unique feature imposed on black American communities, showed little sign of receding; segregation in schooling had increased. Intermarriage rates between African Americans and other racial/ethnic groups remained anomalously low. So firmly embedded is the racial divide in U.S. society that a book on race in the early 1990s borrowed a phrase from the Kerner Commission report of 1968—"separate and unequal"—for its subtitle.[44]

But why did extreme poverty in the late twentieth century increasingly take the form of homelessness among young black males, especially in light of the robust legacy of the black extended family? The few accounts that explicitly examined the linkage between race and homelessness offer some clues. A study in Ohio found that, compared to whites, homeless black respondents were younger, had somewhat better schooling, were more likely to be Vietnam veterans, were longer-term local residents, and were more recently homeless; they were also "more likely to move in and out of homeless conditions." Like the pattern in African American poverty generally, recurring homelessness tended to be less "event-driven" than a matter of "reshuffling." A Detroit study found homeless African Americans more likely than whites to have sustained ties with relatives and to have been in alcohol or drug detoxification units, jail, or prison, but less likely to have a psychiatric history. Although frequently resorting to makeshift alternatives with friends and families, blacks nonetheless accounted for a third of a Birmingham sample; blacks in a neighboring city were disinclined to use local missions and so were overrepresented on the street. Racial/ethnic differences were less clear in Chicago, where both black and Hispanic families were "more likely [than whites] to subsidize their dependent adult members."[45]

Work and kinship remain critical gauges of the risk of homelessness. In some regions, decades-old trends in segmented labor markets have been exacerbated by the growth of the informal sector and influx of new immigrants, who compete for cheap housing and menial jobs in service and "downgraded manufacturing" sectors.[46] In the 1980s and early 1990s, single males especially were disadvantaged by the growing scarcity of affordable housing and cutbacks in income-maintenance programs for the unattached and/or disabled poor. By that time, too, a cultural turn had occurred in the guise of the "underclass" debate—that ghetto residents were beset not only by "concentrated" poverty but by singularly disabling cultural deficits as well.

Trends in the Labor Market

But for a brief upturn at the end, during the last quarter of the twentieth century, rates of unemployment, underemployment, and long-term joblessness for black males rose dramatically. This was especially true for young men and any who lacked timely skills or adequate schooling. Since the mid-1970s, earnings of young black males relative to whites had steadily deteriorated, across all education groups. In the central cities, the picture was even bleaker. If one included discouraged and involuntary part-time workers, nearly a quarter of black males were jobless in the first quarter of 1992, twice the rate of white men. Even this figure misrepresents, owing to the number of black men behind bars: nearly half of all state/federal correctional inmates in June 1991 were black, a rate nearly four times their representation in the general population.[47]

Economists debated the reputed causes of the dismal employment prospects of the black worker, but few questioned the severity or the tenacity of the trend. When the percentage of black men of prime laboring age who are idle leaps *fivefold*—from 6.8 to 32.7 percent—from 1963–1965 to

1985–1987,[48] doubt is reserved for the professionally contrary. Explanations ranged from changes in the supply of workers (skills, wage expectations, acceptable work) in local and global settings, to the effects of plant relocation or closure, to changing demands on workers within industries or occupations (tending toward both high-end "information processing" and low-end work in service or downgraded manufacturing), to the competing lure of "underground" or other "nonwork" sources of income, to the continuing preference of employers for nonblack workers. In none of these scenarios could the enabling hand of government in shaping the postwar job and housing markets be ignored.

Whatever the proper proportions of causal ingredients in this instance, the preemptive power of aggregate labor market demand is evident. Two studies from Boston showed that a tight local labor market substantially improved the employment picture for young black men in the inner city, especially those with poor education. Poverty rates declined as well.[49] Such findings confirmed survey research showing the work ethic to be alive and well in minority neighborhoods. They animated enthusiasts of full-employment policy, despite the dismal history of efforts to implement it. And, in the late 1990s, they received an unexpected real-world boost, with the upsurge of young black employment in a recovering economy.[50]

Absent that substantial economic upturn, exactly how and where to stimulate demand was a much-vexed issue. Take, for example, the findings grouped under the "spatial mismatch" hypothesis. Thirty years ago, John Kain first argued that the "postwar dispersal" of jobs to the suburbs, coupled with persisting (if not worsening) patterns of residential segregation, meant that black employment prospects, already handicapped by employer discrimination and poor education, could well deteriorate. Studies of cities undergoing deindustrialization showed that job displacement and job elimination occurred much earlier and more severely for African American blue-collar workers. But was race or location at fault? Ironically, black gains in manufacturing in the industrial North in the immediate postwar period meant that they were disproportionately employed by industries that had stagnated or declined since then. Whether they were auto workers in Detroit, steel workers on the South Side and West Side of Chicago, production workers in Philadelphia, or blue-collar operatives in New York City, the effect was the same; only the scale of plant closures and lost jobs varied. Outside the rust belt, "deproletarianization" was not so widespread and played less of a role in the economic fortunes of blacks in the 1970s. Still, four cities in the industrial North accounted for 35 percent of the ghetto poor in 1980. By then, other factors were at work as well.[51]

Two "cultural" aspects of the changing work environment merit note here. First are the secondary costs that a dearth of laboring men imposes on a local neighborhood. Fewer workers mean a reduced supply of those vital informal connections to entry-level positions for the upcoming generation of job seekers. It also means a loss of visible embodiments of respectability, of handy means to enforce informal social sanctions, and of object lessons dispelling the notion that playing by the rules is just for chumps. Second, service-sector work imposes a different kind of discipline than that demanded by blue-collar work. Proper attitude and comportment matter more. Performance standards are more personalized. Greater visibility and more frequent customer contact not only up the ante on appearance and demeanor but also restrict the time and space available for compensatory face-saving maneuvers and curtail the worker's ability "to stamp [the job] as his own."[52]

In a culture that places a high premium on work for males, prolonged periods of enforced idleness damages self-esteem and erodes the regard of others. Nor were legitimate "nonwork" sources of support any refuge for able-bodied men in the early 1990s. Unemployment benefits were reaching a smaller proportion of the jobless than at any time in the prior twenty years. State-administered "general assistance" (GA) programs were devalued by inflation and cut by governments throughout the 1980s and early 1990s. In not a single one of forty-four metropolitan areas were maximum monthly GA benefits sufficient to meet fair market rent for an efficiency apartment.[53]

All this made it increasingly unlikely that jobless young black males could meet their responsibilities for shared household expenses. Kinship may be flexible, but tested by time and trouble its patience knows bounds.

Changes in the Black Extended Family

Kinship has historically provided the first line of defense against misfortune and the bedrock of social security. In times of turmoil, loss, relocation, and adaptation to new forms of work, kin ties provide the indispensable connections to obligated others—"diffuse, enduring solidarity"—that enable people to carry on. Its resources are myriad. Its claims may be contested but are difficult to ignore. Local and geographically dispersed members may be brought into play. And even long-dormant ties can prove available in times of trouble. But maintaining kinship takes work, and that crucial labor is typically performed (and regulated) by women. The point, critical to an understanding of "social capital," is that kinship cannot simply be inserted into the subsistence equation as a bankable asset. Its circuits of obligation and reciprocity require proper maintenance and cultivation.[54]

Bondage imposed singular difficulties on African American families, difficulties that did not end with Emancipation. Even so, the celebrated legacy of the black family is one of resiliency and innovation. Its "flexibility and strength" not only anchored the Great Migration north, but continue to distinguish present-day black communities. If details of slave family culture remain to be clarified; if, in their zeal to correct a portrait of black family life as little more than a "tangle of pathology," some analysts have underplayed the toil, trouble, and strain inherent in managing extended households; if too little attention has been paid to the uneven ledgers of reciprocity in practice and the difficulties of extracting oneself from overdemanding networks—if, in short, too much has been made of the contrivances of kinship and too little of its costs—still, the strength and durability of kinship in the black community are undeniable.[55]

What strains the ties that bind are not the normal processes of economic growth, but the dislocations that arise from irregular or suddenly interrupted employment. In the 1970s, such households suffered severe setbacks, which then worsened in the next decade. Between 1969 and 1979, the prevalence of extended households among the urban jobless or marginally employed increased by 24 percent (from 17 to 21 percent); among blacks, the increase was 44 percent (from 18 to 26 percent). At the same time, if one sets aside public "transfer payments," their pooled ability to raise household income above poverty level was nearly halved. In 1969, 30 percent of extended household heads earned sufficient income to lift them above the poverty line, but an additional 39 percent of such households were kept out of poverty by the combined effect of other family earnings and the contributions of nonfamily household members. In 1979, by contrast, fewer extended households (24 percent) avoided poverty through the earnings of their heads, and just over another fifth (22.5 percent) were held above poverty by ancillary earnings and nonfamily contributions.[56]

Domestic social capital had been pummeled. This "precipitous decline in the antipoverty effectiveness" of the informal resources of extended households meant that substantially more people were at risk of displacement and homelessness. For a while, a series of makeshift accommodations, "reshuffling" the burden of support, may have sufficed to keep frank homelessness at bay. But faced with a renewed assault on its carrying capacity from both the market and the state in the 1980s, even families renowned for their tenacity and resourcefulness in the face of adversity were courting exhaustion. To judge from shelter demographics, many of the single men they put up arrived with a serious drug or alcohol problem, suffered from a severe psychiatric disorder, or confronted the reentry problems of an ex-offender—none of which can have eased the prior burden on kin.[57]

Housing

Highway construction, mortgage guarantees, revisions in the tax code to allow write-offs for property taxes and mortgage interest, assessment practices biased against urban areas—all of these reveal the heavy hand of the federal government in the postwar suburban housing boom in the United States. Race, not merely geography, was also a factor. Housing development in the last fifty years betrays the actions of a government "anxious to use its power and resources for the social control of racial minorities." Its legacy is a pattern of residential segregation tenacious enough to earn the appellate "American apartheid."[58]

Affordability and habitability in the dwellings of the urban poor have suffered in consequence. In the past twenty years, the rental housing gap—the number of available, affordable units relative to the need—has widened appreciably.[59] Nationwide, in 1990 an estimated 5.1 million low-income households were classified by the Department of Housing and Urban Development (HUD) as having "worst case housing needs." Their incomes were below 50 percent of the area median, *and* they paid at least half their income on housing or lived in severely substandard dwellings, or both. As a rule, federal housing subsidies fail to offset affordability difficulties for poor families, fewer than a fifth of whom live in subsidized units. Nearly two-thirds of welfare households live in unsubsidized housing and pay over half of their income for the privilege; a third of that housing is "substandard." Blacks are much more likely than whites to live in physically deficient or overcrowded dwellings, and nearly three-quarters of poor black households pay more than 30 percent of income for housing.[60]

A more telling measure is "shelter poverty." This refers to households who, having met their housing costs, are unable to satisfy nonhousing needs at a minimal level of adequacy. By this standard, approximately *half* of all black households were shelter poor in 1972–1991, a rate 20 percentage points higher than that of all households. Blacks account for only 11 percent of total households, but make up 19 percent of shelter-poor households.[61]

Precariously housed poor households are obviously limited in their capacity to offer assistance to others. Of more direct relevance to the residential options of young black men is the fate of low-cost residential hotels, which had provided housing of last resort for people whose habits and incomes complicated the business of making ends meet. In the 1970s, fueled by gentrification and urban "revitalization" movements, that stock was virtually depleted in many large urban areas. Nationwide, an early estimate placed the loss of units of "one and two rooms lacking facilities" during the 1970s at over a million, or nearly half the total. Subsequent studies, detailing the loss in specific cities, have generally confirmed this estimate. Options for poor singles in New York narrowed considerably. Nearly two-thirds of low-cost residential hotel units were lost (to conversions, abandonment, demolition) between 1975 and 1981.[62]

SROs were not the only stock hit hard. Between 1978 and 1987 in New York City, low-rent units declined by 26 percent; vacancies in that range fell by 72 percent. During the same period, the pool of poor renters increased slightly, and the income distribution grew more polarized. Housing stock losses and inflation coupled to reduce the supply of units affordable by households on public assistance by 60 percent. Notwithstanding modest gains in the prior two decades, compared to whites, in the late 1980s black renter households were still five times as likely to be occupying dilapidated units, three times as likely to be overcrowded, and more than twice as likely to be living in physically inadequate conditions. At the same time, signs of owner disinvestment (the withdrawal of essential services, failure to pay taxes, or defaulting on mortgage payments) were found in one of every six rental properties, all concentrated in poor neighborhoods with high proportions of African American and Latino residents. During the same period, public shelters expanded from a single Bowery-based intake center in 1979 to two dozen facilities scattered throughout four boroughs. Nightly shelter census topped ten thousand in the late 1980s.[63]

Not known for their irony, some poverty analysts took to referring to shelters as the public housing initiative of the 1980s.

Culture

Serious research on African American communities in the United States all but halted in the early 1970s in the wake of the bitter dispute over the "culture of poverty." The exceptions that subsequently appeared were for the most part corrective in nature, bent on countering the image of the dysfunctional black family. By default, power to define the terms of the renewed debate in the early 1980s was ceded to conservative scholars. When rejoined in the 1990s, the debate was fueled by free-wheeling comments on underclass ways of life, blunt calls for rectifying "the moral environment of the poor," and forays into the new politics of dependency.[64]

Battered about in this fracas, twisted to purposes of retailers with no sense of its history and a limited one of its meaning, was the resuscitated term "culture." Often as not it was used as the social equivalent of computer hardware. But if anthropology has anything to teach, it is that culture is not the symbolic equivalent of silicon circuitry. It is not a tight, hypercoherent program for action and thought, but rather a "tool kit" of images, frames, skills, and worldviews from which people assemble heuristic "strategies of action." Though these stores of motives and explanatory constructs, of reasons *for* doing and compulsions *to* do, have inertial force (tradition, received lore), they are also subject to editing and correction in the daily round of living. Even for matters that go to the heart of American culture—kinship, marriage, work, initiative, dependency, livelihood, dealings with the state, harmful habits, individualism—meanings are not fixed but unsettled, rattled by circumstance, shaken by new technologies, contested by myriad stakeholders. Culture's imprint is to be sought locally, in documented practice, not ecologically as an aspect of habitat.[65]

Few observers deny that some of the poor (at least some of the time) "hold values and take actions far outside the mainstream," that for some these can become characteristic patterns, and that such behaviors add to the injuries and deepen the captivity of ghetto life. How best to interpret these behaviors, how prevalent they may be, how tightly coupled to present-day contextual variables, how long they persist in the absence of such supporting contingencies, and how tolerant or condemnatory the local moral world is toward such behaviors—these remain contested issues.[66]

For field-based social scientists, looking to the limits and pressures exerted by context and history, trying imaginatively to project both the influence of tradition and our hide-bound sensibilities into alien turns of mind, the trick is to read long and hard in ways that unsettle the reader and disturb preconceptions. This may be the moral justification for ethnography,[67] but it derives from the imaginative project more broadly. Nonanthropologists (and not just novelists, artists, historians) make the effort, as when economists struggle to imagine the incentive structure and adult models confronted by young black men. But done casually, it borders on caricature; unbending, inscrutable culture is invoked to explain itself.[68]

Five problems continue to plague the invocation of culture in underclass discourse:

1. How *distinctive* are portrayals of present-day black "underclass" culture? Although much is made in today's debate of the "social isolation" of contemporary ghetto culture, ethnographic accounts of its predecessor in the postwar period offer not contrasting cases but familiar ones: coexisting but hardly commingling communities, divided along class lines.[69] Cross-sectional analysis may reveal, but cannot decode, shifts in population. Absent longitudinal ethnographic research, it isn't clear how geographic distance will modify patterns of enduring interactions.
2. Hyperbolic, contradictory images of *individual agency* hobble the discussion. In accounts hedged against victim blaming, ghetto dwellers appear largely as victims, buffeted by macroeconomic and microcultural

forces only dimly within their ken and far outside their control. Adaptation in such analyses is largely unconscious, transmitted through unseen wires to flesh-and-blood puppets, an operation imputed from without. Only rarely does adaptation take shape as a strategic posture, actively weighing choices and deliberating a course of action. In dialectical contrast, ghetto dwellers may be portrayed as adepts schooled in the art of cultural resistance. Segregation may have imposed the conditions of their confinement, but it cannot dictate the terms. Far from merely "adapting" to unyielding circumstance, an oppositional culture develops in response: rich, innovative, and defiant. Too often lacking in these accounts is an appreciation of the tragic costs of such defiance, an awareness that separate is rarely equal and that refusal may serve to perpetuate the structure of exclusion.[70]

3. *Anomalies in the ethnographic record* abound, suggesting either that textual coherence seen elsewhere has been had at the cost of ill-fitting data or that a great deal of genuine variation across place and time remains to be accounted for. Consider, for example, the competing accounts of young black fatherhood offered by Elijah Anderson and Mercer Sullivan: The first does so in terms of "sex codes" (chiefly, "the peer-group ethic of 'hit and run'"); the second identified a dominant pattern of quietly honored paternity among young black fathers, a pattern thrown into sharp relief through the use of a comparative design that varied configurations of class, ethnicity, and social ecology.[71] These may prove to be not misreadings but discordance: genuine points of contention, fault lines of divergent practice, tokens of dispersed and divided communities. Critical site differences, for example, appear to be at work in studies of schooling. Contrast accounts of oppressive high schools and defiant, disengaged students for whom race has become a caste status, with the surprising story of inner-city black students for whom the same legacy of race has become a liberating force.[72] In the latter, the unavailability of discrimination as excuse helps explain diminished aspirations among white teenagers.[73]
4. *Unresolved measurement issues* have surfaced as hypotheses become more refined. Classification and causal inference problems persist, whether describing neighborhoods or developing indices for tracking changes over time, or demonstrating the strength and direction of alleged effects. The personal impact of local disorder may be intuitively obvious, but reliably measuring it is another matter. Many analysts continue to use data banks of convenience (census-based reports on household composition or labor market participation especially), despite stubborn evidence of their limitations as faithful representations of phenomena at the margins. Conversely, to recall the theme with which

this chapter began, the ethnographic record on African American communities is sorely in need of updating (though progress is being made).[74]

5. Finally, when one turns away from the object of inquiry and looks instead at the subject making it, certain *distancing maneuvers* become apparent. Common enough in the annals of homelessness (see Chapter 2), these work to impart an artificial "otherness" to something of which the observer remains a necessary part. For the most part, such maneuvers serve to mask those implicit connections that make the world of the observer complicit in the suffering of the observed. On occasion, an anxiety betraying a more intimate recognition can be detected. In a late nineteenth-century society still unsettled by the dislocations introduced by industrialization, for example, the affront of the tramp owed much to the fact that his mobility "reminded Americans of the potential fragility of community bonds." A similar "distorted mirror" logic has recently been applied in a social psychological analysis of the "underclass" literature. Jennifer Hochschild argues that it would be wrong to dismiss certain features of underclass life as merely strange or pitiable. To the contrary: The discipline and work ethic of the drug trade, the wiles devoted to outwitting government regulations, and the taste for pain-numbing pastimes make their practitioners "not only inhabitants of an alien culture or innocent victims of the capitalist juggernaut . . . [but] in an exaggerated and distorted way, us."[75]

This recognition should not be allowed to obscure a larger point. Like "beliefs," values do a job.[76] Durable dispositions to act they may be, but they are also subject to modification, hedging, and reinterpretation as circumstance (and self-respect) demand. Whether they match those of the dominant or mainstream culture seems largely beside the point. The anthropological literature is full of accounts of how dissonance, born of unaccommodating circumstance, gives rise to doubled lives. This can mean, variously, retreat to "shadow values," maddening attempts to marry the dictates of "respectability" with the means of local repute, open repudiation of standards of class-based expected performance, subtle efforts at subterfuge and insubordination, and reinterpretation of dominant values in terms that make sense on the home front, however alien they may seem from without or harmful they prove within.[77] Such relative autonomy also suggests that the levers of change are not solely structural in nature.[78]

In summary, then, the verdict is still out and likely to be mixed on the versions of the cultural turn advanced so far. But it would be foolhardy to ignore certain strands of evidence:

- In some ghetto communities, paternal and avuncular embodiments of "respectability" are in scarce supply.
- Absent males (and, with them, foregone connections to work) mean that informal sanctions of antisocial behavior and effective means of countering it are often absent too, shifting disciplinary responsibility to female heads of households.
- In some places, a linguistic divide tending toward "mutual incomprehensibility" has opened between whites and blacks.
- Language confusions can be compounded by misunderstandings rooted in nonverbal aspects of communication (e.g., gestures of deference, indices of respect, face-saving maneuvers), which are central to those "cultural conflicts" between boss and employee that so often derail early employment prospects.
- Even if endemic drug use is interpreted as part of a culture of "repudiation"—against those "pervasive assaults to self-esteem and dignity inherent in the narrow legitimate options for poor [ghetto] youth"—that hardly negates the damage to self, family, and neighborhood.[79]

To the extent that any of these factors works further mischief with one's chances in the job market or jinxes one's welcome at home, it increases risk of homelessness.

A Working Hypothesis

Owing to a confluence of factors—structural, familial, and individual—homelessness among black men rose markedly in the 1980s. Labor and housing markets grew progressively more hostile to men of low skill and modest means. Ghetto neighborhoods reeling under the impact of concentrated poverty saw commercial investments decline, public services cut back, and sectors of a physical landscape reduced to ruins.[80] Extended households struggled to make ends meet, as nonfamily member earnings and government benefits both declined in value. When focus shifts from the material base to informal governance, other factors become salient. With the social regulatory function of work degraded and the disciplinary function formerly played by senior males (employed or retired) attenuated, the burden of informal control shifts progressively to the shoulders of women. One of the most effective sanctions they wield is ejection from the household. The upshot: When market losses in affordable housing and decent work are coupled with the mounting strains on extended families, feminization of familial discipline, the growth in the drug trade, and continued failures of community-based mental health services, homelessness seems an all but foregone conclusion.

Although absent or long-severed family ties figure in the histories of some of the homeless poor, for many others—especially those for whom homelessness is local and episodic—such ties are not only maintained, but spell the difference (sometimes recurrently) between a berth amid kin or friends and a cot among strangers. Far from suffering from "a pathology of connectedness," these men avoid homelessness and/or "exit" from it periodically thanks largely to the resiliency of such networks. As was the case with their forebears in the late 1930s, it is the generosity of extended households in the 1980s that impresses.[81]

But even obligations anchored by kinship have their limits. Tolerating demanding or overcrowded situations is easier if one can expect them to be short-lived—if, that is, viable alternatives to doubling up exist. A local surplus of affordable housing was essential to the fluid residential arrangements that preserved the elasticity of the African American extended family, free to expand and contract as need and domestic discipline required.[82] In many cities in the 1980s, that changed. The accommodating inefficiencies in the formal housing market that had made it possible for informal kin-based system to operate so flexibly virtually disappeared. This loss of housing, however disreputable it may have been, badly hedged the options of circulating family members. What "slack" remained in household carrying capacity was soon exhausted.[83]

Even if one supposes that disruptiveness could be contained, men remain at higher risk of homelessness. Should hardship persist in extended households, eventually a kind of triaging may be instituted. As declining resources make it impossible to meet the needs of all, the circle of kin is drawn more tightly. Those better able to fend for themselves are expected to do so. For good reason, triaging is gender biased. Differences in expectations of independence on the part of men and women persist in both larger (American) and local (African American) cultures. Women are more valued and versatile as household members. And, until recently at least, they were less prone to disabling drug or alcohol use.[84] More to the point here, *women do the work of kinship;* their investment in the social capital of family ties—and thus their expected return—is greater and more durable than that of men.[85] In any event, it is surely stronger than that of young men, many of whom have yet to secure the foothold in the labor market that would enable them to perform as "responsible" (and hence, "respectable") members of the family. By the same token (reliability of female kin, instability of male livelihood), marital prospects may be viewed by young black women as decidedly bleak. For these and related reasons, then, a lengthy sojourn with family immediately precedes the homelessness of women far more often than it does with men.[86]

But neither can it be said that men are immune to the nagging claims of kinship. Pride bristles at prolonged dependency when one has little with which to reciprocate. Under such circumstances, leaving a sorely strapped household and seeking public shelter may be one way of repaying hospitality.[87] Given a scarcity of market units and severe pressure on informal resources, the appeal of nonmarket alternatives grows. Military service was one such option, although it came at the cost of a heavy commitment. By the mid-1970s, another had surfaced. Absent any change in the operating rules of the institution itself but concurrent with a decline in its traditional clientele, functional patterns of use in public shelters began to shift dramatically in that decade. From a terminal station for elderly, poor, and friendless white men, the shelters became way stations for young black men in flux—a modern, relatively unstructured version of the nineteenth century police station houses for tramps.

The upshot is a pattern of intermittent official homelessness (staying in the shelters or on the street) that can make distinctions between housed and homeless somewhat arbitrary—a confusion evident in the following press account: "Although he described himself as homeless when he was arrested Monday, friends and neighbors at his parents' house . . . said yesterday that he had been living there off and on recently." In the late 1980s, over half the city shelter residents reported that they make use of the system on a part-time or occasional basis. If only one in seven residents then considered the shelter "home," nearly a third did so from time to time.[88]

Conclusion

Arguably foremost among the "complexities of need" that Mark Stern argued had escaped the scrutiny of advocates and analysts of homelessness in the 1980s was race.[89] Not that they were the first to overlook it. Despite a steady—at times robust—representation in the ranks of skid row men and transients, African Americans have been a shadow presence in the chronicles of homelessness. Until recently, that disregard was easier to understand: Black men were, after all, a minority population among skid row men, although not nearly as negligible as some accounts have led us to believe. But the persistence of that "blindness" to which Blumberg and colleagues called our attention in 1978 is much harder to account for since then.

Part of the responsibility lies with academic researchers, who (for reasons rehearsed above) were caught off guard by the revival of conservative forays into "underclass" culture. And although William Julius Wilson's rebuttal would spawn a new school of community-oriented research in Chicago, outside of such organized inquiries, neither money nor reputation was likely to be made by revisiting the lifeways of "roving men." For their part, granting agencies were less interested in the structural genesis of homelessness, or in the dynamics of affiliation that made it possible for many to exit from it, than in the epidemiology of its casualties. Such studies were primarily concerned with proper, methodologically sound documentation of pathology.

Part of the fault lies with the press. After a slow start during which reporters dusted off words like "vagrant," stiff from disuse and plainly unequal to the assorted reality on the streets and in the shelters,[90] accounts of homelessness burgeoned in the 1980s. In 1987, *New York Times* coverage averaged an article a day. But a careful content analysis of this coverage revealed that although 75 percent mentioned at least one demographic factor, fewer than 3 percent mentioned African Americans.[91] True, the press' Style Manual mandates that race be mentioned only if strictly pertinent to the story at hand. This makes the omission understandable, but does not excuse the failure to address the nexus of race and poverty expressed in homelessness.

Part of the responsibility, too, must rest with the African American political leadership. In February 1988—when the Atlanta March for the Homeless drew Joseph Lowery, Jesse Jackson, and Andrew Young, trudging alongside homeless advocates Mitch Snyder, Robert Hayes, Luisa Stark, and Chris Sprowal—prospects for an alliance between civil rights and housing rights advocates seemed bright. They have dimmed considerably since. No doubt, some black leaders viewed a revived linkage to poverty issues as the last thing needed by a movement badly burned by the conservative ascendancy of that decade. Among homeless advocates, the lapse occurred for less considered reasons.

The choice may have been strategic, the motives beyond reproach, and the collateral damage unwitting, but the net effect of advocacy's focus on a "just like us" image of homelessness during the 1980s was to reinforce a tacit racism in the public perception of the needy. This point has been well made by Lucie White:

> When [hardworking, displaced white families] become one's mental image of those homeless families whom the citizenry should feel moved to help, one is likely to resist poverty policies that shift goods and power to groups that depart from that image in obvious ways.[92]

The indirect effect of an appeal couched in such terms was to sanction the division of the urban poor into deserving and undeserving, this time along implicitly racial lines.[93]

Eager for a hearing in precincts seemingly deaf to the entreaties of the poor (and, until recently, unconcerned with more unruly expressions of discontent) and bent on expanding its base of support, advocacy parlayed the urgency of suffering on the streets into a general movement for "housing justice." In the process, a few troublesome, potentially derailing issues got left along the wayside.[94] Drug abuse and alcoholism was one; HIV/AIDS was another.[95] Deeply entwined with both of them, race was a third. In the end, as critics within its own ranks are quick to point out, ceding to others the rights of commentary on such "complexities" left the movement open to charges that it had sanitized the issue, purging homelessness of its more difficult and disturbing aspects. From the left came the opposite charge: that advocates badly underestimated the structural forces (in government and the marketplace) arrayed against substantive housing reform. From either side, the claim at heart was that the movement lacked serious measure of what it was up against. Homelessness in America was not about to yield to a Children's Crusade.

Corrective work began in the 1990s within the house of homeless advocacy.[96] But whatever shape that work may take, the larger debate remains poverty, and the contributions of homeless advocates will be subject to the defining terms of that debate. In the late 1990s, at least for while, matters seemed a bit more hopeful. Not that the guns on either side of the divide had been silenced. But recognitions of fresh complexity abounded, race seemed an unavoidable element of such complexities, and newly founded entities—like the Poverty and Race Research Action Council in Washington, D.C.—were committed to keeping it on the political agenda. There seemed room, too, in the space vacated by stridency, for that principled, fiercely argued brand of critical pragmatism being reinvented by Orlando Patterson, Cornel West, Henry Louis Gates, and others to get a real hearing. The critical task, Gates argued, was not only securing cultural standing and multiplying "authorized subjectivities," but the broader one of "rethinking the larger structures that constrain and enable our agency."[97]

If African Americans must confront the limits of "otherness" as credential before such rethinking can begin, different barriers apply for other Americans. To begin with, as this brief review of the erasure of race in the discourse on homelessness has shown, we would do well to recover the lesson that Ralph Ellison tried to teach nearly half a century ago—that invisibility is not an accident, but the product of a determined refusal to see.[98] Dispelling invisibility, we have slowly learned, isn't so much a matter of shedding light as it is choosing, deliberately, to look.

PART III

ADVOCACY AND ENGAGEMENT

[7]

Negotiating Settlement: Advocacy for the Homeless Poor in the United States, 1980–1995

No one is living in the streets.
—HUD official Philip Abrams,
to a Boston audience, June 1982

Although many groups were barred from that masked ball of false prosperity that was the United States in the 1980s, few proved as successful at crashing the party than the homeless poor. They were the spoilers, insistent reminders of the unruly night outside. Try as its officials might—by denying their existence, ascribing it to pathology (alcohol, drugs, and mental illness), interpreting it as a perverse exercise of "individual choice"—the state was hard pressed to conjure away the evidence of the streets. Most of the damage done to the poor in that decade took the form of a quiet, unobtrusive violence, and as such escaped notice. Unwitting exception though it may have been, the visible suffering of the street-dwelling poor inconveniently had no place else to go. It may be time to ask how well that impudence has worn and what was won on its behalf.

Not that the times are especially auspicious for such a retrospective.[1] The utility of emergency-based definitions of "homelessness" has just about run its course. Hard-won reforms of courts and state houses, the results of years of public-interest litigation and legislative work, are routinely being undone in practice. Where they are able to garner funding to continue their work, advocacy organizations find themselves fighting rear-guard actions, girding repeatedly to retake ground thought to have been secured long ago. Policing of public space has intensified. A massive reconfiguration of social insurance and social assistance programs is under way throughout the country, its effects buffered (for the time being) by an unusually robust economy. Social policy in the United States today seems a time machine bent on returning to the storied mercies of the nineteenth century do-nothing state.[2]

In 1980, it was a different story. Homelessness had just barreled onto the scene. And, like a young contender fresh from the gym, flush with early round victories and pumped by hype, advocacy was aching for a fight—mercifully unaware how long this one would last.

By the mid-1980s, the numbers of homeless poor in the United States had outstripped anything seen since the Great Depression. Disease, infirmity, even death were becoming regular features of life on the streets and in the shelters. In certain cities, homeless mothers and their children occupied waiting rooms in emergency assistance units for days on end and, once placed, found themselves living in quarters that in times past had been the exclusive preserve of "transients." The importunings of street beggars, antics of the wandering mad, and sprawling assemblies of shanty settlements were remaking some urban vistas in the image of the prior century.[3] Psychiatric hospitals, detoxification facilities, and jails played host to people who—psychoses quelled, cravings checked, or time served—were discharged with little hope of finding housing on their own, let alone of managing a household for long. Crack cocaine appeared as a cheap, repeatable high, wrecking lives and wreaking havoc with already unstable housing arrangements.

Yet for all that startled, there remained something wearily familiar about the face of homelessness. Strip away the veneer of pathology, and the hard grain of a more enduring reality stood exposed. Appearances may have suggested otherwise, but what the country glimpsed on the streets and in the shelters in the 1980s was not some new species of disorder, but the usually hidden face of poverty, ripped from its customary habitat. Advocacy's task, as simple to state as it was to prove elusive to accomplish, was to capitalize on the urgency to "do something" about the spectacle of homelessness, while not forgetting that the more difficult and essential target of redress was the durable stage of inequality and all its props. The demands of agitating on two fronts—piecemeal but winnable skirmishes on the one, a dragged-out war of attrition on the other—coupled with organizational isolation and a fitful commitment to wage such campaigns in full connivance with the casualties of homelessness themselves, have made for rocky fortunes.

The Advocacy Record

Any advocacy effort must begin with a defense of the legitimacy of the claim it seeks to have recognized. An anthropologist cannot help but notice that there are obvious cultural aspects to this task. What are prevailing conceptions of the "truly needy"? How are rank orders of "deservingness" set within that group? On what grounds is their support to be justified? What constitutes minimally adequate thresholds of subsistence? If public benefit levels fall manifestly *below* such levels, how (implicitly at least) is the difference to be made up? In that event, too, what kind of compensatory measures should count as unconscionable "cheating" on the part of public assistance recipients?[4] Such questions take us far afield from the somewhat rarefied, rule-riddled terrain of the law, where much of the early homelessness advocacy effort was focused. It is one thing to convince a court that state or local statutes require that certain rudimentary protections apply to the destitute. It is quite another to implement such protections in practice, to safeguard them against de facto "disentitlement" at the level of street bureaucrats who have every reason to resist still another "reform" that merely makes their job harder.[5] And it is yet a third task to mobilize the popular support that is necessary to press beyond the elemental necessities of survival.

Reference to such cultural dimensions of advocacy serves to underscore the time-limited character of such efforts. Conventions of decency are both formal (e.g., regulations in state-run institutions, occupancy limits on overcrowding) and informal (what should count as acceptable work or tolerable living conditions). As they change, so does the warrant of advocacy: what may be legitimately demanded of the state and on what terms. Pragmatism plays no small role, either. New York City, in public defiance of its own regulations, has prudently chosen to ignore the lawless example of the 130,000 persons who are doubled up (illegally sharing quarters rented by friends or family) in *public* housing units alone.[6] Admittedly, the most that might be claimed is that this amounts to an implicit endorsement of a necessary interim measure. Nevertheless, in the absence of a long-term housing plan to produce sufficient affordable housing, this practice must be seen as a tactical retreat from established standards of adequate lodging. The dilemma for advocacy, of course, is how to titrate demands for "housing justice" in the long term with realistic allowances for informal accommodations to satisfy otherwise unmet need in the short term.[7]

Advocacy for the homeless poor in the United States has spanned a wide range of activities: from disruptive street theatre and mass demonstrations; to drafting and lobbying for legislation in local, state, and federal precincts; to protracted legal proceedings; to scholarly articles and popular broadsides; to the auto-instruction implicit in volunteer work. This chapter, as much self-examination as it is movement critique, attempts to take provisional measure of the formative years of such advocacy, roughly the 1980s, and the legacy they left behind.[8]

"If They Only Knew"—Documentation and Mischief

If some charmed point of origin were to be designated for the inauguration of advocacy on behalf of the homeless poor in the United States, it would have to be the occupation of the National Visitors' Center (now part of the Union Station complex in Washington, D.C.) by the Community for Creative Nonviolence (CCNV) in November 1978. Federal police routed them after a few nights, but the warning shot had been fired and an undeclared war joined. Few activists could match CCNV in temerity, style, or commitment to organized confrontation. If other groups lacked the wherewithal to *demand* that the public face up to a scandal, they nonetheless commanded the resources to document what many refused to see. Even academics had skills that could be put to productive use. A flood of reports, broadsides, newspaper articles, and scholarly publications ensued, all with the common intent of taking the measure and showing the face of the new homelessness. If there was an implicit premise to such work it was that houseless poverty was so alien to the American tradition of poor relief that evidence of the betrayal of that legacy would suffice to prompt corrective action. Needless to say, it didn't work out that way.

Within the span of a few years, a revived documentary tradition was flourishing. CCNV released *A Forced March to Nowhere* at a congressional hearing on urban problems in 1980. Testimony and supporting material from subsequent congressional hearings in 1982 and 1984 filled five volumes of proceedings. In 1981 and 1982, detailed reports were published on homelessness in New York City, Baltimore, and Phoenix; in the next few years, dozens more would follow. From industrialized urban areas to farm belt communities, homelessness had broken free of the decades-old confines of skid row.

These early documentary efforts were complemented by a series of political actions and organized demonstrations. Throughout the 1980s, CCNV remained the nerve center of political theater, organized street vigils and punishing fasts, disruptive mischief, and determined evangelizing. In 1980, its members embarrassed local religious leadership by vainly seeking shelter for the homeless in Washington, D.C., churches during a snowstorm. Moral brinkmanship (a fifty-one–day fast that brought CCNV's Mitch Snyder to near-death) effectively extorted a White House commitment to renovate a federal building for use as a shelter in November 1984, but it would take two more publicized fasts before the promised funds were released a year and a half later.[9] CCNV would subsequently (March 1990) return the favor by refusing to allow census takers into the newly refurbished facility on the grounds that official efforts to count the homeless were a sham.

Elsewhere, less extreme measures were the rule. A few highlights: In December 1981, a memorial service was held across from the White House for people who had died on the streets. In January 1983, over 150 demonstrators were arrested for occupying the Capitol to protest the lack of shelter for the poor. A year later, a hundred homeless people and their advocates occupied the mayor's office in Columbus, Ohio, to demand the use of a public facility for shelter. On Christmas eve, 1986, advocates in Atlanta marched in procession behind a black crucifix (the "vagrant Christ") to protest a proposed "derelict-free" zone; fourteen months later, a national March for the Homeless drew thousands of homeless poor, their advocates, and civil rights veterans from across the country to the same venue. Later that summer, campaigns were mounted in Washington, Atlanta, Boston, Cincinnati, San Francisco, and other cities to "take off the boards" and reclaim the unoccupied space of abandoned housing. In March 1988, civil rights leaders joined thousands of homeless people and activists in Atlanta to highlight homelessness as an issue in the upcoming elections. In October 1989, a quarter million advocates, homeless people (some of whom had marched hundreds of miles to get there), and ordinary citizens converged in Washington under the banner of HOUSING NOW! And since 1992, the National Coalition for the Homeless has been spreading the message "You Don't Need A Home to Vote" to groups of disenfranchised citizens everywhere.

Organizing Efforts

Local coalitions to fight homelessness began to proliferate in the early 1980s. In July 1980, the Coalition for the Homeless was formed in New York City; in the next two years, similar organizations emerged in Massachusetts (October 1981), Atlanta (1981), San Francisco (1982), Phoenix (October 1982), and Minneapolis/St. Paul (1982). Allied efforts soon followed in Chicago, Columbus (and then throughout Ohio), Denver, Los Angeles, Richmond, Seattle, and Tucson.

In April 1982, a group of activists declared their intent to form a National Coalition for the Homeless; an organizational meeting in Chicago made it real a year and a half later. Executive directors Robert Hayes (in New York) and Maria Foscarinis (in Washington, D.C.) coordinated a multifront advocacy effort, including litigation, legislative work, and public education. From the start, affordable housing, living wages and/or sufficient public assistance, and accessible health care were the cornerstones of that effort. By the early 1990s, thanks largely to cross-country organizing efforts (chiefly by Michael Stoops), its members represented advocates in nearly every state.

In 1990, the National Coalition's Washington office director split off to form a separate advocacy group, the National Law Center on Homelessness and Poverty.

Other major national advocacy groups for the homeless have included: The National Low-Income Housing Coalition, the National Housing Law Project, the Legal Services Homelessness Task Force, and the National Alliance to End Homelessness. Campus activists formed Students to End Homelessness in the late 1980s; members have done direct service and advocacy in communities across the country.

Self-organizing efforts by homeless people began to take shape as well—notably in San Francisco (November 1982) and Philadelphia (October 1983)—and a national Union of the Homeless was launched in 1985. By the end of 1988, its organizing drive had established affiliated chapters in fourteen cities. Local groups staged demonstrations, conducted strikes at mandatory work programs, organized marches, and engaged in mass sleep-ins to dramatize the plight of their numbers.

By the end of the 1980s, visibility wasn't the issue, although only partly due to advocacy. History played a determined hand as well. Midway through the decade, a *New York Times*/CBS News poll found that only 36 percent of respondents reported personally seeing homeless people in their neighborhoods or on their way to work, while 59 percent knew of the problem only through the press and television. By 1991, those figures were reversed.[10] Homelessness wasn't just something people read about; it had become a routine fixture on the local landscape. But it isn't clear what difference this has made when it comes to remedies. By the end of the decade, "compassion fatigue" had become a fashionable term for the seeming ease with which (some of) the American public had adapted to burgeoning homelessness in the 1980s. While a few studies suggest a more complicated attitudinal picture,[11] it isn't difficult to imagine how ordinary citizens, faced with stubborn evidence of a seemingly intractable problem, could let frustration get the better part of caring. In November 1984, the citizens of Washington, D.C., voted to affirm a right to shelter in a special ballot initiative; six years later, in a referendum vote, the measure was repealed. Not the least of the measure's problems was the host of alternative voices—many of them hostile—on the scene to debate the issue the second time around.

LITIGATION[12]

In October 1979, a relatively inexperienced Wall Street lawyer, Robert Hayes, filed a lawsuit on behalf of homeless men in New York City, *Calla-*

han v. Carey. City and state agencies, which share responsibility for funding, regulating, and operating public shelters, were named as defendants. After a preliminary ruling in favor of the plaintiffs in December directed the city to provide emergency lodging to all "needy, indigent men," the public shelter system began to expand for the first time in fifteen years. But conditions remained dismal, the treatment of applicants harsh and degrading, and deterrence the operative policy. Formal trial proceedings began in December 1980, and in August 1981, a "consent decree" was signed, effectively ratifying a right to shelter and setting minimal standards of decency for public shelter. Over two decades later, local advocates were still locked in legal battles with both city and state officials over conditions in and access to the shelters.[13] (The legacy of *Callahan* is examined later in this chapter.)

By the late 1980s, in at least a dozen communities nationwide, class-action lawsuits had been filed and concessions won with respect to a (de facto) right to shelter, the quality of public shelter, the right to vote, and the removal of barriers to emergency assistance. Litigation efforts were also mounted to ensure emergency shelter for families, sufficient housing allowances for welfare households, education for homeless children, and appropriate housing for persons with severe mental illness or HIV-related illnesses. Most recently, advocates have returned to the courts to fight the revival of vagrancy and antibegging laws.

National Legislation[14]

In 1986, CCNV and the National Coalition for the Homeless joined forces with nine other groups to draft a comprehensive relief bill, the "Homeless Persons' Survival Act," to guide and give substance to a federal role in ending homelessness. The following spring, Congress approved a version of Title I of that act—essentially, the emergency relief provisions—and that summer it was signed into law by a reluctant President Reagan as the "Stewart B. McKinney Homeless Assistance Act" (McKinney Act). It was the first significant piece of federal legislation to address homelessness in fifty years. Appropriated funding for programs sponsored under the McKinney Act increased steadily, from $189 million in fiscal year (FY) 1988 to nearly $1.8 billion in FY 1994, and then dropped to just over $1 billion in FY 2001.[15]

The 1990 reauthorization of the McKinney Act added several new provisions, including funding and protection of schooling for homeless children; two programs to address the specific needs of homeless persons with severe mental illness; and a program designed to demonstrate the effectiveness of neighborhood-based support services in preventing homelessness among families. In 1990, too, Congress expanded the federal housing role for the first time in a decade by passing the National Affordable Housing Act. At the same time, Congress modified the McKinney Act, expanding housing assistance for homeless persons with disabilities (Shelter Plus Care and Projects for Assistance for Transitions from Homelessness [PATH] programs), strengthening provisions for the education and health care of homeless children, and easing access to federal job-training programs.[16] Subsequent modifications bolstered participation of homeless or formerly homeless persons on the boards of recipient agencies, established a new program of "low-demand" accommodations for the street-dwelling homeless ("safe havens"), and created a rural homeless assistance program.

Obscure clauses may reap unexpected benefits. Title V of the McKinney Act required federal agencies to offer first right of refusal on surplus federal property (land and buildings, usually slated for auction or disposal) to states, localities, and nonprofit groups to assist homeless people. Military base closures, for example, offer a ready stock of convertible housing. But when a Navy pier was decommissioned on Lake Michigan, local homeless advocates lay claim to a portion of it to build a solar greenhouse and plant community gardens. The federal government approved the proposal. The City of Chicago had other plans, envisioning a megatourist attraction on the site. Recognizing an opportunity to compound the windfall, the Chicago Coalition for the Homeless traded their plot for an alternative piece of property nearby, a marketing booth on the pier, and the City's agreement to reserve all day-labor jobs at the pier and a convention center for homeless workers.[17]

Hostile times notwithstanding, brave proposals for far-reaching reform continue to make the rounds. A group spearheaded by the National Law Center on Homelessness and Poverty drafted an omnibus proposal to translate the limited emergency measures of the McKinney Act into long-term remedies addressing the causes of homelessness.[18] In what is perhaps the most willfully optimistic action on the cultural front, a group of housing activists circulated a draft manifesto setting out the argument for a right to housing.[19]

Local Homelessness Movements

While national organizations dealt primarily with the federal government, scores of local movements took shape, usually in response to what Rob Rosenthal has called "suddenly imposed deprivations." Of special significance, because of the inherent difficulties involved, were those movements in which homeless people figured prominently.[20] All the usual logistical obstacles to effective organizing by the disenfranchised are magnified when the group in question cannot even count on having a roof over their heads at night. But distinctive problems arise as well.[21] Relations between outside "advocates" and homeless "activists" are strained not only by the usual differentials of class, but by ruder distinctions of urgency of need and ability to make do in the meantime. Means and goals are both affected. "Empowerment" may be freely espoused as a collective organizing principle. But when one group effectively controls access to enabling resources, that principle is difficult to realize in practice and frequently gives way to efficiency. The definition of interests may be hotly contested, especially in the early days when many advocates cast their demands in terms of wholesome shelter, deferring action (it sometimes seemed indefinitely) on the more enduring issues of housing, jobs, and adequate incomes. Suspicions can run high when potential service providers (who have a vested stake in the delivery of goods and services) join forces with would-be clients. Too, homeless activists are wary of allowing the long-standing damage wrought by poverty to be translated into the clinical categories of treatable disorders. Not infrequently, they conclude that advocates are willing to settle for short-term gains that have the effect of blunting the spur of necessity needed to keep the movement alive. With little to lose, activists are nearly always ready to take risks that fall well outside the profit–loss ledgers of conventional politics.

Success can impose costs of its own. Especially of late, local struggles have been targeted at defending access to open space or at preserving programs that were never more than marginal concessions to begin with. In the event, "victory" is tainted by the demoralizing realization that one has once again settled for less than what is really needed—and fought for the privilege of doing so. For their part, homeless activists are caught in the unusual bind of having their authority coupled to a state of situational deprivation from which they (like their compatriots) are anxious to escape. Effective leaders are likely to want to convert any organizing capital they have amassed into jobs and housing, and thus expedite their passage out of homelessness. Their gain is often the local movement's loss. Finally, few demands, no matter how brilliantly orchestrated, can touch the underlying mechanisms of deindustrialization, government cutbacks, and the depletion of low-income housing.

What's Been Won? At What Cost?

If the 1980s taught us anything, it was that emergency relief was at best a necessary stopgap measure. Shelter neither solves homelessness nor prevents further displacement. Absent an adequate supply of affordable housing—and the jobs and income supports needed to sustain households once relocated—remedial efforts are doomed to an endless round of musical chairs. Under such circumstances, "advocacy" stalls, devoting its expertise and moral capital to the task of handicapping some people's needs over others. Neither equity nor neighborhood stability is served in the bargain. For that reason, many local and national advocacy groups have rededicated the bulk of their resources to the struggle for lasting solutions to homelessness. At the same time, whatever the merits of this as a long-term strategy, short-term efforts must contend with the legacy of a decade that saw visible misery burgeon in the streets and contempt for the poor lose its shame.

Still, for a substantial portion of shelter users in cities for which figures are available, the institution appears to work as an emergency resource. For these users, that is, either through their own efforts or those of officials charged with relocation, it adequately serves as a way-station en route to stable rehousing. In New York and Philadelphia, for example, over three-quarters of shelter stays (i.e., the stays of 80 percent of shelter users) are transitory. Relocations appear to be fairly stable. This is especially true when affordable housing can be secured at the end of a shelter stay. A recent five-year follow-up study of sheltered families in New York City found that 80 percent of those who received assisted housing at the end of their shelter stay had stable relocations.[22]

It is thus no small irony that so much of what was accomplished in the 1980s has since receded into the shadows of unremarkable poverty, there to go unnoticed. Why? Once people manage to escape from the streets and shelters, they typically prefer to pick up their new lives as "neighbors," "workers," and "citizens"—and not as tagged specimens of the "formerly homeless." Recent research confirms that a brief bout of homelessness is far more common in American lives than most thought probable.[23] If the markers of the experience do not attract attention once the formerly homeless are rehoused, then evidence of successfully resolved homelessness—although all around us—is bound to be difficult to detect. Unseen, it can offer little reassurance of the worth of the social investment in shelter.

For others, however, attending solely to "shelter" mistakenly assumes that the distress is transitory, that somehow both prehomeless conditions and posthomeless precariousness will be resolved without having to address continuing forces of destabilization. In Westchester County, New York, for example, a de facto "right to shelter" has existed for more than a decade. For families, throughout much of the 1990s, that shelter came with a rigorous training regimen for "housing readiness" that had become the accepted price of queue-jumping in a tight housing market.[24] Until recently, shelters for single people tended to be much less structured, but little in the way of relocation assistance was available. A survey of over two hundred single shelter requesters in 1994 found that, on average, they had spent 21 percent of the last five years on the street or in shelters; for the severely mentally ill among them, that figure rose to 31 percent. For a substantial portion of such people, the shelter system simply fed into a patchwork of institutional resources—jails, rehabilitation programs, psychiatric facilities, general hospitals—from which a sort of institutionalized livelihood could be fashioned. Closely documented residential histories of thirty-six shelter users with severe mental illness showed that for nearly two-thirds of them, stays on this extended "institutional circuit" accounted for 59 percent of their whereabouts for the last five years.[25] Such findings are hardly unique, and suggest that a pattern as old as the institution of poor relief itself is still thriving—that the poor make creative use of the public resources of assistance, which can be quite at odds with the intentions of the state.[26]

We still know little about the transitional resources (formal or informal) that enable individuals and families to "exit" from homelessness or to avoid it in the first place. Without such knowledge, designing—and advocating for—effective programs to resolve or prevent homelessness remains a hit-and-miss affair. A critical review of the literature on prevention is revealing: Even if we ensured that poorly evaluated interventions were 100 percent effective in reaching their targeted groups and allaying evictions, such efforts would still prevent less than half the year's roster of homelessness. More telling, perhaps, they would "target" a host of individuals and families who would never have become homeless. It is difficult to avoid the conclusion, these critics comment, that such programs "merely . . . provide useful services to poor people under a politically convenient rubric."[27]

Taken together with the earlier data on turnover, these findings paint a mixed picture of shelter's utility. In some places, a judicially mediated right to shelter appears to have enhanced the competitive edge of some needy people in a tight housing market. Whether by dint of sheer staying power, willingness to submit to the demands of rehabilitation and training programs, or the luck of the draw locally, these people (families especially) have successfully negotiated stable settlement. Others, young single men in particular, use the shelters as the functional equivalent of crash pads. What has been achieved is a minor (if terribly costly) adjustment at the margins, leaving an uncertain, destabilized core intact. The equity issues raised by allocating a scarce resource in this fashion have barely been touched. The tough challenge of integrating housing and shelter policies has largely been dodged, owing both to entrenched bureaucratic divisions and realistic fears of the potential costs at stake. The deeper issue of livelihood has only fleetingly been raised on the political stage. The upshot is that shelter has become one more institutional segment in a tangled braid of partial survival options, much as the skid row missions had operated in the past.[28]

The Limited Reach of the Language of Rights—The Legacy of *Callahan*

Facing a tradition of state relief founded on exclusion, New York City advocates mounted a campaign premised on its opposite. Some notable exceptions aside, this bid for inclusion was tendered and defended in the courts. Public interest litigation claimed pride of place in the advocacy efforts of the 1980s, and litigation speaks the language of rights. After some stunning initial victories, the limitations of litigation are becoming apparent. Neither the transparent quality of the "needs of strangers" nor the self-evident nature of the means to alleviate them is as unproblematic today as it once seemed. The enforcement power of even vigilant courts is bounded; judicial decrees have proved subject to myriad compromises in practice. Framing constraints go unaddressed. The dilemma is inherent in any reform that relies heavily on the courts and artificial simplification (or partitioning) of complicated social issues that judicial parsing demands. Regrettably, the legal process "leaves many aspects of the underlying problems not only untouched but also unacknowledged."[29]

Improvised as temporary measures under exigent circumstances, the institutional makeshifts put together to check homelessness developed inertial force of their own. *Callahan* is a case in point. After the consent decree was signed, shelter capacity exploded—from a haphazard stock of floor space and flophouse beds in 1979 to a system of two dozen shelters and a handful of armories, capable (at peak demand in 1988) of holding over ten thousand. Satellite programs (health, mental health, drug rehabilitation, and work readiness) were spawned, adding new service density. Detailed attention was paid to those features of shelter for which the consent decree stipulated oversight. Elemental decencies were spelled out in obsessive fashion—space between beds, quality of food, ratio of men to toilet facilities, arrangements for storage of belongings—not only because of the threat of institutional neglect but because that was where legal leverage lay.

But despite the expenditure of over $1.5 billion since the initial lawsuit, including some $40 million for upkeep and repair of armories and warehoused property pressed into service as shelters, conditions (in the deliberately understated opinion of a former state official) remain "far from ideal." She continues, in what must rank as the single most frustrating fact of life for state bureaucrats dedicated (against all odds and stubborn stereotype) to meeting the demand for shelter in a humane way:

> The ability of the city and state to develop homeless policy in a deliberative and rational manner was impeded by the need to respond to frequent motions for enforcement of the Consent Decree. Determining what types of facilities

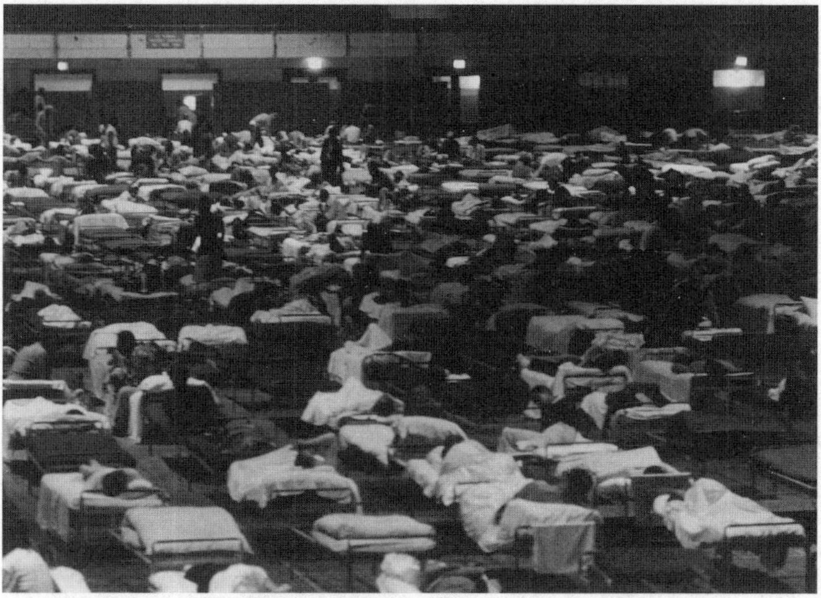

Fort Washington Armory, New York, May 1984

> and programs would truly meet the needs of the residents of adult shelters became a lower priority than ensuring that, for example, there were forty toilets working in the Fort Washington Armory.[30]

The open-ended nature of the agreement, retention of oversight responsibility by the courts, blizzard of subsequent motions to enforce or modify the order, and the ease with which concessions won for this class were transferred to others who were neither parties to nor intended beneficiaries of the original decree, convinced state and city officials that consent decrees would no longer be considered viable means to settle disputed claims.[31]

Without denying the validity of the complaint, one may still object that the former counsel protests too much. Historically, solutions to widespread homelessness have had little to do with what happens inside shelters—strict eligibility criteria, enforcement of make-work rules, provision of programs, disaggregation of residents. Demand for shelter is essentially defined by default, the result of local labor market conditions, supply of cheap housing, adequacy of public assistance, support capacity of kin, commitment practices, and diligence of the police.[32] Bureaucratic bridgework at the governmental level linking departments of housing and economic development with those of health and human services would have been needed. That

East New York Armory, May 1984

bridgework was never seriously contemplated, let alone put under construction. Further, without strong federal leadership and financial support on such fronts, states and localities are limited in what they can do to stem the generative forces of homelessness.

Still, it hasn't been an utterly Pyrrhic victory. For one thing, throughout the 1980s, shelter bed capacity was more elastic than at any time since the 1930s. For another, the open contempt for the homeless man that was the operating premise of public shelter could no longer be avowed as business as usual. Procedures put into place to correct the habitual abuses of the past have had remedial benefits. Shelter workers no longer carry ax handles or routinely hassle applicants with impunity. It may be that genuine "respect" is something that can be exchanged only through the medium of human gesture,[33] but rough approximations of respect are not to be scorned for that reason. Even where imperfectly realized, rights may be interpreted as "communally recognized rituals for securing attention in a continuing struggle over boundaries between people"—especially where one contestant has historically been disenfranchised. If nothing else, "rights claims" such as that secured in *Callahan* wield subversive potential because they highlight a system's contingency and spur awareness of the gap between the shabby reality that is and the dimly glimpsed alternatives that might be.[34]

So the legacy of litigation is only partly that of the war of attrition fought over the terms of bureaucratic compliance. Like the minimum-wage law, the beauty of *Callahan* lay in its simplicity: It established a floor below which public provision of shelter could not be allowed to fall. This, in the aggressively conservative politics of the 1990s, was to prove critical. That decade saw three serious attempts to modify the terms and conditions set forth in the *Callahan* decree: (1) an offer to renegotiate the decree tendered by the newly installed Guiliani administration in 1993; (2) a state proposal to rewrite the eligibility criteria for shelter by declaring an "emergency" in 1995; and (3) an extension of that effort in 1998 to demand that shelter recipients abide by the quid pro quos expected of all relief recipients. The first two, opposed by advocates and stonewalled by the courts, soon died. The third lingered menacingly.

The seeds of this initiative had been planted earlier, when the city issued a plan for "reforming" its system of homeless services. Because, according to a state Department of Social Services (DSS) spokesperson, "scarce shelter beds were often being used by people who did not need them leaving the truly needy on the street,"[35] the new system was to be premised on three provisions:

1. "Eligibility for shelter will [be restricted to] people who have absolutely no other housing alternatives."
2. ". . . access to permanent housing [for homeless individuals] will be provided only when the individual . . . has fully completed a program focused on developing independent living skills necessary to maintain such housing."
3. "We must stop considering people as homeless, and recognize that they may be mentally ill, substance abusers, undereducated or untrained . . ."[36]

Such provisions were squarely at odds with the terms of the original consent decree, which placed no conditions on eligibility for shelter other than need. At the time, the court understood that deciding who may make a claim and under which circumstances it may be honored was superfluous, given the terms and conditions of shelter. Anyone who dared show up to ask for a bed for the night had rendered, by the mere act of petitioning, sufficient evidence of need. As if to anticipate changing times and circumstances, however, the *Callahan* attorneys had stipulated that legitimate need could stem from "physical, mental or *social* dysfunction" (emphasis added). The judicial interpretation of that third key adjective—and the court's tempered faith in bureaucratic discretion and judgment—proved crucial in the decree's staying power.

In August 1998, the Association of Service Providers for Homeless Adults, Inc. (ASPHA, a group of twenty-six service organizations operating drop-in centers and shelters) wrote to the City and State to protest the imposition of "more stringent eligibility criteria." They argued such rules would deny shelter to people in need, especially those most troubled. Specifically, they objected to a provision "discontinuing temporary housing assistance" for thirty days to anyone who fails twice to comply with an independent living plan. Their reasoning was pragmatic, the result of accumulated experience: "At present, we continue to work with these individuals and can, as a result, tell many success stories. Why undercut this process?" The letter concludes by offering their expertise in addressing any continuing problems and in formulating alternative interventions. The offer was politely but firmly refused by both City and State.[37]

Faced with bureaucratic intransigence, the Coalition for the Homeless felt it had no other option but to return to court. By the spring of 1999, it was clear that newly instituted "front-end" eligibility policies—requiring both families and single applicants for shelter to accept an initial placement in temporary, "holding" accommodations—were working as effective deterrents to potential shelter users: nearly a third disappeared before that period was completed. Equally worrisome in the long run were "back-end" behavioral requirements (performing work or participating in treatment) that, for the recalcitrant or deranged, could mean expulsion. The city forced the issue later that fall by threatening to implement the new requirements in both family and single shelters, and the matter went to court.

Arguments in *Callahan* were heard by Judge Sklar (called to the bench from his sickbed) on 7 January 2000. Six weeks later he ruled unambiguously in favor of the plaintiffs. In his opinion, he chided the City and State defendants for "making no acknowledgment of the possibility of *social* impairment, which might make someone *unable*, as opposed to *unwilling* to cooperate with bureaucratic niceties," took account of the changing social realities—a revamped shelter system—but came down foursquare in support of an unconditional right to shelter:

> [A]s admirable as the new system is in comparison to the old, "socially dysfunctional" people continue to exist, and to inhabit the streets of New York in fair weather and foul, and no change in circumstances, social or otherwise, warrants that these individuals should no longer receive succor under the terms of the Consent Decree, or should be subject to termination of their right to shelter if they cannot function within the complex system which defendants have fashioned to alleviate the problem of homelessness.[38]

In effect, because "bureaucratic error is as much a part of bureaucracy as human error is a part of life," the risks of implementing such regulations were "simply too great."[39] "Socially dysfunctional" people could not be expected to navigate their way shrewdly through such thickets.

Not Forgetting the Streets: When the Work of Survival Is Criminalized

If shelter is a bad deal, the streets are worse. Still, in these time of shrinking margins, displaced anger, and unprovoked violence directed against the street-dwelling poor, an aggressive civil rights program has found its way onto many local advocacy agendas.

As a matter of tacit policy, cities are being forced to restore (or reinvent) what urban geographers once called "zones of discard"—those sanctuaries for misfits that patches of the central business districts (the Bowery) once provided for free. The problem, now four decades in the making, is that the cheap housing, spot labor, and rough tolerance that made such places viable refuges are gone. Faced with that depletion and disinclined to use city shelters, growing numbers of the homeless poor have elected a primitive form of self-sufficiency over the official alternatives. Hence, the makeshift assemblies of discarded building material fashioned into rude housing, commonly referred to as "shanties."

These settlements of homeless people are lumpen creations, wrested out of waste spaces and discarded materials in the precarious margins of our urban landscape. By an alchemy born of necessity, their proprietors—people with no property except what they scavenge—have turned these outlaw spaces into places of habitation, respite, and even hope. They do so in the face of the constant threats of eviction, fire, and filth. But let us be clear about the particulars of this choice. In New York, for example, most people who have taken up residence in street dwellings are not strangers to the shelter system. In a street survey conducted jointly by the Coalition for the Homeless and researchers from the Nathan Kline Institute in 1990, we found that the majority of street dwellers had stayed in a city shelter, found them dangerous and overly structured, and had vowed not to return. Nor were these convenient fictions spun for gullible advocates. Careful monitoring of shelter conditions by court observers in the wake of the *Callahan* decree had shown repeatedly that men had good reason to fear such facilities.[40] (See Chapter 3, pp. 85–100.)

Not that the shanty settlements were models of frontier comity. Three years before it was bulldozed, journalist James Lardner drew a fine portrait of one such community, "the Hill" in lower Manhattan.[41] A ramshackle assembly of dwellings at the foot of Manhattan Bridge with about two dozen regular inhabitants, the Hill had its share of deceit, rivalry, and drug dealing. Prevailing norms of civility were roughhewn and uncertain. "[P]eople fight a lot on the Hill," Lardner found, but he also insisted that they "exhibit a degree of neighborliness not to be found in every high-rent apartment building." The former proved the stronger strain. Shortly after Lardner's piece appeared, one of the residents burned to death; his remarkable dwelling, a yurtlike invention of ropes and mattresses, had been set afire.

We should be clear, too, about the affront that such settlements pose. The Hill wasn't another Tompkins Square Park, where in the late 1980s hundreds of homeless people had taken up residence in a residential section of the East Village and resisted pressure to remove them.[42] At the Hill, there were no all-night vigils by self-styled anarchists, no pitched battles with police in riot gear; nor were there any competing land uses at stake. Located at the juncture of several commercial thoroughfares, there wasn't even noise to complain about. What the Hill transgressed was not propriety, or peace, or recreational freedom; it was the simulacra of civic order.[43]

In defending such settlements, some advocates retreated to a default moral stance: Let the settlements stand—not because civil liberty demands that we honor the refusal and ignore the trespass embodied in the shanties; not because their presence in any way enhances our collective claim to civilized status; but because elemental decency moves us to extend allowances to people who prize the residual dignity of a hardscrabble shack over the dubious security of a berth in a modern-day poorhouse. Should they be found to pose a legitimate hazard to health or safety, their residents should be offered relocation services, not shelters. But with no organized constituency behind it, such rhetoric quickly proved no match for aggressive "quality of life" policing.[44] By the winter of 1995–1996 in New York, visible shanty settlements of any size could be found only along the narrow band between highway and waterline on the island of Manhattan. By the following summer (July 1996), most had been dismantled at least once by the police. By 2000, they had disappeared—lock, stock, and barrel—from readily inspected interstices of the urban ecology.

So where have the street-dwelling homeless gone? Part of an answer may be found in journalistic accounts detailing how shanty structures are being relocated to well-hidden sites or places the cops have tacitly agreed to ignore for the time being.[45] Part of it may be found in Mitch Duneier's bracing portrait of the street vendors at Sixth Avenue and 8th Street in Greenwich Village, some of whom had slept in Penn Station until the Amtrak crackdown in the spring of 1990.[46] And part of it may be found in a 1999 report on severe mental illness in jails in New York City.[47] Using published estimates by clinicians and the city's own Department of Mental Health, the report estimates that some 2,850 seriously mentally ill inmates are incarcerated on Rikers Island each night—most, it seems probable given the rise in arrests and convictions for "quality-of-life" violations, for low-level misdemeanors. Nearly half (43 percent) are likely homeless (compared with 20 percent of Rikers Island inmates overall) at the time of arrest.[48]

Taking Stock

Something remarkable has happened to the spectacle of the street-dwelling poor in the two decades since it reappeared on the public stage: Homelessness became domesticated, routine, an all-but-expected feature of the urban landscape. No longer cause for vocal concern, let alone outrage, it has been integrated into that cheerless diorama of unabashed wealth and relentless poverty that now passes for "normalcy" in American cities. (Rural homelessness, like rural poverty in general, remains largely hidden, undetected, much as it was when Michael Harrington surveyed it in the early 1960s.) Instead of spectacle, we have so many tokens of local color: rapid-fire images of sidewalk dwellings in the lead-in footage to cop shows; anti-panhandling signs posted in subways and transportation depots; feature stories about homeless personages who replay classical Grimm-brothers' themes (the hermit who refused help and died alone but not unmourned; the long-lost glories of a former cabaret singer, a pioneer black ballet dancer, a prize-winning photographer who joins the ranks of his portraits; the "wild man" terrorizing a neighborhood whom neither police nor psychiatry can contain). And, domestication writ small, we have the new line of dolls (Homeless Hannah, Steve the Tramp, an assortment of "psycho-killers") designed to appeal to (and foster?) that self-protective sense of macabre otherness in kids everywhere.

Such are among the ironic progeny of persistent advocacy. Impelled by an elemental moralism, we set about telling the story of homelessness in all its unsettling specificity. Like James Agee and Walker Evans before us (if lacking their artistry), we managed to lift the lid on "a portion of unimagined existence" and showed it to be not only imaginable but already here. We gave them names, showed you their faces, ransacked our fieldnotes for arias of heartbreaking tragedy and quiet heroism. Not content merely to document the obvious, we pressed for remedies, adding tools to our kit and half-truths to the things we left behind. Shelters, we soon learned, were necessary stopgaps, no more. The troubles of the displaced were not reducible to the fact of their displacement. An honest offer of assistance was no guarantee of acceptance, nor its refusal the expression of a captive mind's distress. And even with eager clients, huge rents in the social fabric of care and market scarcities made relocation a complicated business, assured only for the comparative few. For all its elemental simplicity, that is, homelessness was proving to be more than a glitch in the otherwise well-oiled machinery of state support. What began as an appeal for rudimentary relief (respite from the streets) was transformed into a mantra for material reform ("housing, housing, housing"). Decent jobs, health care, and income supports rounded out the list. And all the while, the ugly story on the street played on, stubbornly refusing to close out.

On balance, what does the advocacy record look like? As the foregoing discussion suggests, that record invites critical commentary on a number of fronts. There are the difficulties in applying traditional organizing principles when mobilizing the homeless poor; the limits of special pleading, class-action litigation, and rights talk; the problem of scale when applying the lessons of successful demonstration projects; nagging issues of equity that arise with "queue-jumping" remedies; the renewal of antipoor sentiment; the difficulties in tapping the resiliency of traditional informal supports as policy; the complicating factors of substance abuse and severe mental illness.[49] But for me, a product of New Left politics tempered by public health activism and a graybeard partisan on this front, two failures merit particular attention: advocacy's neglect to build the broader alliances that could have moved the enlarged agenda, and its irrelevance to the day-to-day struggles of street workers.

A Marginalized Politics

In taking stock of advocacy's achievements, pride of place must go to its standing refusal to accept an "emergency" idiom as the proper way of framing the issue. Even in the fledging literature of the early 1980s, this insistence on the deeper structural roots of homelessness is apparent. But making the link to broader issues, and opening the familiar store of grievances and interests they tow in their wake, has proved tricky. Embedded in a political environment hostile to any proposal that so much as borrows vocabulary from the lost war on poverty, advocates found themselves repackaging old demands—"You want to curb homelessness among single parents? Try raising welfare benefits to livable levels"—only to be accused of using this fresh misfortune as a pretext for resurrecting defeated causes. Judged from the vantage of preventing future homelessness or stabilizing those resettled, any measure that stood a chance of reducing the risk of displacement seemed fair game. In practice, this meant taking on new battles while repeatedly refighting old ones, as policy terrain thought to have been secured long ago (on vagrancy laws, for example) turned out to have been anything but.

The result was a deadly thinning of advocacy's famously provisional ranks. Even as its reach stretched beyond the wildest imaginings of early advocates—by the mid-1990s, research reports estimated that homelessness had affected millions of Americans in the last half of the 1980s[50]—homelessness was effectively absent from discussions of welfare changes, health care reform, and economic policy, as though decisions in those realms would have no impact on present rates or future trends. Nor could it be argued (though people did, quietly) that remedial measures were obviously failing (just look around, they suggested, at the visibly deranged still on the streets; check out the nearly packed shelters). But persistence of this problem pointed not to the impotence of remedies but to the reservoir of need. The lines of those "exiting" from homelessness were replenished because of the vast numbers of near-homeless who kept joining them, not because relocations failed. "Emergency" measures are stymied by such substitution effects whenever the generative forces behind the "crisis" go unchecked.

If, as advocates insisted, those forces run deep and extend broadly, then their correction requires not only massive public action but a substantial constituency of demand as well. But as advocacy's analysis toughened and its reform agenda ramified, its political infrastructure failed to keep pace. Saints being in limited supply, effectively pressing the case for wholesale reformation of the basic needs–meeting mechanism of a society's poor usually takes more than a moral crusade. It requires an organizational apparatus that lends discipline and structure to a charismatic leadership whose tenure (we learned the hard way) is all too vulnerable to fortune's whimsy. That means either making common cause with broad-based political organizations or inventive coalition building. Neither happened. Intermittent overtures were made to labor, housing, and health care groups, "peace and justice" movements, even (briefly) the leadership of the Democratic party. Fitful attempts were made to shore up grass-roots constituencies, and some local victories scored. But the energy and resources needed to invigorate such ventures, to make them viable enterprises with an inertial force of their own, were never mobilized. We chose to pursue the political game on home turf, if only because no one else took up the cudgels there.

So is it fair to claim, as some have, that although we shifted the ground from charity to justice, we continued to act as though we could shame a nation into responding? That seems too harsh a judgment. Litigation, local action, and relentlessly working Capitol Hill reaped undeniable benefits, and it was secular sweat that pulled off the wins. (Given the political climate, number of advocates on active duty at any moment, and scale of the problem, the wonder perhaps is that so much got done.) Litigation proved a powerful prosthetic device that greatly influenced the leverage of a comparative few. Local skirmishes by rank-and-file advocates racked up concrete concessions and lent hope to similar struggles elsewhere. But for the last decade, the bulk of national advocacy has been deployed within the beltway: drafting legislation, lining up allies, educating (harrying is more accurate) congressional aides, rounding up supporters, negotiating compromises, summoning the grass roots for concerted pressure, reworking regulations—in short, *lobbying* (within the bounds allowed, of course, by nonprofit, 501–C status). But playing Rome's game has its costs in the provinces.

Beltway labor amounts to sustained campaigns for "programs," initially to get them instituted and then, at appointed intervals, to defend them against budget-cutters and opponents caught sleeping the first time around. Some are broad-based (e.g., supportive housing for persons with severe mental illness who are otherwise at high risk of homelessness); others (specialized education for homeless kids, focused health care), the sort of targeted relief that would never happen if we didn't take it on. However urgently needed, success in such ventures ensures a trap of its own making. The McKinney Act made much possible, but for advocates it was a victory purchased on the installment plan. Ensuring that its provisions are renewed and funds reappropriated as expiration dates arrive takes enormous energy and organizational resources. In the process, advocates find themselves not only beholden to a growing constituency of programs dependent on federal funding but also bound to the state in a cross-cousin marriage of political convenience. Inconveniently, special-interest advocacy is one of those unendearing practices that pits potential allies against one another and works against broader movement building.

As it turns out, the only lasting alliance homeless advocates have forged is with that most thankless of activist causes, low-income housing. This preserved the genetic link to shelter and helped shore up the flagging cohorts of a kindred endeavor. But it did so at the cost of emphasizing individual entitlement—something people should be able to claim as a right—rather than collective stake—something they shoulder as part of social membership. When "responsibility" did enter the political discourse of reform, it did so as part of a critique of the moral failures of the poor and of the welfare state's complicity in perpetuating them.

Was there a viable alternative? Perhaps not, but for a brief period in the early 1990s Congress flirted seriously, for the first time in thirty years, with the notion of a broad-based public sector employment program. Impulsive calls rang out to "bring back the WPA," that talisman of the Depression-era can-do state. As has been the rule with such proposals, the flurry of excitement was quickly spent, casualty once more of well-established opposition, an employment policy legacy that emphasizes individual deficits at the expense of structural reforms, and an institutional vacuum at the level of successful (federal) programs.[51] Cultural critiques that located useful work at the heart of civil society[52] found themselves drafted into the service of wholesale welfare reform. While the juggernaut of that restructuring may well have been unstoppable,[53] an opportunity to challenge public opinion by changing the terms of the debate was missed. It may not have amounted to stolen thunder, but at the least it would have been an act of constructive mischief to shift from a demand of passive resettlement ("more housing") to one of active reengagement ("give us a chance to work—and let us worry about a place to live").[54]

Historically, for those whom the market had made redundant or families had failed, *social* alternatives made it possible to lead fully fledged (if somewhat irregular) lives.[55] The signature element of such alternatives was not lodging but useful work (e.g., the WPA) or work equivalents (e.g., higher education under the G.I. Bill). Functioning more as warehouses for the dispossessed, shelters bear little resemblance to them. Except as in-kind currency for earning one's keep, an increasingly common contingency under new welfare regulations, surrogate forms of work play little part. "Guests" at publicly subsidized shelters may be expected to put in their allotted hours doing chores or reporting to work assignments, but this practice essentially reinvents the "work-test" of nineteenth-century lodging houses, with clerical filing replacing woodcutting. (The exception, worth analysis in its own right, is the conversion of guests to "staff"—an occurrence especially common in specialized shelters catering to those with substance-abuse problems.) Most shelters are dismal makeshifts. Assayed as corrective or compensatory measures to a market that fails to provide sufficient work or housing to the unschooled or difficult poor, they're dreadful.[56] Unlike the skid row neighborhoods of a generation ago, they provide not an alternative way of life and work (or, as was truer then, of retirement), but temporary holding mechanisms that tend to morph into domestic equivalents of refugee settlements.

Or so, for much of the period under discussion here, we thought. The shelter turnover rates reviewed earlier suggest a needed refinement to this picture. For many users, the homelessness that leads them to seek public refuge proves a disruptive but transitory experience. Ordinary routines are undone, status distinctions leveled, histories erased, and (unlikely as this may seem) a rude solidarity can take shape.[57] For the fortunate, this is a passage blessed with a terminus, not a "captive state."[58] Assisted exits from homelessness are usually stable—and here, in the brokering specialists newly made available, service-enriched transfers, and limited supply of dedicated housing resources advocates may take some pride of authorship. For those (probably the majority) for whom other options exist, a brief stay in a public facility merely confirms the wisdom of avoiding them. For many, family and friends continue to be the habitual recourse in time of trouble. The exceptions, those for whom the process stalls, are people whose histories, problems, or proclivities make them lousy prospects for "placement" and unwelcome guests at the homes of friends and family. Some have reconciled themselves to a life without roots or reason. Some may have entered an extended period of "woodshedding" (musicians argot for a retreat from public life to explore and hone certain skills) during which much internal reorganization takes place behind the shell of an apparently disengaged self;[59] others, in clinical disrepair, are shuttled from pillar to post. Whether the "socially dysfunctional" beneficiaries of the *Callahan* consent decree, veterans of the institutional circuit in Westchester County, confirmed nomads, or hardened street dwellers, their displacement becomes a limbo. If their former lives were often troubled and unsettled, their present circumstances suspend all entanglements. Living this way turns the twelve-step motto ("one day at a time") into a self-mocking taunt, a state of mind Duneier aptly terms the "Fuck-it" mentality.[60] The old skid-row scholars used to speak of a similar state of "retreatism" as "disaffiliation";[61] this is disaffiliation with a hustler's edge. Disaffiliation, when distilled to a belligerent posture of all demand and no quarter, can greatly stress those who labor on the front lines of succor and shelter.

A worthy cause, committed foot soldiers, appealing rhetoric, and broad-based receptiveness to the notion of a baseline of security are not enough. Of all the suspect premises in our kit, that government could competently do more for the poor may have proved the lethal one. For all the theatrics and hard work, the substantial accomplishments of advocacy came under renewed assault in the late 1990s. Service and shelter are still the watchwords of homeless assistance, and the numbers seeking them remain high.[62] Funds for developing affordable housing, let alone public sector employment, are scarce and getting scarcer. The most visible differences from the early 1980s, such as the street outreach teams now common in major cities, are an odd amalgam of relief and policing. Public funding of once-charitable enterprises proves only that costs can be socialized, even at the margins. What else might one want to claim about the rounds of a mobile soup kitchen in Manhattan that nightly feed eight hundred on the streets?[63]

If the record on substance is uneven, the tally on the political front is dismaying. In harping on the larger picture of poverty, advocates have salvaged a necessary complexity at the cost of exhausting some allies, alarming others, and confirming our enemies in their worst red-baiting fears. We manage, high-handedly and with great regularity, to annoy our friends and exasperate our constituency. (For those who toil on the side of the angels, moral narcissism is a constant occupational hazard.) In the process, homelessness is effectively orphaned as a political issue. Accounting for failure means returning repeatedly to scrutinize goals, strategies, and working ledgers of compromise. It means seeking out those "often invisible linkages that block or redirect the impetus for reform."[64] It means questioning the wisdom of single-issue incrementalism, with its vulnerability to renewed opposition at every turn and divisive effect on potential allies. These days, too, it means confronting the inertial force of the de facto industry that has arisen to deal with homelessness. To say that homelessness has been "domesticated" is both to take rueful stock of our own efforts and to notice that a generation of workers, clients, and their observers cannot recall when it was otherwise.[65]

What has this to do with the day-to-day anxieties of frontline street workers? How do musings on the strategic shortcomings of national advocacy speak to their concerns?

The Heat of Advocacy, The Heart of Everyday Work

"Social mechanisms" are abstract elements in models; "abeyance," "liminality," and "limbo," technical terms to describe the way such mechanisms fit into larger models still ("the market"). In life, corporal works of mercy require agents of flesh and blood, from whom a special toll is exacted. In an extraordinary exchange that took place in 1980, James Rooney and Armand Mauss debated how to reconcile the institutionalized success of rescue missions with the awkward truth that they "fail on a colossal scale in converting derelicts."[66] The facts weren't at issue, the trade being an old one. Skid row preachers browbeat and offer salvation; in return, the men act out. They drink diligently, nod out during services, sing indifferently, feign conversions ("nosedives"), voice contempt for the proceedings, and condemn the missions for staging them. The vast majority of skid row men avoid missions, seizing any option, no matter how menial, to earn their keep—and that, Rooney argued, is precisely the point. By reproducing in religious dress the deterrent hospitality of the nineteenth-century workhouse, the missions bolster the work ethic, subsidize pensions, reduce the official unemployment rate, and ease the burden on public poor relief.

Did Rooney mean to imply that missionaries were merely useful idiots in the service of system maintenance? Mauss asked. (His own preferred interpretation: not stooges, the preachers had a certain slippage affinity with the men they serve, being washouts from mainstream clerical positions themselves.) Given that their preaching not only bore scant fruit, but actively invited mockery as an appropriate response, what could possibly be the return on emotional investment in such poor prospects? If patently fraudulent conversions were countenanced, did that mean that the job required willful self-deception on the part of missionaries? Or was another dynamic at work?[67]

Could it be that the cheap theater of these ersatz congregations ironically confirms the purity of heart of the one preaching? To reap genuine converts yields the sort of satisfaction that could keep anyone going; to fail, repeatedly, and to stick with it requires the tougher fiber of the true believer and attests to motivation that draws its strength from deeper wells. To toil in the company of like-minded marginals ensures back-up persuasion should personal fervor wane.[68]

If this interpretation is correct, the trick at the skid row missions was to reframe the evidence of failure as indirect testament to the otherworldly temper of the effort. Like almsgiving in the Middle Ages,[69] the act is valued for what it revealed about the giver and not for any concrete difference it made in the life of the recipient. Unlike missionaries with little to show for their preachment, however, advocates would be ill-advised to mistake stubborn failure for purity of purpose. For shelter providers of a secular cast of mind, too, the stakes are pragmatic and the challenge sorts out differently. *Laborare est orare* (to work is to pray) may still suffice for a few, but for the unsaintly the decision to stay and work on the front lines of street assistance usually means contending with what actually happens on the ground. Consider the lament of a Los Angeles shelter provider.

Rehearsing the dirty particulars of work almost never witnessed—except by its recipients—Vivian Rothstein found herself wearily questioning the point of it all.[70] Hers was no right-wing screed, nor its author some modern-day Candide (or social work intern) freshly schooled by experience. Rothstein had labored for years to transform the scullery chores of shelter and feeding into rough acts of love. Her doubts were not about giving per se, but about the utility of the gift and so, inescapably, about the value of the gesture. She had come to view herself as a strut in the architecture of their despair—part of the life support apparatus for people who have "adapted to their homelessness," who have come to terms with the "pain of the dispossessed," and who do their best to deaden it. Her work, she believed, was not only complicit but also diverted scarce goods away from equally needy others, less bent on self-destruction. She has not lost sight of the poverty and chains of mishap that drove many to the street, but she's grown weary of being exploited and dubious of the good she tells herself she's doing. Advocacy's rant is of no help, and the reassurance of coworkers rings hollow. Like a stagehand in a Samuel Beckett play, her job enables this grim tableau to be repeated day after day.

An advocate's instinct at this juncture, having paid tribute to the truth of her plaint, is to retreat to the thickets of "the broader political and economic context" from within which her lament issues and recite the sorry history of lost jobs, destroyed housing, gutted programs, dislocated families, and distracted politicians to be found there. But that would reduce her words to mere pretext. People like Rothstein know that history; they helped document it. What one can do—and admittedly, it isn't much—is to acknowledge the huge distance between those macro-order developments and the day-to-day grind of street-level practice. This means bearing witness to the terrible contradictions of such work: for every shelter provider who sees a "ministry of restoration" in her work, there is another who worries that she's doing the backstage chores of system maintenance while having her moral indignation co-opted. Those who come to find the notion of ministry an act of bad faith are ill-suited for the dirty work it both masks and makes possible.

The least we can do is learn from them. But what might this mean, exactly?

It may be small comfort, but the lot of advocates for the homeless poor has an absurdist cast to it these days. None of us is keen to defend the right of anyone who wishes, no matter the soundness of that wish, to live on the street under circumstances that would have shamed a nineteenth-century rag-picker. Few are stirred by the prospect of rehousing the displaced in conditions indistinguishable from those that helped make them homeless in the first place. Many harbor doubts about a calling that, despite its concrete achievements, can sometimes seem an antic sideshow of interest chiefly to its own company of players. It helps to recall that things could be worse—we could be turnkeys in converted asylums—but not much and not for long.

Early in Nadine Gordimer's novel *Burger's Daughter*, there is an account of a tramp's death. The man had passed away quietly in a park one afternoon, while others nearby ate lunch, slept, courted, or simply luxuriated in time off work. The narrator was one such hapless bystander. She is at first stunned: he had "carried through the unspeakable act in our presence"—and no one had noticed, let alone intervened. Not that noticing would have made a difference: The deceased was a homeless ex-miner who "drank methylated spirits and slept in bus shelters." But in the narrator's family, it was believed that "the revolution we lived for" would change everything. That day in the park she slowly comes to see that there are kinds of damage (even unremarked deaths) that a remade world will never reach.

It may be useful, then, to distinguish between essential/unavoidable suffering and the needless/gratuitous type. Yes, this is just the sort of bright line that advocacy notoriously favors and the analytic mind questions.[71] But before dismissing it out of hand, consider two opposing moments that might help us draw the distinction.

Call the first the *limit of politics*. There are grievances (death if not taxes) that pragmatic culture is impotent to redress, species of adversity that the tools of market, state, or community cannot repair. Some are categorically beyond reach—the pain, moral outrage, and bafflement written indelibly into the life script. Faced with these trials, the work of culture takes on a distinctive color. Where practical remedies are not viable and common sense flummoxed, we reach for symbolic accounts that ground suffering in a different order of justification—in religion, for example.[72]

Clearly, with respect to the scarcity of affordable housing in the United States, we are well short of that limit. Practical remedies are well within our reach, and politics can legitimately be tasked with realizing them. But in addressing other needs, things are not so clear.

Most cultures admit of outsiders, people for whom life on the margins can become a kind of calling or commitment. The offer of community disinterests them. They occupy a zone where misfits, defiance, and the unassimilable thrive.[73] This preference for being left alone defines what might be called the *limit of solidarity,* where the perceived benefits of belonging are outweighed by the freedom to dissent in ways that divide and mark one as "other." Rothstein's clientele may be among them. That this attitude may itself be both an adaptation to failure and an ordeal holding hope of a recovered respectability (as with some of *Sidewalk*'s street venders[74]) complicates the picture. (For them, an outsider status is a liminal experience.) Either way, a judicious measure of tolerance seems called for. In times past, such a measure was embodied, in effect if not by design, in the waste spaces and disreputable lodgings of central business districts. Although traces survive, those places are rare today.[75] Here, too, advocacy has its work cut out. As such spaces vanish, advocates find themselves in the unusual position of calling on government to preserve, even develop, substandard resources it once actively sought to upgrade or eliminate.

Admittedly, in distinguishing species of suffering, advocacy favors the simpler calls: the need that goes unmet because degradation is exacted as an intrinsic condition of its satisfaction; the offer of assistance that enlists coercion in the interest of efficiency; the bureaucratic practice that routinely sabotages hard-won statutory remedies; the grotesque inequities in state-mediated housing assistance; the refusal to see that settles on a citizenry faced with the spectacle of extreme privation. To recognize that such suffering is gratuitous—to say that its origin is *social*[76]—is not to claim that its generative structures are readily correctable or its effects easily undone. But this is only to point out that advocacy is work, not a walk in the park.

Rothstein's lament is different. Hers is the unhappy realization that committed work (what an outsider might recognize as "harm reduction") demands not simple acts of mercy, but complex ones of connivance. She confronts a need deformed by denial, a misery that has come to prefer (and so cultivates) its own company, a willfulness bent on defeating the gentlest of overtures. In such quarters, empathy can wither, compassion flag. That these are enduring quandaries fails to cheer.

In the face of such stoicism, advocacy had best hold counsel: There are no words of relief.

At the end of his canon-worthy ethnography, *Tally's Corner,* Elliot Liebow shook off his functionalist traces and reached for a wartime appeal from poet W.H. Auden. In context, the line reads more as commentary than conclusion:

> "We must love one another or die."

But this, as E.P. Thompson has noted, "is still only to state the problem." He continues: "The central place of cultural conflict is the place where the arguments of 'love' and the arguments of necessity contend."[77] Whether as political action or the scullery chores of kitchen work, organized movement or human gesture, advocacy on behalf of the homeless poor has set itself against the argument of necessity. Its tragedy is that the skills so essential to the one task are so poorly suited for the other.

[8]

Limits to Witnessing: From Ethnography to Engagement

The dogs bark, but the caravan moves on.
—Bedouin proverb

For over twenty years now,[1] ethnographers have plied their trade in the briar patch of homelessness across the United States. Working against a cultural tradition of denial and confinement, one that readily accommodates unobtrusive poverty, we seized on this novel spectacle—rude, visible, burgeoning homelessness—as a vehicle for reopening the book on poverty and dysfunction. If we had a guiding preoccupation, it was to bear witness: to render faithfully the "Minute Particulars" (William Blake) of a reality that, structurally, was not supposed to exist (not in these numbers, at any rate). We never sought to segregate these margins, quite the contrary. Ironically though, in the rush to refine focus we may have sacrificed depth of field, cheated time, cut some essential pathways, and shortchanged practical application. This concluding chapter takes up the task of reconnection.

In retrospect, the temptation to traffic in some eth-notional land of the homeless is understandable. Like the skid row sociologists of the 1960s, we found ourselves taken aback by the convenient *foreignness* of the phenomenon.[2] For those of us denied an "over there," here was an opportunity to do some real anthropology on a subject that readily lent itself to such scrutiny. With some exceptions, the homelessness portrayed in these studies tends to be sequestered, captive, estranged. It's an exotic world, but one that has been safely domesticated; its protagonists, tantalizingly different from, yet plainly recognizable to, those of us secure at home. Within that world, a warping holds sway. Events and practices unfold in a zone of hysteresis, where successive adjustments to an initial destabilizing force have the effect of nudging a system (the lived world of the officially homeless) ever further off course. Actions in this borderland become progressively out-of-the-ordinary, while remaining within reach: strange enough to sustain ethnographic curiosity, yet sufficiently familiar to yield to interpretation. Lately, the scope of work has broadened. Early accounts of the gritty particulars of subsistence have been joined by chronicles of aestheticized pain, verbal inventiveness, and ironic cultural commentary.

The common subject of these reports is a contained disorder, its metes and bounds set by officialdom and sanctioned by social science as "literal homelessness"—the unaccommodated men, women, and (sometimes) children of the street and shelters. But in the effort to get the jarring particulars right, causal analysis is scanted (the arduous work of making the necessary connections being typically shunted off to others), practical correctives ignored, and alternatives left unplumbed. Instead of the stubbornly abrasive substance we may have fancied ourselves producing, the ethnographic product is readily accommodated as local color, prepackaged compassion, or reassuring narratives of resiliency on the margins.

Like Dante's underworld visitor, we have wandered through this fresh hell, taking note of familiar faces, ruined lives, and dashed hopes, leaving little trace behind. Writing well may be a kind of revenge—but against whom, exactly?

For that matter, writing is hardly the end of it. Working as we do with natives and activists in an era "when they read what we write,"[3] and as the hard-won stock of provisions for the poor is undergoing "devolution" before our eyes, it obviously behooves us to examine the practical implications of our parasitic texts. I want to explore a stronger claim here: that ethnographic work is essentially unfinished if it pulls up short at description and commentary. Engagement must be the complement to witnessing in a discipline that prizes the well-being of "those whose lives and cultures they study" above all else and deems it an affirmative obligation of its members "to speak out publicly" on matters within their field of expertise.[4] Reckoning with the demands of citizenship, with the transfer of anthropological aptitude into political reason and political action, isn't just a nice idea. It goes to the heart of who we anthropologists say we are.

Genesis

This chapter began as a rueful stocktaking by a slow learner. Improbably, its immediate impetus was working on a review of a book about homeless women, *Tell Them Who I Am* (1993), by the late Elliot Liebow. It's a book about toil and trouble, about the prospects of solidarity in difficult straits, about grit and humor. Energy, effort, and resolve punctuate its pages as surely as failure, frustration, and disappointment. As the shelters, the streets, thoughtless passersby, skinflint employers, service providers, and other assorted grifters put these women through their paces, we learn (safely, from afar) what it means to do the *work* of homelessness. That is the book's true subject, the portrayal of which is among its singular achievements.

At the same time, one can't help but suspect that the implied target and original motivation was the "social factory" that exacts such work of these women—the shelters, welfare institutions, peripheral labor markets, and grudging families. Shelters aside, except as they emerge in fragments of narrative that compose these women's stories, we learn little about the institutions and practices that account for their homelessness in the first place. The focus remains fixed on the world of official homelessness: the streets and shelters, and what it takes to survive there. Hysteresis reigns. The work these women do simply to stay afloat ultimately counts for very little. With few exceptions, it returns little on the investment, persuades few of their worth, amasses no equity. It matters only because of what it allows them to reap in the process: the dividends of a tentative self-regard and, if only in the sharing of stupidities endured, a precarious kind of sisterhood.

Liebow's tacit argument is a fiercely moral one: Forget about how they got here, no one deserves to be treated like this.[5] There is no fair measure. For these women, each day brings new challenges, only rarely muted by (let alone advancing upon) the exertions that went into surviving the day before. Resolutions of their predicament are not the cumulative product of sustained effort, but a haphazard mix of luck and timing and living long enough to see them. Homelessness is unworthy of the work these women put into it. Unto such labors, more should flow.

In the deliberately blunt rubric with which I mean to end this book, so what?

The conclusion to *Tell Them Who I Am* contains no statements about the work of homelessness, or about solidarity on the margins, or about grit in the face of adversity. These things are missing for the simple, exasperating reason that they *have nothing to do with solving homelessness.* Faithful though they may be to the ethnography of street life, they are mute guides to its eradication. Instead, we are given a number of impatient if accurate reflections (e.g., more affordable housing) that could have been forged without the painstaking account of toil and trouble that precedes them. (In fact, Liebow claimed he wrote them before completing the ethnography.)

To be sure, Liebow's book teaches much about life on this gendered margin: about homeless women as active collaborators in a documentary effort;

about the lure and hazards of work; about the many ways in which powerlessness hedges the prospects of dignity and connectedness; about the obscure mandate and casual "brutishness" of shelter; about the uneven trade in emotional support; about the divisiveness of race even at the bottom; about the hard-won wisdom of not expecting too much that the staff often mistakes for "failure to plan"; about amateur theodicies spun to account for the hopelessly arbitrary quality of their daily lives; about uncertainty as a way of life, hopes scuttled, and disbelief come to ground as depression. Though they go to the heart of what it means to be homeless, none of them has a thing to do with resolving it.[6] Liebow was no fool; what on earth did he have in mind in organizing his book this way?

Or is this all a bit forced and parochial, a petty cavil voiced about an otherwise splendid valedictory volume that ought rightly to be celebrated? After all, it's not as though the field had lain fallow until the author of *Tally's Corner* showed up and "backed into it."[7] What have the other ethnographers of homelessness been up to?

Some Noteworthy—If Limited—Accomplishments

With few exceptions, recent ethnographies of homelessness may be mapped along three axes of interest: clinical, subsistence, and literary. In varying proportions, these concerns—with damage, with resourcefulness, and with wrested significance—have shaped our inquiries.

Highlights of these ethnographies, by now familiar, include the following:

- The resurgence of institutional demoralization ("manufactured dependency") in men grown accustomed to "shelterized" life[8]
- The temporal dislocations of street life[9]
- The sheer ingenuity and doggedness of those who redefine the use-value of public spaces and discarded waste products into survival goods—converting airports and train terminals into group quarters, public parks and facilities into campgrounds[10]
- The untrustworthiness of appearance as a key to resilience—the deployment of "crazy" behavior as a protective device, for example[11]
- The resurgence of soup kitchens, shanty-structures, and encampments in urban areas, sometimes erected with the help of outlaw construction gangs[12]
- The evolution of distinctive ethics of survival in different homeless ecologies—street, private shelter, and municipal warehouse[13]
- The development of informal economies in municipal shelters[14]
- The demands of "identity work" on those who would survive with their

dignity intact on the street, and the contrivances by which damage to one's sense of connectedness can be repaired[15]

- The innovations of street outreach work and importance of being able to offer—and deliver on—real choices in efforts to engage street-dwelling homeless[16]
- The prizing of privacy and safety by formerly homeless persons forced to shared residential quarters, and the difficulties of hewing consistently to an ethic of empowerment in such shared settings[17]
- The keen observations nested in the rapid-fire speech of shelter residents "talking ragtime"[18]
- The plotting of longitudinal courses of homelessness for single adults with severe mental illness, and identifying of predictors of "exits" from homelessness[19]
- An early call for elucidating field-based "economies of makeshift" has been answered with a fine study of street vendors.[20]

Some have made the crossing into practice, but not many and not often. The exceptions merit note: a seasoned anthropologist gone native, transforming herself into a full-time housing developer in her home community (Stark[21]); ethnographers who have tested their mettle as "expert witnesses" in public interest litigation (myself,[22] Koegel, DeHavenon among them); and investigators who have tackled real-life dilemmas of practice—the vagaries of street outreach (Lovell, Barrow, Rowe), the hazards and promise of self-governance in contrived communities of those formerly homeless and still severely mentally ill (Ware and her colleagues); the worn and troubled mercies of harm reduction (Koester, Feldman). Some have tested the boundaries of official homelessness (Hopper and Baumohl, Gounis, Williams); others looked at organizing efforts among the homeless poor themselves (Rosenthal, Wagner, Wright, Mathieu). A number have wrestled directly (though without noticeable effect) with policy quandaries. Some have ghost-written official reports.

To What Avail?

But for the most part, ethnographies of American urban homelessness conducted in the 1980s and 1990s fell prey to the pull of *hysteresis.* Economists borrow the term from physics to describe the cumulative (or developmental) complexity of a destabilized system, careening from one induced adjustment to another, getting progressively further off course and out of balance, such that restoration to its original state is an ever more costly and difficult affair.[23] My contention is that the location of ethnographies of homelessness in the inherently unstable zone of hysteresis may have made for vivid documentation and lively analyses, but at the cost of ensuring that the product could be safely ignored. By restricting the scope of work in this way, we lose (and thus encourage others to forget) the fact that both the margins and the displaced poor who occupy them are historical, contingent products. Disorder tends to be taken as a given, its genesis of secondary import to the task of capturing its manifold intricacies and plumbing its secrets. To the extent that they are addressed at all, the details of the causal antecedents of widespread homelessness and the shape of plausible social remedies tend to be borrowed, synoptic, breezed through by way of historical prelude. The excitement lies elsewhere: in redeeming the currency of actions and utterances whose face value would seem to be reckless, stupid, self-destructive, or crazy.

We anthropologists seek to decipher camouflaged utilities, to "ferret out the unapparent import of things";[24] to identify unseen, even disavowed, force fields of power;[25] to uncover "hidden transcripts" of resistance and cultural commentary, whose existence (it transpires) may be unknown even to the native authors themselves.[26] In doing so (exceptions noted), we give short shrift to the tedious work of backtracking—tracing erstwhile connections to labor and housing markets, to kin and friends, to unofficial sources of subsistence. Such work might reveal the delicate shape of "but fors"—elements of everyday life that, had they remained in place or been shored up, could have averted the displacement of homelessness.

We've ignored such traditional topics of ethnographic inquiry as the following: the degradation of habitat (the depletion of crucial "marginal" resources); the growth of precariously accommodated populations at risk of displacement (from their own or shared housing) and of competition for affordable housing; the workings of informal alternatives to official homelessness (specifically, the elaboration of those makeshifts that have been the historical legacy of the urban poor);[27] and careful examination of rectification strategies proposed (from emergency relief to income, housing, service policies, and police practices).

As I argued in Chapter 1, such topics require framework as well as fieldwork, expanding the usual circle of informed natives, attending to history, political economies, and the swamplands of bureaucracy. I mean something more modest than, say, "The Postmodern Leviathan." To cite only five topics ripe for ethnographic inquiry: (1) the unprecedented appearance of large numbers of African Americans in contemporary shelter populations (see Chapter 6); (2) the visibility cast on domestic violence by the availability of specialized shelters; (3) neighborhood opposition to the siting of "special needs" housing;[28] (4) the enabling circumstances and administrative skills that transform a superior "demonstration" project into a newly accepted standard; and (5) the operation (and potential for both support and exploitation) of the shadow housing market.

Linking Fieldwork to Framework

If we expect linguistic competence of fieldworkers dispatched to far-flung lands, or (closer to hand) insist that ethnographers of "scientific work" come equipped with (or prepared to master) the requisite knowledge and competencies demanded in the laboratory,[29] why not expect ethnographers of poverty to develop the technical expertise, clinical knowledge, and familiarity with regulatory and procedural constraints to evaluate proposed interventions? I'm suggesting that it is time for the ethnography of homelessness to extend itself into the realm of defensible reforms—without yielding our critical perspective or falling into the squirrel cage of system maintenance. If the first task is to understand *what stands in the way* of consequential reform in housing,[30] not far behind is an assessment of what the new regimens of managed care will mean for troubled populations in a habitat of diminished margins. But to entertain such extensions means acquiring the requisite skill needed to assess proposed remedies and fashion reasonable alternatives. This is an application of ethnographic tradecraft quite distinct from that needed to document the work of homelessness. As it stands, we ethnographers of homelessness tend to know little about measuring unmet need for affordable housing, let alone assembling the financing for housing development (where a *bond,* we soon learn, is not something mediated through kinship). We know less about labor markets, almost nothing about bureaucracies of assistance, and surprisingly little about the informal communities of support and sustenance that often spell the difference between a berth among friends or family and an anonymous cot in a barrack shelter. We pay ritual homage (as anthropologists must, if only as an article of faith) to the provenance of homelessness as "a sociopolitical condition—a set of *historical relations* and *categories* resulting from struggles over the production and allocation of social wealth"[31]—but fail to follow through on the logical and empirical implications of such a claim.[32] Like "the urban" in Richard Fox's early critique,[33] "the margins" we study tend to be taken as unanalyzed givens: the *there* we labor to make our own. "Imagine yourself suddenly set down" indeed . . .

Without such practical extensions into the dirty particulars of habitat history, policy, and program design—under circumstances never of our own choosing and rarely to our liking—even impassioned narratives of homelessness may become little more than detailed registers of grievances, sustained *études* into the aesthetics of suffering, pointless exercises in critical exegesis, or feckless hand-wringing. When coupled with the righteous anger so often provoked by serious acts of witnessing, applied work in this arena risks the "seduction of moral disgust" which, in turn, can become an excuse for withdrawal from the field of effort and compromise. Referring to "failures" of witnessing on a much graver scale, Ignatieff pleads:

> . . . policy-makers often exaggerated our impotence as an excuse to do less than we could have done; those demanding intervention often failed to understand that we could not have done more. Between those who said we could do nothing and those who said we could do it all has to lie a position where the ethics of commitment meets the ethics of responsibility, where the commitments we make to strangers in danger can be backed up by believable, achievable strategies of rescue.[34]

In the case of homelessness, "strangers" is too strong and "rescue" too ambitious. There is no question of our being "saliently related" to the peril we so assiduously document. These people are our neighbors. We ethnographers are citizens of the state constitutionally charged with their welfare, and if any stable "local" resolution is to happen we need to be part of it. But as noted earlier, the utility of emergency-based definitions of "homelessness" has been exhausted, the forward-leaning reforms of courts and state houses are now routinely taken apart in practice, and social policy has taken a huge step backward.[35]

In the end, it may be that the most we can hope for is to be prepared to subvert the premises of some bad policy,[36] but I'm reluctant to concede the point. An ethnographic corrective—to stereotypes, to psychiatric imperialism, to the presumed sufficiencies of the welfare state—is one thing; an active, engaged ethnography of how this present mess might be corrected (or improved on) would be quite another.[37] Sure, the latter runs the risk of losing its soul, but we've already seen what it's like to hold onto it at the expense of being rendered redundant. Admittedly, working within existing bureaucracies of assistance is like waltzing with a monster: the footwork can be tricky, there's no doubt about who's leading whom, and all the while one part of you is trying to work out who's calling the tune. So what? When you're done, and if so moved, write about *that.*

Second Thoughts?

This concluding screed may well be overargued.[38] It is, after all, not an easy thing to trace influence or locate the distant imprint of a well-told tale, especially when it undoes bias or damage that would have otherwise gone undetected. (We part-time teachers are wont to place great stock in such ambiguities of effect.) Nor should we gainsay efforts that simply keep an issue alive, seeding the popular imagination with half-appreciated notions of how things might be otherwise. Still, I think it worthwhile to pursue the implications of the position outlined here, if only to highlight its infirmities.

Not to put too fine a point on it, facts in the polis are so much timber. It takes a special kind of finishing work to fashion them into the fitted struts, braces, joists, and planks that are eventually assembled as policy statements. There is, in short, a *rhetoric* to useful—or, better, persuasive—research, and those of us who would aspire to have an impact on disputed issues of public policy had better learn to attend to its laws. Ethnographers of homelessness have done yeoman's work in depicting the shadowed details of life on the street and in the shelters. We've made passing attempts to measure the generative forces that shape homelessness in the United States today. But sheaves of thick description and heroic structural analyses are not enough. The nuance, shading, and complexity that make for fine ethnography also compose an open invitation to willful misreading. (If the rhetoric of policy-relevant research has one presiding rule, it is to restrict the possibilities of misreading to a minimum.) Further, by some perverse law of the excluded middle, we have failed to look at intermediary forces linking macro and micro,[39] virtually ignoring the fields and mechanisms of engines of reform, locally and nationally. What are our alternatives?

There are at least two obvious ones. The first, alluded to above, would entail deliberate forays into the thickets of political reason. This would mean taking seriously the translation process itself—the derivation of practical implications of research results, the distillation of core findings, the delineation of essential qualifiers of context or design, the identification of specific relevancies to current policy deliberations. These are not chores best left to legislative aides or jousting attorneys.

The second would mean heeding calls for political action, public interest anthropology, collaborative ethnographies, engaged advocacy.[40] Method as well as action is at stake. What might a multivocal evaluation study—with different versions crafted for different audiences—look like? How might we best safeguard that prospect when writing contracts for evaluation work? The promises and pitfalls of "studying up" need to be revisited; ethical issues of infiltration, investigation, and documentation confronted directly; and defensible means of access negotiated. All these potential fields of action merit closer scrutiny than I can give here. But the larger point should not be lost: The time for ever more refined accounts of marginalia has passed.

Fresh recruits to the cause are one thing; corrective measures that take root and grow, quite another. A further piece of anthropological business, one that gives the arrow of inquiry a recursive twist, might return to those surfaces where the dominant culture meets the margins. We go there if only because solidarity, as one of our tribal elders reminds us, "is only gesturing when it involves no sacrifice."[41]

From Shelter to Solidarity

Largely because of seismic changes in the labor and housing markets, the cultural landscape shifted in the 1980s, allowing us—as the Great Depression had allowed Agee, Evans, and their readers—a glimpse into "a portion of unimagined existence" ordinarily unavailable. In neither case was the poverty new, nor was its normal unavailability accidental. Whether it was tenant farmers in 1930s Alabama or African American families in contemporary Chicago or Boston (or, for that matter, working-class families in nineteenth-century Massachusetts), the travails that so stunned a middle-class readership were part of what it meant to make do on the rough edge of subsistence.[42] It was out of such contrivances, unseen and unheralded, that the poor managed to survive. That this was largely unknown, at times even actively concealed, was as it should be: This was the way cultural (and class) "boundaries" were supposed to work. The seventeenth-century cleric George Herbert may have lamented the fact that "one half knows not how the other half lives," but he was certainly not surprised by it.

When such boundaries are eroded, the shock of meeting poverty on the street—"unaccommodated," its hand outstretched, the plea for assistance made personal and immediate—is both edifying and disingenuous. It is edifying because people who have lived with the convenience of not seeing can prove quick studies when they confront it in the flesh. There is, after all, a linkage to be prized in the sudden realization of a Presbyterian elder at a Salt Lake City soup kitchen that "I am one job and one divorce away" from the people she was serving.[43] It is disingenuous because, plainly, the poverty had always been there for the seeing. It was not the case (much press to the contrary) that some previously unknown, long festering "underclass" had emerged. What was new, was that poverty had become an unavoidable fact of everyday life. Culture could no longer shield it from sight; in order to turn a blind eye to suffering these days one had to *cultivate* the habit of not seeing. That takes time, and it isn't simple or painless.

If, as Lilian Brandt once argued,[44] little is new in the corrective measures each era adopts to cope with the burden of the homeless poor, it is also true that recycled policy often goes unrecognized as such. Forced to cultivate the habit of not seeing, Americans have rediscovered how difficult that is and how easily resentment displaces sympathy. Like the citizens of sixteenth-century Bruges, we have rushed to institutionalize measures that, whatever their long-term costs, at least promise the short-term gain of removing the spectacle of poverty from the street. Like his counterparts in the nineteenth century, New York City's mayor, reading portents of general "disorder" in the example of unrestricted panhandling, went to court to secure a ban against begging in the subways.[45] Like irate townspeople combating the tramp menace, local governments have returned to the practice of "warning out" the undomiciled, on the premise that it is much cheaper to "move on" those who otherwise must be assisted or suffered. And like relief officials in the 1930s, states and municipalities have turned first to private charity and then to the long-discredited practice of storing surplus persons in warehouses and armories.

Driven by a mounting sense of things whirling out of control, such measures have as their object, whether as underlying logic or explicit design, the reestablishment of proper boundaries between a well-hidden poor and a no-longer-uneasy settled citizenry. Whatever their immediate value as instruments of relief, these measures fall far short of seeking to rectify—or even to address—the structural roots of the poverty attested to by widespread homelessness. More pernicious still, they may have the effect of soothing the abrasion needed to motivate the search for a more lasting and inclusive resolution. The issue is not mere lack of shelter. It isn't the absence of a prescribed set of rules, services, and medications in carefully structured environments that will enable the chronically ill or afflicted to live decently, if apart from the rest of us. It isn't the lack of specialized assistance for troubled families. It is something far more fundamental than that: the barely noticed loss of a sustained, determined commitment to make available to all the material resources and social tools needed to fully participate in this society.

Put plainly, the opposite of homelessness is not shelter but home. Understood culturally, *home* must entail some claim to inclusion. The principled question underlying homelessness policy, then, is not, what does charity demand? but rather, what does solidarity require? And so it no longer suffices (if it ever did) to ask what it is about the homeless poor that accounts for their dispossession. One must also ask what it is about "the rest of us" that has learned to ignore, then tolerate, only to grow weary of, and now seeks to banish from sight the ugly evidence of a social order gone badly awry.[46]

Phrased this way, the question unsettles. For some time now, other than infrequent and terrible preparations for invasions abroad or, more recently, terrorism on the home front, American culture has been markedly short on solidarity. Is it simply that common decency has become such an uncommon commodity? Or might it be rather that mobilizing it, animating it, putting it to constructive use in collective action, requires both a will and sense of urgency that are absent, even unmentionable, in the ranks of political leadership. (With rare exceptions, we have always lacked [in William James's fine phrase] "the moral equivalent of war"[47]—at *home,* on the *domestic* front.) Or is it rather that any semblance of vital solidarity, of the sort that somehow manages to take in and harbor what it might not yet understand, will be firmly local in recognition and equipage? That it must take in more than "security" and be, to borrow an old phrase, "community based"?

That Lear was banished to the heath was a transgression of kinship. He took refuge there in the cave of Poor Tom, who himself was masquerading as a homeless lunatic to escape the treachery of his half-brother. Is this as far as the legacy of tradition can take us—are answers to be found in disciplining kinship to meet its obligations? Or in trusting to the comfort found only in the hovels of similarly kinless strangers? Let us grant that the welfare state has made some progress since Elizabethan times. What *would* solidarity—in the sense of inclusiveness, not merely safety—dictate, here, at home?

Some durable themes have been sounded throughout this book: distancing and abandonment; utility, work, and worth; the limits of kindness and reach of kinship; the redemptive power of what happens when history and hope, for want of a better coupling, unite. Though only occasionally glimpsed in these pages (but all too evident in the work of outreach), another should be mentioned: the complications introduced when misery comes to prefer its own company. What do they suggest about future avenues of inquiry? Whither the anthropology of homelessness?

If this book's argument (if so lumpy a gladstone of history, field dispatch, reportage, and commentary can be said to have one) has any merit, its forward impulse should be clear: We should be looking elsewhere. *Not* toward closer/edgier documentation of natives of odd habits in unfamiliar habitats (who are increasingly likely, in any event, to be there for *shorter* periods of time than the fieldworker,[48] making for a postmodern encounter of a forced and artificial sort). Instead, we should be driving toward better understandings of alternatives, both "preventive" arrangements and engagements unrecognized as such, and corrective measures explicitly designed for the purpose.

"Solving" homelessness—at least the sort that does not arise out of liminal breakdowns, late-adolescent adventure, or exceptional occupation[49]—is moronically simple in principle. "Housing," to steal a slogan, "works." The trickier tasks are recognizing *how* it was solved (or prevented) in the past; what about those practices or policies might be resurrected and retooled to the specifications of the present; and what newly fashioned remedies might be needed, and how, if they work, they might be replicated. (We may not choose to reinvent skid row, but functional equivalents of low-cost, low-demand accommodation are surely needed.) The model, to say it again, should be *employment,* not flood or famine relief; the mistaken notion—regnant for two decades—that a passing crisis might be waited out has not only incurred huge social costs but created a massive artificial relief industry with a perverse interest in sustaining demand for its services.[50]

Shifting ethnographic attention may amount, in the main, to what was referred to in Chapter 1 as an "anthropology of makeshifts," with homelessness either a nonissue or making its entrance as a by-product of peculiar existential commitments or contingencies. In some cases, though, the inquiry will have a markedly recherché feel, the themes familiar even if the stage and players are not.

Nowhere is this clearer than in the lives of those coping with severe mental illness, whose predicament on the street first drew me to this work some twenty-odd years ago. In the wreckage of deinstitutionalization, a de facto mental health system had taken shape and a serious debate over the terms of inclusion had ignited. In falling first casualty to the former, homelessness derailed the latter.

To confront the limits of supportive housing today is to enter a time warp and reclaim that lost debate. Once homelessness is solved, one realizes with a start, all those once unsettling questions crop up again with new urgency and distinctive inflections. What does it mean to belong, to claim full adult membership, in a noninstitutional world? What metes and bounds of care ought to apply once the warrant of custody is lifted? How best extend the social contract to include those whose lives are disrupted by disorder (sometimes repeatedly) and who struggle to negotiate terms of reentry? How does madness change when welcomed back into "the community"? How, in turn, might community be transformed? This time, too, the voices of service users are being heard.

The critical literature of the mid- to late 1970s catalogued the social failures of deinstitutionalization with the expectation that speaking truth to power would usher in reform. It found small-scale replicas of old-style asylums tucked away in rundown quarters of light industry, failed resorts, and shabby residences. It railed against "service-dependent ghettoes" of the formerly confined. It charged the community mental health movement with defaulting on its founding charter, catering to the walking wounded instead of those making the difficult passage from hospital to home or doing without the former altogether. It identified an emergent ramshackle affair of off-loaded responsibility and convenience (the de facto mental health system) and asked who was in charge.

In response, the National Institute of Mental Health (NIMH) championed a nascent "community support" movement and set out to rectify, or at least demonstrate the feasibility of rectifying, the glaring defects of current practice. Even as that corrective took root, its own deficiencies were scrutinized. For a brief bracing period—epitomized in the upstart scholarship of a gifted skeptic with an eye for unkept promises, Sue Estroff's *Making It Crazy* (1981)—the debate was on. It ranged widely: Medication as package deal not magic bullet: controlling symptoms perhaps, but with side effects that shouted out one's status. The subtler arts of influence and constraint in noninstitutional settings, once restraint and seclusion no longer obtain. The "lure and haven" of disorder—how sickness can be cultivated as a career and identity—and with what costs. The hazards of dumbed-down work. The difficulties of crafting a social life across the stigmatized divide separating "normals" and "crazies."

The quarrel flared, then crashed. By the time the paperback edition of Estroff's path-breaking work appeared a few years later, its epilogue was already grappling with a new complication—not the benevolent paternalism of the intrusive state, but the wreckage of an absent one. Once the historic association of madness and vagrancy was restored, and in numbers never before seen in this country, the debate over living life to the fullest and planning for the uneven uphill course of recovery suddenly seemed a luxury, a starry-eyed holdover of the utopian '60s. Homelessness meant that all bets were off. The urgency lay elsewhere, and properly so. Better grateful than dead.

But a quarter century has passed. And, under circumstances hostile to social experimentation of any but the most strapped and utilitarian sort, we've shown homelessness among this population to be a practical matter of resources and skills, and not some postmodern variant of madness. We know how to reach those left out, how to house and support them, how to improve prospects of recovery. We have better tools for symptom management, a better feel for pathologies of place, renewed appreciation of the ruder constraints of budgets. We can see what needs to be done, what gains consolidated. None of this is to suggest that the project of solving homelessness is in endgame or that completing it will be easy. (And none of the old questions makes sense unless it's resolved.) But it is to insist that we can already see what success in that venture will leave undone and, with the benefit of hindsight, what we cannot settle for. This time around, it will not suffice to rest content with stable "placements" or to return to those great hulking arks—board-and-care facilities and the other beached ships of fools—where the still-dispossessed but no longer institutionalized tarried while their lives ran out.

Solving homelessness will mean returning, at long last, to first principles and foundational questions. It will mean reexamining the initial term in what now passes for a geographical phrase—"community psychiatry"—and asking what range of meanings it might hold for persons too often denied the usual passports of worth. (We could do worse, for example, than to consider Adam Smith's notion of the "semblance of real regard" in measuring the "support" in contrived living arrangements.) It means rethinking patienthood as an ambiguous and contested state, revisiting the terms of moral agency, looking anew at issues of coercion, autonomy, and the balance of power and respect in treatment decisions.

Homelessness may have forced a moratorium, but the old questions never went away.

Notes

Chapter 1. This Business of Taking Stock

1. At about this time, British journalists had taken to characterizing that country's deinstitutionalization policies as transforming "patients into vagrants."

2. Advice from one urbane vade mecum: ". . . to be a New Yorker is to be a person who frequently asks himself, 'What am I doing here?' A diehard New Yorker has learned to live with that question, the way one learns to live with a bone spur" (*The New Yorker*, 23 February and 1 March, 1999, 41).

3. Hufton 1974, 12.

4. Bruns 1980, 17.

5. Bureau of Applied Social Research 1965, 1, 17.

6. Caplow 1970, 6.

7. Harlow 1931, 529; Anderson 1934, 58.

8. *New York Times* 25 February 1972, 1.

9. Jackson 1987, 71; Bonner 1990; Isay et al, 2000.

10. As Roger Sanjek nicely argues in an essay on "ethnographic validity" (Sanjek 1990).

11. Rist 1994, 550.

12. Bouwsma 1990.

13. Mizruchi 1987.

14. Turner 1967, 93–111; 1969, 94–203; 1974, 166–271; 1985, 158–162, 264f, 294f.

15. Stocking 1983, 92.

16. Barrett 1996, 73.

17. Jackson 1990.

18. Sanjek 1990; DeVita 1990.

19. Barrett 1996, 179. In the course of conducting such research, grounding epistemological issues are bracketed and elemental questions of methodology are "managed by a fundamental neglect"—as is typically the case with "normal science" (Rock 1979, 172, 178).

20. Wood 1999, xiii.

21. Stott 1973; Geertz 1998, 22; Coles 1997; Rorty 1998. None of this, it needs be said directly, is meant to deny the constructive (not "merely" mimetic) element in any representa-

tion. The predicament, I'm fairly sure, is a common one: you've read enough of critical self-examinations and apologias in your own discipline, and sampled the wares of merchants in the philosophy and history of science, to know that your account will always and inevitably be "not the way it really was" (Neumann 1992). You're convinced nonetheless that with sufficient industry you can produce something "a little less false" than competing accounts (to borrow Sandra Harding's characterization, as cited in Wolf 1992, 125). So you soldier on, accumulating the debts of readers . . .

22. Elsewhere, I've offered an insider's view of working for the state. Not one likely to be mistaken for a recruiting poster, it reviews some common predicaments of contract anthropology, makes a pitch for applying ethnographic methods to core concerns in mental health services research, and argues that the circumstances of litigation can call for a distinctive sort of applied anthropology (Hopper, 2002).

23. Blau 1992.

24. The term "literal homelessness" is Rossi's (1989, 10).

25. Nicely exemplified by Duneier's *Sidewalk* (1999).

26. Note, too, that to appreciate the relevance of a secure income, affordable housing, and the availability of social support we must move well beyond the domain of the individual household. I realize as well that this is not the only lesson that can be drawn from this story, though it is the one I intended to be drawn. A physiologist with whom I once taught, after reading an early version of this account, looked at me bewildered: "So what's the big deal? She's a schizophrenic."

27. E.g., Kozol 1988.

28. Marin 1991; Moss and Tilly 1991.

29. Coser 1965, 141.

30. See Bahr 1970 for review essays and a useful annotated bibliography.

31. Davis 1968; Hufton 1974; Mollat 1986.

32. Tawney 1912; Webb and Webb [1927] 1963; Polanyi 1944; Beier 1985.

33. Ringenbach 1973; Kusmer 1987; Monkkonen 1984.

34. In part this appears to be due to the tendency of both local chroniclers and later historians to be more interested in her common trade—prostitution—than in the destitution and homelessness she would otherwise suffer. "Like peddling, scavenging, and ragpicking [the trades more commonly associated with homelessness], prostitution turned something with little value into something with cash value. When work was slow or money slack, milliners, servants, and peddlers alike resorted to prostitution." Nearly half of the prostitutes committed to the almshouse in 1859 were former servants (Gilfoyle 1992, 60). See also Golden 1992; Liebow 1993; Waterston 1999.

35. Rossi 1989, 10.

36. A recurrent theme in Nels Anderson's studies (1923, 1932, 1934).

37. See Monkkonen 1984; Bruns 1980; Hoch and Slayton 1989; Groth 1994.

38. During the worst of the Depression, these were nontrivial numbers: of the roughly 21,000 people I estimate to have comprised the city's "homeless" caseload in June 1935, some 5,200 were members of families relieved in their own homes—what we would later commonly refer to as "emergency assistance" or, perhaps, as "homeless prevention assistance." (See Hopper 1987, Table 3, pp. 238 A and B, for details.)

39. Sometimes all these varieties occur in the same setting. Homeless relief rolls in Westchester County in 1995 included those who: have "made their own arrangements" in rent-sharing agreements, stay in privately run shelters in the county, reside in public shelters and motels in adjacent New York City, live in motels in the county, participate in service-enriched "transitional residence" programs in the county, or, for the time being, are in detox, rehab, or work relief programs.

40. See Bogard et al., 1995.

41. Bahr 1973. "Disaffiliation" was their definitive characteristic. Late in the 1980s, Bahr

continued to argue that the contemporary homeless are distinguished by a "pathology of connectedness" (Bahr 1989, xx-xxi).

42. See Groth 1994, 133; Hoch and Slayton 1989. For this reason, Groth emphatically insists that such people "—historically as well as today—have *erroneously* been called 'homeless men'" (1994, 133; emphasis added).

43. This section draws substantially on work done jointly with Jim Baumohl; see Hopper and Baumohl 1994, 1996.

44. To anticipate a later point: Note that abeyance forces us to contend with what otherwise redundant people will do, not merely where or how they will live. That is, it complicates the question of exemption from work by refusing to release those who are still able from the demands of general reciprocity. Even monks performing surrogate penances for "sinner[s] who could afford the price" could pointedly be said to be assigned to "jobs, particularly the kind that required no special talent" (Mizruchi 1987, 33).

As with any number of macrosociological theses, the genius of such an arrangement hinges critically on that old *deus ex theoria,* the latent function of social practices. The difficult policy questions (how one might shape abeyance practices and projects) are thereby dodged. In this regard, it is emblematic that of all the New Deal programs, Mizruchi chose to look only at the Works Progress Administration (WPA) arts projects, which never rose to compete with the private sector or raised questions about unions, prevailing wages, inefficiencies, etc. Oddly enough, given the disruption-averting function that Mizruchi discerns for such projects, advocates for unemployment relief in this country have repeatedly had to argue both the danger that idleness poses and the injustice that it represents (Keyssar 1987, 214).

45. Mizruchi 1987, 157–158. Mizruchi is deliberately following Marx here: "Pauperism is the hospital of the active labour-army and the dead weight of the industrial reserve army. . . . It forms part of the *faux frais* [incidental expenses] of capitalist production: but capital usually knows how to transfer these from its own shoulders to those of the working class and the petty bourgeoisie." ([1867] 1967, 797; cf. [1857–1858] 1973, 609–610).

46. By the same token, it is important *not* to mistake similar cultural practices for solutions to the same local problem. Throughout Latin America, formally illegal "land invasions" on the outskirts of cities provide shelter, serving as in-kind housing subsidies for a low-waged urban proletariat. (Takeovers of abandoned properties within urban areas have recently taken place as well; see *New York Times* 7 April 2001, A7.) In the United States, where the economics of both wage-labor and state subsidies differ, shanty dwellings provide shelter for truly redundant people, people for whom we have yet to devise any alternative use than as recipients of "relief." Put simply, in Latin America such structures are part of the "social wage"; here, they are part of an abeyance process in transition. Similarly, not only the meaning but also the practical utility of "doubling up" can vary markedly among ethnic groups in New York City (Hamberg and Smolenski, 1993).

47. Krueckeberg 1999, 14.

48. Moss and Tilly 1991.

49. For further discussion, see Hopper 1990a.

50. See, e.g., Horton 1984; Karp 1985; Scheper-Hughes and Lock 1989; Kleinman 1992. Sickness was implicitly recognized as a (potentially troublesome) state of "motivated retreat" by Parsons in *The Social System* (1954); hence, his codification of the expectations of the afflicted under the social contract formalized as "the sick role."

51. For the *ordo vagorum,* see Waddell's classic *Wandering Scholars* [1927] 1961). For the Franciscans, see Turner 1974, 245, who saw this as an instance of liminality's "communitarian threat" being turned to the Church's advantage, leaving its impress—"the doctrine of poverty"—in the process. For English wayfaring, see Jusserand 1920.

52. See Katherine Newman's *Falling from Grace* (1988) for extensive examples. Hylan Lewis had earlier used "limbo" to refer to the men whose lives Liebow chronicled in *Tally's Corner* (1967, xii).

53. Thus Weitzman, Knickman, and Shinn (1990) found that 44 percent of their cohort of newly housing single-parent families had never before been a primary tenant, managing a place of their own. Ironically, declaring themselves homeless, and thus receiving preferential consideration for affordable housing, may allow them to complete a transition that, left to their own devices, would have remained stalled.

54. This happened during the Depression, when compulsory attendance of high school was promoted in part to offset the additional competition unemployed teenagers posed to family men out of work (Kett 1977).

55. Lipsky and Smith 1989; Vine 1997; Burt et al. 2001.

56. Modell 1989; Hareven 1991.

57. Stack 1996.

58. *New York Times* 13 March 1999, B1; Hamberg and Smolenski 1993; Sanjek 1998, 190ff.

59. Two examples: the near-absence of homelessness among young black men in *Tally's Corner* (Liebow 1967), and the treatment of home as a moveable feast in Peter Hainer's *Sharing Kith and Kin* (1991).

60. And which he characterizes as follows: "Knowing how and when to apply rules of thumb in a concrete situation is the essence of *mētis.* The subtleties of application are important precisely because *mētis* is most valuable in settings that are mutable, indeterminate (some facts are unknown), and particular" (Scott 1998, 316).

61. Updating Lipsky (1980). How, for example, would a (pre–"welfare reform") bureaucrat have read Edin and Lein's (1997) account, detailing the unauthorized ways in which welfare recipients "make ends meet"?

62. This is the notion that evident disorder—an unrepaired window—sends the message that "nobody cares" and invites more of the same (and worse) (Wilson and Kelling 1982). For a critique, see Harcourt 2001.

63. See, e.g., Rothstein 1993, discussed at the conclusion of Chapter 7.

64. See, e.g., Lyon-Callo's account of his work in Northamptom (1998).

Chapter 2. Unearned Keep

1. According to this principle, provisions for the dependent poor were to be "less eligible" (attractive) than the lot of the most menial laborer.

2. Piven and Cloward 1971, 173, 346; Gordon 1994.

3. Rothman 1971, 14; cf. Hareven 1991,255–256; Davis 1968.

4. Modell and Hareven 1973, 165; Rothman 1987,18; *N.Y. Col. Laws* III, 645, as cited in Morris 1946,12–13; Kusmer 1980; Way 1993, 10, 99; Booth 1859, 347; Lawrence 1892, 245.

5. Anderson 1934, 5; Brandt 1933, 34.

6. Anderson 1934, 6; Committee on the Almshouse 1901, 519; Carlisle 1893, 7; *Minutes of the Common Council,* 20 November 1789, as cited by Pomerantz 1938, 331.

7. Imported from English prisons, this was a large rotary drum, connected by gears and rods to a grinding mill, and driven by the forced labor of inmates "stepping" on raised edges on the surface of the drum. Its "terror" and deterrent power, according to a contemporary champion, lay in the "*monotonous steadiness*" it required of those assigned to it (*Sixth Annual Report of the Society for the Prevention of Pauperism,* 1823, 15, emphasis in original). For an illustration, see Beard and Kapsis 1987, 118.

8. Morris 1946, 13; Rothman 1971, 195.

9. Anderson 1934, 6; Cray 1988; Greenblatt 1948, 23.

10. Crapsey 1872; Boyer 1978, 89–90; Spann 1981, 35–41; Hagen 1982, 111.

11. Richmond 1872, 524; *Guide to the Charities of New York and Brooklyn* 1886.

12. Klips 1980, 340, 346; Johnson 1911.

13. Raborg 1872; Bonner 1990.
14. Greenblatt 1948, 23; Monkkonen 1981, 10, 86–91.
15. Richardson 1970, 265; Derby 1877, 68–69, 73; Crapsey 1872, 128.
16. Richardson 1970, 152, 264.
17. Anderson 1932, iii-iv; Mohl 1985, 36; Gutman 1965, 257.
18. Feder 1936, 65; Richardson 1970, 265; Reynolds 1893, 122; *Annual Reports* of the COS for 1894, 18, and 1895, 21–22; Gutman 1965, 257; Schneider 1984, 221.
19. Rosenzweig and Blackmar 1993; Sante 1991, 314; Zeisloff 1899, 516; Pinkerton 1878, 57; McCabe 1882, 653; Campbell, Know, and Byrnes 1891, 654. Observers put the summer population of homeless people living in Central Park in the early 1990s at about five hundred (Swerdlow 1993, 23).
20. Zeisloff 1899, 192.
21. Seligson 1940, 14–15; Nascher 1909, 70–79; Kingsbury 1915, 30; Kellor 1915, 7–12; Public Welfare Committee 1917; Brandt 1933, 115–116; Ringenbach 1973, 165–166; Rice Archives, Box 36.
22. Kingsbury 1915; Rice 1922, 361n.; 1918, 141.
23. McCook 1895, 289; Wyckoff 1897; Committee on Statistics 1896, 60; Kent 1903, 670.
24. Ringenbach 1973, 70; COS *Annual Report* for 1894; Lescohier 1935, 271; Advisory Social Service Committee 1915; Whiting 1914; Rice 1918; CSS Archives, Columbia University, Box 131.
25. Barnes 1914, 78.
26. Rice 1922, 360.
27. Keyssar 1986, 156; Hareven 1987, 42.
28. Schneider 1984; Hareven 1982; 1987; Monkkonen 1984, 240, 242.
29. Hareven 1991, 274, emphasis in original.
30. Illich 1981, 113; Modell and Hareven 1988.
31. Ringenbach 1973; Klein 1923, 150; McElvaine 1984, 46–50; Garraty 1986, 28–49; Bremer 1984, 25.
32. Seligson 1940; Anderson 1932, xiii; 1934, 76–77; Josephson 1933, 15–16.
33. Crouse 1986, 133, 173–176, 209; Governor's Commission on Unemployment Relief 1936, 209; Brandt 1939, 390.
34. Reed 1934, 38; Brown 1940, 262–263; Anderson 1934, 59–64; Crouse 1986, 100–102; *New York Times* 22 September 1932.
35. Breines 1932; Still 1956, 300.
36. Leff 1932, 63.
37. Editorial, *Shelter* 1932, Vol. 2(5):61.
38. McMillan 1934, 75; Herlands 1940, 114–128; Wilson 1935, 210; Governor's Commission on Unemployment Relief 1936, 145.
39. Anderson 1934, 430; Wilson 1935, 214.
40. Reed 1934, 72.
41. Welfare Council 1949; Bahr 1973. One curiosity of this approach, at least to contemporary eyes, is that even longtime SRO residents—precisely the niche whose loss present-day analysts of homelessness bewail—were considered "homeless" if they had shed social entanglements. For the corrective, see Groth 1994.
42. Nash 1964a, b, c; Anderson 1934; Kromer [1935] 1986; Dees 1948; Markel 1964; Schneider 1986. The last observation is Jim Baumohl's.
43. Barnes 1915–1916, 26.
44. Ingram 1910–1911, 837; Fabian 1983, 17–18, emphasis added.
45. McCook 1895; Kusmer 1995.
46. Monkkonen 1981, 88; Schneider 1984, 212; Kusmer 1987, 14–15.
47. Barnes 1912; 1914.
48. Gould 1981, 196–197; 199–223; Lubove 1977, 67–71.

49. Sutherland and Locke 1936, 142.

50. Van Kleeck 1934.

51. See Gounis and Susser 1990.

52. Kent 1903; Kromer [1935] 1986; Anderson 1923, 261; Rice Archives, Box 34; Lovald 1960. Cf. Warner 1985.

53. Rice Archives, Boxes 34–40, 115; Anderson 1961, xiii; 1975, 165. Unfortunately, Anderson's papers in the Special Collections Department of the University of Utah Libraries show a gap for his New York years, 1930–1934, and the historical files of the Community Council (successor to Welfare Council) were apparently discarded at the time of the agency's demise in 1989 (letter from H. Lautard, 30 May 1995; telephone interview with Jerry Schroeder, spring 1995).

54. And not, Rothman (1987) and Culhane (1992) to the contrary, the almshouse.

55. By 1992, 58 percent of those surveyed in a New York Times/CBS News poll regularly saw homeless people in their communities or while commuting to work (*New York Times,* 20 January 1992, B7).

56. In November 1999, the Giuliani administration intensified measures to relocate—by arrest if necessary—the visible homeless. City "streets are not for sleeping," the mayor dutifully informed the public. Some two hundred homeless persons were arrested in the initial phase of the crackdown; over twice that number were taken to shelters (*New York Times,* 2 December 1999, A34; 9 December 1999, B5).

57. As best I can trace it, Sydney Schanberg started the trend when he compared the street homeless to a scene from Jakarta or Calcutta (*New York Times,* 25 August 1981). It was soon picked up by the politicians—City Comptroller Harrison Goldin at a press conference in 1985: "New York City doesn't have to look like Bombay" (*Albany Times Union,* 23 September 1985). And it was the heading for a series of editorials in the *New York Times* (beginning on 15 July 1987, A26) decrying the paucity of treatment alternatives for the street-dwelling poor.

58. Sante 1991; Liebow 1993, 147; Fogelson 1989.

59. John Sayles, *The Brother From Another Planet,* 1985. Contrast with the following, from a psych resident on an acute psychiatric unit: "This guy's hopeless. I'm sending him to the mission" (Rhodes 1991, 137).

Introduction: Ethnography in the Annals of Homelessness

1. Stott 1973.

2. 1987, 215, n.5.

3. Solenberger 1911; Advisory Social Service Committee 1915; Laubach 1916.

4. Barnes's report, prepared for the Russell Sage Foundation, never saw the light of day. The same is true of both of Anderson's reports for the Welfare Council. Sections of the original typescript of the first volume of his 1934 study are heavily edited, replete with marginal corrections, rephrasings, excisions, and notations that "Mr. Anderson is to rewrite" certain passages. To a distant reader, his critical remarks (confined mainly to a single concluding chapter) are reasoned and well supported. But it is easy to see how the agencies that commissioned the study may have felt exposed. Anderson argues that the private agencies serving the homeless have achieved no consensus over goals or means; frequently duplicate (where they do not sabotage) each other's work; cull their intake rolls to boost rates of success; and adapt their programs as budgetary constraints, not the size of the problem, demand. Self-preservation, he concludes, regularly trumps their responsibility to report accurately, develop innovative programs, and educate the public. As contemporary ethnographers working under contract continue to discover (Hopper 1997), suppression of purchased but unwelcome findings is an effective form of censorship.

5. Barnes 1914; Anderson 1932; 1934; Anderson 1923.

6. Sutherland and Locke 1936.

7. Bruns 1980; Kusmer 1980; Monkkonen 1984.
8. Flynt 1899; Wyckoff 1897; McCook 1901; Stiff [Anderson] 1931; Minehan 1934; Outland 1934–1935; Kromer [1935] 1986; cf. Feied 1964 and Stott 1973.
9. Anderson 1940; Caplow 1940; cf. Allsop 1967.
10. Lovald 1960; Rooney 1970; Hayner 1945.
11. Caplow 1970, 3.
12. Bahr and Caplow 1974.
13. Levinson 1966b.
14. Merton 1957, 153.
15. Spradley 1970; Wiseman 1970.
16. Harper 1976.
17. Mathers 1974; Leen 1979; Harper 1982; Conover 1984. The number of contemporary freight-hoppers is reckoned at between fifteen and twenty thousand according to Ted Rose 1989, 43.
18. Hand 1976.
19. For specific citations, see Hopper 1991d, 794–795, n.76.
20. Cohen and Sokolovsky 1989.
21. Snow et al. 1986; Koegel, Burnam, and Farr 1990; Koegel 1992 ; Morrissey et al. 1985; Gounis 1992; Ware et al. 1992; Barrow et al. 1989.
22. Fitchen 1991.
23. Snow et al. 1989; Fischer 1992.
24. Wright and Devine 1992.
25. Lovell, Barrow, and Struening 1992; Koegel, Burnam, and Farr 1990.
26. Hopper 1991a; Lovell 1992; Koegel 1992.
27. Cohen and Thompson 1992; Mossman and Perlin 1992.
28. Sosin, Piliavin, and Westerfelt 1990.

Chapter 3. Streets, Shelters, and Flops

1. State Democratic Task Force 1976, 4–5, 7.
2. New York State, Office of Mental Health internal memo, 12 October 1979; Schwam 1979.
3. Littman 1979, 210; U.S. Census Bureau n.d., 19, 79, 223; 1983, 26; 1984, 808, Table 43; U.S. HUD 1984, 16.
4. Bahr and Caplow 1974, 57–58.
5. Bahr 1968; 1973; Patch 1970, 437; Cumming 1974.
6. Engels [1845] 1969; Booth 1859; Orwell [1933] 1961; Bogue 1963; Blumberg, Shipley, and Barsky 1978.
7. Lindenbaum 1979, 128, 145; cf. Douglas 1966, 3, 113; Bahr 1973, 61–64, 83; Cook and Braithwaite 1979, 7; cf. Thompson 1978, 55, 93. As Bahr notes, this image was fed by common pillory of "the skid row derelict" in contrast to the "worthwhile person suffering from an illness which can be successfully arrested" (1973, 80).
8. Wallace 1965; Spradley 1970; Bahr 1973, 9–13, 287–292.
9. Levinson 1963; O'Connor 1963.
10. Anderson 1923; Conroy [1933] 1963; Algren [1935] 1965; Kromer [1935] 1986.
11. Bahr 1973, 67–86.
12. Bahr 1973, 86, 15, 29, 41–42, 120.
13. *Soho Weekly News* 28 April 1977; 8 May 1980; *Safety Network* June 1983.
14. *New York Times* 23 October 1973; 9 April 1980; 20 April 1979; *Daily News* 9 July 1977; *Natural History* November 1978; *New York Times* 20 April 1979; *Chelsea Clinton News* 6 December 1979; *New York Post* 18 December 1979.

15. In the remainder of this chapter I draw heavily on the work I did jointly with Ellen Baxter, from 1979 to 1982, which was sponsored by the Community Service Society. Special thanks are due Frank Caro for his guidance and patience in dealing with unorthodox research methods and a sometimes unruly crew of self-deputized research assistants.

16. Baxter and Hopper 1980.

17. We spent little time in Harlem or in Spanish Harlem, partly due to limited resources and partly to lack of familiarity and contacts. This proved a mistake: soon, the majority of clients at the Men's Shelter and Wards Island would be black or Hispanic and to have only interviewed them there, away from home grounds, was to have missed part of what was distinctive about their homelessness. Hainer's (1991) is the only study of precariously housed single men in those areas, except as they make their way to public shelters.

18. Winberg and Wilson 1981, 46–47, 51, 64–65, 88–90.

19. Rosenhan 1973, 252; Henry 1980.

20. Garraty 1978, 116; Carlin 1979; Salerno, Hopper, and Baxter 1984; *New York Times* 7 February 1981; Dembo and Morehouse 1993.

21. Kasl, Gore, and Cobb 1975; Dooley and Catalano 1980; Brenner 1977; Pearlin and Radabaugh 1976.

22. Jackson 1976; Marcuse 1979.

23. New York City Office of the Comptroller 1979.

24. Crystal and Goldstein 1982, 13; U.S. HUD 1984, 27.

25. Reich and Siegel 1978, 193.

26. Love 1956.

27. Coalition for the Homeless and SRO Tenants Rights Coalition 1985.

28. Lovell and Makiesky-Barrow 1981.

29. Vera Institute 1977, 5.

30. Hopper, Susser, and Conover 1985.

31. The warning, it turned out, was an old one in the annals of homelessness. Nels Anderson, who had proposed a much-used typology of homeless men in *The Hobo* (1923), came to reconsider the wisdom of such schemes. Whether devised by the men themselves, by treating agencies, or by outside "experts," such classifications suffered from a "snapshot" artificiality. They ignored the changes—in residence patterns, in means of procuring income—that are the only real constant in this way of life. "All such terms, like 'hobo,' 'tramp,' or 'bum,'" Anderson concluded, "are really designations for conditions in which a man may find himself at any one time" (1934, 152).

32. Henshaw 1968.

33. By the end of 1979, a fair number of men at the shelter were eligible for benefits that they were not receiving. A city-commissioned survey, conducted on 28 December 1979 of over five hundred shelter clients, showed that while over one-third were veterans, only about half of those men were drawing pensions. Approximately a fifth of the men surveyed were then receiving assistance from other government agencies; over half of them were drawing SSI (disability benefits). Those receiving welfare or disability checks had room and board deducted at the rate of $13 a day—equivalent, roughly, to per-capita operating expenses at the shelter at the time (Bock Associates 1980).

34. The text accompanying a 1982 exhibition of a German photographer's study of the street stated confidently that "a new Bowery is in the making," although, the writer added: "Traces of the old persist, and they will remain as long as the city's Men's Shelter stays near the corner of Bowery and Third Street" (Marx 1982).

35. Cf. Parker 1970, 9.

36. Warner 1985, 91–92.

37. *Jablonsky v. Brezenoff,* Index No.41132/80, "Complaint," 22 May 1980, 3; "Order," 23 July 1980, 2.

38. WCBS-TV 4 August 1980. Subsequently, huge concrete planters were put on the

benches that had been occupied by sleeping figures, greatly reducing the area available to them. The reduction was evidently insufficient. In the summer of 1983, the owner of One Penn Plaza (the towers that, along with the Garden, occupy the space where formerly stood the old Pennsylvania Station) approached the general director of the agency for which I worked. It seems he had become increasingly disturbed by the continuing presence of homeless men and women sleeping in the public plaza area and wanted to do something about it. He was prepared to put up some money and urge other business associates to join him. His concern was fueled by complaints by one of his more prestigious tenants that he was "tired of stepping over derelicts" on his way to work. At the behest of our boss, another staff member and I prepared a set of feasibility studies—setting out a number of options, involving various combinations of drop-in centers, temporary shelters, and permanent housing—of projects that would offer alternatives to the homeless people making use of the plaza. We were offered breakfast in the conference room of a Park Avenue bank, thanked profusely for our efforts, and sent on our way. Six months later, a chain-link cyclone fence was erected around much of the plaza area.

39. Letter from Jack Harris [Amtrak security] to Nina Roth-Dornfeld, 10 October 1983; personal communication from Marcia Martin (Manhattan Bowery Corporation) 20 March 1984.

40. *New York Times* 29 November 1977, B1; 17 March 1980, B1.

41. Later that year, some of the men, including Ken on occasion, returned. Indeed, one or two would be interviewed on camera in the spring of 1981. For a later glimpse of this habitat, see Swerdlow 1997.

42. 1923; 1934, 210.

43. [1935] 1986, 43–53.

44. Goffman had noted the same phenomenon in mental hospitals in 1961.

45. For a series of assessments of alcohol-related problems among the homeless, see the spring 1987 issue of *Alcohol Health and Research World* (published by the National Institute on Alcohol Abuse and Alcoholism).

46. One former Bowery man who regularly made the Catskill circuit recalls that after a full summer's work, he would return to the city with perhaps $100 in his pocket (Kopperdahl 1987, 31).

47. For an account of one such "refusal," which eventuated in the death of the homeless woman involved, see Hopper 1982.

48. Orwell [1933] 1961, 17.

49. On December 30, 1980, Deputy Mayor Nat Leventhal reported to a meeting of city mental health and social service officials that in a phone conversation with Mayor Koch (in Israel at the time), the mayor had sworn that he would go to jail before opening an additional shelter in the city.

50. The report made front-page news in the Sunday *New York Times* (8 March 1981); in the next two weeks, that story was followed by three others and an editorial. In its draft form, the report had received prior coverage in the *Christian Science Monitor* (6 February 1981, B4), and would be picked up by *Newsweek* (23 March 1981, 71) and a host of local news programs and neighborhood papers.

51. *New York Times* 21 March 1981, A26; 28 June 1981, A1.

52. *New York Times,* 12 June 2002, B6.

Chapter 4. The Airport as Home

1. Baumohl 1992; Baumohl and Huebner 1991; Koegel, Burnam, and Farr 1988; 1990; Koegel, Burnam, and Baumohl 1996; Lovell 1989; Snow et al. 1986; Snow, Baker, and Anderson 1988, 1989; Snow, Anderson, and Koegel 1994; Susser et al. 1991; Tessler and Dennis 1989; National Institute of Mental Health 1990.

2. Rollin 1970. A 1979 report from the office of the city council president compared the Men's Shelter to a nineteenth-century asylum (Bellamy 1979).

3. For exemplary reviews, see Bachrach 1978; S.M. Rose 1979; Estroff 1981; Lerman 1982; Dear and Wolch 1987; and National Institute of Mental Health 1990.

4. Spradley 1970; Wiseman 1970; Stark 1985; Koegel 1989; Snow and Anderson 1993; Dordick 1997.

5. As early as 1927, the Travelers Aid Society had noted the peculiar problems presented by emotionally disturbed travelers and had made efforts to tailor its usual methods of hospitality and relocation to their special needs (Sands 1927; Kimble 1935). Reports of the homeless poor living in the subways likewise date from the Great Depression (e.g., Federal Writers' Project [1939] 1982), although accounts in the popular press appeared a decade earlier.

6. *New York Times,* 26 October 1971, 82; 23 May 1973, 50; 9 November 1987, B1.

7. Flinn 1962; Miller and Zarcone 1968, 364.

8. Shapiro 1976, 455–456.

9. Shapiro 1976, 455.

10. Jauhar and Weller 1982; Weller 1987; Weller and Jauhar 1987, 38–39.

11. Shapiro 1982.

12. Lamb 1984, 65.

13. Schwartz 1989, I:48; II:169ff; Michael Marubio, personal communication, 8 November 1989; *New York Times,* 6 July 1987, 33; 23 November 1989, A22; 9 March 1991, 25; John Donohue, personal communication, 28 March 1991; Mike Fabricant, personal communication, 22 March 1991; HRA April 1988. Note that HRA's recorded rate of acceptance (12 percent) for the airport outreach team was considerably lower than that for similar teams operating in Pennsylvania Station, Port Authority Bus Terminal, Grand Central Terminal, and the subways. At these four sites, acceptance ran at about 50 percent.

14. Anonymous 1987.

15. Berger 1988.

16. This category included the rather extraordinary case of a man of late middle age who wintered at the terminal, receiving regular checks from his family (sent to the airport American Express office), and was picked up by the same family in late May or early June to spend the next three or four months at a summer home in Connecticut.

17. Anonymous 1988, 1.

18. Income opportunities (such as panhandling—rare, in my experience—and baggage cart returns) and free transportation between terminals are other amenities.

19. Goffman 1964. That the generosity of airport staff extended to even obviously disturbed dwellers suggests too that stigma's impact may be blunted in liminal spaces.

20. *Village Voice* 26 December 1989, 35; Port Authority Press Release, 30 January 1988.

21. *New York Times,* 12 February 1999, E36.

22. *City and Society* 1996; Hopper 1997.

23. Shattuck 1996.

24. Brettell 1993; Scott 1990.

25. As any number of contributors to Robert Borofsky's 1994 volume attest.

26. Witness, for example, the continued controversy over the role anthropologists played in the War Relocation Authority (Spicer 1979; Starn 1986; and the responses of Opler 1987 and Sady 1987, together with Starn's rejoinders).

Chapter 5. Out for the Count

1. "The Census of the Homeless Men in the Bowery District . . ." Rice Archives, Box 36; McCall 1989; Hopper 1991b; 1991c. See also Caplow, Lovald, and Wallace 1958.

2. Spradley 1970; Wiseman 1970; Hopper 1990a; Hopper, Susser, and Conover 1985; Koegel 1990.

3. Curiously, in *Night as Frontier* (Melbin 1987), the chapter "Who Is Active at Night?" makes but one mention of "vagrants" or the homeless poor seeking shelter outdoors. For a different impression, see the 30 April 1990 edition of *New York Magazine,* "A Night in the Life of New York."

4. Erikson 1967; 1968; Denzin 1968.

5. Cassell and Wax 1980; Fluehr-Lobban 1991; Nader 1974; Favret-Saada 1990.

6. As noted above, this difficulty was accentuated by the uniform decision to pass as homeless that the ethnographic team made.

7. Lardner 1991; Dordick 1997.

8. Kennedy fieldnotes, 24 March 1990.

9. Grieshof, Stevens, and Tejada fieldnotes. If there is a single index to the relative security many street dwellers felt about their sites, it may be the widespread practice of taking off their shoes before bedding down for the night. Unlike most residents in the public shelters, these men and women do not always make a point of securing their shoes (under bedposts, under their mattresses, as part of their pillows).

10. Though the rules of exchange are a bit tricky: At one site, giving away cigarettes when the going rate was 15 cents was viewed as an indicator of naiveté by the residents; sharing food, which could be gotten from merchants or charity kitchens, was not (Dush, Lee fieldnotes).

11. Lambert fieldnotes. Subsequent investigation of a rather large (some 15–20 residents) midtown shanty settlement disclosed that at least two of the regular women residents there did "drive-by" street sex work along the avenues fronting the settlement itself. Their income was probably the most reliable of the group.

12. Dozier, Herrera fieldnotes.

13. Salmon fieldnotes.

14. Welle fieldnotes, 25 March 1990.

15. Welle fieldnotes, 25 March 1990.

16. Greshof, Salmon fieldnotes.

17. Seber 1982; Hopper 1991b; Martin et al. 1997. All of which may be moot for the time being in the wake of the 1999 Supreme Court ruling against statistical estimation—at least for purposes of apportionment.

18. Salo and Schwede 1991.

19. Ignatieff 1984; Toth 1990. Scavenging has not always been their lot: for nearly two-thirds of those interviewed in the companion study, a job was given as their last source of steady income.

20. Hopper 2000.

21. Griffin 2001. Compare, e.g., Kuhn and Culhane 1998.

22. *New York Times,* 28 June 2001, A12.

23. U.S. Bureau of the Census, October 2001, 1.

Chapter 6. Homelessness and African American Men

1. Liebow 1967, 58, 60.

2. Hainer 1991. Even in Tally's time, the resentment that some African Americans felt toward such men was a little noted feature in Liebow's account, a fact some of his women readers—irked too by what they saw as Liebow's complicity in too readily "understanding" such men—were quick to point out to him (personal communication, 1992). The costs of the new depredations of the intensified drug trade in inner city African American communities are yet to be reckoned (Hamid 1990; Tidwell 1992; Currie 1993).

3. Kleinman 1992, 171–173.

4. Sassen 1993; Wolch and Dear 1993; Lynch 1994.

5. Hochschild 1988; 1991, 561 n.3; Landry 1991; Gans 1991; Katz 1989, 185–186; Katz 1993b. It should be clear, too, that "race" is used here not in the discredited sense of biological difference but in the public health sense as "social fact" (Muntaner 1999).

6. In New York and Philadelphia, for example, most public shelter stays (some 70 percent of users) are transitory and relocations appear to be fairly stable—at least to the extent of not eventuating in another shelter stay in that year (Culhane et al. 1994; Burt 1994).

7. Burt 1992, 17; Shlay and Rossi 1992, 135; North and Smith 1994.

8. MacLeod 1987; Williams 1988; Sullivan 1989a; Burton 1990; Fine 1991; Hainer 1991.

9. Wilson 1987; Maxwell 1988; Gephart 1989; Pearson 1989; Sanjek 1990b; Moffatt 1992; Newman 1992; Williams 1992; Katz 1993a; Sullivan 1993.

10. Kusmer's authoritative history (2001) is the exception. More typical is a Brookings Institution volume on domestic policy: In it, Berlin and McAllister note early on that "over half the homeless are minorities" (1992, 65) and then proceed to ignore that fact. Contrast that with the attention given to race in chapters in the same volume dealing with children and families, education and training, and crime. Nor did it make an appearance in Jencks' volume (1994), despite his considerable experience with issues of poverty and race.

11. As in life, so in death: A public burial ground (or "potter's field") was established in New York City sometime before 1755, in what had been the Old Negroes Burial Ground, just north of present-day City Hall. It "serv[ed] as a burial place for slaves, paupers, and criminals . . ." (Dean 1981). Over two centuries later, the casual labor exchange patronized by homeless men in Minneapolis would be known as "the slave market" (Lovald 1960, 352ff).

12. Kusmer 1980, 27; Booth 1859, 347; Anderson 1934, 5.

13. Bahr 1970; Clement 1984; Kusmer 1987; Solenberger 1911, 216, 306; Barnes 1914, 41; Ringenbach 1973, 60, 70–71; Monkkonen 1984; Schneider 1984; McCook 1895.

14. Monkkonen 1984, 14; Blumberg, Shipley, and Barsky 1978, 123; Clement 1984, 70; Schneider 1984, 213–215; Kusmer 1987, 22.

15. Frazier's attention to the marginally situated (1932, 1939) is of a piece with the University of Chicago's urban ethnographic studies during this era; three of the eight studies cited by Wilson as illustrative of the productivity of this school dealt exclusively with homeless men (1987, 215, n.5). Drake and Cayton also make reference to the "notorious and widespread wandering" of Negro men, a pattern which, although originating in the search for more or better work, had become "a custom which runs on its own steam" (1945, 583). But their source is Frazier, not their own fieldwork.

16. The reasons behind mobility of the two groups were different, however. For white men, tramping often meant a means of escape from (even defiance of) the new regime of industrial work. Much more than a reflexive response to unemployment, tramping was for them "a clear indication of worker discontent" (Kusmer 1990, 101). Barred from industrial employment and "reduced to peonage" by a new sharecropping system that left them but one remove from slavery, blacks were motivated by a different impulse. "The tendency of blacks to join the underclass [of tramps] must thus be viewed as part of a much larger spectrum of rebellion against their economic and political repression in the South. . . . In the immediate aftermath of slavery, freedom of movement *per se* seemed especially important to a race that had been denied geographic mobility during the long centuries of bondage" (Kusmer 1980, 223; cf. Jones 1993, especially her discussion of "shifting"). Even when they secured industrial jobs—say, in Chicago's meatpacking firms—"[c]hanging jobs . . . constituted an extension of migration itself, with movement remaining a metaphor for freedom" (Grossman 1989, 197).

17. Monkkonen 1984; Kusmer 1980, 225; Anderson 1923, 8; Frazier 1932, 118; Grossman 1989, 134; Lemann 1991.

18. Anderson 1934, 134; Sutherland and Locke 1936, 38, 42; Webb 1935, 33; Crouse 1986, 9; Turkel 1970, 56–60; Caplow 1940, 737; Peery 1994, 89–129.

19. Although most public shelters accepted black men, only one—the Salvation Army's Harlem Lodging House on 124th Street (or Hotel for Colored Men), which operated at full capacity—was located in or near Harlem, a fact hardly conducive to ease of access (Anderson 1934, 76; Crouse 1986, 82; Greenberg 1991, 56, 155). A "colored mission" opened on West 131 Street in 1925 (Greenberg 1991, 263, n.35); the Bowery Mission also accepted blacks (Anderson 1934, 219).

20. Aaron 1935; Schubert 1935; Clarke 1937; Anderson 1934, 138–140, 135.

21. Louis LeCount, as cited in Anderson 1934, 135.

22. Frazier 1939, 285. Trotter (1991, 12) argues that Frazier tended to underappreciate the role of family and neighborhood networks in resettlement, and his account of "solitary" men and women should be read with this caveat in mind.

23. Lovald 1960, 449; Rooney 1969; Bahr 1973, 105.

24. The literature here abounds and is increasingly attentive to differences in the move north depending on conditions in the cities settled. For a sampling, see: Liebow 1967; Hannerz 1969; Stack 1974; Gutman 1976; Borchert 1980; Kusmer 1986; Lemann 1991; Billingsley 1992; Trotter 1993. An especially valuable cross-section of urban case studies may be found in Trotter 1991.

25. Borchert 1980, 81–82; Grossman 1989, 133ff; Trotter 1993, 78; Jones 1993. The resiliency of informal supports was a core theme of *Tally's Corner* (1967), but even then, in Washington, D.C., there was a black minister (Lewellyn Scott) who opened a free flophouse for black men down on their luck—the "Blessed Martin de Porres Hostel (for homeless men)" (Liebow 1967, 245). He took no public funds and operated apart from the established church (personal communications, Elliot Liebow 1993, and Michael Kirwin, 1994). Memory is the only archive where such records are kept.

26. Wilson 1987, 177–178; Piven and Cloward 1971, 281.

27. Schneider 1986, 181; Pittman and Gordon 1958; Bigart 1961; Levinson 1963; 1966a, b; Kean 1965; Rooney 1969, n.2.

28. Bogue 1963, 106–108; Hoch and Slayton 1989, 98–99; Rooney 1969.

29. Bahr and Caplow 1974, Table 2–1; Nash 1964a, b; Markel 1964; Aronow 1967; Henshaw 1968. Such findings flatly contradict the thesis of "the underrepresentation of blacks" on skid row (Bahr 1973, 105).

30. *New York Times* 27 January 1969, p.21. Bahr and Caplow 1974, 35. Regarding the younger age of black homeless men, a city official is quoted by the *Times* as observing: "Negro derelicts reach the last stop quicker"—an opinion I will argue was almost certainly wrong.

31. Blumberg, Shipley, and Barsky 1978, 122. Working in New York and Philadelphia, James Rooney (1969, 1970, 1980a,b) was a notable exception.

32. Nash 1964c, D-26ff.

33. Blumberg, Shipley, and Barsky 1978, 175.

34. Anderson 1978. Accurate figures are hard to come by. A third of Chicago's nearly four thousand skid row men in the early 1970s were "by rough estimate" nonwhite. But this included significant numbers of Puerto Ricans, Mexicans, and Native Americans in addition to American blacks (McSheehy 1979, 43, passim). By the late 1950s, Native Americans already accounted for a fifth of the nonwhite skid row population in Chicago (Bogue 1963, 108).

35. Hamburger 1983; Shapiro 1971, 24; Siegel 1978, xix-xxi, 65.

36. See Koegel, Burnam, and Baumohl 1996.

37. Cohen and Sokolovsky 1989; Bonner 1990.

38. Vera Institute of Justice 1977; 1980; Office of Mental Health 1982; Crystal, Goldstein, and Levitt 1982; Crystal and Goldstein 1982.

39. Barrett, Anolik, and Abramson 1992; Rosenheck et al. 1989, Table 5–5; Shlay and Rossi 1992, 135.

40. Gounis 1993, 125.

41. Hainer 1991, 223–224.

42. Sharff 1987; Jones 1992.

43. Census Bureau figures used in calculating such rates are notoriously unreliable for adult black males. In the 1990 census, official estimates of the undercount of African Americans range from 4.4 to 5.7 percent, depending on the method used; the comparable figures for the general population are 1.6 to 1.8 percent (Hogan and Robinson 1993). Use of household data from the Current Population Survey (CPS) is even more hazardous: the March 1986 CPS is thought to have missed from 18 to 20 percent of black men age 16 and higher (Panel on Census Requirements in the Year 2000 and Beyond 1993, 15n).

44. Jones 1992, 270; Sawhill 1992, 156; Massey and Denton 1993; Orfield 1993; *New York Times*, 25 September 1992, A12; Sanjek 1994; Hacker 1992.

45. Figures in this paragraph are from: First, Roth, and Arewa 1988; Bane 1986; Douglass and Hodgkins 1991; LaGrory et al. 1989; Wilson, McCallum, and Bolland 1991; Rossi 1989, 125.

46. Sassen 1988; 1991.

47. Kasarda 1985, 1989; Hirschman 1988; Lichter 1988; Moss and Tilly 1991; Tidwell and Jackson 1992; U.S. Census Bureau 1992.

48. Jencks 1992, Table 5.3.

49. Freeman 1991; Osterman 1991.

50. Tienda and Stier 1991; Weir 1992; *New York Times* 23 May 1999, 1.

51. Bluestone and Harrison 1982; Kain 1968; Sugrue 1993; Wacquant and Wilson 1989; Wacquant 1989; Kasarda 1989; Stern 1993, 224–226; Jargowsky and Bane 1991, 254. In New York City, it was the relative loss of jobs in personal services that hit native blacks hardest, while their concentration in the public sector offered some shielding, as Bailey and Waldinger 1991 have argued.

52. Tilly and Tilly 1994, 306. This isn't just a matter of "misunderstandings" between boss and employee, but implicates the severely constrained sphere of service work when compared to the old blue-collar settings or dirty work. As Fine nicely documents, for example, the cramped quarters of kitchen work still allow for horseplay, pranks, teasing, and "deviance" (Fine 1991, 118f), unlike the closely regulated social space of face-to-face retailing. See also Jencks 1992, 128; MacLeod 1995, 179, 227, 243; Bourgois 1995; and especially MacDonald and Siriani 1996.

53. See *New York Times* 2 December 1990, A1; Shapiro et al. 1993; Leonard and Lazere 1992, 43

54. Gans 1962; Bott 1971; Keyssar 1986; Schneider 1968; Hareven 1982. Micaela diLeonardo coined the term "the work of kinship" (1984, 194ff), and it is apt here. The centrality of women in that work and the extraordinary burden it can place on them is clear in historical accounts of textile workers (Hareven 1982, esp. 105ff), as well as in contemporary portraits of Italian American (Gans 1962; diLeonardo 1984), Japanese American (Yanagisako 1985), and African American families (Stack 1974; Aschenbrenner 1975; Martin and Martin 1978; Williams 1988; Burton 1990; Bourdieu 1990, 96).

55. Grossman 1989, 106–107; Gudeman 1979; Aschenbrenner 1975, 118; Martin and Martin 1978, 111; Belle 1983; Stack 1974, 33.

56. Smelser and Halpern 1984; Stern 1993. Figures calculated from Stern's Table 7.7. Separate data for income source are not reported for black households.

57. Stern 1993, 244; Baumohl and Huebner 1991; Snow and Anderson 1993, 259–261; Dennis, Levine, and Osher 1991. Not only do "alcohol- and drug-abusing poor people have great difficulties maintaining their hold on acceptable housing" in the formal housing market (Wright and Rubin 1991, 942); they are also the source of much friction and grief in the informal economy of friends and family. In this connection, it is instructive that the best research indicates that such problems commonly began before the first bout of homelessness (Baumohl and Huebner 1991, 844). Snow and Anderson, while acknowledging that family resources may be exhausted by some homeless men, also argue that for the majority of their in-

formants, "family relationships appeared to be nonexistent, weak, or, at best, highly ambivalent." Most came from families that were ill-equipped economically to offer much support (1993, 265).

58. Jackson 1985, 191, 219ff; Massey and Denton 1993.

59. In 1970, the number of low-rent units was roughly equal to the number of low-income renters (6.8 and 6.4 million, respectively). In 1989, the supply of such units had shrunk to 5.5 million while the need for them had grown to 9.6 million (Lazere et al. 1991, 4–5).

60. Lazere et al. 1991, 4, 8, 63–64; Alker and Dolbeare 1990.

61. Stone 1993, 147–150.

62. Pharr [1971] 1998; Green 1982; Hoch and Slayton 1989, ch.9; Blau 1992, 75; Burt 1992, 33–34; Kasinitz 1984.

63. Weitzman 1989; Bach and West 1993; Human Resources Administration 1993. The shelter figures cited do not include numbers for homeless families receiving emergency shelter.

64. Wilson 1987, 4–19; Schwartz 1991; Mead 1992a, b.

65. Swidler 1986; Geertz 1973; Rosaldo, 1989; Bourdieu and Wacquant, 1992; Kleinman 1992; Ortner, 1999.

66. Hochschild 1991, 565; Wilson 1987, 138; Patterson 2000.

67. Geertz 1994.

68. Williams 1977; Greenstone 1991; DeVine and Wright 1993; Kasarda 1985, 62; 1989, 45. Example of the absurd account: "Evidently, the worldview of blacks make them uniquely prone to the attitudes contrary to work, and thus vulnerable to poverty and dependency" (Mead 1992a, 148). For a historically rigorous, well-grounded account of African American culture, attuned to both the promise and pitfalls of recent deliberations on culture, see Patterson 2000.

69. Hannerz 1969; Duneier 1992, 129f; Newman 1992. Intriguingly, so does one of the few studies of white underclass culture at that time (Howell 1973).

70. Burton 1990; Massey and Denton 1993, 165ff; Kleinman 1992. Duneier 1999 has a nice analysis of what it means for some street vendors to "choose" to be homeless.

71. Anderson 1989, 65; Sullivan 1989b.

72. On the one hand, it explains past familial failures to achieve; on the other, the achievements of the civil rights movement are believed to have removed past barriers and expanded one's individual potential. Ogbu 1986; Fine 1991; MacLeod 1987, 129–135.

73. Not that completing high school, or even some college, guarantees success: MacLeod's bleak extended ethnography confirms that service economy jobs place a premium on "good attitude" in exchange for "low wages, infrequent raises, awkward working hours, minimal training, and high turnover" (1995, 243). But it is the disaffected white teenagers he follows into the labor market—and not their black counterparts—who turn in substantial numbers to the drug trade.

74. Gephart 1989, 87; Tienda 1991; Kotlowitz 1991. See also Wilson's 1996 mixed methods study of Chicago.

75. Kusmer 1990, 103; Cook and Curtin 1987; Hochschild 1991, 573. Nor, Hochschild later points out (1995, 193f), is there a bright line between legal and illegal work. See also Currie 1993, 143f; Nightingale 1993, 135–165; and MacLeod 1995, 231).

76. As Luhrmann (1989) persuasively argues in a different context. See Hochschild 1995, 218f, for application to the case at hand.

77. Liebow 1967; Rainwater 1970; Wilson 1974; Willis 1977; Scott 1990; Hainer 1991. But so, too, can mimicking the mainstream exact "hidden injuries" of its own (Bourdieu and Wacquant 1992, 80; Sennett and Cobb 1972). These are not especially original observations. In his classic analysis of deviance, Merton (1949) pointed out that (when it doesn't retreat or turn in on itself) frustrated ambition will seek the spoils of success by forbidden channels.

78. Patterson 2000.

79. Anderson 1989; Hainer 1991; Sullivan 1989a; Fagan 1993; Massey and Denton 1993, 163; Jencks 1992, 128; Currie 1993, 11.

80. See Wallace's discussion of "urban desertification" (1990).

81. See Bahr 1989 for "pathology." For resiliency of networks, compare Forestall on D.C.'s alley dwellers—"They feed their own hungry, house their own homeless, lend to their penniless, and shelter their own refugees from the law" (1938, 32)—with Stern: "Faced with an increasing number of individuals and families unable to survive on their own resources, urban jobless householders opened their homes to friends and kin even though it did nothing to improve the economic status of their immediate family" (1993, 248).

82. See especially Stack 1974, 61 (that kin live in proximity to one another is key to their effectiveness in mutual-aid networks); and Hainer 1991, 297 (housing surplus must exist to accommodate changing family rosters and preserve family unity as "a movable feast").

83. Compare Wallace and Bassuk: "[A]s the housing famine progresses, social networks become 'congested' as virtually everybody who can house a displaced friend or relative does so" (1991, 489).

84. Psychiatric hospitalization and victimization, however, figure more highly in women's prehomeless careers. The rise of crack cocaine may have weakened some of these sex differences by the time they were reported (Burt 1992, 111–116). If journalistic accounts are borne out, the subsequent increase in virtually abandoned kids, a kind of forced fosterage, has placed great strains on grandmothers in black communities (Minkler and Roe 1993).

85. In this connection, an early observation by Crystal merits note. In examining intake assessments of a 1982–1983 cohort of shelter applicants in New York, he found that the women were more than twice as likely as the men (7.4 percent versus 2.8 percent) to have had institutional or foster care placements as the "*principal* living arrangement in which they grew up" (1984, 4; emphasis in original). Many more, Crystal adds, had spent at least part of their childhood in such settings. He also found that severe psychiatric disorder was more common among the women, a finding since replicated in other studies (Fischer and Breakey 1991). Insofar as they erode one's social margin, both would increase one's risk of homelessness.

86. "On the street and in the shelters, one meets many homeless women who had been kept afloat by family members until, for one reason or another, the family had to let go. For most women, living with relatives or receiving significant financial or other support from them was the last stage in their descent into homelessness" (Liebow 1993, 81–82; cf. Golden 1992). For African American women, the hardship associated with "multiple family occupancy" and domestic violence appear to be the most common precipitants of homelessness (Milburn and D'Ercole 1991, 1164). In New York, black mothers with children applying for emergency shelter report not a dearth of family ties, but a dire shortage of kin with the capacity to put them up—usually because they had already relied on such kin for a place to live or help with rent in the previous year (Shinn, Knickman, and Weitzman 1991, 1183–1185). Other sources for this paragraph: Stack, as cited in Hochschild 1989, 149; Fischer 1989, 366; Bourdieu 1986; Hainer 1991; Burton 1990.

87. Or, as Gounis (1993) argues, public shelter itself may be converted into a kind of respite service in the makeshift economies of the marginally situated.

88. *New York Times* 11 January 1989, B3; Struening and Pittman 1987.

89. Stern 1984, 299.

90. Until 1983, *The New York Times Index* listed articles on homelessness under the heading "Vagrants and Vagrancy"; that year it was changed to "Homeless Persons."

91. Lee, Link, and Toro 1991, 670–671.

92. 1990–1991, 306.

93. White is worth citing at length:

> [W]e identified ourselves with the cause of "homelessness" because, in an adverse situation, we could not see any better strategic option. Having made that reactive judgment, we promoted the cause of "the homeless" with single-minded determination. . . . We

> didn't intend, through all these efforts, to construct a new moral category of the poor, to impose a new stigma on already beleaguered people, or to introduce new divisions between them. There simply seemed to be no better way, in the 1980s, to picture the urgency of housing market failure and to give new lustre to the very old struggles of the poor. (1990–91, 292)

94. In advocacy's defense, this occurred not simply, as is often claimed, because such issues sullied the legitimacy of need of a newly christened deserving poor, but because whatever their afflictions, those poor required safe and secure housing if they were to be effectively treated.

95. They weren't entirely ignored: In New York City, for example, lawsuits were filed seeking right to treatment for drug users and supportive housing for those infected with HIV. Lawyers active in the latter lawsuit were instrumental in setting up a not-for-profit organization (Housing Works) dedicated to housing development for persons with the infection. In the 1990s, the local Coalition for the Homeless was active in resettling HIV-infected Haitian refugees through its own crisis intervention program.

96. Also in the 1990s, the National Coalition for the Homeless, with pro bono assistance from academic researchers, reworked position papers on substance abuse and homelessness, and on race and homelessness. Housing analysts and advocates have been especially active with regard to segregation; see, for example, Massey and Denton 1993.

97. 1992, 193.

98. "When they approach me they see only my surroundings, themselves, or figments of their imagination—indeed, everything and anything except me" (*Invisible Man,* Prologue).

Chapter 7. Negotiating Settlement

1. The discussion in this paragraph draws on Lipsky and Smith 1989; Hopper and Baumohl 1994; Blasi 1987; Bennett 1995.

2. Nothing, that is, except penitentiaries, almshouses, and asylums; "outdoor relief" was almost exclusively the precinct of private charity.

3. Allowing, of course, for changes in fashion and culture: Beggars today (at least in the United States) are more likely to post themselves at the doors to twenty-four–hour automatic banking machines than at the doors of churches.

4. A close study of 214 welfare-reliant mothers in four cities found that benefits alone do not make for a livelihood; instead, recipients must supplement their welfare income with reported and unreported work, covert contributions from boyfriends, friends, or relatives, and aid from various agencies (see Edin and Lein 1997, 20–59). In order to survive, that is, they *must* contrive to "cheat."

5. Lipsky 1984; Blasi 1987; Bennett 1995.

6. *New York Times,* 8 March 1992. In 1991, public housing accounted for less than 9 percent of the city's renter-occupied units. The occupancy survey for 1993 estimated that there were 210,000 doubled-up households in New York City; 86,000 of them harbored an illegal "sub-family," the rest included "secondary individuals" (Stegman 1993, 58, 157).

7. Similar quandaries arise when considering wages and working conditions in the informal economy (Sassen 1991; Portes 1994).

8. I draw on my own experience as an advocate and researcher (mainly in New York City), as well as on the reflections of other advocates, providers, bureaucrats, and academics (see especially Barak 1991; Blasi 1994; Demers 1995; Foscarinis 1993; 1995; Hombs 1992; Hopper and Baumohl 1994; 1996; White 1990–1991).

9. *New York Times,* 5 June 1986.

10. Hombs 1992, 110. Press coverage peaked during this time, averaging a story a day in the *New York Times* in 1987 (Lee, Link, Toro 1991). On the alleged backlash in public at-

titudes, see, e.g., *New York Times,* 2 September 1991, A1; *Washington Post,* 21 May 1990, A1.

11. Blasi 1994; Link et al. 1996.

12. This section draws on Hopper and Cox 1982; Hayes 1987; Hombs 1994; and Simon 1996.

13. Early in February 1996, for example, the court ordered the city to keep an overflow shelter open all day, instead of transferring men there throughout the night (*New York Times,* 3 February 1996, 28). And about the same time, the state began to consider how it might lift or relax regulations governing capacity and amenities in public shelters, in order (as one critic put it) to "make it easier to run warehouses for people" (*New York Times,* 14 February 1996, B5).

14. This discussion draws on Foscarinis, 1993; 1995; 1996; Weir 1995; and Duffield 1996.

15. www.nationalhomeless.org/mckinney2001.html

16. The PATH program is formula driven (funding to states is proportionate to a measure of need) and provides mental health and supportive services; Shelter Plus Care provides funds, on a competitive basis, to nonprofit and state applicants for supportive housing for homeless persons who have severe psychiatric disorders, substance abuse problems, or HIV-related illnesses.

17. Donohue 1996. Earlier, the same group had parlayed a 20 percent low-income set-aside in a huge housing development (Presidential Towers) into 165 units in the development for low-income renters, 1,014 rental subsidies (Section 8, project-based) for low-income housing development, and start-up funds and a commitment of regular contributions to the Chicago Low-Income Housing Trust Fund.

18. See "Beyond McKinney: Policies to End Homelessness" (1993), National Law Center on Homelessness and Poverty, 918 F St., NW, Suite 412, Washington, D.C. 20004; Foscarinis 1993.

19. See "Housing for All: Keeping the Promise" (November 1995), available from the National Housing Law Project, 2201 Broadway, Suite 815, Oakland, CA 94612. Long-time housing advocate Chester Hartman (1998) reargued the case—and challenged those who disagree to make the opposing argument, summoning the empirical evidence for a plausible future absent radical intervention into the housing market.

20. Such efforts have only been sporadically documented. For studies of specific movements in which homeless people themselves played critical roles, see Cress 1990; Mathieu 1994; Rader 1986; Wagner 1993; Rosenthal 1994; Jiler 1997; Wright 1997. For an argument that "top-down" organizing by well-meaning outsiders, apart from a grassroots movement, is bound to fail, see Yeich 1994.

21. I am indebted to Rob Rosenthal's fine analysis (1996) for the following discussion.

22. For shelter stays, see Kuhn and Culhane 1998 and White 1996 for a summary. For stable relocations, see Shinn et al. 1998.

23. Link et al. 1994; Phelan and Link 1999.

24. Bogard et al. 1995. For an earlier report of families strategically seeking shelter as a "route to better housing" in New York City, see Dugger 1991.

25. Haugland et al., 1997; Hopper et al. 1997.

26. Wuerker 1996; Wuerker and Keenan 1997. For the historical precedent, see Lis and Soly 1990; Lis 1986.

27. Shinn et al. 2001.

28. Rooney 1980b.

29. Minow 1990, 366; see also Diller 1995.

30. Demers 1995, 1021.

31. Demers 1995, 1019n.

32. A point not lost on shelter residents themselves. In a visit to the shelters by the presiding judge in *Callahan,* investigating firsthand one of innumerable charges of noncompliance,

he was told by the men that they cared less about shelter amenities than about "access to permanent housing, jobs and treatment for substance abuse" (Demers 1995, 1021n.).

33. Ignatieff 1984.

34. Minow 1990, 383, 307.

35. *New York Times,* 9 November 1995, B10.

36. "Reforming New York City's System of Homeless Services," May 1994.

37. 12 August 1998 letter from ASPHA to Brian Wing, NYS Office of Temporary and Disability Assistance, and to Gordon Campbell, NYC Department of Homeless Services, and from recipients to ASPHA, 21 October 1998 and 9 September 1998, respectively.

38. Sklar Opinion, 18 February 2000, 15, 20, 24.

39. *New York Times,* 23 February 2000, B1.

40. See also Gounis 1993 and Dordick 1997 for more recent depictions of conditions in the shelters.

41. Lardner 1991. See also Fisher 1993.

42. For a detailed recounting of the protracted struggle to reclaim the parkland of Tompkins Square, see Abu-Lughod 1994.

43. In striking down a vagrancy statute in 1967, the New York State Court of Appeals cut closer to the heart of the matter: These people were being removed, the court recognized, because they were "disturbing by their presence the sensibilities of the nicer parts of the community" (*Fenster v. Leary,* as cited in Simon 1992, 642).

44. An internal NYPD memo, "Reclaiming Public Space," lists "dirt, graffiti, homeless people, noise" as among the violations to be targeted (Kunen 1994).

45. *New York Times* 30 March 1997; 28 January 1998. During the TNSOL count of the 2000 census, for example, a sidewalk stretch between 9th and 10th Avenues in midtown Manhattan, well-lit and shielded from the elements by construction scaffolding, was regularly occupied by fifteen to twenty people.

46. See Hopper 1991d, 785; Duneier 1999, 120–154.

47. Barr 1999. In August 1999, that report spurred a class-action lawsuit (*Brad H. v. City of New York,* 117882/99) filed by the Urban Justice Center. In July 2000, a State Supreme Court judge ruled in favor of plaintiffs and ordered the city to continue the treatment of mentally ill inmates after their release so as to prevent "a return to the cycle of likely harm to themselves and/or others, through substance abuse, mental and physical health deterioration, homelessness, indigence, crime, re-arrest and incarceration" (*New York Law Journal* 13 July 2000; *New York Times* 13 July 2000, B1).

48. Colleen Gillespie, personal communication, spring 2000; Martell, Rosner, and Harmon 1995; and Michaels et al. 1992.

49. These and many other aspects of history, problem–framing, and advocacy are extensively treated in *Homelessness in America,* edited by Jim Baumohl (1996).

50. Link et al. 1994.

51. Weir 1992; De Parle 1992.

52. Kaus 1992; Levitan and Gallo 1992.

53. Ellwood 1996.

54. Compare Edsall and Edsall 1992, 278.

55. Again, these are what Mizruchi called "abeyance mechanisms." See Chapter 1.

56. At best, for those deemed unable to work, they provide a sort of secondary or "program citizenship," contingent on their participation in service systems (Rowe 1999, 147)—that is, on providing work for others.

57. For the general phenomenon, see Erikson 1994. For discussions of fleeting (and sometimes enduring) solidarity in shelters or on the street, see Liebow 1993; Snow and Anderson 1993; Dordick 1997; Rowe 1999, 115; and Duneier 1999.

58. Hopper and Hamberg 1986, 14.

59. Strauss 1989.

60. Duneier 1999, 60–62.
61. Bahr 1973.
62. As of February 1996, some forty thousand programs nationwide (mostly nonprofit groups) delivered some form of homeless assistance, with shelter and "family services" listed as the primary mission of 45 percent of the sponsoring agencies (Urban Institute 1999, ch. 14).
63. Personal communication, Patrick Markee, Coalition for the Homeless, New York, September 1999.
64. Weir 1992, 168.
65. Crowley 2000.
66. Rooney 1980a, b; Mauss 1980.
67. I owe Luisa Stark thanks for discussions of this dynamic.
68. See Luhrmann 1989, 307–336, on interpretive drift and serious play among apprentice magicians.
69. Mollat 1986, 70, 113.
70. Rothstein 1993.
71. Luhrmann 2000, 272–293.
72. Obeyeskere 1985; Geertz 1996; Keyes 1985.
73. Marin 1987; Groth 1994; Hopper and Baumohl 1994; Duneier 1999.
74. Duneier 1999.
75. Cohen and Sokolovsky 1989.
76. Kleinman, Das, and Lock 1996.
77. Thompson 1978, 219.

Chapter 8. Limits to Witnessing

1. Recall the early work of Baumohl and colleagues in Berkeley (Baumohl and Miller 1974; Segal, Baumohl, and Johnson 1977).
2. Recall Caplow: "For the price of a subway ride, [the researcher] can enter a country where the accepted principles of social interaction do not apply" (1970, 6). The skid row man was considered "about as different from *Homo Sociologus* as it is possible to be while still remaining human" (ibid.). The descendant of this genre is Giamo's *On the Bowery* (1991), which celebrates the grotesque "otherness" of the place as the dark side of mainstream culture.
3. Brettell 1993.
4. See Code of Ethics, American Anthropological Association (available at www.aaanet.org/committees/ethics/ethcode.htm). This is especially true of applied work, where the explicit aim is to ask: "How can this situation be improved?" (Pelto, as cited by Singer 1996, 82).
5. In approach, his work is much like that of Robert Coles. Even Jencks, in a book otherwise notable for its absence of sentiment, pays lip service to the force of Liebow's claim (1994, 122).
6. On that score, compare *Tally's Corner.* Its watchword was failure—repeated, remembered, bitterly resented failure—and the first test of any policy initiative informed by such testament was whether it pared away at the likelihood of more. The recommendations there had to do, famously and futilely, with the provision of decent work to such men. (For a recent appreciation of which, see Massing 1995.) Ethnography's task might well have been simpler then, if only because the consequences of the next quarter century of ruined work (Moss and Tilly 1991), stressed families (Stern 1993), and revanchist social policy had yet to be tallied. Homelessness was almost nonexistent (Liebow 1967, 36), as were the epidemic proportions of drugs and violence and HIV-related illnesses that have taken root since.
7. Or so he tells us (twice, pp. viii and 319). Happenstance seems enough of a reason:

semi-retired, Liebow was volunteering in a neighborhood women's shelter when he began "out of habit" (and with the women's permission) to take notes.

8. Gounis 1992.

9. Murray 1984; Lovell 1989.

10. Hopper 1991e; Lovell 1992; Snow et al. 1996.

11. Koegel 1992.

12. Wright 1997; Underwood 1990; Balmori and Morton 1993; Phillips and Hamilton 1996.

13. Dordick 1997.

14. Hopper, Susser, and Conover 1985; Gounis 1993.

15. Snow and Anderson 1987.

16. Rowe 1999; Lovell and Cohn 1998.

17. Ware et al. 1992; 1994.

18. Desjarlais 1995.

19. Wolf et al. 2001.

20. Duneier 1999.

21. Though she still finds time to teach and do scholarly work as well.

22. Less than happily or competently in my own case, it must be added (see Hopper 1990b).

23. *Webster's Third New International Dictionary* (1976) defines it more succinctly: "the influence of the previous history or treatment of a body on its subsequent response to a given force or changed condition . . ." There are kindred notions in our own anthropological legacy as well. Bateson's discussion of "schismogenesis" in *Naven* (2d ed., 1958) is the most pertinent. The dynamic is a familiar one in the literature on pragmatics of communication (Watzlawick, Beavin, and Jackson 1967; Watzlawick, Weakland, and Fisch 1974).

24. Geertz 1973, 26.

25. The hidden agendas of bureaucracies, state agents, and service providers, to name a few.

26. Scott 1990. At times, it's as though we revel in our capacity to live as poets must (according to Keats)—"in uncertainties, Mysteries, doubts, without any irritable reaching after fact and reason." Then we profess chagrin when journalists, alerted by our writings, mimic our methods and descend into these same depths to find lost tribes of "mole people" (*Los Angeles Times* 2 September 1990, A1), shelters functioning as "shooting galleries," full of "addicts and AIDS" (Bearak, *Los Angeles Times*, 27–30 September 1992, A1), and streets harried by the "twin" perils of "addiction and homelessness" (Kolata, *New York Times*, 22 May 1989, B1).

27. Again, Duneier 1999 is the exception here.

28. A word might be said here, too, about "community opposition": Too often we practicing anthropologists do a poor job in getting out the word on "what works" (and how) in successful reintegration efforts, and in failing to grasp the depths and history of neighborhood opposition to even well-run programs. Animus to the deranged, especially when disorder is compounded by abandonment, runs deep. Some of it has to do with the vague but unsettling bundle of anxieties set off by standing affronts to bourgeois order; some of it stems from ill-formulated notions of home and threats to that sanctuary; and some of it is doubtless due to coarser stuff, like concerns about property values. In any event, these anxieties are difficult to confront head on in community board hearings. More to the point here, articulated concerns may have nothing to do with the specificities of proposed programs or housing, and everything to do with entrenched patterns of eroding local control.

29. Knorr-Cetina 1983; Lynch 1994.

30. A key lesson from the dismal history of full employment in this country is that intelligent reform must seek first to identify "the often invisible linkages that block or redirect the impetus for reform" (Weir 1992, 168).

31. Bourdieu and Wacquant 1992, 245n, emphasis in original.

32. As has been noted in another context: "The admission of alternatives in principle does not imply their serious consideration in daily practice" (Gould and Lewontin 1979, 586).

33. Fox 1972.

34. Ignatieff 1995, 84.

35. Williams 1995; Walzer 1995; Lipsky and Smith 1989; Lipsky 1984; Blasi 1987; Bennett 1995.

36. As, for example, Koester did recently with respect to ritualistic needle-sharing among IV-drug users in Denver (*New York Times,* 20 September 1995, B10).

37. See also the plea from Blasi 1994. There are promising signs, e.g., Weinberg and Koegel 1995.

38. As Jim Baumohl and Gary Blasi have complained.

39. Such linkages are especially important in understanding how informal markets and sources of assistance work, an understanding that in turn could aid in designing alternatives to formal shelter, supplements to vernacular supports, more cost-efficient allocation of resources, etc. For an intriguing reading of the "institutional" embankments and flows (or "channels") discernible in the apparently idiosyncratic ravings of a man diagnosed with schizophrenia, see Saris (1994).

40. Singer 1996; Berreman 1991, 63; Brettell 1993.

41. Douglas 1986, 4.

42. Agee and Evans [1941] 1966, xiv; Lemann 1991; Hainer 1991; Keyssar 1986.

43. *Iowa Press-Citizen,* 7 May 1983.

44. 1933, 2.

45. *Walley v. New York City Transit Authority,* Index No. 177/91, 1991.

46. See also Blasi 1990.

47. W. James, *Popular Science Monthly,* October 1910. But recall that the attempt to revive the phrase was a miserable failure on the part of the Carter administration.

48. See Desjarlais 1995, for example.

49. Shinn, Baumohl, and Hopper 2001. Kusmer's observation (2001) that in the 1980s the United States returned to what were, historically speaking, more *normal* levels of homelessness is only half-right. When the reasons for homelessness change so profoundly—for the first time, it wasn't driven by economic depression or disruptions of traditional work, having less to do with labor markets than with housing costs—it's arguably not the same thing.

50. Burt et al. 2001, 323.

References

Aaron, H. J., and C. L. Shultze, eds. 1992. *Setting Domestic Priorities.* Washington, D.C: The Brookings Institute.

Aaron, M. 1935. Report of the Mendicancy Project Unit, 18 June. Welfare Island: New York City Department of Corrections.

Abu-Lughod, J. L., ed. 1994. *From Urban Village to East Village.* Oxford and Cambridge: Blackwell.

Advisory Social Service Committee. 1915. *The Men We Lodge.* New York: Advisory Social Service Committee on the Municipal Lodging House.

Agee, J., and W. Evans. *Let Us Now Praise Famous Men.* [1941] 1966. New York: Ballantine Books.

Algren, N. [1935] 1965. *Somebody in Boots.* New York: Berkeley.

Alker, J., and C. Dolbeare. 1990. *The Closing Door: Economic Causes of Homelessness.* Washington, D.C.: National Coalition for the Homeless.

Allsop, K. 1967. *Hard Travellin'.* New York: New Americans.

Alonso, W., and P. Starr, eds. 1987. *The Politics of Numbers.* New York: Russell Sage.

Anderson, E. 1978. *A Place on the Corner.* Chicago: University of Chicago Press.

——. 1989. Sex ccodes and family life among poor inner-city youths. *Annals of the American Academy of Political and Social Science* 501:59–78.

Anderson, N. 1923. *The Hobo.* Chicago: University of Chicago Press.

——. 1932. *Report on the Municipal Lodging House of New York City.* New York: Welfare Council.

——. 1934. *The Homeless in New York City.* New York: Welfare Council.

——. 1940. *Men on the Move.* Chicago: University of Chicago.

——. 1961. *The Hobo.* 2d ed. Chicago: University of Chicago.

——. 1975. *The American Hobo: An Autobiography.* Boston: E. J. Brill.

Anonymous. 1987. Letter to Rita Schwartz, HRA Outreach Coordinator.

Aronow, R. 1967. *Bowery Census 1967.* New York: Columbia University, Bureau of Applied Social Science, May 31.

Aschenbrenner, J. 1975. *Lifelines: Black Families in Chicago.* New York: Holt, Rinehart and Winston.

Bach, V., and S. Y. West. 1993. *Housing on the Block.* New York: Community Service Society.

Bachrach, L. 1978. A conceptual approach to deinstitutionalization. *Hospital and Community Psychiatry* 29: 573–578.

Bahr, H. M. 1968. Homelessness and Disaffiliation. New York: Columbia University, Bureau of Applied Social Research.

——. 1970. Homelessness, Disaffiliation and Retreatism. In Bahr, ed. 39–50.

——. 1973. *Skid Row: An Introduction to Disaffiliation.* New York: Oxford.

——. 1989. Introduction. In Momeni, ed. xvii–xxv.

——, ed. 1970. *Disaffiliated Man.* Toronto: University of Toronto Press.

Bahr, H. M., and T. Caplow. 1974. *Old Men Drunk and Sober.* New York: New York University Press.

Bailey, T., and R. Waldinger. 1991. The Changing Ethnic/Racial Division of Labor. In Mollenkopf and Castells, eds. 43–78.

Balmori, D., and M. Morton. 1993. *Transitory Gardens, Uprooted Lives.* New Haven: Yale University Press.

Bane, M. J. 1986. Household Composition and Poverty. In Danziger and Weinberg, eds. 209–231.

Barak, G. 1991. *Gimme Shelter.* New York: Praeger.

Barnes, C. B. 1912. A Night in the Municipal Lodging House. Unpublished paper.

——. 1914. The Homeless Man. 2 vols. Unpublished ms. Columbia University: COS Archives.

——. 1915–1916. The Homeless Man. In *The Annual* (published by students of the New York School of Philanthropy). 26–33.

Barr, H. 1999. *Prisons and Jails: Hospitals of Last Resort.* New York: the Correctional Association of New York and the Urban Justice Center.

Barrett, D. F., I. Anolik, and F. H. Abramson. 1992. The 1990 census shelter and street night enumeration. Paper presented at the annual meeting of the American Statistical Association, Boston, August.

Barrett, S. R. 1996. *Anthropology: A Student's Guide to Theory and Method.* Toronto: University of Toronto Press.

Barrow, S. M., F. Hellman, A. M. Lovell, J. D. Plapinger, and E. L. Struening. 1989. *Effectiveness of Programs for the Homeless Mentally Ill: Final Report.* New York State Psychiatric Institute, Epidemiology of Mental Disorders Research Department.

Bateson, Gregory. 1958. *Naven.* 2d ed. Stanford: Stanford University Press.

Baumohl, J. 1992. Addiction and the American debate on homelessness. *British Journal of Addictions* 87:7–10.

——, ed. 1996. *Homelessness in America.* Phoenix: Oryx Press.

Baumohl, J., and R. B. Huebner. 1991. Alcohol and other drug problems among the homeless. *Housing Policy Debate* 2:837–865.

Baumohl, J., and H. Miller. 1974. *Down and Out in Berkeley.* Berkeley: City of Berkeley–University of California Community Affairs Committee.

Baxter, E., and K. Hopper. 1980. Pathologies of place and disorders of mind. *Health PAC Bulletin* 11:1–12, 21f.

——. 1981. *Private Lives/Public Spaces.* New York: Community Service Society.

Beard, R., ed. 1987. *On Being Homeless: Historical Perspectives.* New York: Museum for the City of New York.

Beard, R., and S. M. Kapsis. 1987. On Being Homeless in New York: A Pictorial Essay. In Beard, ed. 103–163.

Beier, A. L. 1985. *Masterless Men: The Vagrancy Problem in England, 1560–1640.* New York: Methuen.

Bellamy, C. 1979. *From Country Asylums to City Streets.* New York: Office of the New York City Council President.

Belle, D. E. 1983. The impact of poverty on social networks and supports. *Marriage and Family Review* 5:89–103.

Bennett, Susan D. 1995. "No relief but upon the terms of coming into the house"—Controlled spaces, invisible disentitlements, and homelessness in an urban shelter system. *Yale Law Journal* 104:2157–2212.

Berger, J. 1999. *King: A Street Story.* New York: Pantheon.

Berger, S. 1988. The homeless—a regional crisis. Speech given at Action Day '88, New School for Social Research, October.

Berlin, G., and W. McAllister. 1992. Homelessness. In Aaron and Shultze, eds. 63–99.

Berreman, G. 1991. Ethics versus Realism in Anthropology. In Fluehr-Lobban, ed. 38-71.

Bigart, H. 1961. Grim problems of the Bowery complicate clean-up drive. *New York Times,* 20 November, 1, 36.

Billingsley, A. 1992. *Climbing Jacob's Ladder.* New York: Simon and Schuster.

Blasi, G. L. 1987. Litigation on behalf of the homeless: Systematic approaches. *Journal of Urban and Contemporary Law* 31:137–142.

——. 1990. Social policy and social science research on homelessness. *Journal of Social Issues* 46:207–219.

——. 1994. And we are not seen. *American Behavioral Scientist* 37:563–586.

Blau, J. 1992. *The Visible Poor.* New York: Oxford University Press.

Bluestone, B., and B. Harrison. 1982. *The Deindustrialization of America.* New York: Basic Books.

Blumberg, L. U., T. F. Shipley, and S. F. Barsky. 1978. *Liquor and Poverty.* New Brunswick: Rutgers Center of Alcohol Studies.

Bock Associates. 1980. *Report of a Survey of the Shelter Care Center for Men in New York City for the New York Department of Social Services.* St. Paul.

Bogard, C., J. J. McConnell, N. Gerstel, and M. Schwartz. 1995. Surplus mothers: Assessing family shelters as gendered abeyance structures. Paper delivered at the annual meeting of the Eastern Sociological Association, Philadelphia, March.

Bogue, D. J. 1963. *Skid Row in American Cities.* Chicago: University of Chicago Press.

Bonner, A. 1990. *Jerry McAuley and His Mission.* Rev. ed. Neptune, N.J.: Loizeaux Brothers.

Booth, M. L. 1859. *History of the City of New York.* New York: W.R.C. Clark and Meeker.

Borchert, J. 1980. *Alley Life in Washington.* Chicago: University of Illinois Press.

Borofsky, R., ed. 1994. *Assessing Cultural Anthropology.* New York: McGraw-Hill.

Bott, E. 1971. *Family and Social Network.* 2d ed. New York: Free Press.

Bourdieu, P. 1986. The Forms of Capital. In Richardson, ed. 241–258.

——. 1990. *In Other Words.* Stanford: Stanford University Press.

Bourdieu, P., and L. Wacquant. 1992. *An Invitation to Reflexive Sociology.* Chicago: University of Chicago Press.

Bourgois, P. 1995. *In Search of Respect.* New York: Cambridge University Press.

Bouwsma, W. J. 1990. *A Usable Past.* Berkeley: University of California Press.

Boyer, P. 1978. *Urban Masses and Moral Order, 1820–1920.* Cambridge: Harvard University Press.

Brandt, Lilian. 1933. *Glimpses of New York in Previous Depressions.* New York: Welfare Council, Research Bureau.

——. 1939. *Relief of the Unemployed in New York City, 1929–1989.* Draft ms. New York: Welfare Council Research Bureau.

Bratt, R., C. Hartman, and A. Meyerson, eds. 1986. *Critical Perspectives on Housing.* Philadelphia: Temple University Press.

Breines, S. 1932. The emergencies. Parts 1 and 2. *Shelter* 2(4):21–28.

Bremer, W. W. 1984. *Depression Winters: New York Social Workers and the New Deal.* Philadelphia: Temple University Press.

Brenner, M. H. 1977. Health costs and benefits of economic policy. *International Journal of Health Services* 7:581–623.

Brettell, C. B., ed. 1993. *When They Read What We Write.* Westport: Bergin and Garvey.

Brown, J. C. 1940. *Public Relief 1929–1939.* New York: Octagon.

Bruns, Roger A. 1980. *Knights of the Road.* New York: Methuen.

Bureau of Applied Social Research. 1965. Bowery Project: Summary report of a study undertaken under contract approved by the Board of Estimate, Calendar No. 14, December 19, 1963. New York: Columbia University.

Burt, M. R. 1992. *Over the Edge.* New York: Russell Sage.

——. 1994. Comment. *Housing Policy Debate* 5:141–152.

Burt, M., L. Y. Aron, and E. Lee, with J. Valente. 2001. *Helping America's Homeless: Emergency Shelter or Affordable Housing?* Washington, D.C.: Urban Institute Press.

Burtless, G., ed. 1990. *A Future of Lousy Jobs?* Washington, D.C.: The Brookings Institute.

Burton, L. M. 1990. Teenage childbearing as an alternative life-course strategy in multigeneration black families. *Human Nature* 1:123–143.

Callahan v. Carey. 1979. *New York Law Journal,* Dec. 11, at 10, col.4 (N.Y. Sup. Ct., Dec. 5 1979).

——. 1981. Final Judgment by Consent. August 26. (Reprinted in *One Year Later: The Homeless Poor in New York City, 1982.* New York: Community Service Society.)

Campbell, H., T. W. Know, and T. Byrnes. 1891. *Darkness and Daylight: Lights and Shadows of New York Life.* Hartford: A.D. Worthington.

Caplow, T. 1940. Transiency as a cultural pattern. *American Sociological Review* 5:731–739.

——. 1970. The Sociologist and the Homeless Man. In Bahr, ed. 3–12.

Caplow, T., K. A. Lovald., and S. E. Wallace. 1958. A general report on the problem of relocating the population of the lower loop redevelopment area. *Minneapolis: Minneapolis Housing and Redevelopment Authority.*

Carlin, P. E. 1979. Social outcasts: The tramp in American society, 1873–1910. Paper presented at the annual meeting of the American Historical Association, December 28.

Carlisle, R. J. 1893. *An Account of Bellevue Hospital.* New York: Society of the Alumni of Bellevue Hospital.

Cassell, J., and M. Wax, eds. 1980. Ethical problems of fieldwork. *Social Problems* 27:259–377.

Clarke, D. A. 1937. Men on relief in Lackawanna, N.Y., 1934–1935. *University of Buffalo Studies* 14(4):67–119.

Clement, P. F. 1984. The Transformation of the Wandering Poor in Nineteenth-Century Philadelphia. In Monkkonen, ed. 56–84.

Coalition for the Homeless and SRO Tenants Rights Coalition. 1985. *Single Room Occupancy Hotels: Standing in the Way of the Gentry.* New York: Coalition for the Homeless.

Cohen, C., and J. Sokolovsky. 1989. *Old Men of the Bowery.* New York: Guilford.

Cohen, C., and K. S. Thompson. 1992. Homeless mentally ill or mentally ill homeless? *American Journal of Psychiatry* 149:816–823.

Cohen, N., ed. 1990. *Psychiatry Takes to the Streets.* New York: Guilford.

Coles, R. 1997. *Doing Documentary Work.* New York: Oxford University Press.

Committee on the Almshouse. 1901. Report. In *Annual Report of the State Board of Charities for 1900.* Albany: J. B. Lyon.

Committee on Statistics. 1896. Report. In *Fourteenth Annual Report of the Charity Organization Society of New York for 1895–July 1996.* Albany: J. B. Lyon, 57–60.

Conover, T. 1984. *Rolling Nowhere.* New York: Viking.

Conroy, J. 1934. *The Disinherited.* New York: Covici Friede.

Cook, T., ed. 1979. *Vagrancy: Some New Perspectives.* New York: Academic Press.

Cook, T., and G. Braithwaite. 1979. The Problem for Whom? In Cook, ed. 1–10.

Cook, T. D., and T. R. Curtin. 1987. The Mainstream and the Underclass. In Masters and Smith, eds. 217–264.

Coser, L. 1965. The sociology of poverty. *Social Problems* 13:140–148.

Crapsey, E. 1872. *The Nether Side of New York.* New York: Sheldon.

Cray, R. 1988. *Paupers and Poor Relief in New York City and its Rural Environs, 1700–1830.* Philadelphia: Temple University Press.

Cress, D. 1990. Look out world, the meek are getting it ready: Implications of mobilization among the homeless. Paper presented at the annual meeting of the American Sociological Association, Washington, August.

Crouse, J. M. 1986. *The Homeless Transient in the Great Depression: New York State, 1929–1941.* Albany: State University of New York Press.

Crowley, S. 2000. Point of View. *Weekly Housing Update: Memo to Members* 5(16)[April 21]:1. (National Low-Income Housing Coalition.)

Crystal, S. 1984. Homeless men and homeless women. *Urban and Social Change Review* 17(2):2–6.

Crystal, S., and M. Goldstein. 1982. *New Arrivals: First-Time Shelter Clients.* New York: Human Resources Administration.

Crystal, S., M. Goldstein, and R. Levitt. 1982. *Chronic and Situational Dependency: Long-Term Residents in a Shelter for Men.* New York: Human Resources Administration.

Culhane, D. P. 1992. The Quandaries of Shelter Reform. *Social Service Review* 66: 428–40.

Culhane, D. P., E. F. Dejowski, J. Ibañez, E. Needham, and I. Macchia. 1994. Public shelter admission rates in Philadelphia and New York City: The implications for turnover for sheltered homeless counts. *Housing Policy Debate* 5:107–140.

Cumming, E. 1974. Prisons, Shelters and Homeless Men. *Psychiatric Quarterly* 48:496–504.

Currie, E. 1993. *Reckoning.* New York: Hill and Wang.

Danziger, S.H., and D.H. Weinberg, eds. 1986. *Fighting Poverty: What Works and What Doesn't.* Cambridge: Harvard University Press.

Davis, N.Z. 1968. Poor relief, humanism, and heresy: The case of Lyon. *Studies in Medieval and Renaissance History.* 5:217–275.

Dean, W.J. 1981. Potter's Field: Aisle of the Dead. *New York Times*, 25 May.

Dear, M., and J. Wolch. 1987. *Landscapes of Despair.* Princeton: Princeton University Press.

Dees, J. 1948. *Flophouse: An Authentic Undercover Study of "Flophouses," "Cage Hotels," Including Missions, Shelters and Institutions Serving Unattached (Homeless) Men.* Francestown, N.H.: Marshall Jones.

DeHavenon, A.L., ed. 1996. *There's No Place Like Home.* Westport: Bergen and Garvey.

Dembo, D., and W. Morehouse. 1993. *The Underbelly of the U.S. Economy.* Croton-on-Hudson, N.Y.: Council on International and Public Affairs.

Demers, S. 1995. The failure of litigation as a tool for the development of social welfare policy. *Fordham Urban Law Journal.* 22:1009–1050

Dennis, D., I.S. Levine, and F.C. Osher. 1991. The physical and mental health status of homeless adults. *Housing Policy Debate* 2:815–835.

Dennis, D., and J. Monahan, eds. 1995. *Coercion and Aggressive Community Treatment.* New York: Plenum.

Denzin, N.K. 1968. On the ethics of disguised observation. *Social Problems* 15:502–504.

Denzin, N.K., and Y.S. Lincoln, eds. 1994. *Handbook of Qualitative Research.* Thousand Oaks: Sage.

De Parle, J. 1992. Nostalgia and need conjure up thoughts of the W.P.A. *New York Times* 3 May, E6.

Derby, R.H. 1877. Final Report of the Committee on Out-Door Relief Upon Night Refuges. In *Fifth Annual Report of the State Charities Aid Association.* Albany: J.B. Lyon, 67–81.

Desjarlais, R. 1995. *Shelter Blues.* Philadelphia: University of Pennsylvania Press.

Deutsch, M. 1975. Equity, equality, or need? *Journal of Social Issues* 31:137–149.

DeVine, J.A., and J.D. Wright. 1993. *The Greatest of Evils.* New York: Aldine de Gruyter.

DiLeonardo, M. 1984. *The Varieties of Ethnic Experience.* Ithaca: Cornell University Press.

Diller, M. 1995. Poverty lawyering in the golden age. *Michigan Law Review* 93:1401–1432.

Dooley D., and R. Catalano. 1980. Economic change as a cause of behavioral disorder. *Psychological Bulletin* 87:450–468.

Dordick, G.A. 1997. *Something Left to Lose.* Philadelphia: Temple University Press.

Douglas, M. 1966. *Purity and Danger.* London: Routledge & Kegan Paul.

——. 1986. *How Institutions Think.* Syracuse: Syracuse University Press.

Douglass, R. L., and B. J. Hodgkins. 1991. Racial Differences Regarding Shelter and Housing in a Sample of Urban Elderly Homeless. In Keigher, ed. 43–57.

Drake, St. C., and H. R. Cayton. 1945. *Black Metropolis: A Study of Negro Life in a Northern City.* New York: Harcourt, Brace and Company.

Duffield, B. 1996. National Coalition for the Homeless, personal communication, 8 February.

Dugger, C. 1991. Families seek out shelters as route to better housing. *New York Times,* 4 September, A1.

Duneier, M. 1992. *Slim's Table.* Chicago: University of Chicago Press.

——. 1999. *Sidewalk.* New York: Farrar, Straus and Giroux.

Edin, K., and L. Lein. 1997. *Making Ends Meet.* New York: Russell Sage.

Edsall, T. B., and M. D. Edsall. 1992. *Chain Reaction.* New York: W.W. Norton.

Ellison, R. 1952. *Invisible Man.* New York: Random House.

Ellwood, D. T. 1996. Welfare reform as I knew it. *The American Prospect* 26:22–29.

Engels, F. [1845] 1969. *The Condition of the Working Class in England in 1944.* Stanford: Stanford University Press.

Erickson, J., and C. Wilhelm, eds. 1986. *Housing the Homeless.* New Brunswick: Center for Urban Policy Research, Rutgers University.

Erikson, K. 1967. A comment on disguised observation in sociology. *Social Problems* 14:366–373.

——. 1968. A reply to Denzin. *Social Problems* 15:505–506.

——. 1976. *Everything in Its Path.* New York: Simon and Schuster.

——. 1994. *A New Species of Trouble.* New York: W. W. Norton.

Estroff, S. E. 1981. *Making It Crazy.* Berkeley: University of California Press.

Fabian, J. 1983. *Time and the Other.* New York: Columbia University Press.

Fagan, J. 1993. Crime, drugs, and neighborhood change: The effects of deindustrialization on social control in inner cities. Background memorandum prepared for the Social Science Research Council, Policy Conference on Persistent Urban Poverty, Washington, D.C., November 9–10.

Favret-Saada, J. 1990. On participation. *Culture, Medicine, and Psychiatry* 14:189–199.

Feder, L. H. 1936. *Unemployment Relief in Periods of Depression.* New York: Russell Sage.

Federal Writers' Project. [1939] 1982. *The WPA Guide to New York City.* New York: Pantheon.

Feied, F. 1964. *No Pie in the Sky.* New York: Citadel.

Fine, M. 1991. *Framing Dropouts: Notes on the Politics of an Urban Public High School.* Albany: State University of New York Press.

First, R. J., D. Roth, and B. D. Arewa. 1988. Homelessness: Understanding the dimensions of the problem for minorities. *Social Work* 33:120–124.

Fischer, P. J. 1989. Estimating the prevalence of alcohol, drug, and mental health problems in the contemporary homeless population. *Contemporary Drug Problems* 16:333–389.

——. 1992. Criminal behavior and victimization among homeless people. In Jahiel, ed. 87–112.

Fischer, P. J., and W. R. Breakey. 1991. The epidemiology of alcohol, drug, and mental disorders among homeless persons. *American Psychologist* 46:1115–1128.

Fisher, I. 1993. Shantytowns, bulldozers, and patience: A dilemma. *New York Times*, 19 September, E6.

Fitchen, J. M. 1991. Homelessness in rural places: Perspectives from upstate New York. *Urban Anthropology* 20:177–210.

Flinn, D. E. 1962. Transient psychotic reactions during travel. *American Journal of Psychiatry* 119:173–174.

Fluehr-Lobban, C., ed. 1991. *Ethics and the Profession of Anthropology.* Philadelphia: University of Pennsylvania Press.

Flynt, J. 1899. *Tramping with Tramps.* New York: Century.

Fogelson, R. M. 1989. *America's Armories.* Cambridge: Harvard University Press.

Forestall, M. R. 1938. Trends in housing: Delinquency and health in the central northwest area in Washington, D.C. Master's thesis, Catholic University. (Courtesy of James Borchert)

Foscarinis, M. 1993. Beyond homelessness: Ethics, advocacy, and strategy. *St. Louis University Public Law Review* 12:37–67.

——. 1995. Shelter and housing: Programs under the Stewart B. McKinney Homeless Assistance Act. *Clearinghouse Review* 29(7–8):760–770.

——. 1996. The Federal Role: The Stewart B. McKinney Homeless Assistance Act. In Baumohl, ed. 60–171, 247–250 (notes).

Fox, R. G. 1972. *Urban Anthropology.* Englewood Cliffs, N.J.: Prentice-Hall.

Frazier, E. F. 1932. *The Negro Family in Chicago.* Chicago: University of Chicago Press.

——. 1939. *The Negro Family in the United States.* Chicago: University of Chicago Press.

Freeman, R. B. 1991. Employment and Earnings of Disadvantaged Young Men in a Labor Shortage Economy. In Jencks and Peterson, eds. 103–121.

Gans, H. J. 1962. *The Urban Villagers.* New York: Free Press.

——. 1991. *People, Plans, and Policies.* New York: Columbia University Press.

Garraty, J. A. 1978. *Unemployment in History.* New York: Harper.

——. 1986. *The Great Depression.* New York: Harcourt, Brace, Jovanovich.

Gates, H. L. 1992. *Loose Canons: Notes on the Culture Wars.* New York: Oxford.

Geertz, C. 1973. *The Interpretation of Cultures.* New York: Basic Books.

——. 1994. The Uses of Diversity. In Borofsky, ed. 454–465.

——. 1996. *After the Fact: Two Countries, Four Decades, One Anthropologist.* Cambridge: Harvard University Press.

——. 1998. *Works and Lives: The Anthropologist as Author.* Stanford: Stanford University Press.

Gephart, M. A. 1989. Neighborhoods and communities in concentrated poverty. *Items* (Social Science Research Council) 43(4):84–92.

Giamo, B. 1991. *On the Bowery.* Iowa City: University of Iowa Press.

Gilfoyle, T. J. 1992. *City of Eros: New York City, Prostitution, and the Commercialization of Sex, 1790–1920.* New York: W. W. Norton.

Glasser, I. 1989. Locating the homeless in a small city. Paper presented at the annual meeting of the American Anthropological Association, Washington, D.C., November.

Goffman, E. 1961. *Asylums.* Garden City, N.J.: Doubleday.

——. 1964. *Stigma: Notes on the Management of a Spoiled Identity.* Englewood Cliffs, N.J.: Prentice-Hall.

Golden, S. 1992. *The Woman Outside.* Berkeley: University of California Press.

Goldschmidt, W., ed. 1979. *The Uses of Anthropology.* Washington, D.C.: American Anthropological Association.

Good, M-J.D., P.E. Brodwin, B.J. Good, and A. Kleinman, eds. 1992. *Pain as Human Experience: An Anthropological Perspective.* Berkeley: University of California Press.

Gordon, L. 1994. *Pitied But Not Entitled.* New York: Free Press.

Gould, S.J. 1981. *The Mismeasure of Man.* New York: W.W. Norton.

Gould, S.J., and R.C. Lewontin. 1979. The spandrels of San Marcos and the panglossian paradigm: A critique of the adaptationist programme. *Proceedings of the Royal Society of London.* 205:581–598.

Gounis, K. 1992. The manufacture of dependency: shelterization revisited. *New England Journal of Public Policy* 8:685–693.

——. 1993. The domestication of urban marginality: New York shelters for homeless men. Ph.D. diss., Columbia University.

Gounis, K., and Susser, E. 1990. Shelterization and Its Implications for Mental Health Services. In Cohen, ed. 231–255.

Governor's Commission on Unemployment Relief. 1936. *Public Relief for Transient and Non-Settled Persons in the State of New York.* Albany: J.B. Lyon.

Green, C.B. 1982. Housing single, low-income individuals. Paper prepared for conference on New York State Welfare Policy, Sterling Forest Conference, Harriman, October 1–2.

Greenberg, C.L. 1991. *"Or Does It Explode?" Black Harlem in the Great Depression.* New York: Oxford University Press.

Greenblatt, W. 1948. Social aspects of the panic of 1957. Master's thesis, Columbia University.

Greenstone, J.D. 1991. Culture, Rationality, and the Underclass. In Jencks and Peterson, eds. 399–408.

Gregory, S., and R. Sanjek, eds. 1994. *Race.* New Brunswick: Rutgers University Press.

Griffin, R.A. 2001. *Census 2000: Service Based Enumeration Multiplicity Estimation.* Washington, D.C.: U.S. Census Bureau, February 28.

Grossman, J.R. 1989. *Land of Hope.* Chicago: University of Chicago Press.

Groth, P. 1983. Forbidden housing. Ph.D. diss., University of California, Berkeley.

——. 1994. *Living Downtown: The History of Residential Hotels in the United States.* Berkeley: University of California Press.

Gudeman, S. 1979. Herbert Gutman's *The Black Family in Slavery and Freedom, 1750–1925*: An anthropologist's view. *Social Science History* 3(3&4):56–65.

Gutman, A., ed. 1988. *Democracy and the Welfare State.* Princeton: Princeton University Press.

Gutman, H.G. 1965. The failure of the movement by the unemployed for public works in 1873. *Political Science Quarterly* 80:254–276.

——. 1976. *The Black Family in Slavery and Freedom, 1750–1925.* New York: Vintage.

Hacker, A. 1992. *Two Nations.* New York: Random House.

Hagen, J.L. 1982. Whatever happened to 43 Elizabeth I. c. 2? *Social Service Review* 56:108–119.

Hainer, P. 1991. Sharing kith and kin: A study of kinship behavior, an approach to explanation. Ph.D. diss., Brandeis University.

Hamberg, J., and C. Smolenski. 1993. Illegal SROs and other illegal occupancies in New York City. Unpublished ms.

Hamburger, R. 1983. *All the Lonely People: Life in a Single Room Occupancy Hotel.* New York: Ticknor and Fields.

Hamid, A. 1990. The political economy of crack-related violence. *Contemporary Drug Problems* 17:31–78.

Hand, J. 1976. Shopping bag ladies: A study in interstitial urban behavior. Paper presented at the annual conference of the Society for the Study of Social Problems. New York, September.

Hannerz, U. 1969. *Soulside.* New York: Columbia University Press.

Harcourt, B. E. 2001. *Illusion of Order.* Cambridge: Harvard University Press.

Hareven, T. K. 1982. *Family Time and Industrial Time.* New York: Cambridge.

——. 1987. Historical Analysis of the Family. In Sussman and Steinmetz, eds. 37–55.

——. 1991. The history of the family and the complexity of social change. *American Historical Review* 96:95–124.

Harlow, A. 1931. *Old Bowery Days.* New York: Putnam's Sons.

Harper, D. A. 1976. The homeless man: An ethnography of work, trains, and booze. Ph.D. diss., University of Chicago

——. 1982. *Good Company.* Chicago: University of Chicago.

Harrington, M. 1962. *The Other America.* New York: Macmillan.

Harrison, L. E., and S. P. Huntington, eds. 2000. *Culture Matters: How Values Shape Human Progress.* New York: Basic Books.

Hartman, C. 1998. The case for a right to housing. *Housing Policy Debate* 9:223–246.

Haugland, G., C. Siegel, K. Hopper, et al. 1997. Mental illness among single homeless adults in a suburban county. *Psychiatric Services* 48:504–509.

Hayes, R. M., ed. 1987. *The rights of the homeless.* New York: Practicing Law Institute.

Hayner, N. S. 1945. Taming the lumberjack. *American Sociological Review.* 10:217–225.

Henry, N. 1980. Down and Out. (series of articles) *Washington Post* 27 April—8 May.

Henshaw, S. K. 1968. *Camp LaGuardia: A Voluntary Total Institution.* New York: Bureau of Applied Social Research, Columbia University.

Herlands, W. B. 1940. *Administration of Relief in New York City.* New York: New York City Department of Investigation.

Hirschman, C. 1988. Minorities in the Labor Market. In G. Sandfour and M. Tienda, eds. *Divided Opportunities.*

Hoch, C., and R. A. Slayton. 1989. *New Homeless and Old.* Philadelphia: Temple University Press.

Hochschild, J. L. 1988. Race, Class, Power, and the American Welfare State. In A. Gutman, ed. 157–184.

——. 1989. Equal opportunity and the estranged poor. *Annals of the American Academy of Political and Social Science* 501:143–155.

——. 1991. The politics of the estranged poor. *Ethics* 101:56–78.

——. 1995. *Facing Up to the American Dream.* Princeton: Princeton University Press.

Hogan, H., and G. Robinson. 1993. What do the Census Bureau's evaluations tell us about the differential undercount? Paper presented at the Research Conference on Undercounted Ethnic Populations, Richmond, May 5–7.

Holzer, H. J. 1991. The spatial mismatch hypothesis: What has the evidence shown? *Urban Studies* 28:105–122.

Hombs, M. E. 1992. Reversals of fortune: The homeless poor and their advocates in the 1980s. *New Formations* 17:109–125.

——. 1994. *American Homelessness.* 2d ed. Santa Barbara, Denver, Oxford: ABC-Clio.

Hopper, K. 1982. Commentary on "The Woman Who Died in the Box." *Hastings Center Report* 12:18–19.

——. 1987. A bed for the night: Homeless men in New York City, past and present. Ph.D. diss., Columbia University.

——. 1990a. Public shelter as a 'hybrid institution': Homeless men in historical perspective. *Journal of Social Issues* 46:13–30.

——. 1990b. Research findings as testimony: The ethnographer as expert witness. *Human Organization* 49:110–113.

——. 1991a. A poor apart: The distancing of homeless men in New York's history. *Social Research* 58:107–132.

——. 1991b. *Final Report: Monitoring and Evaluating the 1990 S-Night in New York City.* Washington, D.C.: U.S. Bureau of the Census, Center for Survey Methods Research.

——. 1991c. *Final Report: Repeat Enumeration, Structured Interview, and Brief Ethnographic Studies of the Street Census Project.* Washington, D.C.: U.S. Bureau of the Census, Center for Survey Methods Research.

——. 1991d. Homelessness old and new: The matter of definition. *Housing Policy Debate* 2:757–813.

——. 1991e. Symptoms, survival, and the redefinition of public space. *Urban Anthropology* 20:155–176.

——. 1992. Marginalia: Notes on Homelessness in the United States. H. Norden, M. Järvinen, and C. Tigerstedt, eds. *NAD Publication* 22:123–156. Helsinki.

——. 1997. On contract knowing. *Anthropology Newsletter.* 38(6):34–35.

——. 2000. When the mental health system breaks down, *Social Policy* 30:20–27.

——. 2002. When (working) in Rome: Applying anthropology in Caesar's realm. *Human Organization.* 63:196–209.

Hopper, K., and J. Baumohl. 1994. Held in abeyance: Rethinking homelessness and advocacy. *American Behavioral Scientist* 37:522–552.

——. 1996. Redefining the Cursed Word: A Historical Interpretation of American Homelessness. In Baumohl, ed., 3–14, 221–224 (notes).

Hopper, K., and L. S. Cox. 1982. Litigation in advocacy for the homeless: The case of New York City. *Development: Seeds of Change, Village Through Global Order* 2:57–62.

Hopper, K., and J. Hamberg. 1986. The Making of America's Homeless: From Skid Row to New Poor, 1945–1984. In Bratt et al., eds. 12–40.

Hopper, K., J. Jost, T. Hay, S. Welber, and G. Haugland. 1997. Homelessness, severe mental illness, and the institutional circuit. *Psychiatric Services* 48:659–665.

Hopper, K., E. Susser, and S. Conover. 1985. Economies of makeshift: Homelessness and deindustrialization in New York City. *Urban Anthropology* 14:183–236.

Horton, C. F. 1984. Women have headaches, men have backaches: Patterns of illness in an Appalachian community. *Social Science & Medicine* 19:647–654.

Horwitz, A.V., and T.L. Scheid, eds. 1999. *A Handbook for the Study of Mental Health.* New York: Cambridge University Press.

Howell, J. T. 1973. *Hard Living on Clay Street.* Garden City: Anchor.
Huber, J., ed. 1991. *Macro–Micro Linkages in Sociology.* Newbury Park, Calif.: Sage.
Hufton, O. 1974. *The Poor in Eighteenth Century France, 1750–1789.* Oxford: Clarendon.
Human Resources Administration. 1993. Internal Shelter Census Reports.
Hymes, D., ed. 1974. *Reinventing Anthropology.* New York: Random House.
Ignatieff, M. 1984. *The Needs of Strangers.* New York: Viking.
——. 1995. The seductiveness of moral disgust. *Social Research* 62:77–98.
Illich, I. 1981. *Shadow Work.* Boston: Marian Boyers.
Ingram, T. A. 1910–1911. Vagrancy. In *Encyclopedia Brittanica,* 11th ed. 27:837.
Isay, D., S. Abramson, and H. Wang. 2000. *Flophouse: Life on the Bowery.* New York: Random House.
Jackson, A. 1976. *A Place Called Home: A History of Low-Income Housing in Manhattan.* Cambridge: MIT Press.
Jackson, J. E. 1990. "I Am a Fieldnote": Fieldnotes as a Symbol of Professional Identity. In *Fieldnotes: The Makings of Anthropology,* R. Sanjek, ed., 3–33. Ithaca: Cornell University Press.
Jackson, K. T. 1985. *Crabgrass Frontier.* New York: Oxford.
——. 1987. The Bowery: From Residential Street to Skid Row. In Beard, ed., 68–79.
Jahiel, R. I., ed. 1992. *Homelessness: A Prevention-Oriented Approach.* Baltimore: Johns Hopkins University Press.
Jargowsky, P. A., and M. J. Bane. 1991. Ghetto Poverty in the United States, 1970–1980. In Jencks and Peterson, eds. 235–273.
Jauhar, P., and M.P.I. Weller. 1982. Psychiatric morbidity and time zone changes: A study of patients from Heathrow Airport. *British Journal of Psychiatry* 140:231–235.
Jencks, C. 1992. *Rethinking Social Policy.* Cambridge: Harvard University Press.
——. 1994. *The Homeless.* Cambridge: Harvard University Press.
Jencks, C., and P. E. Peterson, eds. 1991. *The Urban Underclass.* Washington, D.C.: The Brookings Institute.
Jiler, J. 1997. *Sleeping with the Mayor: A True Story.* New York: Hungry Mind.
Johnson, A. 1911. *The Almshouse: Construction and Management.* New York: Russell Sage.
Jones, J. 1992. *The Dispossessed.* New York: Basic Books.
——. 1993. Southern Diaspora: Origins of the Northern 'Underclass.' In M. B. Katz, 27–55.
Josephson, M. 1933. The other nation. *The New Republic* 75(May 15):14–16.
Jusserand, J. J. 1920. *English Wayfaring Life in the Middle Ages.* Rev. ed. London: Ernest Benn.
Kain, J. F. 1968. Housing segregation, negro employment, and metropolitan decentralization. *Quarterly Journal of Economics* 82:175–197.
Karp, I. 1985. Deconstructing culture-bound syndromes. *Social Science and Medicine* 21:221–228.
Kasarda, J. D. 1985. Urban Change and Minority Opportunities. In Peterson, ed. 33–67.
——. 1989. Urban industrial transition and the underclass. *Annals of the American Academy of Political and Social Science* 501:26–47.

Kasinitz, P. 1984. Gentrification and homelessness. *Urban and Social Change Review* 17:9–14.

Kasl, S.V., S. Gore, and S. Cobb. 1975. The experience of losing a job: Reported changes in health, symptoms, and illness behavior. *Psychosomatic Medicine* 37: 106–122.

Katz, M.B. 1989. *The Undeserving Poor.* New York: Pantheon.

——. 1993a. Reframing the 'Underclass' Debate. In Katz, ed. 440–447.

——. 1993b. The Urban 'Underclass' as a Metaphor of Social Transformation. In Katz, ed. 3–23.

——, ed. 1993. *The 'Underclass Debate.'* Princeton: Princeton University Press.

Kaus, M. 1992. *The End of Equality.* New York: Basic Books.

Kean, G.G. 1965. A comparative study of negro and white homeless men. Ph.D. diss., Yeshiva University, New York.

Keigher, S.M, ed. 1991. *Housing Risks and Homelessness among the Urban Elderly.* New York: Haworth.

Kellor, F.A. 1915. *Out of Work: A Study of Unemployment.* Rev. ed. New York: G.P. Putnam.

Kent, M. 1903. The making of a tramp. *The Independent.* 55:667–670.

Kett, J.F. 1977. *Rites of Passage.* New York: Basic Books.

Keyes, C. 1985. The Interpretive Basis of Depression. In Kleinman and Good, eds. 153–174.

Keyssar, A. 1986. *Out of Work: A Century of Unemployment in Massachusetts.* New York: Cambridge.

——. 1987. Unemployment before and after the Great Depression. *Social Research* 54:201–222.

Kimble, G.E. 1935. *Social Work with Travelers and Transients.* Chicago: University of Chicago Press.

Kingsbury, J.A. 1915. Rehabilitation of the Homeless Man. In *Proceedings of the Fifteenth New York State Conference on Charities and Corrections, 1914.* Albany: Brandon, 29–38.

Klein, P. 1923. *The Burden of Unemployment.* New York: Russell Sage.

Kleinman, A. 1992. Pain and Resistance: The Delegitimation and Relegitimation of Local Worlds. In Good et al., eds. 169–197.

Kleinman, A., V. Das, and M. Lock, eds. 1996. *Social Suffering.* Special Issue of *Daedalus* 125(1).

Kleinman, A., and B. Good, eds. 1985. *Culture and Depression.* Berkeley: University of California Press.

Klips, S.A. 1980. Institutionalizing the poor: The New York City almshouse, 1825–1860. Ph.D. diss., City University of New York.

Knorr-Cetina, K.D. 1983. The Ethnographic Study of Scientific Work: Towards a Constructivist Interpretation of Science. In Knorr-Cetina and Mulkay, eds. 115–140.

Knorr-Cetina, K.D., and M. Mulkay, eds. *Science Observed.* Beverly Hills: Sage.

Koegel, P. 1989. Ethnographic perspectives on the adaptations of the homeless mentally ill. Paper presented at the annual meeting of the American Public Health Association, Chicago, October.

——. 1990. Broadening perspectives on the problem of the homeless. Presented at the Interdisciplinary Symposium, Los Angeles: University of California, December.

——. 1992. Through a different lens: An anthropological perspective on the homeless mentally ill. *Culture, Medicine, and Psychiatry* 16:1–22.

Koegel, P., and M.A. Burnam. 1987. *The Epidemiology of Alcohol Abuse and Dependence among Homeless Individuals: Findings from the Inner-City of Los Angeles.* Rockville: National Institute on Alcohol Abuse and Alcoholism.

Koegel, P., M.A. Burnham, and J. Baumohl. 1996. The Causes of Homelessness. In Baumohl, ed. 24–33, 225–226.

Koegel, P., M.A. Burnam, and R.K. Farr. 1988. The prevalence of specific psychiatric disorders among homeless individuals in the inner city of Los Angeles. *Archives of General Psychiatry* 45:1085–1092.

——. 1990. Subsistence adaptation among homeless adults in the inner city of Los Angeles. *Journal of Social Issues* 46:83–107.

Kopperdahl, P. 1987. The Bowery remembered. *Village Voice* (28 July) :29–37.

Kotlowitz, A. 1991. *There Are No Children Here*. New York: Doubleday.

Kozol, J. 1988. *Rachel's Children: Homeless Families in America.* New York: Crown.

Kromer, T. [1935] 1986. *Waiting for Nothing and Other Writings.* A.D. Casciato and J.L.W. West III, eds. Athens: University of Georgia Press.

Krueckeberg, D.A. 1999. The grapes of rent: A history of renting in a country of owners. *Housing Policy Debate* 10:9–30.

Kuhn, R., and D.P. Culhane. 1998. Applying cluster analysis to test a typology of homelessness by pattern of shelter utilization. *American Journal of Community Psychology* 26:207–232.

Kunen, J.S. 1994. Quality and equality. *The New Yorker* 28 November, 9–10.

Kusmer, K.L. 1980. The underclass: Tramps and vagrants in American society, 1865–1930. Ph.D. diss., University of Chicago.

——. 1986. The Black Urban Experience in American History. In *The State of Afro-American History,* D.C. Hine ed., 91–135. Baton Rouge: Lousiana State University Press.

——. 1987. The Underclass in Historical Perspective. In Beard, ed. 20–31.

——. 1990. Conceptualizing Social History: Homeless Men in America, 1865–1940, as a Case Study. In Lenz, Keil, and Bröck-Sellah, eds. 94–109.

——. 1995. The homeless unemployed in industrializing America, 1865–1930: Perception and reality. *American Studies (Amerikastudien)* 40:667–694.

——. 2001. *Down and Out, On the Road.* New York: Oxford.

LaGrory, M., F.J. Ritchey, T. O'Donoghue, and J. Mullis. 1989. Homelessness in Alabama. In Momeni ed. 1–20.

Lamb, H.R. 1984. Deinstitutionalization and the Homeless Mentally Ill. In Lamb, ed. 55–74.

——, ed. 1984. *The Homeless Mentally Ill.* Washington, D.C.: American Psychiaric Association.

Landry, B. 1991. The Enduring Dilemma of Race in America. In Wolfe, ed. 185–207.

Lardner, J. 1991. Shantytown. *The New Yorker,* July 1, 67–76.

Laubach, F.C. 1916. Why there are vagrants. Ph.D. diss., Columbia University.

Lawrence, E. 1892. William Cosby and the Freedom of the Press, 1732–1936. In Wilson, ed. 2:209–258.

Lazere, E.B., P.A. Leonard, C.N. Dolbeare, and B.A. Zigas. 1991. *A Place to Call Home.* Washington, D.C.: Center on Budget Priorities and Low-Income Housing Information Service.

Lee, B. A., B. G. Link, and P. A. Toro. 1991. Images of the homeless: Public views and media messages. *Housing Policy Debate* 2:649–682.

Leen, D. 1979. *The Freighthoppers Manual for North America.* Santa Barbara, Calif.: Capra.

Leff, R. 1932. When winter comes. *Shelter* 2(5):61–63.

Lemann, N. 1991. *The Promised Land.* New York: Knopf.

Lenz, G. H., H. Keil, and S. Bröck-Sellah, eds. 1990. *Reconstructing American Literary and Historical Studies.* New York: St. Martin's Press.

Leonard, P. A., and E. B. Lazere. 1992. *The Low-Income Housing Crisis in 44 Major Metropolitan Areas.* Washington, D.C.: Center for Budget and Policy Priorities.

Lerman, P. 1982. *Deinstitutionalization and the Welfare State.* New Brunswick: Rutgers University Press.

Lescohier, D. D. 1935. *Working Conditions.* Vol. 3 of *History of Labor in the United States, J. Commons ed.* New York: Macmillan.

Levinson, B. M. 1963. The homeless man: A psychological enigma. *Mental Hygiene* 47:590–600.

——. 1966a. A comparative study of northern and southern negro homeless men. *Journal of Negro Education* 35:144–150.

——. 1966b. Subcultural studies of homeless men. *Transactions of the New York Academy of Sciences* 29:165–182.

Levitan, S. A., and F. Gallo. 1992. *Spending to Save.* Washington, D.C.: George Washington University.

Lewis, H. 1967. Foreword. In Liebow 1967, vii–xiii.

Lichter, D. T. 1988. Racial differences in underemployment in American cities. *American Journal of Sociology* 93:771–792.

Liebow, E. 1967. *Tally's Corner.* Boston: Little, Brown.

——. 1993. *Tell Them Who I Am: The Lives of Homeless Women.* New York: Basic Books.

Lindenbaum, S. 1979. *Kuru Sorcery: Disease and Danger in the New Guinea Highlands.* Palo Alto: Chandler.

Link, B. G., J. Phelan, A. Stueve, R. Moore, M. Bresnahan, and E. Struening. 1996. Public knowledge, attitudes, and beliefs and homeless people. In Baumohl, ed. 143–148, 246 (notes).

Link, B. G., E. Susser, A. Stueve, J. Phelan, R. E. Moore, and E. Struening. 1994. Lifetime and five-year prevalence of homelessness in the United States. *American Journal of Public Health* 84:1907–1912.

Lipsky, M. 1980. *Street-Level Bureaucracy.* New York: Russell Sage.

——. 1984. Bureaucratic disentitlement in social welfare programs. *Social Service Review* 58:3–27.

Lipsky, M., and S. R. Smith. 1989. When social problems are treated as emergencies. *Social Service Review* 63:5–15.

Lis, C. 1986. *Social Change and the Labouring Poor: Antwerp: 1700–1860.* New Haven: Yale University Press.

Lis, C., and H. Soly. 1990. "Total Institutions" and the Survival Strategies of the Labouring Poor in Antwerp, 1700–1860. In Mandell, ed. 38–67.

Littman, M. S. 1979. The 1980 Census of population: Content and coverage improvement plans. *Journal of Consumer Research* 9:204–212.

Lovald, K.A. 1960. From hobohemia to skid row: The changing community of the homeless man. Ph.D. diss., University of Minnesota.

Love, E.G. 1956. *Subways Are for Sleeping.* New York: Harcourt Brace.

Lovell, A.M. 1989. Seizing the moment: Power and spatial temporality in street life. Paper presented at the annual meeting of the American Ethnological Association, Santa Fe, March.

——. 1992. Marginal arrangements: Homelessness, mental illness, and social relations. Ph.D. diss., Columbia University.

Lovell, A.M., and S. Makiesky-Barrow. 1981. Psychiatric disability and homelessness: A look at Manhattan's Upper West Side. Paper presented at conference, "The Community Support Population: Designing Alternatives in an Uncertain Environment." Syracuse, N.Y., November 19.

Lovell, A.M., S.M. Barrow, and E. Struening. 1992. Between Relevance and Rigor: Methodological Issues in Studying Mental Health and Homelessness. In Jahiel, ed. 372–395.

Lovell, A.M., and S. Cohn. 1998. The elaboration of "choice" in a program for homeless persons labeled psychiatrically disabled. *Human Organization* 57:8–20.

Lubove, R. 1977. *The Professional Altruist.* New York: Atheneum.

Luhrmann, T.M. 1989. *Persuasions of the Witch's Craft.* Cambridge: Harvard University Press.

——. 2000. *Of Two Minds: The Growing Disorder in American Psychiatry.* New York: Knopf.

Lynch, O. 1994. Urban anthropology, postmodernism, and perspectives. *City & Society* (Annual Review) :35–52.

Lyon-Callo, V. 1998. Constraining responses to homelessness: An ethnographic exploration of the impact of funding concerns on resistance. *Human Organization* 57:1–8.

MacDonald, C.L., and C. Siriani, eds. 1996. *Working in the Service Society.* Philadelphia: Temple University Press.

MacLeod, J. 1987. *Ain't No Makin' It.* Boulder: Westview.

——. 1995. *Ain't No Makin' It.* 2d ed. Boulder: Westview.

Mandell, P., ed: 1990. *The Uses of Charities: The Poor on Relief in the Nineteenth Century Metropolis.* Philadelphia: University of Pennsylvania Press.

Marcuse, P. 1979. *Rental Housing in the City of New York: Supply and Condition, 1975–1978.* New York City Department of Housing Preservation and Development.

Marin, P. 1987. Helping and hating the homeless. *Harper's* 274 (January) :39–49.

——. 1991. The prejudice against men. *The Nation* 8 July, 46–50.

Markel, N. 1964. *A Preliminary Study of New York City's Hospitals and Their Contact with Homeless Men.* New York: Columbia University, Bureau of Applied Social Science, December.

Martell, D.A., R. Rosner, and R.B. Harmon. 1995. Base-rate estimates of criminal behavior by homeless mentally ill person in New York City. *Psychiatric Services* 46:596–601.

Martin, E.P., and J.M. Martin. 1978. *The Black Extended Family.* Chicago: University of Chicago Press.

Martin, E., E. Laska, K. Hopper, M. Meisner, and J. Wanderling. 1997. Issues in the use of a plant-capture method for estimating the size of the street-dwelling population. *Journal of Official Statistics* 13:59–74.

Marx, H. 1982. *The Bowery: Portrait of a Changing Street.* New York: Museum for the City of New York and Goethe House.

Marx, K. [1867] 1976. *Capital.* Vol. 1. B. Fowkes, trans. Harmondsworth: Penguin.

——. [1857–1858] 1973. *The Grundrisse.* M. Nicolaus, trans. New York: Vintage.

Massey, D. S., and N. A. Denton. 1993. *American Apartheid: Segregation and the Making of the Underclass.* Cambridge: Harvard University Press.

Massing, M. 1995. Hanging out. *New York Review of Books.* 25 May 1995.

Masters, J. P., and W. P. Smith, eds. 1987. *Social Comparison, Social Justice, and Relative Deprivation.* Hillsdale, N.J.: Lawrence Erlbaum.

Mathers, M. 1974. *Riding the Rails.* Boston: Houghton Mifflin.

Mathieu, E. 1994. Parents on the move. Ph.D. diss., New York: New School for Social Research.

Mauss, A. L. 1980. Salvation and Survival on Skid Row: A Comment on Rooney. *Social Forces* 60: 898–904.

Mauss, M. [1950] 1990. *The Gift.* New York: W. W. Norton.

Maxwell, A. H. 1988. The anthropology of poverty in black communities. *Urban Anthropology* 17:171–191.

McCabe, J. D. 1882. *New York by Sunlight and Gaslight.* Philadelphia: Thayer, Merriam and Co.

McCall, G. J. 1989. Keeping track: What can ethnographers learn through tracking homeless individuals? Paper presented at the annual meeting of the American Anthropological Association, Washington, D.C., November.

McCook, J. J. 1895. The Tramp Problem: What It Is and What to Do With It. *Proceedings of the National Conference on Charities and Corrections.* 288–302. Boston: Ellis.

——. 1901. Leaves from the Diary of a Tramp. *The Independent.* 53: 2760–2767; 2880–2888; 3009–3013.

McElvaine, R. 1984. *The Great Depression.* New York: Times Books.

McMillan, W. 1934. Single blessedness. *Survey* 70:74–75.

McSheehy, W. 1979. *Skid Row.* Cambridge: G.K. Hall.

Mead, L. 1992a. *The New Politics of Poverty.* New York: Basic Books.

——. 1992b. [Op ed] *New York Times,* 19 May 1992.

Melbin, M. 1987. *Night as Frontier.* New York: Free Press,

Merton, R. K. 1949. The Sociology of Social Problems. In Merton and Nisbet, eds. 5–43.

——. 1957. *Social Theory and Social Structure.* Rev. Ed. Glencoe, Ill.: Free Press.

Merton, R. K., and R. Nisbet, eds. *Contemporary Social Problems.* 4th ed. New York: Harcourt Brace Jovanovich.

Michaels, D., S. R. Zoloth, P. Alcabes, C. A. Braslow, S. Safyer. 1992. Homelessness and indicators of mental illness among inmates in New York City's correctional system. *Hospital and Community Psychiatry* 43:150–155.

Milburn, N., and A. D'Ercole. 1991. Homeless women: Moving toward a comprehensive model. *American Psychologist* 46:1161–1169.

Miller, W. B., and V. Zarcone. 1968. Psychiatric disorders at an international airport. *Archives of Environmental Health* 17:360–365.

Minehan, T. 1934. *Boy and Girl Tramps of America.* New York: Farrar and Rinehart.

Minkler, M., and K. M. Roe. 1993. *Grandmothers as Caregivers: Raising Children of the Crack Cocaine Epidemic.* Beverly Hills: Sage.

Minow, M. 1990. *Making All the Difference.* Ithaca: Cornell University Press.
Mizruchi, E. H. 1987. *Regulating Society.* 2d ed. Chicago: University of Chicago Press.
Modell, J. 1989. *Into One's Own: From Youth to Adulthood in the United States, 1920–1975.* Berkeley: University of California Press.
Modell, J., and T. K. Hareven. 1973. Urbanization and the malleable household. *Journal of Marriage and the Family.* 35:467–479.
Moffatt, M. 1992. Ethnographic writing about American culture. *Annual Review of Anthropology* 21:205–229.
Mohl, R. A. 1985. *The New City: Urban America in the Industrial Age, 1860–1920.* Arlington Heights, Ill.: H. Davidson.
Mollat, M. 1986. *The Poor in the Middle Ages.* A. Goldhammer, trans. New Haven: Yale University Press.
Mollenkopf, J. H., and M. Castells, eds. 1991. *Dual City: Restructuring New York.* New York: Russell Sage.
Momeni, J., ed. 1989. *Homelessness in the United States.* Westport, Conn.: Greenwood Press.
Monkkonen, E. H. 1981. *Police in Urban America, 1860–1920.* New York: Cambridge University Press.
——. 1984. Introduction and Regional Dimensions of Tramping. In Monkkonen, ed. 1–17, 189–211.
——, ed. 1984. *Walking to Work: Tramps in America, 1790–1935.* Lincoln: University of Nebraska.
Morris, R. B. 1946. *Government and Labor in Early America.* New York: Columbia University Press.
Morrissey, J. P., D. Dennis, K. Gounis, and S. Barrow. 1985. *The Development and Utilization of the Queen's Men's Shelter.* Albany: New York State Office of Mental Health, Bureau of Evalution of Research.
Moss, P., and C. Tilly. 1991. Why black men are doing worse in the labor market: A review of supply-side and demand-side explanations. Working paper, Social Science Research Council. New York.
Mossman, D., and M. L. Perlin. 1992. Psychiatry and the homeless mentally ill: A reply to Dr. Lamb. *American Journal of Psychiatry* 149:51–57.
Mullings, L., ed. 1987. *Cities of the United States.* New York: Columbia University Press.
Muntaner, C. 1999. Invited commentary: Social mechanisms, race, and social epidemiology. *American Journal of Epidemiology* 150:121–126.
Murray, H. 1984. Time in the street. *Human Organization* 43:154–161.
Nader, L. 1974. Up the Anthropologist—Perspectives Gained from Studying Up. In Hymes, ed. 284–311.
Nascher, I. L. 1909. *The Wretches of Povertyville.* Chicago: J. J. Lanzit.
Nash, G. 1964a. *The Bowery in the Small Hours of the Morning.* New York: Columbia University, Bureau of Applied Social Science, August.
——. 1964b. *Spot Job Employment Agencies.* New York: Columbia University, Bureau of Applied Social Science.
——. 1964c. *The Habitats of Homeless Men in Manhattan.* New York: Columbia University, Bureau of Applied Social Science.

National Institute of Mental Health. 1991. *Two Generations of NIMH-funded Research on Homelessness and Mental Illness: 1982–1990.* Rockville, MD: NIMH.

Neisser, U., ed. 1986. *The School Achievement of Minority Children.* Hillsdale, N.J.: Lawrence Erlbaum.

Neumann, K. 1992. *Not the Way It Really Was: Constructing the Tolai Past.* Honolulu: University of Hawaii Press.

Newman, K. 1988. *Falling from Grace.* New York: Free Press.

——. 1992. Culture and structure in *The Truly Disadvantaged. City & Society* 6:3–25.

New York City Office of the Comptroller. 1979. *Performance Analysis of Programs for New York State Assistance to New York City Agencies Serving Deinstitutionalized Psychiatric Patients.* New York: Office of the Comptroller.

Nightingale, C. H. 1993. *On the Edge.* New York: Basic Books.

North, C. S., and E. M. Smith. 1994. Comparison of white and nonwhite homeless men and women. *Social Work* 39:639–647.

Obeyeskere, G. 1985. Depression, Buddhism, and the Work of Culture in Sri Lanka. In Kleinman and Good, eds. 134–152.

Ochs, E., and L. Capps. 2000. A dimensional approach to narrative. Paper presented at the annual meeting of the American Anthropological Association, San Francisco, November 17.

O'Connor, P. 1963. *Britain in the Sixties: Vagrancy.* London: Penguin.

Office of Mental Health. 1982. *Who Are the Homeless?* Albany: New York State Office of Mental Health. June.

Ogbu, J. U. 1986. The Consequences of the American Caste System. In Neisser, ed. 19–56.

Opler, M. 1987. Engineering internment. *American Ethnologist* 14:383.

Orfield, G. 1993. *The Growth of Segregation in American Schools: Changing Patterns of Separation and Poverty Since 1968.* Alexandria: National School Boards Association.

Ortner, S. 1995. Resistance and the problem of ethnographic refusal. *Comparative Studies in Society and History* 37:173–203.

——, ed. 1999. *The Fate of "Culture": Geertz and Beyond.* Berkeley: University of California Press.

Orwell, George. [1933] 1961. *Down and Out in Paris and London.* New York: Harcourt Brace Jovanovich.

Osterman, P. 1991. Gains from Growth? The Impact of Full Employment on Poverty in Boston. In Jencks and Peterson, eds. 122–134.

Outland, G. E. 1934–1935. Sources of transient boys. *Sociology and Social Research* 19:429–434.

Panel on Census Requirements in the Year 2000 and Beyond. 1993. *Planning the Decennial Census: Interim Report.* Washington, D.C.: National Academy Press.

Parker, P. 1970. A view from the Bowery. Unpublished paper.

Parsons, T. 1952. *The Social System.* New York: Free Press.

Patch, I. C. 1970. Homeless men: A London survey. *Proceedings of the Royal Society of Medicine* 63:437–441.

Patterson, O. 2000. Taking Culture Seriously: A Framework and an Afro-American Illustration. In Harrison and Huntington, eds. 202–218, 321–323.

Pearlin, L. I., and C. W. Radabaugh. 1976. Economic strains and the coping functions of alcohol. *American Journal of Sociology* 82:652–663.

Pearson, R.W. 1989. Economy, Culture, Public Policy, and the Urban Underclass. *Items* (Social Science Research Council) 43(2):23–29.

Peery, W. 1994. *Black Fire.* New York: The New Press.

Peterson, P. E., ed. 1985. *The New Urban Reality.* Washington, D.C.: Brookings Institution.

Pharr, R. D. [1971] 1998. *S.R.O.* New York: W. W. Norton

Phelan, J., and B. G. Link. 1999. Who are "the homeless"? Reconsidering the stability and composition of the homeless population. *American Journal of Public Health* 89:1334–1338.

Phillips, A., and S. Hamilton. 1996. Huts for the Homeless: A Low-Technology Approach for Squatters in Atlanta, Georgia. In DeHavenon, ed., 81–104.

Pinkerton, A. 1878. *Strikers, Communists, Tramps, and Detectives.* New York: G.W. Carleton.

Pittman, D. J., and T.W. Gordon. 1958. *Revolving Door: A Study of the Chronic Police Case Inebriate.* New York: Free Press.

Piven, F. F., and R. Cloward. 1971. *Regulating the Poor.* New York: Vintage.

Polanyi, K. 1944. *The Great Transformation.* Boston: Beacon.

Pomerantz, S. I. 1938. *New York: An American City, 1783–1803.* New York: Columbia University Press.

Portes, A. 1994. The Informal Economy and Its Paradoxes. In Smelser and Swedborg, eds. 426–449.

Prewitt, K. 1987. Public Statistics and Democratic Politics. In Alonso and Starr, eds. 261–274.

Public Welfare Committee. 1917. *Humanizing the Greater City's Charity.* New York: Public Welfare Committee.

Raborg, S. A. 1872. The homeless poor of New York City. *Catholic World* 16:206–211.

Rader, V. 1986. *Signal Through the Flames: Mitch Snyder and America's Homeless.* Kansas City: Sheed and Ward.

Rainwater, L. 1970. The problem of lower class culture. *Journal of Social Issues* 26:133–137.

Reed, E. F. 1934. *Federal Transient Program: An Evaluative Survey.* New York: Committee on Care of Transient and Homeless.

Reich R., and L. Siegel. 1978. The emergence of the Bowery as a psychiatric dumping ground. *Psychiatric Quarterly* 50:191–201.

Reynolds, M. T. 1893. *The Housing of the Poor in American Cities.* Baltimore: American Economic Association.

Rhodes, L. A. 1991. *Emptying Beds.* Berkeley: University of California Press.

Rice, S. A. 1918. The homeless. *American Academy of Political and Social Science* 77:140–153.

——. 1922. The failure of the municipal lodging house. *National Municipal Review* 11:358–362.

Richardson, J. F. 1970. *The New York Police: Colonial Times to 1901.* New York: Oxford University Press.

Richmond, J. F. 1872. *New York and Its Institutions, 1609–1872.* New York: E. B. Treat.

Ringenbach, P.T. 1973. *Tramps and Reformers, 1873–1916.* Westport, Conn.: Greenwood Press.

Rist, R.C. 1994. Influencing the Policy Process with Qualitative Research. In Denzin and Lincoln, eds. 545–557.

Rock, P. 1979. *The Making of Symbolic Interactionism.* Totowa, N.J.: Rowman and Littlefield.

Rollin, H. 1970. From patients into vagrants. *New Society* 15(381):90–93.

Rooney, J.F. 1969. Race relations in skid row. Unpublished ms.

——. 1970. Societal Forms and the Unattached Male: An Historical Review. In Bahr, ed. 13–38.

——. 1980a. Organizational success through failure: Skid row rescue missions. *Social Forces* 58:905–924.

——. 1980b. Reply [to A. Mauss]. *Social Forces* 60:905–907.

Rorty, R. 1998. *Achieving Our Country.* Cambridge: Harvard University Press.

Rosaldo, R. 1989. *Culture and Truth.* Boston: Beacon.

Rose, S.M. 1979. Deciphering deinstitutionalization: Complexities in policy and program analysis. *Milbank Memorial Fund Quarterly* 57:429–461.

Rose, T. 1989. Hoboes, tramps, and bums. *Locomotive and Railway Preservation.* November-December:36–43.

Rosenhan, D.L. 1973. On being sane in insane places. *Science* 179:250–258.

Rosenheck, R., P. Gallup, C. Leda, L. Gorchov, and P. Errera. 1989. *Reaching Out Across America: The Third Progress Report on the Department of Veterans Affairs Homeless Chronically Mentally Ill Veterans Program.* West Haven, Conn.: Department of Veterans Affairs Medical Center.

Rosenthal, R. 1991. Straighter from the source: alternative methods of researching homelessness. *Urban Anthropology* 20:109–126.

——. 1994. *Homeless in Paradise.* Philadelphia: Temple University Press.

——. 1996. Dilemmas of Local Antihomelessness Movements. In Baumohl, ed. 201–212, 253–255.

Rosenzweig, R., and E. Blackmar. 1993. *The Park and the People.* Ithaca: Cornell University Press.

Rossi, P.H. 1989. *Down and Out in America.* Chicago: University of Chicago Press.

Rothman, D.J. 1971. *The Discovery of the Asylum.* Boston: Little, Brown.

——. 1987. The First Shelters: The Contemporary Relevance of the Almshouse. In Beard, ed. 11–19.

Rothstein, V. 1993. Where should the homeless sleep? Their space is ours, too. *New York Times* 19 December, 13.

Rousseau, A.-M. 1981. *Shopping-Bag Ladies.* New York: Pilgrim Press.

Rowe, M. 1999. *Crossing the Border: Encounters Between Homeless People and Outreach Workers.* Berkeley: University of California Press.

Sady, R. 1987. Comment on "Engineering Internment." *American Ethnologist* 14:560–562.

Salerno, D., K. Hopper, and E. Baxter. 1984. *Hardship in the Heartland.* New York: Community Service Society.

Salo, M., and L. Schwede. 1991. Analysis of in-place-observer debriefings on S-night procedures in five cities during the 1990 decennial census. Presented at the U.S. Bureau of the Census Annual Research Conference, Arlington, Va., March 18.

Sandfour, G., and M. Tienda, eds. 1988. *Divided Opportunities: Minorities, Poverty, and Social Policy.* New York: Plenum Press.

Sands, I. J. 1927. Manifestations of mental disorder in Travelers Aid Society clients. *Mental Hygiene* 11:728–744.

Sanjek, R. 1990a. On Ethnographic Validity. In. R. Sanjek, ed. 385–418.

——. 1990b. Urban anthropology in the 1980s: A world view. *Annual Reviews in Anthropology* 19:151–186.

——. 1994. Intermarriage and the Future of Races in the United States. In Gregory and Sanjek, eds. 103–130.

——. 1998. *The Future of Us All: Race and Neighborhood Politics in New York City.* Ithaca: Cornell University Press.

——, ed. 1990. *Fieldnotes.* Ithaca: Cornell University Press.

Sante, L. 1991. *Low-Life.* New York: Vintage.

Saris, J. 1994. Telling stories: Life histories, illness narratives, and institutional landscapes. *Culture, Medicine, and Psychiatry* 19:39–72.

Sassen, S. 1988. *The Mobility of Labor and Capital.* New York: Cambridge.

——. 1991. The Informal Economy. In Mollenkopf and Castells, eds. 78–102.

——. 1993. *Cities in a World Economy.* New York: Pine Forge/Sage.

Sawhill, I. V. 1992. Young Children and Families. In Aaron and Shultze, eds. 147–184.

Scheper-Hughes, N., and M. Lock. 1989. The mindful body: A prolegomenon to future work in medical anthropology. *Medical Anthropology Quarterly,* n.s., 1(1):6–41.

Schneider, D. M. 1968. *American Kinship: A Cultural Account.* Englewood Cliffs, N.J.: Prentice-Hall.

Schneider, J. C. 1984. Tramping Workers, 1890–1920: A Subcultural View. In Monkkonen, ed. 212–234.

——. 1986. Skid Row as an Urban Neighborhood, 1890–1920. In Erickson and Wilhelm, eds. 167–189.

Schubert, H. J. P. 1935. *Twenty Thousand Transients.* Buffalo: Emergency Relief Bureau.

Schwam, Keith. 1979. *Shopping Bag Ladies: Homeless Women.* New York: Manhattan Bowery Corporation.

Schwartz, J. 1991. The moral environment of the poor. *The Public Interest* 103:21–37.

Schwartz, R. 1989. *The Homeless: The Impact on the Transportation Industry.* 2 vols. New York: Port Authority of NY&NJ.

Scott, J. C. 1990. *Domination and the Arts of Resistance.* New Haven: Yale University Press.

——. 1998. *Seeing Like a State.* New Haven: Yale University Press.

Seber, G. A. F. 1982. *The Estimation of Animal Abundance and Related Parameters.* 2d ed. London: Ch. Griffen.

Segal, S. P., J. Baumohl, and E. Johnson. 1977. Falling through the cracks: Mental disorder and social margin in a young vagrant population. *Social Problems* 24:387–400.

Seligson, I. 1940. The care of the homeless man in New York City. Master's thesis, New York School of Social Work.

Sennett, R., and J. Cobb. 1972. *The Hidden Injuries of Class.* New York: Random House.

Shapiro, I., M. Sheft, L. Summer, R. Greenstein, and S. D. Gold. 1993. *The States and the Poor. II.* Washington, D.C., and Albany, N.Y.: Center on Budget and Policy Priorities and Center for the Study of the States.

Shapiro, J. H. 1971. *Communities of the Alone.* New York: Association Press.

Shapiro, S. 1976. A study of psychiatric syndromes manifested at an international airport. *Comprehensive Psychiatry* 17:453–456.

——. 1982. Airport wandering as a psychiatric symptom. *Psychiatric Clinics* 15:173–176.

Sharff, J. W. 1987. The Underground Economy of a Poor Neighborhood. In Mullings, ed. 19–50.

Shattuck, R. 1996. *Forbidden Knowledge: From Prometheus to Pornography.* New York: St. Martin's Press.

Shinn, M., J. Baumohl, and K. Hopper. 2001. The prevention of homelessness revisited. *Analyses of Social Issues and Public Policy* (*ASAP*) 1:95–127.

Shinn, M., J. R. Knickman, and B. C. Weitzman. 1991. Social relationships and vulnerability to becoming homeless among poor families. *American Psychologist* 46:1180–1187.

Shinn, M., and B. Weitzman. 1994. You can't eliminate homelessness without housing. *American Behavioral Scientist* 37:435–442.

Shinn, M., B. C. Weitzman, D. Stojanovic, J. R. Knickman, L. Jimenez, L. Duchon, S. James, and D. H. Krantz. 1998. Predictors of homelessness among families in New York City: from shelter request to housing stability. *American Journal of Public Health* 88:1651–1657.

Shlay, A. B., and P. Rossi. 1992. Social science research and contemporary studies of homelessness. *Annual Review of Sociology* 18:129–160.

Siegel, H. A. 1978. *Outposts of the Forgotten.* Totowa, N.J.: Transaction Books.

Simon, H. 1992. Towns without pity. *Tulane Law Review* 66:631–676.

Simon, H. 1996. Municipal Regulation of the Homeless in Public Spaces. In Baumohl, ed. 149–159, 246–247.

Singer, M. 1996. The evolution of AIDS work in a Puerto Rican community organization. *Human Organization* 55:67–75.

Sklar, S. L. 2000. Opinion, in *Callahan* v. *Carey* (Index No. 42582/79), and *Eldredge* v. *Koch* (Index 41494/82), February 18, pp. 1–24, Supreme Court of the State of New York, New York County.

Smelser, N. J., and S. Halpern. 1984. The historical triangulation of family, economy, and education. *American Journal of Sociology* 84(Supplement):5288–5315.

Smelser, N. J., and R. Swedborg, eds. 1994. *The Handbook of Economic Sociology.* Princeton: Princeton University Press, and New York: Russell Sage.

Snow, D. A., and L. Anderson. 1987. Identity work among the homeless. *American Journal of Sociology* 97:1337–1371.

——. 1993. *Down on Their Luck: A Study of Homeless Street People.* Berkeley: University of California Press.

Snow, D. A., L. Anderson, and P. Koegel. 1994. Distorting tendencies in research on the homeless. *American Behavioral Scientist* 37:461–475.

Snow, D. A., L. Anderson, T. Quist, and D. Cress. 1996. Material Survival Strategies on the Street: Homeless People as Bricoleurs. In Baumohl, ed. 86–96, 234–236.

Snow, D. A., S. G. Baker, and L. Anderson. 1988. On the precariousness of measuring insanity in insane contexts. *Social Problems* 35:192–196.

——. 1989. Criminality among homeless men: An empirical assessment. *Social Problems* 36:532–549.

Snow, D., S. Baker, L. Anderson, and M. Martin. 1986. The myth of pervasive mental illness among the homeless. *Social Problems* 33:407–413.

Solenberger, A. W. 1911. *One Thousand Homeless Men.* New York: Russell Sage.

Sosin, M., I. Piliavin, and H. Westerfelt. 1990. Toward a longitudinal analysis of homelessness. *Journal of Social Issues* 46:157–174.

Spann, E. K. 1981. *The New Metropolis.* New York: Columbia University Press.

Spicer, E. H. 1979. Anthropologists and the War Relocation Authority. In Goldschmidt, ed. 217–237.

Spradley, J. P. 1970. *You Owe Yourself a Drunk: An Ethnography of Urban Nomads.* Boston: Little, Brown.

Stack, C. 1974. *All Our Kin.* New York: Harper and Row.

——. 1996. *Call to Home.* New York: Basic Books.

Stark, L. 1985. Tents and tepees: The organization of a homeless community. Paper presented at the annual meeting of the American Anthropological Association, Washington, D.C., November.

Starn, O. 1986. Engineering internment: Anthropologists and the War Relocation Authority. *American Ethnologist* 13:700–720.

Senate Democratic Task Force on the City of New York. 1976. *Shelter Care for Men.* Albany: State Senate of New York.

Stegman, M. A. 1993. *Housing and Vacancy Report, New York City, 1991.* New York: Department of Housing Preservation and Development.

Stern, M. J. 1984. The emergence of the homeless as a public problem. *Social Service Review* 58:291–301.

——. 1993. Poverty and Family Composition Since 1940. In Katz, ed. 220–253.

Stiff. D. [pseud. for Anderson, N.] 1931. *The Milk and Honey Route: A Handbook for Hobos.* New York: Vanguard.

Still, B. 1956. *Mirror for Gotham.* New York: New York University Press.

Stocking, G. W. 1983. The Ethnographer's Magic: Fieldwork in British Anthropology from Tylor to Malinowski. In Stocking, ed. 70–120.

Stocking, G. W., ed. 1983. *Observers Observed.* Madison: University of Wisconsin Press.

Stone, M. E. 1993. *Shelter Poverty.* Philadelphia: Temple University Press.

Stott, W. 1973. *Documentary Expression in Thirties America.* New York: Oxford.

Strauss, J. S. 1989. Mediating processes schizophrenia: Toward a new dynamic psychiatry. *British Journal of Psychiatry* 155(suppl. 5):22–28.

Struening, E., and L. Pittman. 1987. *Characteristics of Residents of the New York City Shelter System, Summer 1987.* New York: Epidemiology of Mental Disorders Department, New York State Psychiatric Institute.

Sugrue, T. J. 1993. The Structures of Urban Poverty. In Katz, ed. 85–117.

Sullivan, M. L. 1989a. *Getting Paid: Youth, Crime and Work in the Inner City.* Ithaca: Cornell University Press.

———. 1989b. Absent fathers in the inner city. *Annals of the American Academy of Political and Social Science* 501:48–58.
———. 1993. The social organization of poor neighborhoods: A forgotten object of ethnographic study? Paper prepared for the conference "Meaning and Context," Oakland, Calif., June 9–13.
Susser, E., S. P. Lin, S. A. Conover, and E. L. Struening. 1991. Childhood antecedents of homelessness in psychiatric patients. *American Journal of Psychiatry* 148:1026–1030.
Sussman, M. B., and S. K. Steinmetz, eds. 1987. *Handbook of Marriage and the Family.* New York: Plenum Press.
Sutherland, E. H., and H. J. Locke. 1936. *Twenty Thousand Homeless Men.* Chicago: J. B. Lippincott.
Swerdlow, J. L. 1993. Central Park. *National Geographic* 183(5):2–37.
———. 1997. Under New York. *National Geographic* 191(2):110–131.
Swidler, A. 1986. Culture in action: Symbols and strategies. *American Sociological Review* 51:273–286.
Tawney, R. H. 1912. *The Agrarian Problem in the Sixteenth Century.* London: Longmans Green.
Tessler, R. C., and D. L. Dennis. 1989. *A Synthesis of NIMH-Funded Research Concerning Persons Who Are Homeless and Mentally Ill.* Rockville: National Institute of Mental Health.
Thompson, E. P. 1978. *The Poverty of Theory and Other Essays.* New York: Monthly Review Press.
Tidwell, B. J., and M. L. Jackson. 1992. *Perils of Neglect: Black Employment in the Nineties.* Washington, D.C.: National Urban League.
Tidwell, M. 1992. *In the Shadow of the White House.* Rocklin, Calif.: Prima Publishing.
Tienda, M. 1991. Poor People and Poor Places: Deciphering Neighborhood Effects on Poverty Outcomes. In Huber, ed. 244–262.
Tienda, M., and H. Stier. 1991. Joblessness and Shiftlessness: Labor Force Activity in Chicago's Inner City. In Jencks and Peterson, eds. 135–154.
Tilly, C., and C. Tilly. 1994. *Work Under Capitalism.* Boulder: Westview.
Toth, J. 1990. N.Y.'s "mole people" shun society in transit tunnels. *Los Angeles Times* 7 September, A1.
Trotter, J. W., Jr., ed. 1991. *The Great Migration in Historical Perspective.* Bloomington: Indiana University Press.
———. 1993. Blacks in the Urban North. In Katz, ed. 85–117.
Turkel, S. 1970. *Hard Times.* New York: Avon.
Turner, V. 1967. *The Forest of Symbols.* Ithaca: Cornell University Press.
———. 1969. *The Ritual Process.* Ithaca: Cornell University Press.
———. 1974. *Dramas, Fields, and Metaphors.* Ithaca: Cornell University Press.
———. 1985. *On the Edge of the Bush.* Tucson: University of Arizona Press.
U.S. Census Bureau. n.d. *1980 Census Special Place Operations Manual.* Washington, D.C.
———. 1983. *Special Tabulations from the 1980 Census of Population: People at Shelters, Campsites, Etc.* Washington, D.C.: Government Printing Office.
———. 1984. *Persons in Institutions and Other Group Quarters.* PC80-2-4D. Washington, D.C., April.

——. 1992. *Poverty in the U.S. 1991.* P60, #181, Washington, D.C., August.

——. October 2001. *Emergency and Transitional Shelter Population: 2000.* Washington, D.C.: Government Printing Office.

U.S. Department of Housing and Urban Development. 1984. *Report to the Secretary on the Homeless and Emergency Shelters.* Washington, D.C.

Underwood, J. 1990. An ethnography of a homeless camp. Ph.D. diss., University of California, Los Angeles.

Urban Institute. 1999. *Homelessness 1996: People and Programs.* Draft Document.

Van Kleeck, M. 1934. Our Illusions Regarding Government. *Survey* 70:190–193.

Vera Institute of Justice. 1977. Report to the Office of Family and Adult Services on the Men's Shelter. New York.

——. 1980. First-Time Users of Men's Shelter Services: A Preliminary Analysis. New York.

Vine, P. 1977. A "cure" for the homeless. *City Limits* January. <http://www.citylimits.org/content/articles/articleView.cfm ?articlenumber=126>

Wacquant, L. J. D. 1989. The ghetto, the state, and the new capitalist economy. *Dissent* 36 (Fall): 508–520.

Wacquant, L. J. D., and W. J. Wilson. 1989. The cost of racial and class exclusion in the inner city. *Annals of the American Academy of Political and Social Science* 501:8–25.

Waddell, H. [1927] 1961. *The Wandering Scholars.* New York: Doubleday.

Wagner, D. 1993. *Checkerboard Square: Culture and Resistance in a Homeless Community.* Boulder: Westview.

Wallace, R. 1989. A synergism of plagues: Planned shrinkages, contagious housing destruction and AIDS in the Bronx. *Environmental Research* 47:1–33.

——. 1990. Urban desertification, public health and public order: "Planned shrinkage," violent death, substance abuse and AIDS in the Bronx. *Social Science & Medicine* 31:801–813.

Wallace, R., and E. Bassuk. 1991. Housing famine and homelessness: How the low-income housing crisis affects families with inadequate supports. *Environment and Plannning* A 23:485–498.

Wallace, S. E. 1965. *Skid Row as a Way of Life.* Totowa, N.J.: Bedminister Press.

Walzer, M. 1995. The politics of rescue. *Social Research* 62:53–66.

Ware, N. C., R. R. Desjarlais, T. L. AvRuskin, J. Breslau, B. J. Good, and S. H. Goldfinger. 1992. Empowerment and the transition to housing for homeless mentally ill people: An anthropological perspective. *New England Journal of Public Policy* 8:297–314.

——. 1994. Discipline and practice in mental health services. Paper delivered at the annual meeting of the American Anthropological Association, Atlanta, November.

Warner, R. 1985. *Recovery from Schizophrenia.* Boston: Routledge & Kegan Paul.

Warner, R., and P. Pollack. 1995. The economic advancement of the mentally ill in the community: II. Economic choices and incentives. *Community Mental Health Journal* 31:477–492.

Warsh, C., ed. 1993. *Drink in Canada: Historical Essays.* Montreal: McGill-Queens University Press.

Waterston, A. 1999. *Love, Sorrow, and Rage: Destitute Women in a Manhattan Residence.* Philadelphia: Temple University Press.

Watzlawick, P., J. H. Beavin, and D. D. Jackson. 1967. *Pragmatics of Human Communication.* New York: W. W. Norton.
Watzlawick, P., J. H. Weakland, and R. Fisch. 1974. *Change.* New York: W. W. Norton.
Way, P. 1993. *Common Labour: Workers and the Digging of North American Canals, 1780–1860.* New York: Cambridge University Press.
Webb, J. N. 1935. *The Transient Unemployed.* Washington, D.C.: Works Project Administration.
Webb, S., and B. Webb. [1927] 1963. *English Poor Law History. Part I: The Old Poor Law.* Hamden: Archon Books.
Weinberg, D., and P. Koegel. 1995. Impediments to recovery in treatment programs for dually diagnosed homeless adults: An ethnographic analysis. *Contemporary Drug Problems* 22(2):193–236.
Weir, L. 1995. Update on using military base closures to aid homeless people. *Clearinghouse Review* 29 (7–8):771.
Weir, M. 1992. *Politics and Jobs.* Princeton: Princeton University Press.
Weitzman, B., C. James, R. Knickman, and M. Shinn. 1990. Pathways to homelessness among New York City families. *Journal of Social Issues* 46:125–140.
Weitzman, P. 1989. *Worlds Apart: Housing, Race/Ethnicity and Income in New York City, 1978–1987.* New York: Community Service Society.
Welfare Council. 1949. *Homeless Men in New York City.* New York: Welfare Council.
Weller, M. P. I. 1987. A biochemical hypothesis of wandering. *Medicine, Science and Law* 27:40–41.
Weller, M. P. I., and P. Jauhar. 1987. Wandering at Heathrow Airport by the mentally unwell. *Medicine, Science and Law* 27:37–39.
White, A. 1996. Perception vs. reality. *City Limits* January:110–112.
White, L. 1990–1991. Representing "The Real Deal." *University of Miami Law Review* 45:271–313.
Whiting, W. A. 1914. Summary of the Report of William Alberti Whiting of the Investigation of the Homeless Unemployed Which Was Held at the Municipal Lodging House in March 1914.
Williams, B. 1988. *Upscaling Downtown.* Ithaca: Cornell University Press.
——. 1992. Poverty among African Americans in the Urban United States. *Human Organization* 51:164–174.
Williams, B. R. 1999. The public I/eye: Conducting fieldwork to do homework on homelessness and begging in two U.S. cities. *Current Anthropology* 36:25–51.
Williams, R. 1977. *Marxism and Literature.* New York: Oxford University Press.
Willis, P. 1977. *Learning to Labor.* New York: Columbia University Press.
Wilson, J., D. M. McCallum, and J. M. Bolland. 1991. *The Magnitude and Demographics of Homelessness in Huntsville.* Tuscaloosa: University of Alabama, Institute for Social Science Research.
Wilson, J. G., ed. 1892. *Memorial History of the City of New York.* 4 vols. New York: New York History Company.
Wilson, J. Q., and G. Kelling. 1982. Broken windows. *The Atlantic Monthly* February: 29–38.
Wilson, P. J. 1974. *Oscar: An Inquiry into the Meaning of Sanity.* New York: Random House.
Wilson, R. S. 1935. Problems in co-ordinating services for transient and resident unat-

tached from the point of view of individual service. *Proceedings of the National Conference of Social Work, 62nd Annual Session,* 210–223. Chicago: University of Chicago.

Wilson, W. J. 1987. *The Truly Disadvantaged.* Chicago: University of Chicago Press.

——. 1996. *When Work Disappears: The World of the New Urban Poor.* New York: Knopf.

Winberg, E., and T. Wilson. 1981. *Single Rooms: Stories of an Urban Subculture.* Cambridge: Shenkman.

Wiseman, J. 1970. *Stations of the Lost: The Treatment of Skid Row Alcoholics.* Englewood Cliffs, N.J.: Prentice-Hall.

Wolch, J., and M. Dear. 1993. *Malign Neglect: Homelessness in an American City.* San Francisco: Jossey Bass.

Wolf J., A. Burnam, P. Koegel, G. Sullivan, S. Morton. 2001. Changes in subjective quality of life among homeless adults who obtain housing: a prospective examination. *Social Psychiatry and Psychiatric Epidemiology.* 36:391–398.

Wolf, M. 1992. *A Thrice Told Tale.* Stanford: Stanford University Press.

Wolfe, A., ed. 1991. *America at Century's End.* Berkeley: University of California Press.

Wood, J. 1999. *The Broken Estate.* New York: Random House.

Wright, J. D., and J. A. Devine. 1992. Counting the homeless: The Census Bureau's "S-Night" in five U.S. cities. *Evaluation Review* 16:355–364.

Wright, J. D., and B. A. Rubin. 1991. Is homelessness a housing problem? *Housing Policy Debate* 2:937–956.

Wright, T. 1997. *Out of Place: Homeless Mobilizations, Subcities, and Contested Landscapes.* Albany: State University of New York Press.

Wuerker, A. K. 1996. The changing careers of patients with chronic mental illness. *Journal of Mental Health Administration* 23:458–470.

Wuerker, A. K., and C. K. Keenan. 1997. Patterns of psychiatric service use by homeless mentally ill clients. *Psychiatric Quarterly* 68:101–116.

Wyckoff, W. A. 1897. *The Workers: An Experiment in Reality.* Vol. 1, *The East.* New York: Scribners.

Yanagisako, S. J. 1985. *Transforming the Past: Tradition and Kinship Among Japanese-Americans.* Stanford: Stanford University Press.

Yeich, S. 1994. *The Politics of Ending Homelessness.* Lanham, Md.: University Press of America.

Zeisloff, E. T. 1899. *The New Metropolis.* New York: D. Appleton and Co.

Zimmerman, M. A., and J. Rappaport. 1988. Citizen participation, perceived control and psychological empowerment. *American Journal of Community Psychology* 16:725–750.

Zweig, P. 1986. *Departures.* New York: Harper and Row.

Index

The Anthropology of Contemporary Issues
A Series Edited by
Roger Sanjek

Wanderings: Sudanese Migrants and Exiles in North America by Rogaia Mustafa Abusharaf

A Neighborhood Divided: Community Resistance to an AIDS Care Facility by Jane Balin

Chinatown No More: Taiwan Immigrants in Contemporary New York by Hsiang-shui Chen

Farm Work and Fieldwork: American Agriculture in Anthropological Perspective edited by Michael Chibnik

The Varieties of Ethnic Experience: Kinship, Class, and Gender among California Italian-Americans by Micaela di Leonardo

Lord, I'm Coming Home: Everyday Aesthetics in Tidewater North Carolina by John Forrest

Chinese Working-Class Lives: Getting By in Taiwan by Hill Gates

Looking for Chengdu: A Woman's Adventures in China by Hill Gates

Accommodation without Assimilation: Sikh Immigrants in an American High School by Margaret A. Gibson

Praying for Justice: Faith, Order, and Community in an American Town by Carol J. Greenhouse

Ginseng and Aspirin: Health Care Alternatives for Aging Chinese in New York by Zibin Guo

Distant Companions: Servants and Employers in Zambia, 1900–1985 by Karen Hansen

Rx: Spiritist as Needed: A Study of a Puerto Rican Community Mental Health Resource by Alan Harwood

Reckoning with Homelessness by Kim Hopper

Lady Friends: Hawaiian Ways and the Ties That Define by Karen L. Ito

Dismantling Apartheid: A South African Town in Transition by Walton R. Johnson

Caribbean New York: Black Immigrants and the Politics of Race by Philip Kasinitz

Antler on the Sea: The Yup'ik and Chukchi of the Russian Far East by Anna M. Kerttula
Becoming American, Being Indian: An Immigrant Community in New York City by Madhulika S. Khandelwal
The Solitude of Collectivism: Romanian Villagers to the Revolution and Beyond by David A. Kideckel
Nuclear Summer: The Clash of Communities at the Seneca Women's Peace Encampment by Louise Krasniewicz
Between Two Worlds: Ethnographic Essays on American Jewry edited by Jack Kugelmass
American Odyssey: Haitians in New York City by Michel S. Laguerre
From Working Daughters to Working Mothers: Immigrant Women in a New England Industrial Community by Louise Lamphere
Sunbelt Working Mothers: Reconciling Family and Factory by Louise Lamphere, Patricia Zavella, Felipe Gonzales, and Peter B. Evans
Creativity/Anthropology edited by Smadar Lavie, Kirin Narayan and Renato Rosaldo
Cities, Classes, and the Social Order by Anthony Leeds
Lesbian Mothers: Accounts of Gender in American Culture by Ellen Lewin
Civilized Women: Gender and Prestige in Southeastern Liberia by Mary H. Moran
Blood, Sweat, and Mahjong: Family and Enterprise in an Overseas Chinese Community by Ellen Oxfeld
The Magic City: Unemployment in a Working-Class Community by Gregory Pappas
The Korean American Dream: Immigrants and Small Business in New York City by Kyeyoung Park
Hispanas de Queens: Latino Panethnicity in a New York City Neighborhood by Milagros Ricourt and Ruby Danta
Inside the Revolution: Everyday Life in Socialist Cuba by Mona Rosendahl
Brokered Homeland: Japanese Brazilian Migrants in Japan by Joshua Hotaka Roth
State and Family in Singapore: Restructuring an Industrial Society by Janet W. Salaff
The Future of Us All: Race and Neighborhood Politics in New York City by Roger Sanjek
Medicalizing Ethnicity: The Construction of Latino Identity in a Psychiatric Setting by Vilma Santiago-Irizarry
Diamond Stories: Enduring Change on 47th Street by Renée Rose Shield
Children of Circumstances: Israeli Emigrants in New York by Moshe Shokeid
Rum and Axes: The Rise of a Connecticut Merchant Family, 1795–1850 by Janet Siskind
History and Power in the Study of Law: New Directions in Legal Anthropology edited by June Starr and Jane F. Collier
"Getting Paid": Youth Crime and Work in the Inner City by Mercer L. Sullivan
Breaking the Silence: Redress and Japanese American Ethnicity by Yasuko I. Takezawa
Underground Harmonies: Music and Politics in the Subways of New York by Susie J. Tanenbaum
Generations in Touch: Linking the Old and Young in a Tokyo Neighborhood by Leng Leng Thang
City of Green Benches: Growing Old in a New Downtown by Maria D. Vesperi
Strawberry Fields: Politics, Class, and Work in California Agriculture by Miriam J. Wells

Renunciation and Reformation: A Study of Conversion in an American Sect by Harriet Whitehead

Upscaling Downtown: Stalled Gentrification in Washington, D. C. by Brett Williams

Women's Work and Chicano Families: Cannery Workers of the Santa Clara Valley by Patricia Zavella